Understanding American Politics

UNDERSTANDING AMERICAN POLITICS

Stephen Brooks

UTP

University of Toronto Press

LIBRARY AND ARCHIVES CANADA CATALOGUING IN PUBLICATION
Brooks, Stephen, 1956-
        Understanding American politics / Stephen Brooks.

Includes bibliographical references and index.
ISBN 978-0-8020-9671-5

        1. United States—Politics and government—Textbooks.
I. Title.

E178.1.B76 2009   320.973   C2009-900442-9

We welcome comments and suggestions regarding any aspect of our publications—please feel free to contact us at news@utphighereducation.com or visit our internet site at www.utphighereducation.com.

North America
5201 Dufferin Street
Toronto, Ontario, Canada, M3H 5T8

2250 Military Road
Tonawanda, New York, USA, 14150

ORDERS PHONE: 1-800-565-9523
ORDERS FAX: 1-800-221-9985
ORDERS EMAIL: utpbooks@utpress.utoronto.ca

UK, Ireland, and continental Europe
NBN International
Estover Road, Plymouth, PL6 7PY, UK
TEL: 44 (0) 1752 202301
FAX ORDER LINE: 44 (0) 1752 202333
enquiries@nbninternational.com

This book is printed on paper containing 100% post-consumer fibre.

The University of Toronto Press acknowledges the financial support for its publishing activities of the Government of Canada through the Book Publishing Industry Development Program (BPIDP).

Every effort has been made to contact copyright holders; in the event of an omission or error, please notify the publisher.

Cover design by Em Dash Design.
Interior design by Em Dash Design.

Printed in Canada

CONTENTS

APPENDICES

In some ways, writing a book that sets as its goal an understanding of American politics is an immodest and impossible task. "There is so much more in America than any one man can know," says Harold Laski in *The American Democracy* (1948). "There is so much in it, both of beauty and ugliness, of good and evil, that he cannot put into words." But the ambitiousness of the enterprise has not stopped many from trying. Alexis de Tocqueville's magisterial *Democracy in America*, written in the 1830s, is surely the best known and many believe the most successful of such attempts. It was followed by books on American politics and society written by many of the leading thinkers of their times, including James Bryce, H.G. Wells, Georges Duhamel, and Gunnar Myrdal, to mention only a handful. The effort has continued in more recent decades, generating a prodigious mountain of scholarship, commentary, and polemic.

Laski's caution about the challenge that faces anyone who seeks to add to this mountain deserves to be taken seriously. At the same time, however, a sober appreciation of the scale and, according to Laski, impossibility of the task should not produce despair or paralysis. I chose the title *Understanding American Politics* in the belief that this attempt is always worthwhile and perhaps never more so than in the times in which we currently live. I do not expect that readers will reach the end of this book and proclaim, "Now it all makes sense to me." But if he or she understands better the confusing eddies that flow beneath the surface of American politics, then the effort of writing this book will have been worthwhile. Perfect understanding is for the omniscient and the deluded, who are sometimes the same. Along with Harold Laski, the rest of us may be content with a level of insight more suited to the mortal condition.

Part of that condition involves what Max Lerner once described as the ideas that we associate with America and the sentiments that are stirred by our perceptions of its actions and their consequences. It is impossible, Lerner argued, to view the United States with detachment. Inevitably our hopes and fears for the American enterprise, an enterprise that is now several centuries in the making, intrude and color our judgments. When French President Nicolas Sarkozy visited the United States in 2007 and spoke of "l'Amérique qu'on aime" (the America that we love), he thereby acknowledged the hopes and expectations that his compatriots, and many non-Americans throughout the world, have for the United States. These hopes and expectations are also held, even more fervently, by Americans. Indeed, Americans have often been the sharpest and least forgiving critics when they perceive that their country has failed to achieve the ideals that they expect of it.

When I conceived the idea for this book I had in mind chiefly the thousands of non-American students at universities throughout the world. Courses on the politics and government of the United States are frequently taught in English even in many countries where this is a second language for most or all students. These students prefer to approach the study of American politics from a comparative perspective, something that is uncommon in the standard textbooks on the politics and government of the United States. But when I began to teach courses on Foreign Perceptions of America and on Canadian Politics at the University of Michigan, I immediately discovered that American students also appreciated the comparative approach. Too often the politics and government of the United States are taught in a way that ignores the rest of the world. This approach impoverishes students by failing to make them aware of other cultural and institutional possibilities that exist. Moreover, it does nothing to help them understand how others view them and their country, a failure whose consequences are more appreciated these days than in years past.

As a result, I revised my original plan and attempted to write a book that would help non-Americans *and* Americans to better understand the politics and government of the United States. To achieve this aim I weave my analysis around the concept of American exceptionalism—not American superiority, but American difference—that is at least as old as Tocqueville's monumental study of American democracy. Whether this book succeeds in providing a better understanding of American politics than those offered by competing interpretations is up to instructors and students to judge.

Acknowledging the debts that one owes to others should always be a pleasure and it certainly is for me in connection with this book. My first thanks must go to Michael Harrison of the University of Toronto Press, who encouraged me to write this book. Michael also happens to be the person who signed me to write *Canadian Democracy*, now in its sixth edition. He is truly one of the most respected people in Canadian academic publishing. Greg Yantz helped shepherd this project from proposal to the final manuscript and his background in the University of Michigan's strong tradition of quantitative research made him an ideal editor for this book.

Copy editors always play a crucial role in ensuring that readers are not subjected to careless writing, sloppy thinking, and the multitude of errors and omissions that can seriously mar a book. I was privileged to work with an exceptionally good one on this project. Betsy Struthers was a meticulous reader, with a strong sense of how thoughts ought to be expressed. The first quality is one that is expected in a copy editor. To be fortunate enough to work with someone who has the second quality is a true blessing.

As is often the case with my books, this one is replete with figures and tables. Luc Quenneville of the Document Services Department at the University of Windsor was indispensable in helping me construct these, taking my hand-drawn graphs, bar charts, and tables and converting them into something intelligible. Never once did he complain, although I am certain that he had reason to on more than one occasion.

Most of this book was written while I held the Chaire en études canadiennes at the Sorbonne's Institut du monde anglophone. I am grateful to my colleague Jean-Michel Lacroix of l'Université de Paris III for the opportunity to spend a year in circumstances that were so conducive to work on this book. I would also like to thank Professor Romain Huret of l'Université de Lyon for the opportunity to present some of my ideas on religion and American politics to his seminar on the United States.

Finally I would like to thank the students who have taken my American politics courses in Ann Arbor, Brussels, Leuven, Paris, and Windsor. Teaching them provided me with the motivation to write this book and kept me focused on the comparative approach that is woven throughout its chapters. I dedicate this book to them.

Stephen Brooks
Paris and Windsor

UNITED STATES OF AMERICA

PHOTOS (LEFT TO RIGHT)

1. Among the symbols most often associated with the United States, the Statue of Liberty is perhaps the foremost. For about 12 million newcomers to America it was one of their first views of the country as they approached the immigration station at Ellis Island.
2. Americans do not hold a monopoly on patriotism, but Tocqueville's observation that they tend to be more overtly patriotic, as seen in public displays of the flag everywhere from private homes to hardware stores, continues to distinguish them from citizens of other Western democracies.
3. Alexis de Tocqueville visited the United States in 1831. His book *Democracy in America* is the best known and most cited interpretation of the country ever written by a foreign observer.
4. The election of Barack Obama, seen here taking the oath of office as the 44th president of the United States, was widely seen in America and abroad as the most important step forward in race relations since the passage of the 1964 *Civil Rights Act*. Image courtesy of Master Sergeant Cecilio Ricardo, US Air Force/Department of Defense.

PART ONE

Introduction

CHAPTER ONE

American Exceptionalism

Several days before reaching the coast of New England in the year 1629, John Winthrop wrote what would become one of the most famous journal entries of all time. Winthrop was a Puritan who became the first governor of the Massachusetts Bay Colony. In his journal he expressed confidence that the hand of Providence had guided him and his fellow pilgrims to the New World where they would build a "shining city on a hill." With these words was born the idea of American exceptionalism. Winthrop believed that those he led were part of a singular destiny that would unfold in North America. They were not simply exporting the Old World—its values, institutions, and ways—to a new land. Rather, he believed, a new chapter in human history was about to be written.

Almost four centuries later, this notion of American exceptionalism is still strong. Indeed, recent years have seen a flurry of books that take as their theme the gap between the United States and countries with which it shares a common Western heritage: *American Vertigo: In the Steps of de Tocqueville*, by Bernard-Henri Lévy; *America Alone*, by Mark Steyn; *America Against the World*, by Andrew Kohut and Bruce Stokes; Jeffrey Kopstein and Sven Steinmo's, *Growing Apart? America and Europe in the 21st Century*; and my own book, *As Others See Us: The Causes and Consequences of Foreign Perceptions of America*.[1]

The notion of American exceptionalism is almost always anchored to ideas. G.K. Chesterton put it well when he wrote, "America is the only nation in the world that is founded on a creed. That creed is set forth with dogmatic and even theological lucidity in the Declaration of Independence."[2]

Gunnar Myrdal echoed these sentiments in *An American Dilemma*, where he examined in exhaustive detail the ways in which what he called the "American creed"[3]—faith in individual freedom and the equality of persons—excluded black Americans and the reasons for their exclusion. Harold Laski, Simone de Beauvoir, Jean Baudrillard, and others have made similar arguments, emphasizing the difference between the values and beliefs of Americans and those of other national populations. The World Values Survey project, directed by Ronald Inglehart over the last three decades, provides solid empirical proof that, when it comes to culture, the United States is in many important respects an outlier among advanced democratic societies (see Figure 1.1).

FIGURE 1.1:   INGLEHART-WETLZEL CULTURAL MAP OF THE WORLD

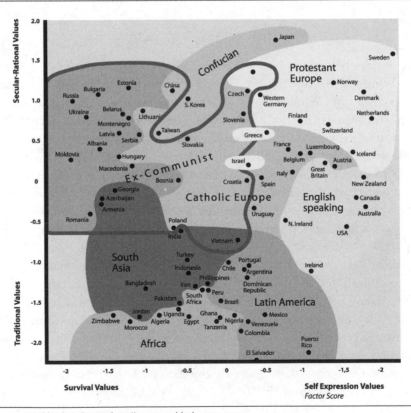

Source: World Values Survey, http://www.worldvaluessurvey.org.

The American exceptionalism thesis includes several elements relating to the history and contemporary conditions of the United States. They include the following:

- the absence of a history of rigid class hierarchy;
- the lack of a tory tradition that would have legitimized such a class hierarchy;
- the weakness of socialism, both as a political movement and an ideology;
- the nature of America's religious tradition, which has been more pluralistic and democratic compared to that in other Western societies;
- a national identity—"Americanism"—constructed on the basis of universal values rather than ethnicity, religion, or some other ascriptive criteria;
- exceptional geographic and socio-economic mobility;
- the ability to integrate unmatched number of immigrants into American society; and
- a belief in the special mission and destiny of the United States.

Some of these elements of American exceptionalism have been challenged on the grounds that they no longer accurately describe an important difference between the United States and the rest of the developed world. In particular, the claims about its unmatched level of socio-economic mobility and its capacity to integrate successfully new immigrants are disputed by critics at home and abroad. Others criticize the notion of American exceptionalism on the grounds that it is often used as a justification for American interventions abroad (ironically, perhaps, it has just as often been used as a reason not to meddle in foreign affairs), as in President George W. Bush's 2002 address to Congress in which he spoke of America's mission to export democracy. Still others object to what they see as the inescapable parochialism and arrogance that accompanies Americans' belief that their country is somehow special. Shortly after 9/11, British novelist Doris Lessing wrote:

> The judgment "they had it coming," so angrily resented, is perhaps misunderstood. What people felt was that Americans had at last learned that they are like everyone else, vulnerable to the maker of Envy and Revenge, to bombs exploding on a street corner ... or in a hotel housing a government (as in Brighton). They say themselves

that they have been expelled from their Eden. How strange they should ever have thought they had a right to one.[4]

Another criticism of the American exceptionalism thesis comes from those who maintain that the special condition of the country and, in particular, its prominent status in the world are temporary and passing. Harold Laski, one of the greatest left-wing thinkers of the twentieth century, argued in his 1948 book, *The American Democracy*, that the United States would eventually become "Europeanized."[5] By this he meant that class conflict would break through what he believed to be the clutter of false consciousness and misinformed contentment generated by the American media, the educational system, and organized religion, producing a reorganization around class interests and identities of the political party system and of politics more generally. Many social scientists on both sides of the Atlantic shared this expectation. The fact that it has not come about two generations after Laski made his prediction may be interpreted in a couple of ways. One possibility is that the power of the interests that Laski believed prevented class politics from assuming a more prominent role in the United States has been greater than he imagined. But the other possibility is that what critics from Laski to historian Howard Zinn and activist writer Noam Chomsky dismiss as a false consciousness nurtured and reproduced through capitalist manipulations is in fact a durable and deeply rooted culture difference that tends to inoculate Americans against class politics.

The emergence of the United States as the world's foremost economic and military power during the twentieth century was immediately linked to ideas of American exceptionalism. However, there has been no shortage of critics who have predicted the decline and fall of the United States, interpreting American dominance as a passing phase in world history rather than evidence of exceptionalism. The first major wave of skeptics emerged during the 1960s when American forces were bogged down in an increasingly unpopular war in Vietnam. Critics at home and abroad argued that this war showed that the United States had become an imperialist power and that its leaders had turned their backs not only on Washington and Jefferson's advice not to meddle in quarrels far from America's shores and distant from its domestic interests but had also abandoned the internationalism of Woodrow Wilson and Franklin Delano Roosevelt. As the costs mounted in money and lives, those who insisted that the United States had a responsibility to combat the spread of communism throughout the world found fewer sympathetic ears.

The ignominious withdrawal of American troops from Vietnam occurred at a time of major economic uncertainty and racial tensions that continued to roil the surface of American life after the riots and assassinations of the 1960s. The United States seemed to many people, both within and outside its borders, to be less exceptional than similar to other big, aggressive powers that had come before it. The fact that this free fall in America's international reputation coincided with years of major economic uncertainty during the 1970s and the post-Watergate scandal increase in public cynicism about politics made arguments about America's decline seem even more convincing. In a 1976 Swedish television animated documentary entitled, "The American Dream," Sweden's foremost political cartoonist, Leif Zetterling, expressed the view of many Western intellectuals. He portrayed American history as five centuries of violence, oppression, dispossession, and aggression, finally culminating in domestic collapse. Simone de Beauvoir, Herbert Marcuse, and many other prominent left-wing thinkers of this period agreed with Zetterling's assessment of American decadence and inevitable decline.

The1980s saw a rebound of faith in American exceptionalism. Ronald Reagan was the living embodiment of the doctrine, expressing the sunny optimism, idealism, and uncomplicated virtues associated with the premise of American greatness and belief in its unique role in the world. Reagan's 1984 re-election slogan captured the national mood: "It's morning again in America." When the Berlin Wall came down in 1989 and the Soviet Union collapsed two years later, American triumphalism under Reagan's successor, George H.W. Bush, was running at full throttle. Francis Fukuyama argued that the age of ideology was dead, that communism had been vanquished by capitalism and liberal democracy embodied in their most successful form by the United States.

But the end of the Cold War and the apparent victory of democratic capitalism were interpreted differently by some. When the American economy slipped into recession at the beginning of the 1990s and with the old certainties of the bipolar world swept away, a new wave of declinist thinking emerged. Paul Kennedy's *The Rise and Fall of the Great Powers*[6] led the way. Published in 1989, this book argued that the decline of past empires came about as a result of military overstretch and that the United States was heading down the same path. Kennedy's view of an American empire in decline was echoed by others at home and abroad. Here is a short list of some of the gloomy assessments, from conservatives and liberals alike, published during those years:

- John Kenneth Galbraith, *The Culture of Contentment* (1992). An American liberal's lament over what he saw as the short-sighted unwillingness of conservative administrations in the United States to address the real and worsening problems of the poor.

- Allan Bloom, *The Closing of the American Mind* (1987). A conservative philosopher's call to arms against what he argued to be the evisceration of American principles and in particular the impoverishment of higher education.
- A similar argument was made by Daniel D'Souza in *Illiberal Education* (1991), although he focused on what he called the damaging consequences of political correctness and its contribution to making the United States a country of balkanized tribal enclaves.
- Robert Reich, *The Work of Nations* (1991). This Berkeley professor, who became President Clinton's first Secretary of Labor, argued that its failure to adapt to the forces of globalization was contributing to class polarization in the United States.
- Arthur Schlesinger, Jr., *The Disuniting of America* (1993). Rampant multiculturalism and an emphasis on group identities over universal values were, this Harvard historian argued, undermining the foundations of America's pluralistic democracy.

Prognostications of doom and gloom did not have the field all to themselves, but voices of dissent such as James Galbraith's *The Myth of America's Decline* (1990) were drowned out by the much louder chorus of the declinists.[7]

However, as in previous decades, predictions of America's decline soon appeared to be premature. A resurgence of triumphalism swept across the United States in the 1990s as the country's economy experienced the longest period of sustained robust growth in decades. The nature of the post-Cold War world seemed to have only one certainty: the unrivalled power of the United States. The terms "uni-polar world," "American hegemony," and American "hyper-power" (*hyper-puissance*, as coined by the French politician and writer Hubert Védrine) became common at the end of what *Time* magazine's one-time editor, Henry Luce, called the "American century." The unmatched wealth and international influence of the United States were, the triumphalists argued, the rewards of American exceptionalism.

The years since 9/11 and the 2003 invasion of Iraq re-energized the debate on American exceptionalism in many important ways. The failure of the United States to capture Osama bin Laden and the persistence of

Taliban influence in Afghanistan several years after the regime was ousted from Kabul, combined with the protracted war in Iraq, illustrated the limits to American military power. The inevitable comparisons of Iraq to Vietnam grew even stronger after President George W. Bush's Republican Party experienced serious losses in the 2006 congressional elections. Predictably, a fresh cycle of declinist analysis accompanied these years, focusing not only on what was seen as imperial overstretch but also on severe problems at home. Foremost among these domestic problems, critics argued, were crippling economic problems and class polarization. The conditions that had always been central to American exceptionalism—democratic idealism, a leading role in the world, and the promise of widely shared opportunities and affluence at home—were imperiled. Variations of this argument have been advanced by such prominent thinkers as Emmanuel Todd, *Après l'empire* (2002); Paul Krugman, *The Great Unraveling* (2003); Immanuel Wallerstein, *The Decline of American Power* (2003); Jeremy Rifkin, *The European Dream* (2004); and Stanley Hoffman in *America Goes Backward* (2004).[8]

The idea of American exceptionalism, we have seen, is as old as the European settlement of America. It has been explained and endorsed over the years by some of the Western world's most distinguished thinkers, including Alexis de Tocqueville, H.G. Wells, Gunnar Myrdal, and Harold Laski, as well as such prominent American scholars as Seymour Martin Lipset, Louis Hartz, and Daniel Boorstin. The idea of American exceptionalism easily shades into a conviction that providence has marked out the United States for a special role in the world and that the American model is destined to triumph over its rivals. This is how American exceptionalism is often understood by politicians, radio talk show hosts, and motivational speakers.

This is not, however, the meaning of American exceptionalism that is used in this book. By American exceptionalism I mean simply that the circumstances of America's historical development have ensured that its voices and institutions continue to be significantly different from those of the European societies whose immigrants and ideas gave it birth. What was true when Tocqueville visited the United States in 1831–32 continues to be true today. Although the nature of American exceptionalism is no longer identical to that described by Tocqueville,[9] much of what sets American politics apart from the politics of other wealthy democracies can be traced to that earlier America.

The idea of American exceptionalism has been reinforced in recent years by empirical studies of the values and beliefs of Americans compared to those of other democracies. The World Values Survey (WVS) based at the University of Michigan has been surveying national populations—democratic and non-democratic, rich and poor—for three decades. Data from the WVS tends to corroborate the American exceptionalism thesis. So too does the survey data collected for the Global Attitudes Project of the Pew Center for the People and the Press. A number of recent analyses of the United States, both American and foreign, concur in varying ways with the American exceptionalism thesis.

American exceptionalism provides a framework for making sense of what might otherwise seem anomalous behaviors and outcomes. Gunnar Myrdal recognized this in *An American Dilemma*, his sweeping analysis of race relations in the United States. The fact that Americans had elevated the values of freedom and equality to the status of a national creed, a sort of civic religion whose principles were explicit and known to all, was indicative of this exceptionalism. "The American Creed is not merely—as in some countries— the implicit background of the nation's political and judicial order," says Myrdal, "But as principles which *ought* to rule, the Creed has been made conscious to everyone in American society."[10] But it also cast a harsher and less forgiving light on the treatment of the country's black minority, a lived reality that was so much at odds with the ideals embodied in the creed.

American Exceptionalism and the Playing Field

In the course of the twentieth century, especially among countries of the advanced industrial world, a set of common icons has developed that have become part of what we call Western culture. While this has been true on all levels, elite as well as mass, this commonality has been particularly pronounced in what has come to be known as popular culture.... [I]t would be erroneous to see this development as purely a one-way street in which an all-powerful America imposes its cultural icons on the rest of the world. Any visit to the United States, where wine drinking, coffee culture, sushi, and other aspects of the European as well as the Far Eastern culinary worlds have become commonplace from coast to coast, demonstrates that global culture—though featuring American items—is far from identical with American culture. Moreover, important pockets of popular culture exist that have remained completely resistant to any kind of Americanization in the course of the twentieth century. Nowhere is this more pronounced than in the crucial world of mass sports.... Americans know details and become passionate about the World Series ... and March Madness, and they remember and revere—perhaps even idolize—legends such as Mickey Mantle ... and Wayne Gretzky ("The Great One").... Europeans have identical relationships of affect and admiration for the likes of Bobby Charlton ... and other greats of the world of soccer. While to Americans, Fenway Park ... and Madison Square Garden invoke history, memory, and awe, Europeans experience identical sentiments and associations with names such as Old Trafford, ... Maracana, and the Boekelberg.

Andrei Markovits and Stephen Hellerman, Offside: Soccer and American Exceptionalism *(Princeton, NJ: Princeton University Press, 2001) 42.*

American military interventions abroad have often been explained as the simple and brutal expression of the economic and strategic interests of the United States. Such explanations, while often containing a large element of truth, are misleading and incomplete when they do not take seriously the idealism that has long been an important element of American thinking about America's role in the world. From President McKinley's 1898 decision to send American ships and troops to the Philippines to the 2003 invasion of Iraq under George W. Bush, democratic idealism has been part of the explanation—not merely the justification—for American actions abroad.

The point is this: in order to understand politics and governance in the United States, one needs to be aware of and take seriously these values that make America exceptional. I do not mean exceptional in any absolute sense. To say that Americans tend to be idealistic or religious or populist, for example, does not mean that these attributes are absent in other national populations but that they assume greater importance in the United States or they take a form that is significantly different there compared to other societies. For example, it would be wrong to say that Americans are more egalitarian than Swedes. However, egalitarianism tends to assume a different form in the United States, being much less about equality of socio-economic conditions and much more about perceived equality of opportunity. To give another example, by such measures as church attendance, importance attached to prayer, and belief in absolute standards of good and evil, the Irish are as religious as Americans. However, the nature of religious belief and participation in the United States tend to be different from in Ireland and the relationship between religion and politics is also not the same.

In *American Exceptionalism*, Seymour Martin Lipset identifies the five values that he believes constitute American exceptionalism:

- liberty,
- egalitarianism,
- individualism,
- populism, and
- laissez-faire.[11]

In the spirit of Louis Hartz's argument that America is pure eighteenth-century liberalism—basically John Locke plus Adam Smith—reinforced by a frontier experience that reinforced these values, Lipset makes the case that these five elements of American exceptionalism hold the key to solving the puzzles of American politics.

Without wanting to challenge in any fundamental way Lipset's characterization of American exceptionalism, the analysis in the following chapters
is based on a slightly different set of values. They are listed and explained
in Table 1.1.

America the Baffling

More than is true for any other country in the world, people outside the
United States are likely to have an opinion about it. This is not surprising.
The American military presence and the economic activities of American
businesses are found in all corners of the world. But, most importantly, in
terms of its impact on why and what others think about the United States
and its people, American culture spans the globe. It has been said that, after
God, Coca-Cola is the most recognized word in the world. Not only such
corporate symbols, but American films, music, video games, television programs, and computer software and websites find markets throughout the
world. Measuring the scope and value of American cultural exports in all
their forms is extremely difficult, but they are acknowledged by all trade
experts to be vast. To give but one example, in 2004 all of the top 20 films
in the world, measured by box-office gross and excluding revenues earned in
the United States, were products of Hollywood's dream machine.[12]

Little wonder then that people everywhere tend to have opinions about—
and often think they understand—America and Americans. After watching
countless films where settings, stories, and stars are Americans and listening to hours of music from Elvis Presley to Christine Aguilera, such a belief
is not surprising. It is reinforced by the fact that political leaders, teachers, journalists, and religious leaders in virtually all countries communicate
information, ideas, and images of America to their populations.

The sentiments that foreign populations have toward the United States
are wide-ranging and often quite different within a single country. Indeed,
ambivalence—admiration of some American traits, institutions, values, and
accomplishments and dislike of others—is common in many countries. But
even among those who, on the whole, hold positive views of America, there
is widespread bafflement over what are seen to be characteristic features of
American politics and society. This bafflement assumes the form of a number
of questions that one encounters constantly when traveling abroad. Among
the most frequent are the following:

TABLE 1.1:   THE ATTRIBUTES OF AMERICAN EXCEPTIONALISM

Attribute	
Idealism	While often skeptical about human nature ("If men were angels, there would be no need for government," Madison, *Federalist Paper* no.10), Americans tend to have faith in progress, in personal and social improvement—what Tocqueville called the idea of human predictability—and in the effectiveness of well-designed constitutions and institutions. Their generally optimistic outlook is related to their idealism.
Populism	The absence of hereditary aristocracy and title, the Lockean liberalism of the founders, the early equality of social conditions that so struck Tocqueville, and the leveling influences of the frontier all combined to create and sustain a strong belief in the idea of popular sovereignty. Government belongs to the people, it should never be something that is apart from or above them.
Materialism	The pursuit of wealth has always been considered legitimate and, in the eyes of most Americans, a sign of success. They are not alone in this, but economic freedoms, property rights, profits, and the attainment of wealth as a good in itself tend to be valued more highly in the United States than in other democratic societies.
Individualism	The rights and freedom of individual citizens have always been central to the American value system. But individualism also, and even more fundamentally, involves their tendency to think of the individual as the basic unit of society, primarily responsible for his or her own welfare and success in life.
Egalitarianism	Relatively few Americans think that the good society is one in which differences in the material well-being and social conditions of individuals are small. They do believe, however, that people should have equal opportunities to pursue their dreams or at least as equal as is feasible in an imperfect world. Abraham Lincoln called this the "civic religion" of Americans: their belief that they too could move from modest means as a wage-earner to wealth as a business owner or property holder.
Openness	Americans expect that actions, motives, and consequences will be out in the open, transparent for all to see. They mistrust authority that cloaks itself in secrecy. Their openness extends to personal and political relationships.
Religiosity	Traditional religious values and practices—including belief in absolute standards of good and evil, in the existence of God, the importance of prayer, regular church attendance, and volunteer work and charitable giving through churches—are found more frequently in the United States than in other developed democratic societies. Moreover, Americans are more likely than others to expect political leaders to be motivated by religious values and to express their faith in the public sphere.

- Why are Americans so hypocritical, professing to believe or stand for one thing, but behaving in ways that are so different from their words?
- Why do they so often elect mediocre and even stupid people?
- Despite all the talk about government by and for the people, it's the "golden rule," right? That is, those with the gold rule in America.
- Why don't Americans understand or even care about the selfish consequences of their lifestyles and actions abroad?
- Why are Americans, or at least their governments, so often out of sync with other democracies when it comes to important issues like capital punishment, landmines, global warming, the International Criminal Court, and more?
- Why does a country that is so rich tolerate such poverty in its midst?
- Why is there so much violence in America, and why don't governments take some obvious steps to reduce it, like stricter gun control?
- Why are judges, sheriffs, and even county drain commissioners elected?
- Why is racism so prevalent in America?
- Why don't Americans vote?
- Why are there only two political parties in America, and how can Americans expect to have all points of view represented by so few parties?

Questions like these reflect the fact that non-Americans often see the United States as exceptional, but not always in a good way. They are sometimes puzzled by the values and behavior of Americans and the actions of those who govern them. The Belgian cartoonist Hergé's famous character, Tintin, expressed this bafflement when he said "Qu'ils sont fous, les Américains!" (Americans are crazy!) The chapters that follow are a modest effort to help readers outside the United States—and Americans too—understand the fundamental ideas, institutions, and processes of politics and government in America. Whether you decide that Americans and their politics are, indeed, exceptional, and that this is on the whole a good or bad thing, is of course up to you.

Notes

1 Bernard-Henri Lévy, *American Vertigo: Traveling America in the Footsteps of Tocqueville* (New York: Random House, 2006); Mark Steyn, *America Alone: The End of the World As We Know It* (Washington, DC: Regnery Publishing, 2006); Andrew Kohut and Bruce Stokes, *America against the World: How We Are Different and Why We Are Disliked* (New York: Times Books, 2006); Jeffrey Kopstein and Sven Steinmo (eds.), *Growing Apart? America and Europe in the 21st Century* (Cambridge: Cambridge University Press, 2007); Stephen Brooks, *As Others See Us: The Causes and Consequences of Foreign Perceptions of America* (Peterborough, ON: Broadview Press, 2006).

2 G.K. Chesterton, cited in Gunnar Myrdal, *An American Dilemma: The Negro Problem and American Democracy* (New York: Harper and Brothers, 1944).

3 Myrdal.

4 Doris Lessing, "What We Think of America," *Granta* 77 (2002): 54.

5 Harold Laski, *The American Democracy* (New York: Viking, 1948).

6 Paul Kennedy, *The Rise and Fall of the Great Powers: Economic Change and Military Conflict from 1500 to 2000* (New York: Vintage, 1989).

7 John Kenneth Galbraith, *The Culture of Contentment* (New York: Houghton Mifflin, 1992); Allan Bloom, *The Closing of the American Mind* (New York: Simon and Schuster, 1987); D'Souza, Daniel. *Illiberal Education* (New York: The Free Press, 1991); Robert Reich, *The Work of Nations* (New York: Vintage, 1991); Arthur Schlesinger Jr., *The Disuniting of America* (New York: Norton, 1993); James Galbraith, *The Myth of America's Decline* (New York: Oxford University Press, 1990).

8 Emmanuel Todd, *Après l'empire* (Paris: Gallimard, 2002); Paul Krugman, *The Great Unraveling* (New York: Norton, 2003); Immanuel Wallerstein, *The Decline of American Power* (New York: The New Press, 2003); Jeremy Rifkin, *The European Dream* (New York: Tarcher, 2004); and Stanley Hoffman, *America Goes Backward* (New York: New York Review of Books, 2004).

9 Alexis de Tocqueville, *Democracy in America*, Books I and II, from the Henry Reeve Translation, revised and corrected, 1899; University of Virginia, American Studies Program http://xroads.virginia.edu/~HYPER/DETOC/colophon.html. All references to and quotes from Tocqueville in this text come from this source.

10 Myrdal 3.

11 Seymour Martin Lipset, *American Exceptionalism* (New York: Norton, 1996).

12 Based on data at http://www.boxofficemojo.com and http://www.moviemarshal.com.

PHOTOS (LEFT TO RIGHT)

1. Abortion continues to be a politically divisive issue in America, and one that, unlike in other democracies, regularly arises during election campaigns.
2. Americans are far more likely than people in other rich democracies to say that they pray on a regular basis. Prayer circles, where people pray together publicly—for example, at a sporting event or social gathering—are common in many parts of the United States. Image courtesy of the Holy Ghost Riders.
3. Dr. Martin Luther King, Jr., was both the most prominent spiritual leader in black America and the political leader of the civil rights movement. This photo was taken during his 1963 March on Washington that culminated in his famous "I have a dream" speech. Image courtesy of the National Archives and Records Administration.
4. Millions of Europeans took to the streets in 2003 to protest the looming American-led invasion of Iraq. President Bush's characterization of Saddam Hussein's regime as part of the "axis of evil" resonated with many Americans but was considered to be simplistic and inappropriately moral in tone by most Western Europeans.
5. Rates of volunteerism are higher in the United States than in other democracies.

PART TWO

Ideas and Behavior

CHAPTER TWO

Political Culture

Introduction

In recent years there has been a spike in the number of analyses purporting to find a large and growing gulf between the political values and beliefs of Americans and those of their counterparts in other affluent democracies. The title of a recent book asks, *Growing Apart? America and Europe in the 21st Century*.[1] Analyses such as this have tended to stress what is argued to be the gap between secular Western Europe and traditionally religious America; the greater pacifism and multilateralism of Europeans versus the tendency toward militarism and unilateralism among Americans; and the communitarian ethos of Europeans and their greater willingness to rely on the state to achieve collective goals—whether economic, environmental, cultural, or social—compared to the stronger individualism of Americans and their tendency to mistrust the state. Many of these analyses have compared America unfavorably to other affluent democracies, arguing that its values and policies are increasingly retrograde and out of sync with the realities of the contemporary world. Others, however, judge America positively, particularly with respect to what is argued to be its superior ability to integrate newcomers into American society and what some believe to be the necessity of Americans' willingness to maintain the world's most formidable military in defense of the values that America stands for.

There is a sense that America is an outlier: an anomalous case that does not conform to a pattern of change observable in countries that have a broadly similar standard of living, democratic political institutions, and a common Western heritage. This assessment is in large measure correct, but it is also rather misleading. When speaking of the political values and beliefs of Americans, which Americans does one have in mind? Someone flying from Burlington, Vermont to Amarillo, Texas might find it difficult to believe that the people living in these two communities belong to the same country. America is a society in which Michael Moore on the left and Mark Steyn on the right can both draw a standing-room-only crowd, although not always in the same city or on the same college campus. Assessments of American political culture need to be mindful of the important variations that exist regionally and along other fault lines cutting through the American population. Such variations exist in any diverse society, but they tend either to be overlooked, caricatured, or assigned insufficient importance by outside observers.

Openness

European visitors to the United States have long been struck by what might be called the openness of its people and their mores. Openness here refers to the quality of lacking guile and artifice, of allowing oneself and one's actions, motives and sentiments to be open to others and expecting such openness in return. Many of the attributes that foreign observers have argued characterize American culture are linked in some important way to this quality of openness. They include the following:

Naiveté. Americans have often been portrayed as naïve and lacking in sophistication. Alexis de Tocqueville remarked on the lack of guile and artifice on the part of those Americans he met. Charles Dickens also recognized openness as a typically American attribute, but he was inclined to see in their open and frank manner a sort of boorish lack of breeding and uncouth quality. The naïve American versus the worldly and sophisticated European has long been a pretty standard trope. But it has not always contained a critical judgment on Americans.

Naiveté may be associated with gullibility and simple-mindedness. Ronald Reagan and George W. Bush are two recent presidents who have been characterized by some, in the United States and abroad, as rather simple-minded in their understanding of the world. In his memoirs, former Canadian Prime Minister Pierre Trudeau tells of how he and French President François Mitterand were dumbfounded at a NATO meeting when President Reagan launched into a sincere discourse on the evils of communism.[2] Reagan's tendency to understand issues in dichotomous terms and to communicate his vision of America and its place in the world in terms of right and wrong, good and bad, virtue versus vice is one of the qualities that his many admirers like most. George W. Bush is another president who has often been portrayed as naïve and simpleminded. In the eyes of his critics, these qualities made him incapable of understanding the complexity of issues and of the world. According to this interpretation, Bush's lack of sophistication left him open to the manipulations of people in his administration like Donald Cheney, Paul Wolfowitz, and Donald Rumsfeld, who effectively pulled the strings in the White House. During his second term as president, Bush often said, speaking of the war in Iraq, that he would rather be right than popular. His defenders maintained that what critics interpreted as naiveté and

American Melting Pot and Canadian Mosaic?

All Canadian schoolchildren learn that their society is more diverse and accommodating toward cultural diversity than that of the United States. Indeed, along with schoolchildren in France, the United Kingdom (UK), and probably most other countries, Canadians learn that the United States, despite its vast size, is culturally a rather homogeneous place. It is the great melting pot where immigrants have long been expected to cast off the cultural baggage they bring with them from abroad, speak English, and share in a common set of values and beliefs and a more or less uniform lifestyle. To do otherwise would be un-American.

The problem with this image is that it is a caricature that ignores the considerable diversity that exists within the United States and between regions of that country and, moreover, exaggerates the difference between the cultural experiences of immigrants in that country compared to those in a country like Canada, which has an official policy of multiculturalism. Survey data show that the regional variations in values and beliefs between different regions of the United States are not narrower than those that exist within the predominantly English-speaking regions of Canada (omitting Quebec). Comparing rates of language retention, ethnic group identification, participation in ethnically based social networks,

and attitudes and behavior toward racial and ethnic minorities, Raymond Breton and Jeffrey Reitz argue that there is almost no empirical basis for Canadians' cherished self-image of their society as being more tolerant and less assimilationist than that of the United States.[3] Traveling across the United States, it is true that one is struck by elements of homogeneity—the Wal-marts, McDonald's, Starbucks, and other chains—but this is equally true of Canada.

The image of the American melting pot is not false; it just ignores important aspects of American society that emphasize diversity and difference rather than uniformity and sameness. The United States is, after all, the birthplace of multicultural studies, going back to the emergence on college campuses of Black Studies in the 1960s. Even a cursory glance at university course guides is enough to convince anyone that multicultural studies is a vast enterprise in American academe. This has been lamented by some, who believe that this emphasis on difference is socially and politically divisive. The same phenomenon and reaction may be observed in Canada. The point is that the so-called melting pot is not as homogenous as many foreign and even some American observers appear to believe. Nor is the Canadian mosaic immune from the same assimilationist pressures that exist within the United States.

simplemindedness—when more venal motives were not attributed—was, in fact, the same strength of character that Reagan's admirers saw in him.

The judgment that Americans are naïve and simpleminded is not one reserved for some of their leaders. The day after George W. Bush's re-election the front page of the London tabloid *The Sun* read, "How could 59,054,087 people be so stupid?" Openness as simplemindedness, naiveté, and a capacity to be taken in by arguments that a more sophisticated and worldly people would reject continues to be seen by some as an important aspect of American culture and, moreover, one that impedes Americans' ability to understand the world.

Transparency, equality, and accountability. Openness has, however, another side that is far more positive. It may connote frankness, candor, transparency in one's dealings with others, and an absence of barriers. Americans have often applied such qualities to their culture and their ideal American. Every American learns that George Washington, as a boy, is said to have replied to the question of whether he cut down the cherry tree by declaring, "I cannot tell a lie. I cut it down." Americans admire this sort of candor and lack of concealment. This does not mean that American politicians are less likely than their counterparts elsewhere to dissemble and deceive, or that bad behavior is less likely to be denied and concealed. Instead, it means that transgressions against idealized standards of frankness and transparency are more likely to be judged negatively and even harshly.

It is undeniable that concealment is present in much of American political life, including CIA involvement in various successful and failed coups, the Watergate cover-up of the Nixon years, the Iran-Contra scandal of the second Reagan administration, and allegations of lying and spin brought against every administration. But the culturally interesting point is not that bad behavior happens—where does it not?—but rather the reaction to it. Every democracy that observes the rule of law will, of course, censure and punish such behavior. But concealment, deception, and cover-up are considered to be particularly scandalous and unacceptable in America precisely because they transgress the value of transparency. The image that some have of America as a society in which the rich and powerful receive a pass for bad behavior simply does not square with the facts of a country in which, at any given time, numerous investigations of the powerful—in Congress, through the courts, and in the media—are ongoing. One need only listen to a few hours of National Public Radio (www.npr.org), watch CNN, or peruse the pages of the *New York Times* to know that investigating and exposing what is alleged to be wrongful behavior is a staple of American news. Of course, the rich and the powerful may avoid punishment in the end, but they are not spared the harsh spotlight of public scrutiny.

Friendliness and egalitarian manners. A third dimension of openness involves what James Bryce referred to as the habitually easy manner of Americans.[4] This is a quality that has been commented on countless times and that is, in fact, a standard part of the image of the American as found in literature and cinema. Wealth, occupation, and status—certainly not birth—do not determine how Americans deal with others. Jean Baudrillard provides an interesting description of these democratic manners, free from the self-consciousness and psychological barriers that class creates, in comparing restaurant servers in the United States and France:

> Just look at this girl who serves you in the guest-room: she does so in total freedom, with a smile, without prejudice or pretentiousness, as though she were sitting opposite you. The situation is not an equal one, but she does not pretend to equality. Equality is part of the way of life here. Precisely the opposite of Sartre's [French] waiter, who is completely alienated from his representation and who only resolves the situation by calling on a theatrical metalanguage, by affecting in his gestures a freedom and an equality he does not really enjoy ... In America—and this is a commonplace—you are astonished by the almost natural way status is forgotten, by the ease and freedom of personal relations.[5]

It is probably fair to say that this difference that Baudrillard observes and that commentators from Crèvecœur to Bernard-Henri Lévy have remarked on, has diminished over time as the hierarchical traditions of Europe have receded and democratic manners, as Tocqueville predicted, have sunk deeper roots in what formerly were aristocratic societies. Moreover, it is not true that Americans are never conscious of differences of status based on wealth, education, or position in their dealings with one another. But, on the whole and certainly compared to other Western democracies, the American style in personal relations is relaxed and casual.

The political significance of this was apparent in the 2004 presidential election that pitted George W. Bush—the folksy, occasionally tongue-tied president who was obviously comfortable at a southern barbeque and a football game—against Senator John Kerry—rather patrician, somewhat aloof in his manner of speaking and his bearing, and unconvincing in his efforts to be just like folks. Despite whatever other character attributes one may associate with Bush, he has always had, in the eyes of many, the quality of openness, understood as the absence of barriers and an ability to connect with people across differences of wealth and position. Bill Clinton had this too, as did Ronald Reagan and Jimmy Carter. John Kerry did not, and the attempt by his Republican opponents to portray him as distant, cold, and aloof—to portray him as French, as that national type is understood by many Americans—was largely successful.

In every society success in political communications depends on achieving a fit between the message, style, and image of the communicator and the expectations of his or her interlocutors. Although there is no one-size-fits-all style of political communication in the United States, there are few parts of the country and not many segments of the population where an open, egalitarian folksiness is not an asset. This style is sometimes seen as inauthentic, empty, and even a sort of manipulative façade. No doubt it is, on occasion, and there is no denying that folksy moments are regularly scripted and orchestrated, as is so much of American political communications. None of this diminishes the fact that Americans, by and large, expect their politicians to appear open and of the people.

Red Nation, Blue Nation: Are There Two Americas? (And Are They At War?)

Edward Kennedy is the senior American senator from Massachusetts. Aside from the president, Kennedy is probably the American politician best known to non-Americans. Part of this comes from the fact that he is the youngest brother of President John F. Kennedy, assassinated in 1963, and in recent years he has been the most prominent member of what is arguably America's best-known family. But part of his renown is due to his reputation as one of the country's foremost liberals. Groups like the American Civil Liberties Union (ACLU), Americans for Democratic Action, and the National Association for the Advancement of Colored People (NAACP) regularly rate Kennedy as one of the country's most liberal lawmakers. Organized labor considers him to be a faithful friend. Groups at the other end of the ideological spectrum, including the Christian Coalition and the National Taxpayers Union, just as regularly find themselves in opposition to the stands Kennedy takes and the votes that he casts in Congress. He voted against the tax cuts implemented during George W. Bush's first administration, he supported the 1973 *Roe v. Wade* Supreme Court decision that established a woman's constitutional right to an abortion, he voted for a ban on civilian ownership of

FIGURE 2.1:　AMERICA: RED AND BLUE, 2004 AND 2008

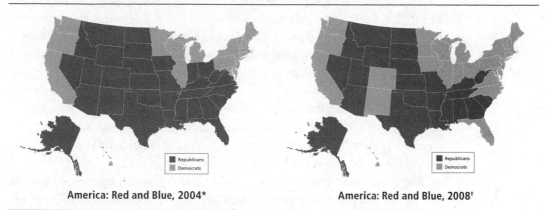

America: Red and Blue, 2004*　　　　　America: Red and Blue, 2008†

*Source: Mark Newman, Department of Physics and Center for the Study of Complex Systems, University of Michigan. Used with permission. † Source: http://www.uselectionatlas.org/RESULTS/.

assault weapons, he voted against a proposal to ban same-sex marriage, and he voted to ban oil drilling in the Alaska National Wildlife Reserve. Kennedy is a politician who would be comfortable in the British Labour Party or the German Social Democratic Party.

One of Kennedy's colleagues in the Senate is Saxby Chambliss, a Republican who represents Georgia. In many ways and on most issues, he is the mirror image of Senator Kennedy. Chambliss gets very high marks from the Conservative Coalition, the National Taxpayers Union, and the Chamber of Commerce, and correspondingly low ones from the liberal groups that rate Kennedy highly. His votes in Congress were exactly opposite to Kennedy's on every one of the issues mentioned above. Just as Kennedy represents "Blue America," Chambliss is one of the standard bearers of "Red America." It is hard to imagine a major Western European political party in which Chambliss would be comfortable. (For historical reasons, blue is the color of the Democratic Party and red of the Republican Party. This creates confusion for non-Americans, of course, because red is generally thought of as the color of the left and blue of the political right.)

The American political values map is both red (conservative) and blue (liberal), with many parts of the country about equally divided between these ideological tendencies and the political parties associated with them. Figure 2.1 shows the map for the 2004 presidential race. The lightly shaded states voted for Kerry and the darkly shaded ones for Bush. Maps like this one have contributed to the idea of a polarized America, with the west coast and the northeast being more liberal and the center of the country more conservative.

But the map is much more complex than can be captured by two broad ideological labels. The Pew Research Center has developed a more nuanced typology that has the dual advantage of recognizing, first, the significantly different value clusters within both Red and Blue America and, secondly, of acknowledging and describing the value attributes of that significant portion of the electorate that does not fall neatly into either camp. The Pew Center typology identifies nine distinct value clusters in the American population, defined by respondents' attitudes toward a range of political, economic, and cultural matters.[6] You may determine which of these groups you fall into by taking the survey online at http://typology.people-press.org.

The values map that emerges is more complex and fragmented than the red versus blue or conservative versus liberal characterizations suggest. Let us look at the value clusters in more detail.

Red America

Enterprisers (9% of adults; 10% of registered voters)

As the label suggests, these citizens believe strongly in the free enterprise system and tend to approve higher taxes and more government regulation of business. More than Americans generally, they believe that individuals are and should be responsible for their own well-being and that welfare programs encourage abuse and laziness. They also support a strong military and the projection of American power in order to protect against terrorism.

The enterprisers are mainly white (91%) and male (76%) and also tend to be more educated and better off financially than most Americans. They are also more likely to be married, own a gun, and have investments in stocks and bonds. About four out of five of them identify with the Republican Party. They voted overwhelmingly for Bush in 2004.

Social Conservatives (11% of adults; 13% of registered voters)

This pod of voters is defined chiefly by their values on morality issues. They are much more likely than the general population to oppose abortion and same-sex marriage. They are also far more likely to believe that immigrants threaten American customs and values. Like Enterprisers, Social Conservatives are skeptical when it comes to welfare state programs, but unlike Enterprisers they tend to think that business corporations are greedy and should be regulated.

Social Conservatives are mainly white (91%) and female (58%) and most attend church weekly. They also tend to be older than members of the other value pods, and close to half of them live in the South. Most own a gun and about half attend Bible study groups. This last figure is not surprising in light of the fact that about four out of 10 members of this group are evangelical Protestants, about twice the national average. About four out of five Social Conservatives identify with the Republican Party.

Pro-Government Conservatives (9% of adults; 10% of registered voters)
This group's label may seem to be an oxymoron. In fact, however, it expresses the complexity that exists inside the broad coalition of groups generally described as conservative and Republican-leaning. The members of this group are sometimes labeled populists and are characterized by stronger than average religious faith combined with skepticism about business and support for government regulation and social programs. They are prepared to ban books from school libraries if they contain "dangerous ideas," and they are more patriotic than most Americans.

These voters are mainly female (62%) and tend to be younger than most other groups in the electorate. They also include a greater proportion of blacks (10%) and Hispanics (12%) than is true of any other part of Red America. They tend to have less education and lower incomes than the general population, and they live disproportionately in the South (42%).

Like Social Conservatives, most Pro-Government Conservatives attend church weekly, but gun ownership is lower than for other conservative groups, and the likelihood that someone in the household has recently been unemployed is higher. Close to six in 10 identify with the Republican Party, but most of the remainder see themselves as Independent or express no party preference. They preferred Bush to Kerry in 2004 by a five to one ratio.

Blue America

Liberals (17% of adults; 19% of registered voters)
This group comprises the heart of Blue America and of the Democratic Party's base. They constitute the most secular group of voters and, therefore, the ones most likely to support same-sex marriage, oppose limits on abortion, and object to policies that limit the rights of accused persons or those convicted of illegal activity. They are strongly in favor of environmental regulation and are the least supportive group when it comes to projecting military force abroad.

Liberals are mainly white (83%) and are much more educated than the general population (about half have at least one college degree). They tend to have higher incomes and are found disproportionately in cities and the West.

In common with Enterprisers, Liberals are more likely than the general population to follow politics and current affairs. They are the group least likely to own a gun (23%), and barely more than one in 10 attends Bible study or prayer meetings. About six in 10 Liberals identify with the Democratic Party, and virtually all of the remainder are Independent or say that they have no partisan preference. In 2004 they voted for Kerry as solidly as Enterprisers and Social Conservatives voted for Bush.

Socially Conservative Democrats (14% of adults; 15% of registered voters)

In some important ways the defining values of these voters resemble those of Pro-Government Conservatives. Both groups have a strong religious orientation and are much more likely than the general population to agree that belief in God is necessary in order to be moral. And like Pro-Government Conservatives, most Socially Conservative Democrats support social spending for the needy (at the same time as they overwhelmingly believe that hard work will enable most people to get ahead in life). Some of these voters are the so-called Reagan Democrats who feel disconnected from the Democratic Party's more liberal bearings on social issues, but whose ties to that party have deep roots in the New Deal coalition that made the Democratic Party the dominant party in American politics from the Great Depression to the 1980s.

It is sometimes said that the black community, in which churches and religious leaders play a major role, is inherently conservative. And, indeed, about 30% of these voters are black, and about one-quarter are older women. Socially Conservative Democrats are somewhat poorer and less educated than the general population.

Close to half of these voters attend church weekly, and almost the same percentage attend Bible study or prayer meetings. About one-third own guns. Although they self-identify as conservatives or moderates, almost nine out of 10 identify with the Democratic Party. They voted for Kerry over Bush by a ratio of more than four to one.

Disadvantaged Democrats (10% of adults; 10% of registered voters)

These voters do not share in the sunny optimism of most Americans and are overwhelmingly skeptical that hard work is the road to success for most people. They have no sense of empowerment and are mistrustful of both business and political elites. They also tend to be the most isolationist group, believing that government should pay less attention to problems abroad and more to those at home. They are strong supporters of welfare state programs and believe that governments do not provide enough aid to those in need.

Disadvantaged Democrats tend to have lower than average incomes, and about three-quarters say that they often cannot make ends meet. This group is disproportionately black (one in three) and female (six out of 10). They are more poorly educated than the general population.

Union membership is comparatively high among these voters, as is unemployment. Gun ownership is comparatively low (27%). About eight in 10 Disadvantaged Democrats identify with the Democratic Party, and almost all of those who voted in 2004 cast their ballots for Kerry.

Independent America

Upbeats (11% of adults; 13% of registered voters)

These voters are defined by their optimism about themselves, their country, and its major institutions. The Pew Center researchers call them "upbeats" precisely because of their upbeat perspective on government and business, which they view more positively than do other groups, and their greater faith in the ability of America and Americans to solve problems and achieve their goals. Given this optimism, it is not surprising to find that their sense of political efficacy is high, at about twice the level of the general population.

The Upbeats tend to be younger, well-educated, and have the highest average income of any group. They are also mainly white and married, living in the suburbs. After Enterprisers they have the second highest level of stock ownership. Most are Catholics (50%) or mainstream Protestants (28%), but they are less likely to attend church regularly than some other groups.

A majority of Upbeats (56%) declare themselves to be Independents or to have no party preference, but a significant number identify with the Republican Party. They preferred Bush over Kerry in 2004 by a greater than four to one ratio.

Disaffected (9% of adults; 10% of registered voters)

Members of this cluster are the mirror image of the Upbeats with one exception: if they vote (and many do not), they too prefer the Republicans over the Democrats. The disaffected are cynical and dissatisfied. They are much more likely than the general population to believe that government is wasteful and inefficient and almost twice more likely to believe that hard work is no guarantee of success. They are also strongly anti-immigration.

These voters are disproportionately male (57%) and tend to be much less educated than the general population. They tend to be found throughout the United States, although more often from rural and suburban communities than urban ones.

The strongly anti-immigration orientation of Disaffecteds is probably related to their perception of immigrants as competition for jobs, housing, and services. Disaffected voters tend to have lower incomes and are more likely than most Americans to have had unemployment in their household over the previous year. They are somewhat more likely than the general population to own a gun and quite unlikely to say that they follow news and current events.

Most Disaffecteds describe themselves as Independents or say that they have no partisan preference. But close to one-third describe themselves as Republicans, and among those who voted in 2004, Bush was preferred over Kerry by a two to one ratio.

Bystanders (10% of adults; 0% of registered voters)

Bystanders are very much like the Disaffected in their core beliefs about politics, but their deep cynicism and disinterest are expressed through withdrawal from civic participation. Some of these Bystanders are not citizens, so they could not vote even if they were inclined to.

The members of this group are, on average, the youngest of all these value clusters and are also the least educated. Only Liberals are less religious. Bystanders are disproportionately Hispanic (about one in five) and concentrated mainly in the South and West. About half say they cannot make ends meet, and just under one-third own guns.

Over half of Bystanders (50%) describe themselves as Independents or as having no partisan preference. Among those who do claim a party identification, they are pretty evenly split between Republicans and Democrats. In the end, however, it does not matter. Bystanders do not vote.

Faultlines Between and Within the United States of America

Writing half a century ago about what he called the liberal tradition in America, Harvard historian Louis Hartz argued that the set of values and beliefs that emerged from eighteenth-century liberalism—particularly the strong support for individualism and the protection of individual rights—constituted the national ethos of America. Liberalism, he maintained, effectively had the field all to itself in the United States, unlike in European

TABLE 2.1:   DIVISIONS WITHIN RED AND BLUE AMERICA

Response Item	Total %	Enterprisers %	Social Conservatives %	Pro-Government Conservatives %	Conservative Democrats %	Disadvantaged Democrats %	Liberals %
Ideology							
Conservative	39	85	66	58	41	27	1
Moderate	37	14	29	38	44	48	35
Liberal	19	1	3	2	9	16	62
ECONOMIC ISSUES							
Outsourcing is...							
Bad for the Economy	69	43	67	71	81	87	72
Good for the Economy	22	44	18	22	10	8	19
Raising taxes in order to reduce deficit							
Favor	31	12	27	32	25	23	56
Oppose	66	87	73	67	71	66	41
Programs designed to help blacks, women, and other minorities get better jobs and education							
Favor	67	31	49	71	74	68	82
Oppose	28	63	45	24	22	25	14
SOCIAL ISSUES							
Making it more difficult for a woman to get an abortion							
Favor	36	54	54	53	37	22	10
Oppose	55	38	40	41	51	67	88
Allowing gays and lesbians to marry legally							
Favor	32	8	12	17	19	37	80
Oppose	61	90	84	76	74	55	15
Teaching creationism along with evolution in public schools							
Favor	57	83	62	64	46	50	49
Oppose	33	12	28	22	33	36	48
FOREIGN POLICY ISSUES							
Spending on national defense							
Increase	20	41	30	24	18	13	10
Keep same	54	54	61	59	55	42	47
Cut back	19	1	4	13	18	38	37
Using military force against countries that may seriously threaten our country but have not attacked us							
Often justified	14	32	24	13	15	5	1
Sometimes justified	46	57	58	54	43	33	32
Rarely justified	21	7	11	16	18	26	44
Never justified	14	3	4	11	14	28	23
Patriot Act							
Necessary tool	33	73	53	38	29	8	15
Goes too far	39	12	13	28	40	60	71

Source: Pew Research Center for the People and the Press, "Beyond Red v. Blue" (10 May 2005). Adapted from data, pp. 67–72.

democracies where it had to compete with and respond to the rival ideologies of conservatism and socialism. The American ideological spectrum was narrower than that of France, the UK, Italy, and other Old World democracies. Value consensus was greater.

This belief in the greater uniformity of political values in the United States, a belief that is at least as old as Tocqueville, probably has three main sources. First, it derives from the undeniable fact that, for much of America's history, the social conditions of its citizens were more equal than in other Western societies. Tocqueville and many others commented on this, believing that the broad similarity in the circumstances and prospects of most Americans generated a uniformity in outlook and even a dangerous tendency toward conformism in thought. Second, the dominance of American politics by two political parties has often been interpreted—quite wrongly as it happens—as proof that the menu of political choice is narrower than in countries with multi-party systems. Finally, the prominence and universal respect paid by Americans of all backgrounds and races to what Swedish economist Gunnar Myrdal calls the American Creed[7]—the conviction that individual freedom and equality are and ought to be the pillars of American society—has often obscured the conflicts and dissent churning below the surface of this universally embraced civic religion.

This image of the United States as a country unmarked by major divisions of cultural and political outlook has never been accurate. The conflict between abolitionists and the defenders of slavery was no minor difference of opinion. Regional differences in political values, leaving aside those between the North and South, have always been significant and are arguably greater than in Canada, where the existence of regional political cultures has long been assumed to be an important feature of the political scene. During the last half-century, important cultural fault lines have opened around morality issues, leading many to argue that a culture war divides America. Moreover, one of the legacies of the Vietnam War has been a sharp division among Americans over their country's role in the world and, more specifically, the use of military force.

Table 2.1 shows that on a range of issues the attitudes of Americans are deeply divided. The Pew Center's typology categories have been retained in order to show that not only is there a gap between Red and Blue America, there are also significant divisions within each values coalition.

The Attitudinal Gap Between Red and Blue America

Conservative Americans tend to be considerably more opposed to abortion, more confident that hard work will pay off for most people, more overtly patriotic, much more likely to believe that the United States should rely on its military strength instead of diplomacy, and more skeptical about the United Nations than liberal Americans. But at least as striking are the value differences within these broad coalitions. Table 2.2 shows that there are wide fissures running through Red and Blue America on social, economic, environmental, and other issues.

There are, of course, some core values and beliefs on which there exists a large measure of consensus among Americans. If we operationalize consensus as the agreement of at least 70% of the population, we find that it is rather elusive. A 2004 survey by the Pew Center found that this test was met on a handful of values ("Religious faith is a very important part of my

TABLE 2.2:   ATTITUDINAL DIFFERENCES BETWEEN DEMOCRATS AND REPUBLICANS

A. Democrats	Liberals (%)	Disadv. Dems (%)	Cons. Dems (%)
Homosexuality is a way of life that ... Should be accepted by society	92	51	34
To be moral and have good values ... It is necessary to believe in God	15	54	74
Government regulation of business ... Is necessary to protect the public interest	72	21	51
Stricter environmental regulations ... Are worth the cost	89	48	60
The growing number of newcomers from other countries ... Threatens traditional American customs and values	9	53	53

B. Republicans	Enterprises (%)	Social Cons (%)	Pro-Gov Cons (%)
Homosexuality is a way of life that ... Should be discouraged	64	65	59
It is necessary to believe in God In order to be moral and have good values	42	61	68
Too much power is concentrated in the hands Of a few large companies	26	88	83
Government regulation of business Is necessary to protect the public interest	16	58	66
Stricter environmental regulations Are worth the cost	16	67	61
The growing number of newcomers from other countries ... Threatens traditional American customs and values	38	68	31

Source: Adapted from Alan Abramowitz and Kyle Saunders, "Why Can't We All Just Get Along? The Reality of a Polarized America," The Forum 1076 (2005): 10.

life," 74%; "Everyone has it in their power to succeed," 78%; "This country should do whatever it takes to protect the environment," 77%; "Too much power is concentrated in the hands of a few large companies," 77%; "The position of blacks in American society has improved in recent years," 73%).[8] A high level of consensus is also found when it comes to national pride, 72% of respondents saying they are very proud to be American and 71% agreeing that competition is good.[9]

FIGURE 2.2:   LIBERAL-CONSERVATIVE POLICY PREFERENCES OF VOTERS IN 2004 ELECTION

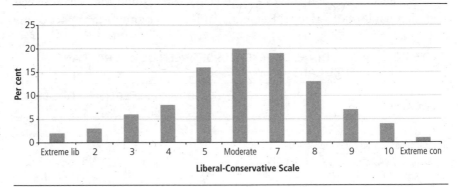

Source: 2004 National Election Study.

But the frequency and degree of division on what are arguably core values is at least as striking as the evidence of consensus. And few claims about American politics have been as generally accepted in recent years as the assertion that Americans are culturally polarized and that the distance between the two Americas has widened over the last generation. *Culture Wars*, the title of a 1991 book by American sociologist James Davison Hunter,[10] are said to pit culturally "orthodox" Americans against "progressive" ones. These culturally orthodox Americans are disproportionately in the middle and southern regions of the country while the progressive elements are more likely to be found on the west coast and in the northeast of the country.

Is there in fact a culture war? Even a casual perusal of public affairs coverage on American television—particularly on the cable news networks Fox, CNN, and MSNBC—or a brief car ride listening to talk radio is enough to suggest that there is. But the appearance may not be the reality. One of the most cited debunkers of the idea of a culture war in the United States is Morris Fiorina. "Publicly available databases," he says, "show that the culture war script embraced by journalists and politicos lies somewhere between simple exaggeration and sheer nonsense." What has happened, he argues, is that the elites who represent and run the Republican and Democratic parties have become more polarized. The values and preoccupation of these elites, amplified by a media system that for commercial reasons has been complicit in the culture wars characterization of American politics, dominate the public conversation. As Fiorina concludes, "By presenting [Americans] with polarizing alternatives, elites make voters appear polarized, but the reality shows clearly when voters have a choice of more moderate alternatives."[11] The issues that allegedly cut deep grooves between Americans are for the most part not ones about which most of these Americans feel very passionately. Polling data that suggests a sharply divided population become much less compelling if it turns out that most people just do not care all that much or that they could be satisfied with a policy or state of affairs that represented some sort of middle ground between the choices framed by elites and offered to citizens by pollsters. Moreover, there is no denying the fact that, attitudinally, most American voters cluster around the moderate middle of the ideological spectrum (see Figure 2.2).

TABLE 2.3:   INCREASING PARTISAN POLARIZATION ON ISSUES, 1972–2004

Issue	1972–1980	1984–1992	1996–2004
Aid to Blacks	.20	.27	.35
Abortion	−.03	.08	.18
Jobs/Living Standards	.28	.34	.40
Health Insurance	.25	.31	.39
Lib/Con Identification	.42	.49	.62
Presidential Approval	.42	.56	.61
Average	.26	.34	.43

Note: Entries shown are average correlations between issues and party identification (strong, weak, and independent Democrats vs. strong, weak, and independent Republicans). A higher score indicates greater polarization.

Source: Adapted from Abramowitz and Saunders, 10.

Fiorina makes a strong case. His observations on the differences between how political elites and the general public view politics are correct, and there is little doubt that values polarization is far greater among elites than ordinary citizens. At the same time, however, the values gap between Red and Blue America and the important fissures within each of these broad coalitions are real and significant. Based on their examination of voters who identify and lean toward the two parties, Abramowitz and Saunders conclude that "the gap between Democrats and Republicans was more than twice as large in 2004 as in 1972."[12] These voters, described by Abramowitz and Saunders as rank-and-file partisans, were more polarized in 2004 than the parties' activists were in 1972. On issues from aid to blacks, abortion, health insurance, whether or not living standards are improving, and approval of the president's performance, polarization between Democratic and Republican partisans—not just activists—increased significantly between 1972 and 2004. Lest it be thought that this increased polarization is merely the product of George W. Bush's presidency, the increase on all of these issues was about as great between 1972–80 and 1984–92 as between 1984–92 and 1996–2004 (see Table 2.3).

Political scientist John White's judgment that "[Americans] live in two parallel universes,"[13] probably overstates the magnitude of the values gap. But in one respect, at least, his assessment is right on. Americans who are religious in a traditional way—who belong to one of the mainstream Christian churches in the United States and who say that they believe in God and in the existence of sin and who attend church regularly—tend to be much more conservative than other Americans. This is the divide that James Davison Hunter emphasized in *Culture Wars*, a divide that is based on very different conceptions of moral authority.

Notes

1   Kopstein and Steinmo (eds.), *Growing Apart?*.

2   Pierre Elliott Trudeau, *Memoirs* (Toronto: McClelland and Stewart, 1993) 332.

3   Raymond Breton and Jeffrey Reitz, *The Illusion of Difference* (Toronto: C.D. Howe Institute, 1994).

4   James Bryce, *The American* Commonwealth (New York: G.P. Putnam's Sons, 1959) 557.

5   Jean Baudrillard, *America*, trans. Chris Turner (New York: Verso, 1988) 93.

6   Pew Research Center for the People and the Press, *Beyond Red v. Blue* (10 May 2005); http://www.typology.people-press.org/.

7   See Introduction, iv.

8   Pew Research Center, *Trends 2005* (20 January 2005): 17; http://www.pewresearch.org/trends/.

9   World Values Survey, 2000.

10 James Davison Hunter, *Culture Wars: The Struggle to Define America* (New York: Basic Books, 1991).

11 Morris Fiorina, "What Culture Wars?," *Wall Street Journal*, 14 July 2004.

12 Alan Abramowitz and Kyle Saunders, "Why Can't We All Just Get Along? The Reality of a Polarized America," *The Forum: A Journal of Applied Research in Contemporary Politics* 3.2 (2005).

13 John Kenneth White, *The Values Divide: American Politics and Culture in Transition* (New York: Chatham House Publishers/Seven Bridges Press, 2003).

CHAPTER THREE

Religion and Politics

"What would Jesus do?" (WWJD). This question and the accompanying acronym are familiar to anyone who regularly follows the American political conversation. Except in the most liberal pockets of the United States, a politician is unlikely to hurt his or her reputation with voters by posing this question out loud. When George W. Bush was asked during the 2000 presidential debates who his favorite philosopher was, he answered without hesitation: Jesus Christ. This was widely seen as an inspired answer and probably the highpoint of his performance in the debates. In Canada, the UK, France or Germany, however, such an answer would have been more likely to set off alarm bells and discredit a candidate in the eyes of many voters as being too religious.

Those who founded America, or at least those who arrived on the shores of Massachusetts, saw themselves as guided by the hand of Providence. The language that they used to described the community they were creating and the destiny they foresaw was not very different from that used by any recent president, Democratic or Republican, in his inaugural address. But their views on the relationship of religion to politics were not identical to those of contemporary Americans. The founding pilgrims came in search of freedom to practice their religion, but they did not believe in the separation of church and state, nor were they particularly tolerant when it came to religious beliefs and practices. By and large, however, contemporary Americans do believe in the separation of church and state and religious tolerance. But, like the founders, they do not believe that religious beliefs should be kept out of the public domain. Indeed, most Americans mistrust political leaders who profess to have no religious beliefs and think that it would be good for the country if more people of strong religious convictions entered public life. "What would Jesus do?" strikes them as an entirely reasonable question for a politician to ask.

Understanding the role that religion plays in American politics is one of the most difficult but also one of the most important challenges for anyone who seeks to understand the United States. The apparent contradictions of a society whose Constitution proclaims the separation of church and state but whose political leaders often use language that would not be out of place in a church and whose money declares "In God We Trust" strikes many observers as rank hypocrisy. This is the country of the Moral Majority, televangelism, and mega-churches that regularly pack upwards of 10,000 worshippers in their pews, the country where political debates over the teaching of evolution and abortion still rage. But it is also the country of the Playboy Channel, the Las Vegas ethic of "What plays in Vegas, stays in Vegas," and rampant materialism. Such a bundle of ill-assorted traits is, at the very least, puzzling.

The Providential Mission of America: Then and Now

Here is a passage from the writings of John Winthrop, who would become the first governor of the Massachusetts Bay Company, from his "A Model of Christian Charity" (1630):

For we must consider that we shall be as a City upon a hill. The eyes of all people are upon us. So that if we shall deal falsely with our God in this work we have undertaken, and so cause him to withdraw his present help from us, we shall be made a story and a by-word through the world. We shall open the mouths of enemies to speak evil of the ways of God and of all professors for God's sake.

And here is an excerpt from President George W. Bush's First Inaugural Address, January 20, 2001:

After the Declaration of Independence was signed, Virginia statesman John Page wrote to Thomas

Jefferson: "We know the race is not to the swift nor the battle to the strong. Do you not think an angel rides in the whirlwind and directs this storm?" ... We are not this story's author, Who fills time and eternity with His purpose. Yet His purpose is achieved in our duty, and our duty is fulfilled in service to one another.

Never tiring, never yielding, never finishing, we renew that purpose today, to make our country more just and generous, to affirm the dignity of our lives and every life.

This work continues. This story goes on. And an angel still rides in the whirlwind and directs this storm.

God bless you all, and God bless America.

The Religious Origins of America

If the early immigrants to America had all been Puritans, like those who settled the Massachusetts Bay Colony, the subsequent history and political development of the country would have been quite different. But while Puritanism dominated in the northern colonies, the Anglican Church was the established state religion in the southern ones. The religion map of colonial America quickly became more pluralistic as a result of divisions within Puritanism and the arrival of immigrants from other Christian groups, including the Quakers. The plurality of religious communities led Tocqueville to declare that "The sects that exist in the United States are innumerable. They all differ in respect to the duties which are due to the Creator; but they all agree in respect to the duties which are due from man to man. Each sect adores the Deity in its own peculiar manner, but all sects preach the same moral law in the name of God."[1]

Today, over 80% of the American population self-identifies with a Christian religious denomination. About 4% identify with a non-Christian religious community, and roughly 15% of the population claim to have no religious affiliation. As Figure 3.1 shows, the percentage of the population claiming to belong to particular religious communities is greater in the American mid-west and south—regions often referred to as the Bible Belt—than in other regions of the country.

FIGURE 3.1: RELIGIOUS ADHERENTS AS A PERCENTAGE OF ALL RESIDENTS, 2000

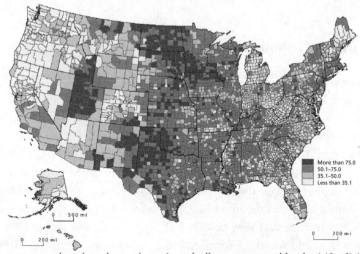

County percentages based on the total number of adherents reported by the 149 religious bodies that participated in a study sponsored by the Association of Statisticians of American Religious Bodies divided by the total population in 2000 reported by the U.S. Census Bureau.

Source: Association of Statisticians of American Religious Bodies, http://www.asarb.org; used with permission.

Religion and the First Amendment

In the conversation on religion and politics in the United States, the First Amendment to the Constitution and how it should be interpreted inevitably arises. The section of the First Amendment dealing with religion states: "Congress shall make no law respecting an establishment of religion, or prohibiting the free exercise thereof." There are two parts to this. The first—"Congress shall make no law respecting an establishment of religion"—is generally referred to as the *non-establishment clause* and is often understood as requiring the separation of church and state. And, in fact, the precise words "wall of separation between Church and State" were used by Thomas Jefferson in 1802. This interpretation and the words "separation of church and state" have been at the heart of many Supreme Court rulings including some of its most controversial ones.

The second part is referred to as the free exercise clause. Its clear meaning is that individuals are free to hold any religious beliefs and to practice them. This is subject, of course—and would have been understood by the generation of those who agreed to this amendment—to limitations that are both legal and cultural. The Church of Satan would have been considered an abomination by eighteenth-century Americans and not deserving of the protection of the free exercise clause. Neither then nor now has the First Amendment been understood as a shield protecting actions that are unlawful. There is, however, a gray area where the dictates of one's religion and the requirements of the law come into conflict and where the law has had to give way.

What Did the Founders Intend?

In debating the Marriage Protection Amendment proposed in 2006, which would have banned the legal recognition of same-sex marriages, most non-Americans found it odd that some of those who supported this proposal thought it relevant to ask how men who lived over 200 years ago would have decided this issue. But one of the important features of American idealism is veneration of the Constitution's founders and of the vision of America that they bequeathed to the nation. *Originalists* argue that lawmakers and judges should cleave to the intentions of the founders and the plain meaning of the Constitution that they wrote. But even those who argue that this is an impractical and too rigid approach to constitutional interpretation often find it convenient to cite history and the words of particular founders to support their case.

Jefferson and the Concept of the Separation of Church and State

Whereas Almighty God hath created the mind free; that all attempts to influence it by temporal punishments or burthens, or by civil incapacitations, tend only to beget habits of hypocrisy and meanness, and are a departure from the plan of the Holy author of our religion, who being Lord both of body and mind, yet chose not to propagate it by coercions on either, as was in his Almighty power to do; that the impious presumption of legislators and rulers, civil as well as ecclesiastical, who being themselves but fallible and uninspired men, have assumed dominion over the faith of others, setting up their own opinions and modes of thinking as the only true and infallible, and as such endeavouring to impose them on others, hath established and maintained false religions over the greatest part of the world, and through all time; that to compel a man to furnish contributions of money for the propagation of opinions which he disbelieves, is sinful and tyrannical ...

... *Be it enacted by the General Assembly*, that no man shall be compelled to frequent or support any religious worship, place or ministry whatsoever, nor shall be enforced, restrained, molested, or burthened whatsoever, nor shall be enforced, restrained, molested, or burthened in his body or goods, nor shall otherwise suffer on account of his religious opinions or belief; but that all men shall be free to profess, and by argument to maintain, their opinion in matters of religion, and that the same shall in no wise diminish, enlarge or affect their civil capacities.

Excerpts from Thomas Jefferson, Virginia Statute for Religious Freedom, *1786.*

When the Bill of Rights was adopted in 1791, several state constitutions already included words similar to the non-establishment clause of the First Amendment. In Virginia, for example, the Statute for Religious Freedom, drafted by Thomas Jefferson, was passed by the state legislature in 1786. The Anglican Church had been the established church in Virginia, as in all the states from Maryland south, and its de-establishment was described by Jefferson as "the severest contest in which I have ever been engaged." In several other states too, official churches had existed during colonial times. However, by the time of the American Revolution most colonists, including their leaders, rejected the idea of an official state religion.

Agreement on the proposition that no particular denomination should have a privileged status in law was not universal. The Congregational Church, descended from the Puritan founders, was not separated entirely from the Massachusetts state government until the 1830s. No less a figure than George Washington supported the idea of state support through taxation for all Christian churches, but the tide had turned against the idea and practice of a state religion. The Enlightenment idea of freedom of conscience was embraced by most of America's leading men. Their views, and the impact that the Revolution had on their thinking, may be seen in James Madison's words to the Virginia Assembly in 1784. "Who does not see," he asked, "that the same authority which can establish Christianity, in exclusion of all other Religions, may establish with the same ease any particular sect of Christians, in exclusion of all other Sects? That the same authority which can force a citizen to contribute three pence only of his property for the support of any one establishment, may force him to conform to any other establishment in all cases whatsoever?"[2]

Thus, the founders were religious men. Washington's speeches and writings suggest that he believed that the individual happiness of Americans and their collective political well-being depended on a healthy Christian culture. Jefferson, although rather unorthodox for the times in his thoughts on religion, is argued by Michael Novak to have seen Christianity as especially suited to the maintenance of freedom and democratic government. Hadley Arkes goes so far as to argue that America's founding documents were based on "a shared belief in a divine lawgiver."[3]

The principle of a wall of separation between church and state, to use Jefferson's words, prevailed among the founders, but they would have been shocked and even outraged at the suggestion that religion and politics should be, or could be, kept apart. They saw America as a Christian nation, and in deliberating on public issues they did not hesitate to use arguments based on religious belief and even scripture. "In the United States," observed Tocqueville in *Democracy in America*, Book II, "religion exercises but little influence upon the laws and upon the details of public opinion, but it directs the manners of the community, and by regulating domestic life, it regulates the state." Writing two generations later, at the end of the nineteenth century, James Bryce arrived at a similar assessment: "Christianity is in fact understood to be, though not the legally established religion, yet the national religion." Bryce went on to observe that Americans believed Christianity to be "one of the main sources of their national prosperity, and their nation as a special object of Divine favor."[4]

The Courts and Religious Freedom

The Pledge of Allegiance has been recited every morning by American schoolchildren for over a century. In 1954 Congress added the words "under God" during an era when Americans saw themselves locked in a struggle of worldviews with "godless communism." This change elicited little comment at the time, but in 2002 the atheist father of a third-grade girl brought suit against the Elk Grave Unified School District in Sacramento claiming that, in the setting of a public school, the pledge's words "under God" violated the non-establishment clause of the First Amendment. After winning his case in the 9th US Circuit Court of Appeals the plaintiff lost on appeal before the Supreme Court. However, the central issue of the case—whether reciting the pledge in schools breaks the wall of separation between church and state—was avoided. The Supreme Court ruled that the father, who was locked in a custody dispute with his daughter's mother, did not have standing to bring the case.

The controversy over this court battle brought back memories of one of the most famous and divisive Supreme Court decisions of modern times, *Engel v. Vitale* (1962). That was the decision that banned from public schools the Lord's Prayer or any official state prayer even if it were denominationally neutral and even if students were allowed to leave the room or remain silent. More than a half century later religious conservatives still think of this as one of the darkest moments in American public life and a serious black mark against the Supreme Court.

Until the middle of the twentieth century the Supreme Court was seldom called on to pronounce upon the meanings that should be assigned the free exercise and non-establishment clauses of the First Amendment. But as the size and scope of state activities grew larger, the opportunities for conflict over these matters increased. Other changes also contributed to an increase in political conflict and litigation over religious rights. One of these involves secularization. Although Americans are more likely to believe in God, attend church, and look to their faith for answers to social and political problems, a significant minority of the population is uncomfortable with God talk, skeptical about organized religion, and doubtful that God even exists. This minority tends to be well-educated and is also well-organized through organizations such as the ACLU and Americans United for the Separation of Church and State. Another factor that contributed to the intensification of the rights culture of the United States in the postwar era was the civil rights movement. This resulted from a combination of forces, but one of its important consequences was an increased tendency to frame political conflicts in the language of civil liberties and civil rights and to use litigation as a means to achieve political goals.

Free Exercise Rulings

The central issue in cases involving the free exercise clause of the First Amendment has tended to be the balance that ought to be struck between a person's right to behave in ways required by his or her faith and the requirements of laws of general application. The issue was first dealt with in the landmark case of *Reynolds v. United States*, 98 U.S. 145 (1878) in which a member of the Mormon Church was charged and convicted of bigamy, an offence under American law in what was then the territory of Utah. The defendant, George Reynolds, argued that his Mormon faith required him to take a second wife and that the First Amendment guaranteed his freedom to practice his religious beliefs. The Supreme Court ruled against him, stating that "to permit this would be to make the professed doctrines of religious belief superior to the law of the land, and in effect to permit every citizen to become a law unto himself. Government could exist only in name under such circumstances."

The spirit of the Reynolds decision was echoed over a century later in *City of Boerne v. Flores*, 521 U.S. 507 (1997). "Where the exercise of religion has been burdened in an incidental way by a law of general application," wrote Justice Kennedy, "it does not follow that the persons affected have been burdened any more than other citizens, let alone burdened because of their religious beliefs." Nevertheless, the courts have found that the burden imposed on a person's religion by a strict unbending application of the law may violate that person's free exercise of religion. The circumstances are key as shown in the following cases.

Sherbert v. Verner, *374 U.S. 398 (1963)*

Sherbert was a member of the Seventh Day Adventist Church who was fired by her employer because of her refusal to work on Saturday, the Sabbath for Adventists. Her application for unemployment insurance benefits was denied on the grounds that she had refused suitable work "without good cause." Sherbert argued that the South Carolina law under which her application for unemployment benefits was denied infringed her free exercise rights. The Supreme Court agreed. The majority found that the challenged law had the effect of impeding the observance of behavior required by the plaintiff's religion and of discriminating between religions by treating Sunday worshippers differently from Saturday ones. Except where some "compelling state interest" exists, said the Court, the state must make reasonable accommodation so that the free exercise of citizens' religious beliefs is permitted without penalty.

Wisconsin v. Yoder, *406 U.S. 205 (1972)*

The State of Wisconsin's compulsory school attendance law, which requires children to attend school until age 16, was challenged on the grounds that it violated the free exercise rights of the Old Order Amish to withdraw their children from school for religious reasons after the eighth grade. The Amish won. The Supreme Court held that "the State's interest in universal education is not totally free from a balancing process when it impinges on other fundamental rights, such as those specifically protected by the free exercise clause of the First Amendment and the traditional interest of parents with respect to the religious upbringing of their children." The plaintiff's case was helped by the facts that the Amish had a long and recognized history as a respected religious community in the United States and that life in the Amish community, after leaving school, provided young people with what the court acknowledged to be "continuing informal vocational education."

Employment Division v. Smith, *485 U.S. 660 (1988)*

The state of Oregon, like every other state, considers peyote to be an illegal drug. Peyote has long been smoked by some Native American communities in spiritual ceremonies. In this case a person was dismissed from his job because of having used peyote and subsequently was denied unemployment benefits because his firing was due to having broken the law. The plaintiff argued, however, that his use of peyote was for religious reasons and therefore protected by the free exercise clause. The Supreme Court ruled that religious freedom did not justify breaking a valid law. Critics charged that the ruling discriminated against Native American spirituality by failing to accord it the respect that the Court had shown toward the Old Order Amish sect in the Yoder case.

Church of the Lukumi Babalu Aye, Inc. v. Hialeah, *508 U.S. 520 (1993)*

The fact that a religious group's practices may be thought rather exotic and even repugnant by most people does not mean that they cannot find shelter under the free exercise clause. That was demonstrated in this case, involving a community of Cuban refugees in southern Florida belonging to the Santería religion. This religion requires ritual animal sacrifice. Authorities in Hialeah, Florida passed a series of ordinances prohibiting animal sacrifice, ostensibly on public health grounds. In finding these ordinances to be an unconstitutional violation of the Santeria community's free exercise rights, the Supreme Court found that the restrictions were aimed at a particular religious group and its practices. "The Free Exercise Clause commits government itself to religious tolerance," said the Court, warning against laws based on animosity toward any particular religion and its practices.

Non-Establishment Clause Rulings

The Supreme Court banned prayer from public schools in 1962. Two decades later it upheld the Nebraska state legislature's practice of beginning each session with a prayer said by a chaplain paid by the state. The Court has ruled that displays of the Ten Commandments in courthouses violate the non-establishment clause of the First Amendment, but the use of public dollars to pay for transportation to bus children to religious schools has been upheld as constitutional. Separating church from state is not always a straightforward matter. And, as the Pledge of Allegiance case demonstrated, conflict over how this line should be drawn can be highly controversial.

West Virginia Board of Education v. Barnette, *319 U.S. 624 (1943)*

Members of the Jehovah's Witnesses faith have often found themselves at odds with the state, particularly in regard to such matters as their refusal to permit blood transfusions or vaccinations for their children and also their objections to public education. At stake in the Barnette case was whether the children of Jehovah's Witnesses parents could be required to salute the American flag and recite the Pledge of Allegiance, actions that they believed violated the requirements of their faith. The school board authorities thought so, and the children were expelled from school. Proceedings were begun against their parents for having contributed to the delinquency of minors.

The Supreme Court thought otherwise. It upheld the right of schoolchildren to abstain on religious grounds from compulsory practices, including

Can American Democracy Survive Religion-Based Dissent?

To believe that patriotism will not flourish if patriotic ceremonies are voluntary and spontaneous instead of a compulsory routine is to make an unflattering estimate of the appeal of our institutions to free minds. We can have intellectual individualism and the rich cultural diversities that we owe to exceptional minds only at the price of occasional eccentricity and abnormal attitudes. When they are so harmless to others or to the State as [refusing to salute the American flag] the price is not too great. But freedom to differ is not limited to things that do not matter much.

That would be a mere shadow of freedom. The test of its substance is the right to differ as to things that touch the heart of the existing order.

If there is any fixed star in our constitutional constellation, it is that no official, high or petty, can prescribe what shall be orthodox in politics, nationalism, religion, or other matters of opinion or force citizens to confess by word or act their faith therein. If there are any circumstances which permit an exception, they do not now occur to us.

From the decision of West Virginia Board of Education v. Barnette *(1943).*

those whose justification was the promotion of national unity and civic-mindedness. The unpopularity or marginality of a group and its religious beliefs were beside the point, said the Court.

Everson v. Board of Education, *330 U.S. 1 (1947)*

The issue of public money being used to support the education of children attending religious schools was the occasion for one of the most memorable Supreme Court rulings on the wall of separation between church and state. In upholding a New Jersey school board's policy of reimbursing parents for the cost of busing their children to Catholic schools, just as the fares of children attending public schools were reimbursed by this board, the Supreme Court looked carefully at the colonial history of church-state relations that led to the inclusion of the non-establishment clause in the First Amendment. Writing for the majority and clearly inspired by Thomas Jefferson's writings on the subject, Justice Hugo Black explained the many ways the state was prohibited from entanglements with religious groups.

The wall of separation, however, did not prohibit all forms of state support for religious schools. The non-establishment clause, said Justice Black, "requires the state to be neutral in its relations with groups of religious believers and non believers; it does not require the state to be their adversary. State power is no more to be used so as to handicap religions, than it is to favor them." Paying the cost of transporting children to fully accredited, non-profit religious schools was, Black said, neutral as between religious and public schools and therefore did not breach the wall of separation.

Engel v. Vitale, *370 U.S. 421 (1962)*

"Almighty God, we acknowledge our dependence upon Thee, and we beg Thy blessing upon us, our parents, our teachers and our Country." This was the prayer that New York state authorities required all children to recite at the beginning of each school day. It was challenged on the grounds that the prayer violated the non-establishment clause because it had been composed by state authorities as part of a policy of promoting religious beliefs through public schools. "It is a matter of history," said the Supreme Court, "that this very practice of establishing governmentally composed prayers for religious services was one of the reasons which caused many of our early colonists to leave England and seek religious freedom in America." The Supreme Court's ruling made very clear that being non-denominational and non-compulsory did not save prayer in public schools from falling outside what the First Amendment requires.

Marsh v. Chambers, *463 U.S. 783 (1983)*

If children may not pray in public schools, what about the men and women who make the laws that apply to these schools? Does the non-establishment clause also prevent them from praying when they are conducting the people's business? Although this case arose in Nebraska as a challenge to that state legislature's practice of beginning each session with a prayer led by a publicly paid chaplain, this same practice was followed in most legislative bodies across the United States, including Congress.

In a six to three ruling, the Supreme Court upheld the constitutionality of paid chaplains and prayer in legislatures. Noting that the practice of opening sessions of Congress with a prayer had an uninterrupted history of almost 200 years, the majority determined that "In light of the history, there can be little doubt that the practice ... has become part of the fabric of our society." Moreover, "To invoke divine guidance for a public body entrusted with making the laws ... is simply a tolerable acknowledgment of beliefs widely held among the people of this country."

Just as the Supreme Court had been very much out of sync with public opinion in the *Engel v. Vitale* case, it was in tune with public opinion in this one. In fact, in using such terms as "tolerable acknowledgment" and beliefs that were "widely held" in the reasons for its ruling, the majority on the Court seemed almost to suggest that the fact that a practice accorded with public opinion should be weighed in the balance when determining its constitutionality. This was not a test that the Court thought appropriate in *Engel*, where it said "fundamental rights may not be submitted to vote; they depend on the outcome of no elections."

Zelman v. Simmons-Harris, *536 U.S. 639 (2002)*

One of the more controversial issues in education policy in the United States over the last couple of decades has involved school vouchers. These are credits issued to the parents of school-age children that may be used to offset the cost of tuition at privately run schools, many of them operated by religious organizations.

Proponents argue that vouchers provide parents with greater choice in their children's education by reducing the cost of selecting a school outside the public system. They also argue that vouchers and the choice they permit should cause the public schools to improve their standards, as a result of having to compete for students with the private tuition schools. They claim that vouchers are particularly beneficial for low-income children, enabling their families to afford a better quality education than is often available through the public schools. The objection is, of course, that these vouchers violate the non-establishment clause when they are used at religious schools, as most of them are.

A deeply divided Court upheld the constitutionality of the Ohio school voucher program by a vote of five to four. Writing for the majority, Chief Justice Rehnquist expressed the view that "the program was one of true private choice, with no evidence that the State deliberately skewed incentives toward religious schools" and that on these grounds it was protected from the claim that it violated the non-establishment clause. Whatever the intentions of Ohio's state lawmakers were, the fact of the matter is that parents generally use vouchers to send their children to a school that has a religious affiliation. With this in mind, dissenting Justice Stevens warned that "Whenever we remove a brick from the wall that was designed to separate religion and government, we increase the risk of religious strife and weaken the foundation of our democracy."

McCreary County, Kentucky v. ACLU of Kentucky, *545 U.S. 844 (2005)*

Once again the Supreme Court was deeply divided on the interpretation of the non-establishment clause, but this time the five to four majority swung toward those who worried that the wall of separation was in jeopardy. The case involved the display of the Ten Commandments in two Kentucky courthouses. In defending their display, state authorities argued that it had a secular purpose, namely, to demonstrate the relationship of the Commandments to Western legal thought, the Declaration of Independence, and the evolution of American law and government. The Court rejected this claim. "This is not to deny," said the majority, "that the Commandments have had influence on civil or secular law.... The point is simply that the original text viewed in its entirety is an unmistakably religious statement dealing with religious obligations and with morality subject to religious sanction. When the government initiates an effort to place this statement alone in public view, a religious object is unmistakable."

As in the case of the *Engel* ruling's ban on prayer in public schools, the ban on the display of the Ten Commandments from the public square generated enormous controversy. Critics charged that the non-establishment clause's meaning was being twisted to discriminate against religious messages in the public square while protecting the constitutionality of any secular message. This, they argued, was a distortion of the founders' original intent by quoting President George Washington's declaration that the "national morality [cannot] prevail in exclusion of religious principle" as proof that the founders did not see affairs of state and religious matters as separate, watertight compartments. But the majority in *McCreary County* is doubtless correct when they write that "there was no common understanding [among the founders] about the limits of the establishment prohibition."

God Talk in American Public Life

> God talk, at least as much as rights talk, is the way America speaks. American politics is unintelligible if severed from America's religions, most importantly Christianity. —Jean Bethke Elshtain[5]

When Al Gore, a Baptist, announced that Senator Joe Lieberman, a Jew, would be his vice-presidential running mate in the 2000 presidential election, he described Lieberman as "someone who believes, as I do, that the Earth is the Lord's and the fullness thereof," and "as I stand next to him today, I believe in my heart that we are one step closer to truly being one nation under God, indivisible, with liberty and justice for all."[6]

When it was his turn to speak, Lieberman spoke in language as suited to the synagogue as the campaign trail: "I ask you to allow me to let the spirit move me as it does to remember the words from Chronicles, which are to give thanks to God. To give thanks to God and declare his name and make his acts known to the people.... To sing to God and to make music to God, and most of all to give glory and gratitude to God from whom all blessings truly do flow." Between the two of them they invoked the name of God over a dozen times, and their brief speeches included many additional religious references.

These, it needs to be emphasized, were the Democratic Party's candidates. It is often thought, particularly by non-Americans, that God talk is the language of Republicans and political conservatives. This is far from being the case. Many liberals and Democratic Party supporters thought that Gore and Lieberman had gone too far in their effusive profession of faith at what was, after all, a political event. But the reality is that God talk in America is bipartisan. In recent years, it has tended to be heard more often and more loudly from the right. Nevertheless, as Jean Bethke Elshtain observes, "God talk.... is the way America speaks."

The truth of Elshtain's observation may be demonstrated in a number of ways. One is to examine what are acknowledged to be classic examples of political rhetoric. It is rarely the case that religious language, references, and symbols are absent and often the case that they are essential elements of the message. William Jennings Bryan's "Cross of Gold" speech, in which the populist 1896 Democratic candidate for the presidency drew on the

language and oratorical style of the Christian religious revival to argue for
the Common Man against the powers of wealth and impersonal capitalism,
is a well-known example. So too is the radio broadcast of Franklin Delano
Roosevelt's prayer for divine assistance on D-Day, June 6, 1944. John F.
Kennedy used God talk often and unselfconsciously in his speeches, as in
his 1961 inaugural address: "With a good conscience our only sure reward,
with history the final judge of our deeds, let us go forth to lead the land we
love, asking His blessing and His help, but knowing that here on earth God's
work must truly be our own." The leader of the black civil rights movement, the Reverend Martin Luther King, Jr., spoke in the style and using the
language of the churches that have created many of black America's most
prominent leaders. His "I Have a Dream," speech delivered against the backdrop of the Washington Monument in 1963, is certainly the most famous
example of his oratory, using religious language and imagery to express a
political message. In Ronald Reagan's televised address to the nation after
the 1986 explosion of the Challenger space shuttle and the death of seven
astronauts, he ends: "We will never forget them, nor the last time we saw
them, this morning, as they prepared for their journey and waved good-bye
and 'slipped the surly bonds of earth,' to 'touch the face of God.'" One of the
more memorable exchanges in the 2004 presidential debates between John
Kerry and George W. Bush involved each man's expression of his faith and
what it meant for his politics. As all followers of American politics know, it
is almost unthinkable that a president does not end any major speech with
the words "God Bless America."[7]

Words like these and the sentiments they express seem not to travel
well. Canada's Conservative Prime Minister, Stephen Harper, discovered
this when he used the words "God Bless Canada" at the close of a couple
of speeches soon after his election in 2006. Not only was he criticized for
injecting inappropriate religious language into politics, but he was accused
of trying to import American ways and values into Canada. This is a red
flag for many Canadians. If the president of France or the chancellor of
Germany were to inject such God talk into their public pronouncements, the
reaction among their respective citizenries would certainly be unfavorable.
Indeed, some would probably question their sanity or at least their fitness
for public office.

God talk in politics is one of the behaviors that sets the United States
and its political leaders apart from other democratic nations. Moreover, it
does not appear that the importance of God talk in the American political
conversation is in decline. On the contrary, in the early stages of the competition for the 2008 Democratic presidential nomination, all of the candidates

talked openly about their faith and what it meant in their lives and for their politics. It went without saying that public confessions of faith were expected from the several candidates for the Republican Party's nomination, but God talk was every bit as evident among the Democrats. Indeed, on the fiftieth anniversary of Martin Luther King's assassination, the two Democratic frontrunners, Hillary Clinton and Barack Obama, both spoke from the pulpit in churches in Selma, Alabama, from which King began his famous civil rights march to Montgomery. Politicians from the president on down, Republican and Democrat, regularly attend prayer breakfasts, and in most parts of the country they are expected to be able to speak comfortably and with an appearance of sincerity about their faith. As Michael Cromartie observed of the 2008 presidential hopefuls, "[A]ny candidate who is tone deaf to religious language and who is uncomfortable speaking publicly about religious themes ... will not be nominated by their party, much less have a chance to win the presidency."[8]

Given all this God talk, it is not surprising that many conclude that the much celebrated separation of church and state in America is just empty hypocrisy. This conclusion is incorrect. Most Americans expect their political leaders to be believers and to find the sources of their morality in their religious faith. But the vast majority would be offended by any attempt to legislate certain advantages for any particular religious denomination over others. Some Americans, such as members of the ACLU, interpret the separation of church and state as requiring the elimination of religious influence from politics. This idea has legitimate roots in the country's history, but it is not held by most Americans and is much more in tune with the European notion of a secular state.

The different histories of Europe and the United States are important for an understanding of this distinction. In European countries, the Church—the Catholic church, not a plurality of competing religions—was long seen as the enemy of democracy and freedom. "In France," writes Tocqueville, "I had almost always seen the spirit of religion and the spirit of freedom marching in opposite directions. But in America, I found they were intimately united and that they reigned in common over the country."[9] The disestablishment of churches in the United States over two centuries ago, combined with the fact that the American religious scene has always been pluralistic and that most religions in the United States have tended to be organized in a comparatively democratic, non-hierarchal fashion, produced circumstances in which the spirit of religion, as Tocqueville called it, is not seen by most Americans as a threat to the spirit of freedom and democracy.

God Talk on the Campaign Trail: George W. Bush and John Kerry in the 2004 Presidential Debates

During the October 13, 2004 debates, President Bush and Senator Kerry were asked "What part does your faith play on your policy decisions?" Here are their responses:

BUSH: First, my faith plays a lot—a big part in my life. And that's, when I was answering that question, what I was really saying to the person was that I pray a lot. And I do. And my faith is a very—it's very personal. I pray for strength. I pray for wisdom. I pray for our troops in harm's way. I pray for my family. I pray for my little girls.

But I'm mindful in a free society that people can worship if they want to or not. You're equally an American if you choose to worship an almighty and if you choose not to. If you're a Christian, Jew or Muslim, you're equally an American. That's the great thing about America, is the right to worship the way you see fit.

Prayer and religion sustain me. I receive calmness in the storms of the presidency. I love the fact that people pray for me and my family all around the country. Somebody asked me one time, "Well, how do you know" I said, "I just feel it."

But when I make decisions, I stand on principle, and the principles are derived from who I am.

I believe we ought to love our neighbor like we love ourself, as manifested in public policy through the Faith-Based Initiative where we've unleashed the armies of compassion to help heal people who hurt. I believe that God wants everybody to be free. That's what I believe. And that's been part of my foreign policy. In Afghanistan, I believe that the freedom there is a gift from the Almighty. And I can't tell you how encouraged I am to see freedom on the march.

And so my principles that I make decisions on are a part of me, and religion is a part of me.

MODERATOR: Senator Kerry?

KERRY: Well, I respect everything that the president has said and certainly respect his faith. I think it's important and I share it.

I think that he just said that freedom is a gift from the Almighty. Everything is a gift from the Almighty. And as I measure the words of the Bible—and we all do; different people measure different things—the Koran, the Torah, or you know, Native Americans who gave me a blessing the other day had their own special sense of connectedness to a higher being. And people all find their ways to express it.

I was taught—I went to a church school and I was taught that the two greatest commandments are: Love the Lord, your God, with all your mind, your body and your soul, and love your neighbor as yourself. And frankly, I think we have a lot more loving of our neighbor to do in this country and on this planet. We have a separate and unequal school system in the United States of America. There's one for the people who have, and there's one for the people who don't have. And we're struggling with that today.

And the president and I have a difference of opinion about how we live out our sense of our faith. I talked about it earlier when I talked about the works and faith without works being dead.

I think we've got a lot more work to do. And as president, I will always respect everybody's right to practice religion as they choose—or not to practice—because that's part of America.

Source: Presidential Debates Commission.

God talk is, in fact, an important language of community in the United States—arguably the most influential language of community. A candidate for office who wishes to convince voters that he or she is compassionate and caring may choose to talk about state programs like welfare, food stamps, public education, and medical care for the poor. This is how his or her counterpart in France, Germany, or Canada would attempt to connect with voters. But in the United States, candidates are more likely than elsewhere to try to establish this connection through the language of faith. "How do you know which candidate will represent your values?," asks Clyde Wilcox. "They need to tell you something authentic about what they care about. Religion is one of the shortcuts we use to determine what people care about."[10]

The line that Americans draw between religion in politics, which most people favor, and the principle of the separation of church and state, which the majority defends, may be seen in the following facts. Close to three-quarters of Americans say that presidents should have strong religious beliefs. About half agree that churches should express their views on political matters. But when asked whether it would be proper for churches to endorse political candidates, about two-thirds say no. Even among those who say that religion is very important in their lives, those who say that it would be wrong for churches to endorse candidates outnumber those who favor religious endorsement by a two to one ratio. Asked whether they thought it proper for Catholic leaders to deny communion to politicians based on their views and actions, about two-thirds of Americans said no.[11]

The "God Gap"

In the 2004 presidential election, Americans who said that they attended church at least once per week (about 42% of the electorate) voted for George W. Bush over John Kerry by a ratio of about three to two. Those who never attended church (15% of voters) preferred Kerry over Bush by a ratio of almost two to one. This finding seemed to corroborate the general belief that a sort of "God gap" divides Red and Blue America. Red America votes Republican and, as we noted in Chapter 2, is more conservative on most issues. Blue America prefers the Democratic Party and is more liberal in its leanings. This ideological divide, according to the God gap thesis, is rooted in religious differences. Red Americans are considerably more likely than Blue Americans to attend church regularly, although the vast majority of voters in Blue America say that they believe in God and that they attend church either weekly or occasionally. The nature of the gap between these two segments is not that one is religious and the other is not; rather, it involves differences in the religious communities within them. On some issues the difference between these communities is great, driving Red and Blue America apart, but on others it is narrow or even non-existent.

Figure 3.2 shows the partisan breakdown of voters in each of the main faith communities, based on a survey conducted in the spring of 2004. Evangelicals, traditionalist Catholics, and mainstream Protestants who attend church regularly are those most strongly supportive of the Republican Party. Modernist Catholics and Protestants who attend church less frequently are the religious groups that lean most strongly toward the Democratic Party.

What is an Evangelical?

Despite having heard countless times that George W. Bush's victories in 2000 and 2004 were due to the "Evangelical vote" and that President Bush himself is an Evangelical, most people have only the foggiest notion what the term "Evangelical" means. The word comes from the Greek New Testament word for the gospel of Jesus Christ. Evangelicals are religious believers for whom the truth about how to live is revealed in the word of God as set down in the Bible. The National Association of Evangelicals declares that Evangelism involves "seeking to apply biblical truth to current events" or, to put it more simply, asking "What would Jesus do?"

Among non-Evangelicals, but especially among people of a more secular disposition, the term "evangelical" tends to carry negative connotations. It is often associated with intolerance, religious extremism, self-righteousness, and even ignorance. Evangelism is often understood as identical to fundamentalism, that is, the belief in the literal truth of the Bible. But although there is overlap between these two communities and their critics are inclined to dismiss any distinction between them as inconsequential, fundamentalism tends to be more dogmatic and conservative than Evangelism.

According to those who study religion and politics, Evangelicals make up just under one-quarter of the American electorate. Whether this figure includes Fundamentalists and whether there is a theological distinction or not between Evangelicals and Fundamentalists, the fact of the matter is that both groups are socially conservative and tend to prefer the Republican Party (or at least Republicans like President George W. Bush; they are not particularly fond of social moderates like Rudolph Guiliani and John McCain).

Evangelicals are not only numerous, they are also well-organized through their churches, advocacy organizations, and schools. Their influence on political conversation in the United States is felt through talk radio, religious television broadcasting, and opinion leaders from President Bush to those who direct the weekly Bible study groups that millions of Americans attend. Although usually thought of as being intellectually lightweight and even reactionary in their thinking, the Evangelical movement may have gained some intellectual heft in recent years through scholarship at such Evangelism institutions as Wheaton College (Reverend Billy Graham's alma mater), Calvin College, Pepperdine University, Baylor University, and Valparaiso University.

The associations between the conservatism of one's religious beliefs and partisan preferences is strong but does not apply across the board. Black Americans tend to hold conservative religious beliefs but prefer Democratic candidates over Republican ones by a large margin. Hispanics also tend to hold conservative religious views, and like black Americans they prefer the Democratic Party, although by a much smaller margin than among blacks.

Mainstream Protestant voters have remained fairly evenly split between Republican and Democratic identifications over the last several decades, but Evangelicals, strongly part of Blue America until the 1980s, are now a bulwark of Red America. The partisan shift among Catholics is no less dramatic, although less often remarked upon. In 1960 about 70% of Catholics identified with or leaned toward the Democratic Party. Under 20% expressed a Republican identification. In recent years the partisan gap among Catholics has narrowed to single digits (44% Democratic and 41% Republican, according to the 2004 Bliss Institute survey).[12]

When it comes to differences on the issues, the conventional wisdom is that Red America is much more preoccupied by and conservative on issues that involve moral values. Same-sex marriage, abortion, and gay adoption are the issues that generally come to mind—these are the *wedge issues* that are said to divide Red and Blue America. But when Americans think of moral issues, these hot-button or wedge issues are not usually the ones that come to mind first. A major 2005 survey on "Faith and the Family in America" found that when asked what moral values meant to them, only 10% of respondents said social issues like abortion and gay marriage. However, 36% mentioned personal values, such as honesty and responsibility; 26% said family values, such as protecting children from sex and violence on television and the Internet; and as many people chose social justice as their idea of moral values as said abortion and gay marriage. Not unexpectedly, evangelical Christians were more likely than others to mention these politically controversial matters. Even among the members of this group only 15% said that abortion and gay marriage shaped their idea of what moral values mean.[13]

Surveys have limitations, however, and it may be that the mere fact that most Americans of all religious persuasions claim to understand moral values in terms of personal and family values does not mean that the gap between these communities on issues like same-sex marriage and gay adoption is not politically significant. The division that roiled the Episcopal Church over the 2003 ordination of an openly gay bishop, Gene Robinson of New Hampshire, and the flurry of court challenges to state laws that limited legal marriage to heterosexual couples and the accompanying calls for a Protection of Marriage Amendment to the Constitution showed just how controversial Americans found these issues to be. The fact that no serious candidate for the presidency from either of the two parties can avoid taking a position on these issues—if a rather ambiguous and evasive one—testifies to their importance in American politics.

FIGURE 3.2:   PARTISAN AFFILIATION BY MAJOR RELIGIOUS GROUPS

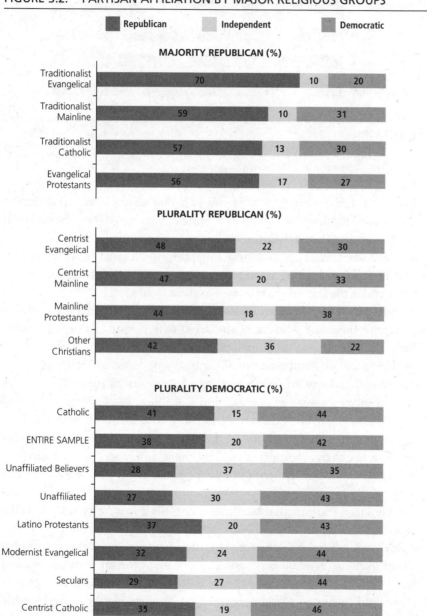

Republican   Independent   Democratic

MAJORITY REPUBLICAN (%)

Group	Republican	Independent	Democratic
Traditionalist Evangelical	70	10	20
Traditionalist Mainline	59	10	31
Traditionalist Catholic	57	13	30
Evangelical Protestants	56	17	27

PLURALITY REPUBLICAN (%)

Group	Republican	Independent	Democratic
Centrist Evangelical	48	22	30
Centrist Mainline	47	20	33
Mainline Protestants	44	18	38
Other Christians	42	36	22

PLURALITY DEMOCRATIC (%)

Group	Republican	Independent	Democratic
Catholic	41	15	44
ENTIRE SAMPLE	38	20	42
Unaffiliated Believers	28	37	35
Unaffiliated	27	30	43
Latino Protestants	37	20	43
Modernist Evangelical	32	24	44
Seculars	29	27	44
Centrist Catholic	35	19	46

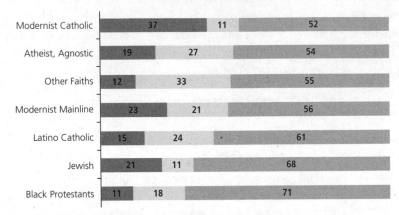

MAJORITY DEMOCRATIC (%)

Modernist Catholic	37	11	52
Atheist, Agnostic	19	27	54
Other Faiths	12	33	55
Modernist Mainline	23	21	56
Latino Catholic	15	24	61
Jewish	21	11	68
Black Protestants	11	18	71

Note: "Democratic" and "Republican" includes those who indicated they were leaning to the party in question.

Source: Adapted from the Fourth National Survey of Religion and Politics, Bliss Institute, University of Akron, March-May 2004. Answers based on replies from all adults.

Table 3.1 and Figure 3.3 show the gap that exists between different religious communities in the United States on these issues. Evangelical Christians and traditional Catholics are the groups most likely to oppose same-sex marriage and gay adoption. Liberal Catholics and those who claim to have no religion or to be atheist or agnostic are the most likely to support equality under the law where it comes to these issues.

Both Red and Blue America include majorities who say that their faith is important to them and who claim affiliation with one or another organized religion. But Red America is more likely than Blue America to depend on the votes of Evangelicals and traditional Catholics opposed to abortion, same-sex marriage, and gay adoption, whereas Blue America includes a greater preponderance of voters who are liberal Catholics, black Protestants, and secular Americans. God is important to most voters in both Red and Blue America, but their moral visions of the world and of the sorts of policies most likely to achieve their preferred vision are different. The God gap that separates Red and Blue America involves precisely this difference in world visions.

Marvin Olasky argues that the difference boils down to what he calls the "religion of reality" in Red America versus the "religion of nicety" in Blue America.[14] Members of the first group, he says, "see poverty as a complex tangle of spiritual, psychological, political, social, historical, institutional and technological factors" that cannot easily be resolved, if it all. On foreign policy, they tend to see the world very much as Thomas Hobbes described life

TABLE 3.1:   DEFINITION OF MARRIAGE BY RELIGIOUS IDENTITY (percentage agreeing)

	Total	Evangelical Christian	Mainline Protestant	Traditional Catholic	Liberal Catholic	No pref/ Atheist/ Agnostic
The law should define marriage as a union between one man and one woman.	59	79	53	70	35	33
The law should define marriage as a union between one man and one woman, but recognize legal agreements between same-sex couples.	14	10	21	11	25	12
The law should define marriage as a union between two people, regardless of their gender.	25	9	25	15	39	52

Source: Adapted from Pew Forum on Religion and Public Life, "Faith and Family in America." Survey directed by John Green, October 2005.

FIGURE 3.3:   GAY ADOPTION BY RELIGIOUS IDENTITY (percentage saying they "strongly" or "somewhat" favor)

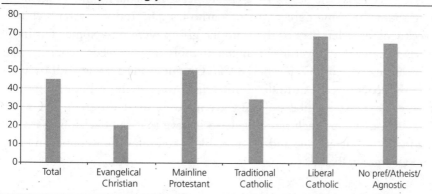

Source: Adapted from Pew Research Center for the People and the Press, The Pew Forum on Religion and Public Life, "Pragmatic Americans Liberal and Conservative on Social Issues," survey released 3 August 2006.

in the state of nature—nasty, mean, brutish, and short—and very much in terms of the sorts of biblical vices—covetousness, deception, and violence— that the faithful are warned against. Those who subscribe to the religion of reality worldview are, Olasky argues, skeptical when it comes to the welfare state as the answer to poverty and inequality and supportive of a strong military over multilateralism and diplomacy as the best way to guarantee national security.

Believers who subscribe to the religion of nicety worldview, Olasky says, believe that "solving the poverty problem is like solving a math problem: Move dollars from X to Y and the job is done."[15] On foreign policy, they tend to believe in the inherent goodness of people and their leaders everywhere and that peace is universally desired. Diplomacy, multilateralism, and international agreements are, they believe, the best way to protect national security.

Olasky clearly thinks that those who subscribe to what he calls the religion of nicety worldview are naïve and wrong. Leaving these matters aside, is he correct in his claim that this is a real divide between religious Americans? The answer is a qualified yes. The Pew Center survey on Religion and Public Life, conducted between 2002 and 2004, provides only tepid support for Olasky's thesis. If Olasky is right, then we would expect to find that white Evangelical Protestants, the most strongly Republican and socially conservative group, hold significantly different attitudes compared to Catholics who do not attend church every week, a group that tends to be more favorable toward the Democratic Party and socially more liberal. In fact, however, the attitudinal differences between them are in some respects quite narrow. About two-thirds of white Evangelicals who attend church at least once per week agreed that the best way to ensure peace is through military strength, but about the same percentage of Catholics who did not attend church weekly agree. Members of the Catholic group were only somewhat more likely to agree that government should do more to help needy people, even if it means more debt (47% versus 39%). On questions dealing with business and the economy, the attitudinal differences were slight at best. But in two respects, at least, members of these groups were quite different. The white Evangelicals were much more likely to believe that the decision to invade Iraq was the correct one and far more likely to prefer the Republican Party and George W. Bush.[16]

The Political Organization and Influence of Organized Religion

Reverend Jerry Falwell, who died on May 15, 2007, was the founder of the Moral Majority, a key component of the conservative movement throughout the 1980s. Indeed, the Moral Majority became almost synonymous with the power of social conservatives during the years of the Reagan presidency. Falwell was a pioneer of political televangelism, broadcasting a message that was uncompromisingly Christian and conservative. Although the Moral Majority ceased to operate in 1989 and Falwell turned much of his attention to building Liberty University, the movement that he launched has become more powerful than ever.

Today, Christian conservatism is no longer associated with one person and one organization, as it was in the 1980s. The movement's influence has been decentralized and institutionalized through a broad network that includes think tanks, universities, lobbying groups, and Christian media. It has resources far beyond those that it possessed during the years of the Moral Majority. Its critics, in the United States and abroad, often portray the religious right as a theocratic leviathan in unholy alliance with the Republican Party to subvert the First Amendment, roll back abortion rights, and replace the teaching of evolutionary biology with a creationist narrative of life's origins and development. This indictment is too sweeping and, among other things, fails to acknowledge the substantial resources that environmentalists, civil rights groups, business and professional organizations, and other interests deploy in American politics. It is, however, true that religious groups have a level of political organization and influence in the United States that far surpasses what is found in other wealthy democracies.

One of the main channels of this influence is through the Christian media. Radio and television broadcasts have a very long history in the United States, almost as long as the media themselves. Regular religious radio programming may have begun in 1920 in Wichita, Kansas, and the first all-religious radio station was WDM which started broadcasting in Washington, DC in 1921. Bishop Fulton J. Sheen's "Life is Worth Living" (1952-58) was one of the first televised religious broadcasts to have commercial sponsors and eventually drew an audience of about 10 million viewers. Televised preachers and "faith healers," including Oral Roberts and Charles Fuller, became popular in the 1950s and 1960s. In 1951 the Baptist Reverend Billy Graham—who became a confidant of almost all American presidents from Dwight Eisenhower to George W. Bush—began his televised crusades. These lengthy sermons, which ended in a call for members of the audience/congregation to pledge publicly their lives to Jesus,[17] drew large primetime audiences for almost five decades. All of this was, however, merely a prelude to the flood of televangelism and Christian radio that took off in the 1980s and has continued since then.

The scope and scale of religious broadcasting in the United States can be measured in various ways. In terms of revenue, it is a multibillion dollar industry that reaches Americans (and some foreign audiences) through local broadcasting, cable, and satellite. One faith network alone, Trinity Broadcasting, has more than 12,000 broadcast outlets throughout the world and a weekly audience that may be in the vicinity of 100 million. One of its most popular programs, "Joel Osteen Ministries," alone draws 7 million viewers a week. Trinity Broadcasting and the Christian Broadcasting Network represent the high end of this industry, but much of what is on faith television is low budget, involving not much more than a preacher and a camera and relying on a production crew of volunteers. The original financial model involved asking viewers to make small donations—$10 is the amount that the "700 Club" suggests—but in recent years the revenue stream has been broadened by sales of DVDs, books, and other products. One of the oldest and most successful religious programs, the Reverend Robert Schuller's "The Hour of Power" from California's Crystal Cathedral, had annual television costs of over $13 million in 2006. A lot of small individual donations are needed to pay the bills for such an operation, and so additional revenue-generating streams have become increasingly important.

The presence of religion in the media system is not limited to broadcasting. Religious fiction is an important segment of the American book industry, and any major bookstore will feature several shelves dedicated to this genre. Among the most popular in recent years are the many volumes in the "Left Behind" series, written by Tim LaHaye and Jerry Jenkins. Christian pop music, although far from having the sales and radio and television playtime of hip hop, rap, or rock, has a significant presence on American Christian airwaves. Country, one of the most popular genres of music in the United States, often conveys a very traditional religious message, frequently mixing patriotism, Christian values, and a skepticism or even condemnation of the sorts of ideas and behavior associated with places like New York and San Francisco. When the Dixie Chicks, a very popular all-female country music group, was publicly critical of President George W. Bush while on tour in Europe in 2003, many country radio stations stopped broadcasting their music. The larger question raised by the boycott of the Dixie Chicks' music and the enormous criticism they received from many erstwhile fans—at the same time as their fan base among those not usually keen on country music, but who liked the Dixie Chicks' message, increased—was whether their criticism of the president and the war in Iraq disqualified their music from the country genre.

In addition to the roles played by country and Christian music, Christian popular literature, and Christian broadcasting on radio and television, much of talk radio has what can only be described as a clearly religious orientation, though this is not always explicitly Christian. Dr. Laura Schlesinger's popular "daily dose of morality," as she describes her program, is premised on the belief that no moral behavior or choice is possible without belief in God and outside the boundaries of conventional religion. But Dr. Laura is a Jew. Mark Levin, another popular conservative talk show host, is also Jewish. Although his program is not about "moral dilemmas," the stated subject of Dr. Laura's, his assessment of political issues and of the choices that should be made in public life are also strongly influenced by religious values. The same is true of Sean Hannity's program, which involves a sort of seamless mixture of patriotism, traditional family values, and small government conservatism.

At the top of the talk radio food chain since the early 1990s is the Rush Limbaugh Show, with an estimated 20 million listeners per day in 2007. Limbaugh's daily and rather humorously delivered claim that his is "talent on loan from God" anchors his program to the socially conservative and traditionally religious values of many, but by no means all, of his listeners. In most ways Limbaugh's style and message are the least obviously religious among the nationally syndicated programs at the top of the talk radio pecking order. His positions on the controversial moral issues that roil American public life are, however, consistently those of the religious right. Moreover, Limbaugh will, on occasion, explain how his belief in God determines his outlook on such matters. Thus, he deserves to be placed toward the center of those parts of the media system that reflect and reinforce the cultural significance of traditional religious values in American public conversation.

Limbaugh and the other parts of the media system mentioned above do more than reflect and reinforce the cultural significance of the religious values they express. They also elevate the political importance of these values by making clear for viewers, listeners, and readers the political dimensions and ramifications of these moral issues, linking them to particular policies, parties, and politicians. The political influence of organized religion in the United States does not operate through dollars given to parties and candidates who take positions favored by a church. Section 501 of the tax code prohibits this in any case, on pain of a group losing its tax-exempt status. Nor does it operate in any other form of directly partisan involvement in politics, although sometimes this boundary line is pushed to the limit as when the members of a church participate in a get-out-the-vote campaign, work the phone banks on behalf of a particular candidate or party, or organize and attend rallies on behalf of a candidate or in support of some stand on an issue.

The political influence of organized religion in the United States is largely indirect, although no less important for that. It operates through the continuous maintenance of a climate of opinion and a public conversation in which the values associated with traditional religion are extremely important and in which, moreover, these values are linked in obvious ways to politics and politicians. The values of religious conservatives—but also religious liberals, although to a much lesser degree—are prominently expressed in the "public square." They are not the views of marginal cranks or discredited hypocrites, although they may often appear so to non-Americans. Main Street, America has churches at both ends, as it did in Tocqueville's time. The majority of Americans, even if they do not attend church every week, see nothing unusual or undemocratic in this.

Key Organizations in the Christian Conservatism Movement

Focus on the Family, http://www.family.org. Founded and directed by Dr. James Dobson, whose books and radio broadcasts are ubiquitous across the United States, this organization describes its mission as "nurturing and defending families worldwide." Based in Colorado Springs and specializing in radio broadcasting and publishing, Focus on the Family has affiliates in 30 states and in Canada. As of 2007, its broadcasts could be heard on over 3,000 radio stations in 116 countries and in 75 languages. Dobson's endorsement is highly valued by many candidates, and he was personally welcomed by President George W. Bush at the 2005 National Day of Prayer observance at the White House.

Family Research Council, http://www.frc.org. This organization is headed by former Louisiana state legislator, Tony Perkins, a graduate of Jerry Falwell's Liberty University. The Family Research Council's 2006 budget was just under $11 million. The Council lobbies on behalf of socially conservative causes; assists in mobilizing voters at election time; and, like many other interest groups on the left and the right, it provides a "scorecard" on the voting records of members of Congress.

Christian Broadcasting Network, http://www.cbn.com. This is run by Pat Robertson, one of America's most successful televangelists. Through such programs as the "700 Club," the CBN raised about $253 million in viewer donations in 2006. Socially conservative politicians often appear on the "700 Club," and the program is, according to the Nielsen ratings, watched by an estimated 1 million viewers per day.

American Center for Law and Justice, http://www.aclj.org. With an annual budget of roughly $15 million, the ACLJ does pro bono legal work on issues relating to religious freedoms. It describes its mission as "working to protect the American family" and has argued cases before the Supreme Court on such matters as the free speech rights of pro-life demonstrators and the right of public school students to form and participate in religious organizations on campus. The organization is active on a wide range of constitutional law issues that all have to do with socially conservative values.

Regent University, Liberty University, Pepperdine University, etc., http://www.regent.edu, http://www.liberty.edu, http://www.pepperdine.edu. Regent was founded by Pat Robertson, Liberty by Jerry Falwell, and Pepperdine by George Pepperdine, a member of the Churches of Christ. They are three of the roughly 1,000 colleges and universities in the United States that have religious affiliations. In many cases, such as Notre Dame and Boston College, both Catholic, and a school like Albion College, affiliated with the United Methodist church, the religious connection is not particularly important in terms of who is hired, how subjects are taught, and the political orientation of the students, faculty, and administration. But in the other cases it matters quite a lot. Regent, Liberty, and Pepperdine all have law schools whose orientation and goals are based on Christian teachings. In 2007 it came to light that about 150 Regent law graduates were employed by the Bush administration.[18] This, replied some, was no more alarming than the fact that graduates from predominantly liberal Ivy League universities have been and continue to be disproportionately represented in the Justice Department.

Being Muslim in America

Dearborn, Michigan is just outside of Detroit and is the home not only of the Ford Motor Company but also for about 30,000 Muslim Americans, making it the city with the largest concentration of Muslims as well as of people of Arab ancestry in the United States (about 60% of Arab Americans in the Detroit area are Christian). Roughly one-third of the students on the University of Michigan-Dearborn campus are Muslims, most of them second-generation Americans.

In the summer of 2007 the administration at the University of Michigan-Dearborn, announced that two footbaths would be installed on the campus so that Muslim students would have a place to wash their feet before prayers, as required of the faithful. Reaction was mixed, but outside the Muslim community most of what was said and written about the footbath decision was highly critical. Generally speaking, there was a sense that it underlined Muslim separateness or what British Prime Minister Tony Blair, in a controversial 2006 statement, had called Muslims' mark of difference. The first strike against Muslims in this footbath story was the breach of the separation of church and state. The second strike was the sense that footbaths were in their small way indicative of an unwillingness to integrate into the society of *e pluribus unum*, but instead to remain apart and different.

Before 9/11, Muslim Americans passed largely unnoticed in American society. Hard numbers are hard to come by—the United States census does not ask about religious affiliation and inferences based on ethnicity are unreliable—but most estimates indicate that Muslims constitute under 1% of the national population.[19] In only a few states are their numbers large enough for them to be considered a community within the larger society. Since 9/11, however, Muslim Americans have received much more attention. Although they constitute a much smaller share of the American population than in such countries as France, Germany, or the UK, many of the same questions have been asked about the relationship of Muslim Americans to the values of the larger society in which they live.

Compared to its counterparts in European countries, not only is the Muslim American population small, it is also better integrated into the larger society both economically and culturally. Figure 3.4 shows that, unlike in the UK, France, Germany, and Spain, Muslims in America are not likely to be poorer than the general population, and they are much less likely than Muslims in all countries but France to think of themselves as Muslims first and citizens of their country second.

FIGURE 3.4:   AMERICAN MUSLIMS MORE MAINSTREAM THAN IN EUROPE

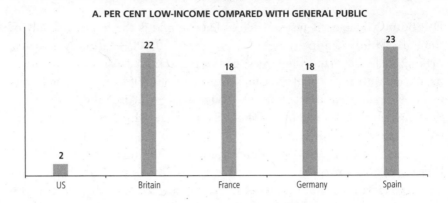

A. PER CENT LOW-INCOME COMPARED WITH GENERAL PUBLIC

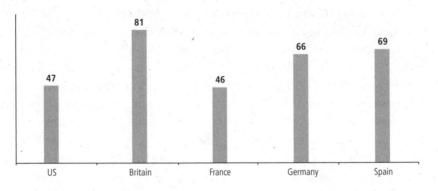

B. THINK OF SELF AS MUSLIM FIRST

Source: "Muslim Americans," Pew Center for People and the Press, May 2007.

The comparatively high integration of Muslim Americans is also seen in the fact that, even more than the general population, they believe that hard work pays off: 71% agree that "most people who want to get ahead can make it if they work hard" compared to 64% for the general population. Just about as many Muslim Americans as members of the general population rate their community as an "excellent" or "good" place to live (72% versus 82%). Finally, Muslim Americans are less dissatisfied with the overall direction of the country (54%) than are Americans generally (61%).[20]

Muslim Americans appear, therefore, to be quite integrated into American society. However, the fact that many more of them think of themselves as Muslims first and Americans second—47% compared to 28%—might be seen as an indication of less than perfect integration into the mainstream. This needs to be set alongside the fact that Muslims are not very different from Christian Americans in this respect: Christians who say that religion is very important in their lives are twice as likely to see their religious identity as more important than their national identity (59% versus 30%). In any case, identities are not mutually exclusive. Consequently, it is an error to assume that people who view religion as the main anchor for their ideas regarding who they are and what beliefs they hold—whether they are Muslim, Christian, or any other religion—have a diminished capacity for citizenship and integration into the larger society. Moreover, Muslin Americans are somewhat less likely to say that mosques should express their views on current social and political matters than members of the general population are to say that churches should do this (43% versus 51%).

TABLE 3.2: "DO YOU BELIEVE GROUPS OF ARABS CARRIED OUT THE 9/11 ATTACKS?"

	Yes %	No %	DK/Ref %
All US Muslims	40	28	32=100
18-29	38	38	24=100
30-39	37	30	33=100
40-54	45	24	31=100
55+	49	16	35=100
College Grad	55	24	22=100
Some College	43	30	27=100
HS or Less	34	30	36=100
Religious Commitment			
High	29	46	25=100
Medium	38	24	38=100
Low	53	22	25=100
Muslims in ...*			
France	48	46	6=100
Germany	35	44	21=100
Spain	33	35	32=100
Britain	17	56	27=100

Question: Do you believe that groups of Arabs carried out the attacks against the United States on Sept. 11, 2001, or don't you believe this?

* Pew Global Attitudes Project, May 2006.

Source: "Muslim Americans," Pew Center for People and the Press (May 2007): 51.

The integrative tendencies of Muslim Americans also may be seen in the fact that only about one-quarter of them agree that Muslims should "mostly try to remain distinct from the larger American society." This figure is even lower if African American Muslims, who tend on all counts to be less favorable toward integration than other Muslims, are excluded. Most surprisingly, perhaps, is the finding that slightly more than six in 10 Muslim Americans believe that it is "okay" for a Muslim to marry a non-Muslim since Islamic Law prohibits a Muslim woman from marrying outside her religion. And just over half of Muslim Americans say that they have relatively few Muslims among their closest friends. All of this adds up to a very different and more integrated picture than is true of Muslim communities in most Western European countries.

Where Muslim Americans depart most significantly from the views of other Americans are on matters relating to politics, particularly America's relationship with the Muslim world. They are far more likely than members of the general population to oppose American involvement in Iraq. Like Muslims elsewhere in the world, Muslim Americans are much more likely than members of the general population to express doubt that Arabs carried out the attacks of 9/11. But as Table 3.2 shows, they are much less likely than Muslims in several European countries to express doubt that Arabs perpetrated these attacks. Support for suicide bombing against civilian targets to defend Islam is low among Muslim Americans and only half the level of support among Muslims in France, Spain, and the UK (8% versus 16%, 16%, and 15%, respectively). But Muslim Americans under the age of 30 are twice as likely as Muslim Americans generally to say that such bombing is often or occasionally justified.

The overall picture is of a Muslim American community that is small and comparatively well-integrated into the mainstream. The radicalism found in Muslim communities in such countries as the UK and France is largely absent in the United States. Occasional issues—like the footbaths on the University of Michigan-Dearborn campus, whether Muslim women who wear the face veil should have to expose their faces for driver's license photos, and the decision to close schools in a predominantly Muslim community in recognition of the Eid holiday—sound alarm bells for some Americans who fear that such actions and behaviors run afoul of essential aspects of Americanism. But it is very possible that these issues would not even have been brought to the American public's attention by the media had it not been for the attacks of 9/11, the war in Iraq, and a backdrop of public hostility toward and mistrust of Muslims—Muslims as a generic category, not necessarily their Muslim neighbors. Indeed, given the comparatively small number of Muslims in America and their concentration in just a handful of urban centers, the foreign Muslims that Americans see on television are much better known to most than are Muslim Americans.

Notes

1 Tocqueville, *Democracy in America*, Book I.

2 "The Papers of James Madison," http://memory.loc.gov/ammen/collections/madison _papers/.

3 See the discussion in Jeffrey Sheler, "Christian Conservatives in 2008," *Religion and Ethics Newsweekly* 1024 (12 February 2007), http://www.pbs.org.

4 Bryce 770.

5 Jean Bethke Elshtain, "Religions in the Public Square," Ronald Reagan Symposium 2007, Regent University; http://www.regents.edu/publications/cl/features/fw_07/reagan_symposium.cfm.

6 Found at http://www.gwu.edu/~action/gore080800.html.

7 Links to all of the speeches mentioned in this paragraph may be found at http://www.americanrhetoric.com.

8 Sheler.

9 Tocqueville, *Democracy in America*, Book I.

10 Quoted in *Religion and Ethics Newsweekly* 1010 (3 November 2006), http://www.pbs.org.

11 Based on data from 2003 and 2004 reported in Pew Center, *Trends 2005: Religion and Public Life*, 33-34; http://www.pewresearch.org/assets/files/trends2005-religion.pdf.

12 Bliss Institute Survey2004, http://www.uakron.edu/bliss/.

13 John Green, "Faith and Family in America," survey conducted for the Pew Forum on Religions and Public Life, 2005 (see note 10).

14 Sheler.

15 Quoted in Sheler.

16 Pew Center, *Trends 2005*, 38–39.

17 http://www.museum.tv/archives/etv/8/htm18/billygraham/billgrahm.htm.

18 Charlie Savage, "Scandal Puts Spotlight on Christian Law School," *Boston Globe*, 8 April 2007.

19 See, for example, the estimates referred to at http://www.adherents.com/largecom_com_islam_usa.html.

20 Pew Center, *Muslim Americans*, 2007. All of the survey data cited in this section are from this report; http://pewresearch.org/pubs/483/muslim-americans.

CHAPTER FOUR

A Values Gap?

Those who have seen *Friday Night Lights*, a film about the Permian Panthers high school football team in Odessa, Texas, will recall that before and after each game the players gather with their coach in a prayer circle. People who have gone to school in the United States and attended football or basketball games will find nothing exceptional in this, but a spectator from France or the UK would probably find it a bit unusual and, on hearing that the team was engaged in group prayer, might even find it rather bizarre. On the other hand, this foreign spectator might find in this very American rite confirmation of his or her view of America as a quaintly—or perhaps disturbingly—religious place. "Religious," in this context, means a traditional, old-fashioned, and rather backward place where abortion is still a political issue; same-sex marriage is extremely divisive; people believe in good and evil instead of striving to understand the complexity of human motivation and behavior; and the president is expected to make regular public reference to the Almighty and end every speech by saying "God bless America."

America is different. This conclusion has been drawn by most foreign commentators from Tocqueville almost two centuries ago to Jean Baudrillard and Bernard-Henri Lévy today. The values and beliefs of Americans, most foreign observers conclude, are somewhat different from those of other societies, including those that are similar to theirs economically and socially and share the same Western heritage. Indeed, there is probably a no more frequent theme in foreign analyses of America than the putative cultural differences between it and other societies and how these differences are reflected in social behavior, world views, and government policies.

Americans seem to share this conviction about their difference. Belief in their own exceptionalism is as old as European settlement in the New World. The line connecting John Winthrop's "shining city on a hill" to America's vision of its place and even mission in the world today, as expressed in any modern president's inaugural address, involves a faith in the extraordinary character of America and the special role that Providence has allotted to America and its people.

America is different, and it is different in ways that interfere with mutual understanding between Americans and their leaders and the peoples and leaders of other societies. The core values and beliefs of Americans are significantly different from those of the French, Germans, Swedes, and even Canadians. These cultural variations are not always very great and should be understood as differences in tendency—for example, the tendency to tolerate economic inequality or to believe that lack of religious faith makes a person less qualified for public office—rather than the presence or absence of some particular attribute. But in some cases the differences are quite sharp, and their cumulative effect interferes with the ability of Americans and some other national populations to understand each other.

For example, in 2003 the French Parliament passed a law prohibiting the wearing of the Muslim hijab in state schools. This law was passed by overwhelming majorities in both chambers of the French legislature and was widely supported by the country's politicians and opinion leaders across the ideological spectrum. In the United States, this law was generally seen as an intolerant violation of minority rights and an indication that the French did not have adequate respect for diversity. Viewed from an American angle and within the prevailing understanding of minority rights and respect for diversity, it was not surprising that Americans would judge the French harshly. But this was, nonetheless, an unfair judgment. France's political culture is quite respectful of minority rights. Its Muslim minority, which constitutes close to 10% of its population, is an important part of French society and, despite occasional tensions, is not the target of official or systematic discrimination by the state. France, like the United States, values the separation of church and state; the important difference, a difference that most Americans did not understand in the hijab controversy, is that France has become a very secular society in which official sanction of religious identities that might be seen as challenging the French civic identity is simply not acceptable to most people. To put this a bit more simply, the dominant understanding of and debate over cultural pluralism is not identical in France and the United States. So it is quite wrong to suggest that the decision to ban the hijab in schools shows that the French are culturally intolerant.

Misunderstanding works both ways. Since the time of Tocqueville, European observers of American politics have remarked on, and been critical of, what they believe to be the tendency of Americans to choose mediocre and even unintelligent leaders. James Bryce even devoted an entire chapter to the subject—"Why the Best Men Do Not Go into Politics"—in *The American Commonwealth*, which was published in 1888. In more recent times, European opinion leaders have shaken their heads over the popularity of Ronald Reagan and George W. Bush, asking how it is that Americans choose to elect men who, in their eyes, are so manifestly dull-witted.

Some Americans share their wonderment. Without getting into the issue of whether these judgments are fair, I would argue that the long-standing tendency of many Europeans to be dismissive and derisive when it comes to the intelligence of American politicians is largely due to differing cultural expectations for and understanding of leadership qualities. This does not mean that Europeans tend to set the bar higher for their political leaders. The root of the difference lies in the American populist tradition, wherein a perceived distance between leaders and those who elect them is quite often a serious liability. The influence of the populist tradition is highlighted in the disparity between the marketing of candidates in the United States and a country like France, and in the ingredients that contribute to an electorally successful image in these respective societies. I do not mean to suggest that those who would be president or prime minister in France, Germany, or Italy can afford to maintain an aloof and distant public persona, apart from and above the people, but there are differences between the sorts of personal attributes that tend to contribute to a politician's electability in the United States and those in other countries. When Ronald Reagan was asked the secret of his popularity with the American people, he answered, "When they look at me, they see themselves." It is hard to imagine Jacques Chirac, Silvio Berlusconi, or even Tony Blair giving the same answer, although the populist style seems to have made inroads in European politics in recent years.

Despite the fact that globalization has contributed to the undeniable convergence of lifestyles in many important ways, significant differences remain in the values and beliefs of societies that are otherwise quite similar in their level of economic development and the nature of their social institutions. In fact, it has become increasingly common in recent years to argue that the values gap between the United States and other rich Western democracies is growing wider. While this conclusion may not be warranted, there is little doubt that such a gap continues to exist and impedes the ability of those on either side to understand each other.

Drawing on data from the most recent round of the WVS (2000), the chief dimensions of this values gap may be examined. Interestingly, these dimensions of difference remain the same as those that foreign observers have remarked on since Tocqueville visited America. They include the following:

- religion,
- moral absolutism,
- civic-mindedness,
- individualism, and
- patriotism.

On each of these dimensions, the values and beliefs of Americans are significantly different from those of people in other developed democracies. These are the differences that contribute to the wall of miscomprehension between Americans and these other societies.

Religion

Tocqueville argued that religion was a bulwark of American democracy in three principal ways. First, the plurality of denominations, none of whom were able to claim a majority of the population, encouraged religious groups to be respectful of diversity and vigilant about state interference with the rights of religious communities. Second, religion was crucial in preventing American individualism and materialism from fatally corroding the sense of community and corrupting the souls of men. Finally, he noted that since most denominations in America were comparatively participatory and non-hierarchical, they acted as training grounds in democratic practice and norms.

Religion continues to be important in the lives of many Americans and a factor in their country's politics. Today, however, most commentary focuses on what is generally believed to be the much greater significance of religious values in America compared to other advanced postindustrial democracies. The evidence in support of this claim is overwhelming. When people in such countries as France, Belgium, and Germany read about the influence of Christian Evangelicals in politics, or hear the president invoke the Almighty several times in a single speech, or see on television thousands of anti-abortion demonstrators massing in Washington, they find it one of the stranger aspects of life in America. They also tend to dismiss it as hypocritical, noting that this is the same society whose rates of divorce and crime are among the highest in the world, whose popular culture churns out vulgarity and irreligiosity at a prodigious rate, and whose leaders take actions and defend policies that fly in the face of the spiritual beliefs they claim to hold dear.

Hypocritical or not, there is no doubt that the role of traditional religion in American politics and culture is greater than in other Western democracies. Only Ireland and Italy have similar levels of church attendance, but even these countries trail considerably behind the United States on most measures of traditional religiousness. Figures 4.1 to 4.8 reveal that Americans consistently report behavior and express views on religion that set them clearly apart from the populations of other Western democracies.

FIGURE 4.1: "RELIGION IS VERY IMPORTANT IN MY LIFE"

US
57
Canada
30
France
11
Germany
9
Britain
13
Italy
33
Japan
7
Spain
19
Sweden
11
0
10
20
30
40
50
60

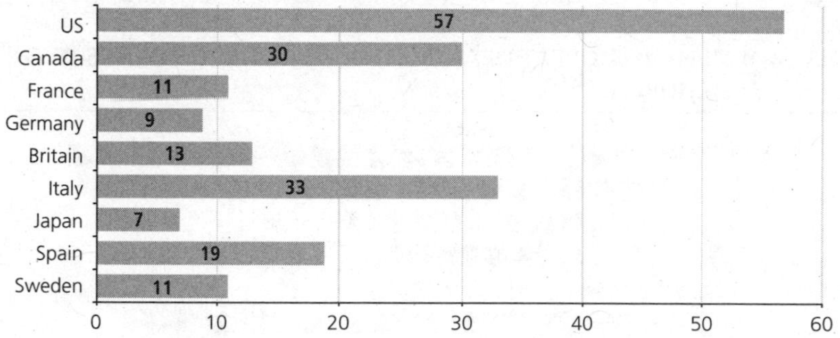

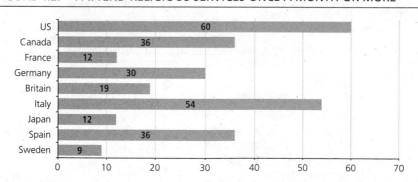

Source: Ronald Inglehart, et al., Human Values and Beliefs *(Mexico: Siglo Veintiuno Editores, S.A. de C.V., 2004). Based on the 1999-2002 World Values Surveys.*

FIGURE 4.2: "I ATTEND RELIGIOUS SERVICES ONCE A MONTH OR MORE"*

US
60
Canada
36
France
12
Germany
30
Britain
19
Italy
54
Japan
12
Spain
36
Sweden
9
0
10
20
30
40
50
60
70

* Not including weddings, funerals, and christenings.

Source: Inglehart, et al.

FIGURE 4.3: "I DO UNPAID VOLUNTARY WORK FOR A RELIGIOUS OR CHURCH ORGANIZATION"

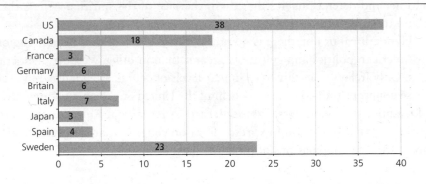

Source: Inglehart, et al.

FIGURE 4.4: "I HAVE A GREAT DEAL/QUITE A LOT OF CONFIDENCE IN THE CHURCHES"

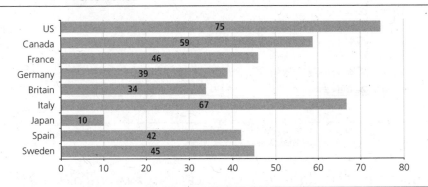

Source: Inglehart, et al.

FIGURE 4.5: "I AGREE THAT MARRIAGE IS AN OUTDATED INSTITUTION"

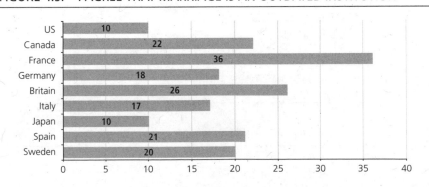

Source: Inglehart, et al.

FIGURE 4.6: "GENERALLY SPEAKING, I THINK THAT CHURCHES ARE GIVING ADEQUATE ANSWERS TO THE SOCIAL PROBLEMS FACING THE COUNTRY TODAY"

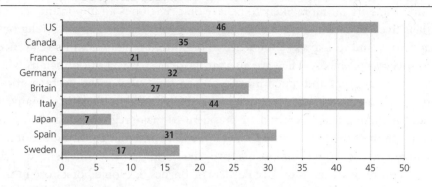

Source: Inglehart, et al.

FIGURE 4.7: "POLITICIANS WHO DO NOT BELIEVE IN GOD ARE UNFIT FOR PUBLIC OFFICE" (% who disagree or strongly disagree)

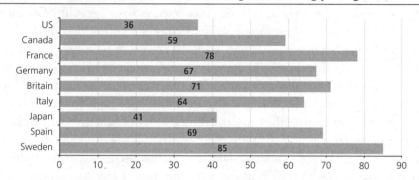

Source: Inglehart, et al.

FIGURE 4.8: "IT WOULD BE BETTER FOR THE COUNTRY IF MORE PEOPLE WITH STRONG RELIGIOUS BELIEFS HELD PUBLIC OFFICE" (% who disagree or strongly disagree)

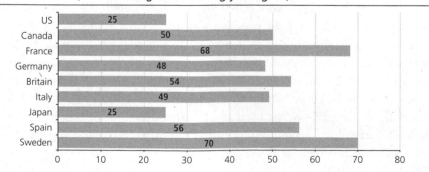

Source: Inglehart, et al.

Thus, when it comes to religion, it is plain that countries like France, Spain, and Sweden are on a very different wavelength from the United States. Americans are far more likely to believe that religion is an important part of their lives, to attend church regularly and volunteer their time to religious activities, and to express confidence in organized religion and its relevance to society's problems. They are also far more mistrustful of politicians who are non-believers and much more likely to think that it would be a good thing if more people with strong religious beliefs held public office. Many, if not most, Americans expect their president to make regular public avowals of his faith. If the president of France were to behave in this way, most of his fellow citizens would think it inappropriate and many would believe such behavior to be dangerous. Any Borders or Barnes & Noble bookstore in the United States includes a section for "Christian fiction." This genre is almost unknown in the popular cultures of most other affluent democracies.

The gap between the traditional religiosity that characterizes much of the American population and the far more secular value system of most other affluent democracies may also be demonstrated in their very different ideas about the creation and evolution of life. Figure 4.9 shows that only about 40% of Americans are in agreement with the theory of evolution, compared to 70–80% in such countries as Italy, France, Germany, Spain, Sweden, and the UK. The 2007 opening of the Museum of Creationism in Kentucky[1] may seem to most non-Americans, and also to some Americans, a rather bizarre and culturally marginal effort to deny the evidence of science. But for many people in America it accords with their skepticism about explanations for life's origins and the existence of human beings that do not assign a determining role to a God who is beyond the understanding of men and women.

The political implications of this are significant. In Canada, Stockwell Day, former leader of the Canadian Alliance Party, had his legitimacy undermined with most voters when it came to light that he had once attended a religious conference at which he had expressed support for the fundamentalist view that the earth is only 6,000 years old. Although it is probable that no serious candidate for the presidency of the United States would express such a view—at least not in so many words—there is no doubt that candidates for lesser offices could not only survive but perhaps even thrive from being associated with such a belief. In terms of public policy, the pressure in some parts of the United States for the teaching in schools of what is called "intelligent design"—what used to be called creationism—as part of the science curriculum, becomes understandable when viewed against a background of such beliefs.

FIGURE 4.9:   BELIEF IN EVOLUTION, 2005 (percentage agreeing it is true)

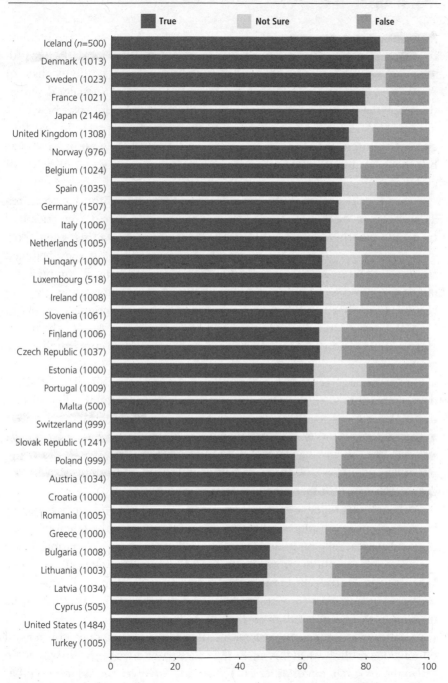

Source: Jon D. Miller, Eugenie C. Scott, and Shinji Okamoto, "Public Acceptance of Evolution," Science II (August 2006), 765-66, used with permission.

Moral Absolutes

European commentators will often remark that Americans are inclined to judge behavior and understand the world in overly simple black-and-white terms. What Tocqueville and Bryce characterized as the idealism of Americans, Simone de Beauvoir interpreted as a sort of adolescent denial of the troubling disorder and complexity of the world. Americans, she wrote, are like "big children." "Their tragedy," she argued, "is precisely that they are not children, that they have adult responsibilities, an adult existence, but they continue to cling to a ready-made, opaque universe, like that of childhood."[2]

When President George W. Bush described Iraq, Iran, and North Korea as an "axis of evil" and claimed that in the war on terror countries had to decide whether they were *with* the Americans or *against* them, foreign critics pointed to these comments as typical of what they believed to be a characteristically American tendency to understand complex circumstances in dichotomous good-versus-bad terms. The president would regularly say that insurgents in Iraq wished to see the country return to "the darkness." His 2005 inaugural address was noteworthy for the moral clarity of his vision for spreading democracy, which he represented as the triumph of good.

Such language resonates powerfully in American public life. To some degree, it is linked to the continuing strength of traditional religious values in American society, as described previously. One would expect that those who are more frequent churchgoers, who have greater respect for the authority of religious leaders, and for whom religion is a more important part of their lives to be also more likely to believe that absolute standards of good and evil, of right and wrong, exist.

Although this tendency to understand circumstances and judge behavior in terms of moral absolutes cannot be disassociated from the religious tradition in America, religion itself does not provide the entire explanation. There runs through the public pronouncements of George Washington, Abraham Lincoln, T.R. Roosevelt, Franklin Delano Roosevelt, Ronald Reagan, and present-day leaders a conviction of the moral rightness of America, of its mission in the world, and its role in world history. It is a conviction that, while often mentioned in the same breath as Providence, does not depend on religious faith. Rather, it is anchored to a sort of civic faith, what Lincoln called the civic religion of America. This "faith" involves the assumption that what Americans have aspired to create is, though imperfect in its execution, fundamentally right and good in its ideals. Jean Baudrillard captures this spirit of moral conviction when he says,

> The Americans are not wrong in their idyllic conviction that they are at the center of the world, the supreme power, the absolute model for everyone. And this conviction is not so much founded on natural resources, technologies, and arms, as on the miraculous premise of a utopia made reality, of a society which, with a directness we might judge unbearable, is built on the idea that it is the realization of everything that others have dreamt of—justice, plenty, rule of law, wealth, freedom: it knows this, it believes in it, and in the end, the others have come to believe in it too.[3]

Figures 4.10 to 4.12 show that Americans are considerably more likely than people in other Western democracies to believe in sin and in the existence of heaven (and hell, although these figures are not shown), and to agree that clear guidelines exist about what is good and evil. When foreign commentators criticize the American government or the president for intransigence, inflexibility, and unilateralism, part of the explanation may be that Americans and their leaders are more likely than others to see the world and particular issues in terms of morally good and bad choices.

FIGURE 4.10: "THERE ARE ABSOLUTELY CLEAR GUIDELINES ABOUT WHAT IS GOOD AND EVIL"

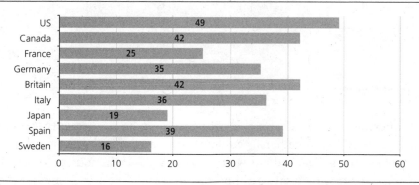

Source: Inglehart, et al.

FIGURE 4.11: "I BELIEVE IN SIN"*

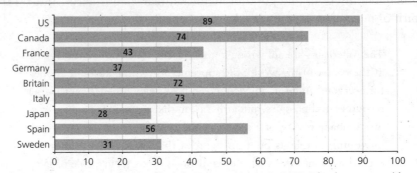

* This question was not asked in all of the WVS countries in 2000. The data reported here is for 1990.

Source: Inglehart, et al.

FIGURE 4.12: "I BELIEVE IN HEAVEN"

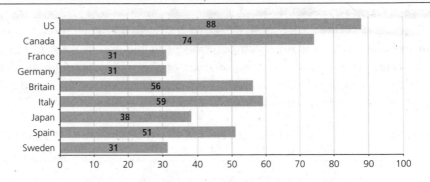

Source: Inglehart, et al.

Social Capital

Tocqueville was struck by the propensity of mid-nineteenth-century Americans to join together in voluntary associations in order to achieve communal goals. They did not wait, he observed, for the state to undertake an endeavor that they saw as important to their well-being, nor did they assume that such community enterprises ought to be the responsibility of public authorities. Tocqueville believed that these voluntary associations were the connective tissue of American democracy. They reminded citizens in immediate and practical ways that they belonged to a community and depended on one another. In doing so they helped overcome the alienating tendency of the individualist ethos that was so strong in America. They also contributed to what commentators today would call the social capital of American society.

But this complex and vibrant web of voluntary associations made another important contribution to American society: it created a particular sort of civic-mindedness that was centered around "we, the people" rather than the state. Part of what has been called American exceptionalism can be attributed to the popular mistrust of government, a sentiment that is often credited to the revolutionary origins of the United States. The historical propensity of Americans to come together in private associations to achieve common objectives reinforced this mistrust and contributed to the idea that citizens *should* be responsible for organizing, financing, and executing many collective activities. More than a century after Tocqueville, American political scientists Gabriel Almond and Sidney Verba argued that this was an important part of democratic citizenship in what they called the "civic culture."[4] Citizens capable of working together to solve common problems and who saw this as an appropriate and important activity were more suited to democratic life than those who tended to view themselves as subjects, dependent on public authorities to organize their civic life.

Today, however, many Americans and people abroad argue that the stock of social capital in the United States has been declining for years. Many go so far as to argue that Americans actually have less of what constitutes social capital than do the populations of many other Western democracies. They point to greater spending on social programs and indications that Americans are less willing than people in these other societies to support and pay for a redistribution of wealth between segments of the population.

This debate over whether the connective tissue that joins citizens is weaker in America than in some other Western democracies often misses an important point related to the nature of American exceptionalism. The communal ethos that exists in America is less dependent on the state as the agency through which it is expressed and the instrument through which its goals are pursued than in other wealthy democracies. In fact, because of their historically grounded mistrust of the state, many Americans are dubious of government programs to achieve collective goals. The debate over faith-based delivery of social programs—a debate that is uniquely American—reflects this sense that social services and aid for the disadvantaged may be better provided by voluntary organizations than the state. It may be a mistake to conclude from America's lower per capita spending on social services that Americans care less than other populations about the communal goals that provide the ostensible justification for this spending.

Perhaps, instead, they are more likely to place their faith and their dollars in non-state responses to social needs.

Data from the WVS demonstrates that Americans are far more likely than their counterparts in other societies to belong to voluntary associations and to participate in their activities. Figure 4.13 shows that a remarkably large share of the American population devotes some of its time to unpaid work for religious, youth, sports and recreation, educational, and cultural groups. In other Western democracies, these activities are more likely to be the responsibility of state agencies and financed by public revenues. If participation in voluntary organizations like these is a reasonable measure of social capital—citizens expressing their support for their communities and collective goals through voluntary efforts—then one would have to conclude that the level of social capital in America is comparatively high.

FIGURE 4.13: MEASURES OF SOCIAL CAPITAL

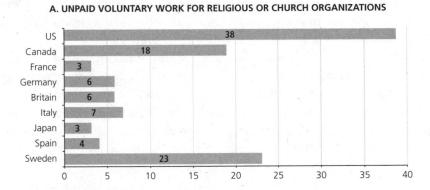

A. UNPAID VOLUNTARY WORK FOR RELIGIOUS OR CHURCH ORGANIZATIONS

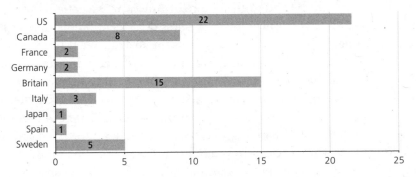

B. UNPAID VOLUNTARY WORK FOR YOUTH GROUPS (scouts, guides, youth clubs, etc.)

C. UNPAID VOLUNTARY WORK FOR SPORTS OR RECREATION GROUPS

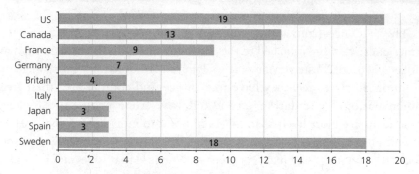

D. UNPAID VOLUNTARY WORK FOR EDUCATION, ARTS, MUSIC, OR CULTURAL GROUPS

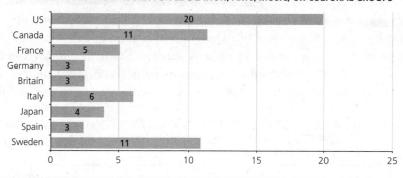

Source: Inglehart, et al.

The fact that Americans are more likely to believe that private citizens and the voluntary associations they create—rather than the state—should be responsible for meeting social needs probably contributes to the misunderstanding between Americans and the populations of other Western democracies. We will have more to say about this in Chapter 17 on civic participation.

Individualism

Individualism is a concept with many dimensions. When Tocqueville wrote about the individualism that he saw in America, he had in mind what was then the rather novel idea that individual persons "owe nothing to any man, they expect nothing from any man; they acquire the habit of always considering themselves as standing alone, and they are apt to imagine that their whole destiny is in their own hands."[5] Commentators since Tocqueville have linked American individualism to such beliefs and attitudes as personal responsibility for success and failure in life, achievement orientation, and support for individual property rights and capitalism.

The evidence from survey research seems to support the claim that Americans are more attached to these dimensions of individualism than are citizens in other Western democracies. Figure 4.14 illustrates that Americans are more likely to feel they have free choice and control over their lives. When national populations are asked why some people are in need, Americans are more likely than others to point to individual laziness or lack of will power, in other words, to say that the person is to blame, not "society," "the system," "bad luck," or some other cause that is beyond individual control (see Figure 4.15). One would expect a society that believes strongly in personal autonomy and individual responsibility for success or failure to be strongly supportive of competition as well. As Figure 4.16 shows, the vast majority of Americans agree that competition is good and that it stimulates people to work hard and develop new ideas. Canadians and Swedes are about as likely to believe this, but skepticism about the virtue of competition is considerably greater in such societies as France, Italy, Japan, and Spain.

FIGURE 4.14: FEELING OF HAVING FREE CHOICE AND CONTROL OVER ONE'S LIFE (percentage saying that they have a great deal of choice and control)*

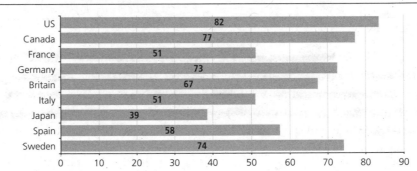

* The question read, "Some people feel they have completely free choice and control over their lives, while other people feel that what they do has no real effect on what happens to them." Respondents answered on a 10-point scale, with 10 being most and 1 being least. Those who answered 7–10 were considered to feel that they had a great deal of choice and control.

Source: Inglehart, et al.

FIGURE 4.15: "PEOPLE ARE IN NEED BECAUSE OF LAZINESS OR LACK OF WILL POWER"*

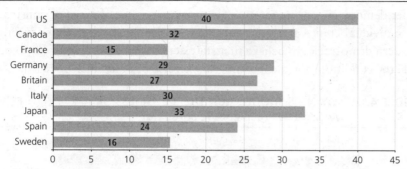

* This question was not asked in all of the WVS countries in 2000. The data reported here is for 1990.

Source: Inglehart, et al.

FIGURE 4.16: "COMPETITION IS GOOD"*

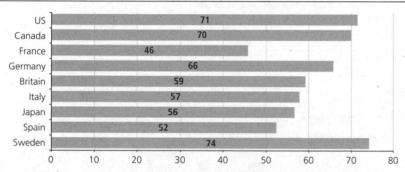

* The response item read, "Competition is good. It stimulates people to work hard and develop new ideas."

Source: Inglehart, et al.

Individualism has always had an important economic dimension in the United States. When Harold Laski commented on what he called the American spirit, he stressed the faith that Americans placed in capitalism, private property, and free markets. He also stressed the skepticism they expressed when it came to state regulation of property rights.[6] This skepticism remains a significant point of difference between the United States and other Western democracies. Americans are considerably more likely to hold the view that owners should determine how their businesses are run, not the state or unions. Only Canadians come close to them in support for ownership rights (see Figure 4.17).

Freedom is a slippery concept, but it is obviously linked to individualism. The language of American public life—and, for that matter, commercial speech in America—is replete with references to freedom. Americans, it is sometimes argued, tend to understand freedom differently than do people in other democracies, being more likely to view it as the absence of constraint on individual choice and behavior. They are less likely than those in other Western democracies to believe that state action is necessary in order to provide the conditions for the meaningful exercise of individual freedom.

FIGURE 4.17: "OWNERS SHOULD RUN THEIR BUSINESS OR APPOINT THE MANAGERS" (percentage agreeing)

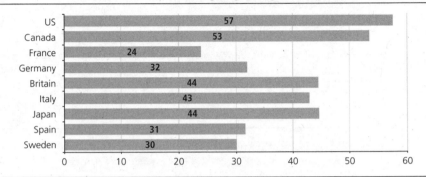

Source: Inglehart, et al.

FIGURE 4.18: "I WOULD CHOOSE FREEDOM OVER EQUALITY"*†

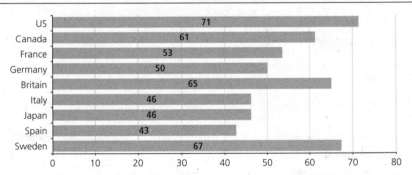

* This question was not asked in all of the WVS countries in 2000. The data reported here is for 1990. † The question read, "Both freedom and equality are important, but if you were to choose one or the other, which of these two statements comes closest to your own opinion? A, personal freedom is more important, or B, equality is more important.

Source: Inglehart, et al.

It appears that Americans are more likely than other national populations to choose freedom over equality when these values are presented in conflict. Figure 4.18 shows that while the differences between Americans and Swedes or Britons are marginal, they are quite dramatic compared to the populations of France, Germany, Italy, Japan, and Spain.

Patriotism

"Nothing is more embarrassing in the ordinary intercourse of life than this irritating patriotism of Americans."[7] Tocqueville's words, many foreign observers would say, still have the ring of truth. Most Americans are very proud of their country and its ideals and accomplishments. Some commentators, both inside and outside the United States, ascribe this high level of patriotism to official and unofficial indoctrination—from reciting the Pledge of Allegiance each morning at school to the celebratory and triumphalist representations of America in much of the popular culture—and to ignorance of and indifference toward the rest of the world.

This was not, however, Tocqueville's explanation of American pride. He located the roots of their enthusiastic patriotism and sensitivity to foreign criticism in the democratic character of the United States. In today's language, one might say that Americans tend to have a sense of ownership when it comes to their society and its accomplishments. They do not see themselves as bystanders or pawns of forces beyond their control but as shareholders in the great American enterprise. Consequently, they feel that its achievements are their achievements. And most Americans believe that these achievements, from the ideals and aspirations embodied in the Constitution to the standard of living they enjoy, are pretty impressive and deserving of pride.

For decades now, survey data have corroborated what one senses from the streetscapes, public language, and behavior of Americans. Figure 4.19 confirms that they *do* tend to be more patriotic and prouder of their country than the citizens of other Western democracies. Some may interpret this as an indication of "blind patriotism," a sentiment that may make Americans more likely than other democratic populations to support their government in military endeavors abroad. But, in fact, Figure 4.19 also shows that Americans are not dramatically more likely than Canadians, Italians, or the French to say that they would be willing to fight for their country. This question was not asked of all the national samples in the 2000 WVS survey, but in the 1990 survey, Swedes were even more likely than Americans to express a willingness to fight for their country, and British respondents were only slightly less likely than Americans to express this sentiment.

FIGURE 4.19: "I AM PROUD TO BE [NATIONALITY]"*

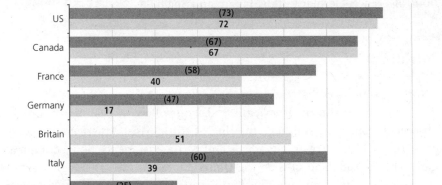

* The lower bar for each country represents the percentage of respondents saying yes to this question: "Of course, we all hope that there will not be another war, but if it were to come to that, would you be willing to fight for your country?

Source: Inglehart, et al.

Materialism and Postmaterialism

In democratic societies across the world it has become common to think of the United States as a rather unprogressive and even culturally reactionary place, a perception quite opposite to that which prevailed in those same countries during most of the twentieth century. The civil rights movement of the 1950s and 1960s, American feminists such as Gloria Steinem and Betty Friedan, a consumer movement pioneered by Ralph Nader, an environmental movement that was louder and better organized politically than elsewhere, and trendsetting on many cultural and lifestyle fronts from music to fashion all suggested that the United States was at the cutting edge of what it meant to be modern and progressive. This has changed. Now, many think that the United States is somewhat backward and rather behind the times on matters from same-sex marriage and stem-cell research to environmental protection and cultural tolerance. The gap between Europe and the United States on the Kyoto Accord and global warming was seen by many as evidence—apologies to Al Gore!—of America's unprogressive mindset. So too was the skepticism of many Americans and their leaders when it came to the multilateral global governance model embodied in the International Criminal Court and the Landmines Treaty favored by Canada and the European Union countries. A once progressive society is now viewed by many outside its borders as a comparatively traditional and even reactionary place.

The truth is far more complicated. We have already seen that Americans tend to be more traditionally religious than the citizens of other Western democracies and, moreover, that national pride is much greater among Americans than in other countries. These more traditional orientations in America distinguish it from the more secular societies of Western Europe and Japan.

These traditional orientations emphasize the *constraints on human behavior*, whereas secular orientations emphasize *choice in human behavior*. "Value change progressing from constraint to choice," says Christian Welzel, "is a central aspect of human development because this value change makes people mentally free, motivating them to develop, unfold, and actualize their inner human potential."[8] This is what is generally meant by a progressive mindset. Americans, it appears, are less likely to have this mindset than are Swedes, Germans, the French, or even Britons. Indeed, the only Western democracy where traditional religion-based notions of community are about as strong as in the United States is Ireland.

But there is a second important dimension to value orientations that is linked to a society's stage of economic development and level of wealth. As societies become wealthier and an increasing share of the population is no longer preoccupied by the challenge of meeting survival needs—shelter, food, security—more priority will be placed on subjective well-being, self-expression, and issues involving the quality of life. *Materialists*—those whose values and behavior are premised on scarcity and insecurity—give way to *postmaterialists*.

The postmaterialist mindset emphasizes individualism and self-expression values—choice over constraint. Measured on this scale of values, Americans are among the most progressive people in the world. Figure 4.20 shows the percentage of the population with postmaterialist values in the United States and several other affluent democracies. Not only is postmaterialist orientation about as likely to be found among Americans as in other democratic societies, the percentage of those with materialist value orientations is dramatically lower in the United States (9% in 2000) compared to Germany

(28%), France (28%), Belgium (23%) or Spain (25%). Only Sweden (6%) has a clearly lower percentage of materialists in its population.

The characterization of the United States as less progressive, as defined here, than other Western democratic societies is not accurate. Or at least the evidence is mixed and even contradictory. Americans are, on the whole, considerably more traditional and less secular than those people in almost all other affluent democracies. This results in their being more likely to oppose individual choices and behavior that violate traditional religious morality (as opposed to standards of secular spirituality). Opposition to abortion and same-sex marriages, calls for the reinstatement of school prayer, and the much greater frequency of religious references in the American political conversation than in that of other Western democracies lead many to conclude that America is a rather backward and intolerant place.

But all this needs to be set alongside evidence of an America that is tolerant of non-conformity, that is highly individualistic, and where levels of interpersonal trust are comparatively high. This is an America in which levels of postmaterialism—emphasizing individual choice over constraint—are as high or higher than in most other affluent democracies.

FIGURE 4.20: PERCENTAGE OF NATIONAL POPULATION WITH
              POSTMATERIALIST VALUES, 1990 AND 2000

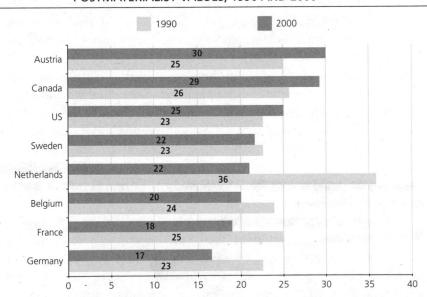

Source: Data from World Value Surveys.

Culture Matters

When trying to understand the ideas and sentiments that foreign populations have concerning the United States and its people, keep in mind that their values and beliefs are not identical to those of Americans. Sometimes this values gap produces serious miscomprehension, and disorientation, summed up in the title of Bernard-Henri Levy's book, *American Vertigo*. At a minimum, it contributes to a certain cultural distance between Americans and other societies. Colin Powell made this point during a 2004 visit to Europe when he acknowledged that Americans needed to do a much better job understanding the others' values and points of view. But, he added, those other societies also need to see the United States more clearly and accurately, not just through the prism of preconceived and sometimes unfounded beliefs and prejudices.

America *is* different. Most foreign commentators and leaders who interpret America to their populations accept this to be true. They know that culture matters and that American behavior, institutions, and policies cannot be explained solely by political interests. Indeed, there is probably no theme that recurs as often in the mountain of foreign commentary on America. The existence of this values gap is unmistakable.

Notes

1 See http://www.creationmuseum.org.

2 Simone de Béauvoir, *America Day by Day*, trans. Carol Cosman (1948; Berkeley, CA: University of California Press, 1999) 313.

3 Baudrillard 77.

4 Gabriel Almond and Sidney Verba, *The Civic Culture: Political Attitudes and Democracy in Five Nations* (Thousand Oaks, CA: Little, Brown and Co, 1965).

5 Tocqueville, *Democracy in America*, Book II.

6 Harold Laski, *The American Democracy* (New York: The Viking Press, 1948), Chapter 2.

7 Tocqueville, *Democracy in America*, Book I.

8 Christian Welzel, "A Human Development View on Value Change Trends (1981–2006)," WVS website, http://www.worldvaluessurvey.org.

PHOTOS (LEFT TO RIGHT)
1. Presidents are expected to provide leadership and reassurance at moments of crisis. President Bush (shown here landing in New Orleans) was criticized by many for being slow to visit the areas ravaged by Hurricane Katrina in 2005. Image courtesy of the Department of Defense.
2. The spirit of the Declaration of Independence, with its emphasis on individual freedom, was reflected in the Bill of Rights, adopted in 1791.
3. Chief Justice John Marshall played a major part in carving out the important role that the Supreme Court very early came to play in the American system of government.
4. "Signing of the Constitution" by Howard Chandler Christy. The founders of the United States believed that they were making history at the 1787 Constitutional Convention in Philadelphia. Most Americans continue to venerate them and the Constitution that they created. Image courtesy of the Architect of the Capitol.
5. Nancy Pelosi, shown here at the President's 2007 State of the Union Address, was the first woman to be Speaker of the House of Representatives.

PART THREE

Structures of Government

CHAPTER FIVE

The Constitution

In August 1814 British troops approached the American capital in Washington, planning vengeance for the Americans' burning of the colonial legislature in York (now Toronto). Aware that the city would be defenseless against superior British forces, Secretary of State James Monroe ordered his staff to find safe places for the original versions of the Constitution, the Declaration of Independence, Washington's correspondence, and other historical documents. One of the clerks in the State Department loaded as much as he could into a cart which he then drove 35 miles from the capital and hid in an empty house, where he believed the documents would be safe from discovery and destruction by the British. Although the United States was barely more than two decades old, its Constitution already was viewed by some as no mere piece of paper but as the inspired product of exceptional men whose deliberations had been guided by the hand of Providence.

The leading figures of the revolutionary generation and many of those who participated in the drafting of the American Constitution saw themselves as "actors in a historical drama whose script had already been written by the gods."[1] In his first inaugural address, Thomas Jefferson described the American government as "the world's best hope," urging his countrymen to put aside their differences—the campaign between the followers of Jefferson and Adams had been vicious—and unite behind the Constitution that had been adopted only a decade earlier. This spirit had been expressed earlier in George Washington's first inaugural address:

Benjamin Franklin Describes the New American Constitution as a "Rising Sun"

James Madison kept a record of the proceedings of the Philadelphia Convention of 1787 where the American Constitution was drafted. In the passage below Madison describes Benjamin Franklin's reflections on the signing of that document.[2]

Whilst the last members were signing, Dr. Franklin, looking towards the president's chair, at the back of which a rising sun happened to be painted, *observed to a few members near him, that painters had found it difficult to distinguish, in their art, a rising from a setting sun. "I have," said he, "often and often, in the course of the session, and the vicissitudes of my hopes and fears as to its issue, looked at that behind the president, without being able to tell whether it was rising or setting; but now, at length, I have the happiness to know that it is a rising, and not a setting sun."*

No people can be bound to acknowledge and adore the Invisible Hand which conducts the affairs of men more than those of the United States. Every step by which they have advanced to the character of an independent nation seems to have been distinguished by some token of providential agency; and in the important revolution just accomplished in the system of their united government the tranquil deliberations and voluntary consent of so many distinct communities from which the event has resulted can not be compared with the means by which most governments have been established without some return of pious gratitude, along with an humble anticipation of the future blessings which the past seem to presage.

This veneration of the Constitution continues today. Senator Robert Byrd of West Virginia, the longest serving member in the history of that legislative body (first elected in 1958), carries a well-thumbed copy of the Constitution in his suit pocket just as a preacher might carry a copy of the Bible in his. Presidents and lesser office-holders speak of the Constitution in reverential tones and of the founders as men of extraordinary genius and wisdom. The mythology of the revolutionary era and of the founders—not mythology as a fanciful story with no basis in fact but as a rather idealized narrative that functions to explain and make sense of the origins and values embodied in the Constitution—runs strong in America. This may be seen by perusing the American history and biography sections of any large bookstore, where literally dozens of volumes on this period in American history and the forces and men that shaped the Constitution will be found. Indeed, such books often reach the non-fiction bestsellers list, as has been true in recent years of books on Washington, Jefferson, and Madison, as well as Joseph Ellis's Pulitzer-winning *Founding Brothers*. In no other country are the intentions of a constitution's founders and the meanings they ascribed to particular sections of their handiwork thought by so many to be so relevant to the determination of present-day constitutional disputes. "What would Madison think?" is a question that few Americans would find to be beside the point.

Veneration of the Constitution is an important part of American idealism. Americans will often be deeply cynical about those who run for and are elected to office. Their faith in important institutions, including such political institutions as Congress, the courts, and the presidency, has declined in recent decades. But their belief that the foundations of their system of government, including the Constitution, remains solid and even inspired and continues to be unshaken. There have been no serious challenges to the legitimacy of the American Constitution since the Civil War. Passionate disagreements about its meanings have been frequent, but few find fault with the Constitution itself. The same may not be said of the modern constitutional histories of such countries as Belgium, Canada, Spain, and the UK, where the legitimacy of the constitution has been challenged by significant regional or ethnic segments of the population.

The Values and Interests Embodied in the American Constitution

Americans have always been ardent believers in the power of paper. Before the Mayflower arrived at Massachusetts Bay in 1620, those on board had written and agreed to a charter that served as the colony's constitution. Almost two decades later, in 1639, the colonists of Connecticut drew up the Fundamental Orders, the first written constitution in America that created a government. A year later the Plantation Agreement of the colonists of Providence included explicit mention of "liberty of conscience." Bills of rights were adopted by most states before the Bill of Rights, the first ten amendments to the American Constitution, was ratified in 1791. Virginia's Bill of Rights, passed in 1776, was influential in America and in France too, where the idea of written guarantees of liberties and rights captured the imagination of Enlightenment intellectuals and revolutionaries.

The Declaration of Independence, agreed to on July 4, 1776, testifies to Americans' belief that the public affairs of men should be governed by written rules, not by tradition, customs, and arbitrary will. This principle may be called *constitutionalism* and has as its corollary the *rule of law*. Most people are at least somewhat familiar with the revolutionary prose of the

Declaration's first two paragraphs (see Appendix 1), but one of the remarkable aspects of that document is its self-consciously historical manner of address: "When in the Course of human events, it becomes necessary for one people to dissolve the political bands which have connected them to another," it begins, "... a decent respect to the opinions of mankind requires that they should declare the causes which impel them to the separation."

The Declaration of Independence was drafted by Thomas Jefferson, and like many of the leading men of his generation he saw himself and America as being in the vanguard of history. The opening words of the Declaration are therefore addressed not merely to the immediate protagonists in the revolutionary war but to "mankind" and posterity. Jefferson had read Thomas Hobbes and John Locke and like them believed that revolution could only be justified by reaction against tyranny, which is precisely the charge that the Declaration levels against Great Britain. The "self-evident" truths that are set forth in the second paragraph of the Declaration—concerning the equality of men; their inalienable right to "Life, Liberty and the Pursuit of Happiness"; and popular consent as the only just basis for government—are its best known parts. But most of the document consists of an itemized list of grievances that the colonists held against the imperial authorities. The rupture with Great Britain was undertaken with full respect for the idea that public actions and the reasons for them should be set down in writing and consented to in a fashion also dictated by written rules (in this case those established by the Continental Congress). The manner of their revolution demonstrated the faith that Jefferson and his contemporaries had in constitutionalism and the rule of law.

Once the colonists' military victory was ensured after the defeat of the British at Yorktown in 1781, the question of what sort of government under what manner of constitution became more pressing. The original 13 states had already agreed in 1777 to be united under the Articles of Confederation, ratified in 1781. This established the first constitution of the newly independent states, although plans for the union of the colonies went back at least as far as William Penn's 1697 Plan of Union and the Albany Plan of Union drafted by Benjamin Franklin in 1754. Under the Articles of Confederation the new confederacy—to call it a country would have begged the question of the attributes necessary to deserve such a description—was called the United States of America, but Article II of this constitution made clear where the power would lie: "Each state retains its sovereignty, freedom and independence, and every Power, Jurisdiction and right, which is not by this confederation expressly delegated to the United States, in Congress assembled."

Those powers, jurisdictions, and rights assigned to the new level of government were, it turned out, extremely feeble. The Articles created a "league of friendship" (Article III) in which each state had equal representation in the Congress and state legislatures, not voters, selected those who would be their delegates. The new level of government had no independent authority to tax or borrow and could not maintain an army, enter into foreign treaties, or declare war except as authorized by delegates of the states. In short, the constitution created under the Articles of Confederation imposed far fewer limits on state governments and assigned incomparably weaker powers to the union government than is the case under the rules of the European Union.

The defects of this first constitution were quickly apparent, and sentiment for its reform led to the convening of the Annapolis Convention in 1786, where representatives from Virginia, Delaware, Maryland, Pennsylvania, New Jersey, and New York met and proposed a meeting of all the states at Philadelphia to "devise such further provisions as shall appear to them necessary to render the constitution of the Federal Government adequate to the exigencies of the Union." This proposed convention convened in late May of 1787 and produced an agreement on the Constitution of the United States, ratified in 1789.

The constitution that was agreed to at the Philadelphia convention represented a compromise not only between the preferences of the larger and smaller states, but also between the *Federalists*—those who saw a new national government with significant powers as necessary for the promotion of public order, economic union, and the defense of the United States—and the *Anti-Federalists*, who mistrusted the idea of a strong central government, preferring to see legislative and revenue-raising powers rest primarily with the states.

The clash of interests and competing visions for the constitution was immediately apparent over the issue of representation in a reformed national congress. The *Virginia Plan* proposed that each state receive a share of seats in the national legislature proportionate to its share of "free inhabitants" of the United States. It also proposed that one branch of the legislature be directly elected by the people, while members of the second branch would be chosen by members of the first from persons nominated by the respective state legislatures. The president would be chosen by the members of the national legislature. This plan guaranteed that the voices of the most populous states, such as New York and Virginia, would be loudest and their interests preponderant in Congress.

Smaller states were alarmed by this prospect. The *New Jersey Plan* defended their interests by proposing that the principle of the equal rep-

resentation of the states and the selection of delegates to Congress by the
state legislatures be retained and that the president continue to be chosen by
Congress. The only concession to the centralist vision held by some of the
convention delegates—but an important one—was a proposed clause declaring that all actions taken by and treaties ratified by the central government,
in accordance with its constitutional powers, "shall be the supreme law of
the respective States ... and that the Judiciary of the several states shall be
bound thereby in their decision" (section 6).

These very different proposals were reconciled through the *Connecticut
Compromise*, also referred to as the *Great Compromise*. This plan proposed that states be represented according to the size of their population
in the House of Representatives, whose members would be elected directly
by the people, and that all states have two representatives in the Senate.
Senators would be chosen by state legislatures (a practice that continued
until the Seventeenth Amendment, requiring the direct election of senators,
was ratified in 1913). This compromise was agreed to by a five to four
vote (two state delegations abstained and two were not present). With this
major obstacle to agreement on a new constitution out of the way, the issue
of how to select the president, who virtually everyone expected would be
George Washington, was then addressed. Some delegates favored the direct
election of the president, although most preferred some system whereby the
state legislatures would do the choosing. The compromise reached was the
electoral college. Each state would be assigned a number of electors in the
electoral college equal to its representation in Congress (two senators plus
the state's number of members in the House of Representatives). The manner of choosing electors was left up to each state (see the discussion of the
electoral college in Chapter 9).

Although no single vision or set of expectations for the new constitution
prevailed, it is possible to identify a number of common principles agreed
upon by most of the founders and that are reflected in the document that
their deliberations produced. They include:

- *Power should be limited.* The American Constitution
  divides power between the legislative, executive, and judicial branches of government, and between the national and
  state levels, in order to reduce the risk that any particular
  branch or level of government might become dominant. This
  is the principle of checks and balances, described by James
  Madison in the Federalist Papers (see Appendix 2). The
  specter of tyranny was still very fresh in the minds of the

founders, and although they were agreed that the Articles of Confederation created too weak a government, they were wary of permitting too much power being concentrated in too few hands.

▪ *Rights should be protected.* Although the Constitution was ratified without the inclusion of a bill of rights, this was an important issue in many of the state ratification campaigns. The promise of a speedy amendment to add a bill of rights was important in winning ratification in some states. But despite the original omission, various sorts of rights were already guaranteed throughout the Constitution. Democratic rights were ensured through provisions requiring periodic elections. The right of equal representation was respected through the assignment of seats in the House of Representatives proportionate to a state's population. The principle of no taxation without representation was acknowledged by the requirement that bills for raising revenue must first be introduced in the elected House of Representatives. The right to a trial by jury was guaranteed.

The omission of a bill of rights from the original Constitution should not, therefore, be interpreted as signifying that the founders were indifferent to the possibility that the national government might, through its actions, infringe on the rights that the Declaration of Independence had pronounced "unalienable" and that were already guaranteed in most state constitutions. As the record of debates at the Philadelphia Convention makes clear and as the concerns and reasoning of many of the articles in the Federalist Papers attest, how to limit power so as to protect rights and liberties while at the same time enabling government to better function for the national defense, the maintenance of public order, and the promotion and regulation of economic activity was central to their deliberations.

▪ *The legislature should be the leading branch of government.* Few among the founders would have agreed with Thomas Paine who said that he smelled the "rat of monarchy" in the constitution agreed to in 1787. Nevertheless, the prospect of an overly powerful executive branch was more worrisome to most delegates than that of a dominant legislative one. The legislature was understood to be the branch of government closest to the people, most responsive to their wishes, and therefore least likely to threaten their rights. The Constitution includes provisions that allow for the impeachment and removal after trial in the Senate of a president found to be guilty of "Treason, Bribery, or other high Crimes and Misdemeanors." The president is able to veto legislation passed by Congress, but his veto may be overridden if there is a two-thirds majority in both the House and the Senate. Even Madison and the other Federalists who wished to see a considerable strengthening of the central government did

Tocqueville on Divided Power and the Presidential Veto

The American Constitution gives the president the right to veto bills passed by Congress. Article I, section 7 states that the president may sign a bill into law or he may veto it within ten days of receiving the bill, "with his Objections to that House in which it shall have originated." This is known as a *veto message*. If the president does nothing, then the bill becomes law after ten days. But if a bill is sent to the president at the end of a session of Congress and there are not ten days between the day it is sent to him and the end of that year's sitting of the legislature, he may veto the bill by not signing it, and in these circumstance need not give reasons for the veto. This has become known as a *pocket veto*.

When Alexis de Tocqueville visited the United States in the early nineteenth century, only seven men had served as president. Between them they accounted for only 22 presidential vetoes, 12 of them by a single president, Andrew Jackson. Although use of the presidential veto was infrequent, Tocqueville understood that it was part of the delicate machinery of checks and balances woven through the Constitution. He wrote:

[T]he struggle between the President and the legislature must always be an unequal one, since the latter is certain of bearing down all resistance by persevering in its plans; but the suspensive veto forces it at least to reconsider the matter, and if the motion be persisted in, it must then be backed by a majority of two-thirds of the whole house. The veto, moreover, is a sort of appeal to the people. The executive power, which without this security might have been secretly oppressed, adopts this means of pleading its cause and stating its motives. But if the legislature perseveres in its design, can it not always overpower all resistance? I reply that in the constitutions of all nations, of whatever kind they may be, a certain point exists at which the legislator must have recourse to the good sense and the virtue of his fellow citizens. This point is nearer and more prominent in the republics, while it is more remote and more carefully concealed in monarchies; but it always exists somewhere. There is no country in which everything can be provided for by the laws, or in which political institutions can prove a substitute for common sense and public morality. —Tocqueville, "The Executive Power," Democracy in America, Book I

Public opinion was, Tocqueville understood, a vital cog in this system of divided power.

not expect that the executive branch would take the initiative in matters of legislation or block the clearly expressed will of Congress.

Ratification of the Constitution required the consent of nine of the 13 states. This proved to be difficult. In each state delegates were chosen by voters to meet in a state convention that would then debate and vote on ratification. Connecticut, New Jersey, Maryland, and Delaware were strongly supportive and ratified early. Ratification was less certain in most of the states, including such large ones as New York, Pennsylvania, Massachusetts, and Virginia. In the end, 11 state conventions ratified the Constitution. Those in North Carolina and Rhode Island initially rejected it, then later ratified rather than be excluded from the union.

The ratification struggle in New York produced what is arguably the most important American contribution to political theory, the Federalist Papers. These consisted of 85 articles written by Alexander Hamilton, John Jay, and James Madison. Published in New York newspapers, they were an attempt to persuade the citizens of that state to support ratification. Federalist Papers no. 10 and no. 51, both written by James Madison, are particularly noteworthy for their exposition of fundamental premises of the Constitution (see Appendix 2).

Was the Constitution of 1789 Racist?

It is well known that many of the founders owned slaves. The Constitution that they agreed to did not abolish slavery nor did it grant rights of any sort to black Americans. Of course it is sometimes said that the Constitution refers to "persons," not white persons or black persons, male persons or female persons, and so the document is not inherently racist or sexist. This is, however, disingenuous. According to the norms and values that prevailed at the time and under the laws that existed, it was understood that black Americans, slave or free, did not enjoy the same rights and constitutional protections as whites. The same was true for women.

Some of the founders were downright racist, and even among the most enlightened of them it is fair to say that not a single one would have found interracial marriage or even racially mixed schools to be acceptable. However, many of them wanted slavery abolished, and the issue was a contentious one during the debates at the Philadelphia Convention. Madison believed that it was *the* chief division between the states: "[T]he States were

Understanding Federalist Papers Nos. 10 and 51

James Madison of Virginia was one of the most influential men of his time. He was instrumental in pushing for a stronger central government than many of the delegates at the Philadelphia Convention would have preferred, and he drafted the Bill of Rights and took the lead in shepherding these first amendments to the Constitution through Congress. Like Thomas Jefferson, he had read all of the classical and contemporary political theorists and had given very careful thought to the nature and consequences of various forms of government.

Federalist Paper No. 10

In Federalist Paper no. 10 Madison explains why a republic—what we would call a representative democracy—is superior to a direct democracy, and why a larger republic is superior to a smaller one when it comes to the protection of rights and liberties.

Madison begins by acknowledging that factions—differing interests, the most important of which tend to be material interests—are bound to arise in any free society. The elimination of factions would require either that everyone have the same interests and opinions, a totally impracticable and undesirable state of affairs, or the abolition of personal freedom, equally undesirable. The "*causes* of faction cannot be removed," he writes, "and ... relief is only to be sought in the means of controlling its *effects*."

In a pure democracy, Madison argues, the likelihood that a majority will recognize that they have interests and opinions in common and legislate in a manner that sacrifices the rights and interests of weaker groups to that of the majority is great. But in a republic, in which citizens elect representatives who then deliberate and legislate on behalf of the people, the likelihood that the rights and interests of individuals and groups will be steamrolled by those of the majority is less for two reasons. First, the fact

that the public's business is conducted "through the medium of a chosen body of citizens" is more likely to ensure wisdom and an appreciation of the general interests of the country in these deliberations.

But Madison was not naïve. He was not ready to count on the good sense, wisdom, and public spiritedness of those chosen to govern. Thus, it was also necessary, he argued, that the republic be of a certain size and that lawmakers represent a number of constituents that is neither too few—otherwise there is the danger that they will behave simply as a tribune for a narrow set of interests and opinions—or too many, in which case the danger is that lawmakers will not be sufficiently in touch with the interests and opinions of those they are elected to represent. Some balance must be struck, but the important advantage of a republic (larger) over a pure democracy (smaller) is that it encompasses a wider set of interests and opinions and thereby reduces the danger that rights and freedoms will be infringed. "Extend the sphere," Madison writes, "and you take in a greater variety of parties and interests; you make it less probably that a majority of the whole will have a common motive to invade the rights of citizens; or if such a common motive exists, it will be more difficult for all who feel it to discover their own strength, and to act in unison with each other."

Federalist Paper No. 51

In Federalist Paper no. 51 Madison returns to the theme of which form of government is best suited to the protection of rights and liberties. He explains how a constitution that divides power between the various branches and levels of government is least likely to threaten freedom.

As in Federalist Paper no. 10, Madison begins with some broad philosophical reflections, this time on human nature, in order to establish the premises of his argument. People, he says, cannot be trusted. "If men were angels, no government would be necessary," he observes. "A dependence on the people is no doubt the primary control on the government: but experience has taught mankind the necessity of auxiliary precautions." Translated into plain English, Madison is saying that the best and most secure method of ensuring that the selfish and unenlightened opinions and motives of those in positions of public authority do not jeopardize the public good is to limit the scope of their powers. Men being as they are, he says, concentrated power is dangerous. "Ambition must be made to counteract ambition."

The independence of each branch of government is crucial, Madison argues. Unitary government or any institutional arrangements that make one branch dependent on another necessarily concentrate power in fewer hands. "[T]he constant aim," he writes, "is to divide and arrange the several offices [of government] in such a manner as that each may be a check on the other." This theory of checks and balances is reflected in the American Constitution.

Madison returns to a theme that he developed in Federalist Paper no. 10, the importance of the range of interests that fall under the authority of the Constitution and therefore of the size of the republic. "In a free government, the security for civil rights must be the same as for religious rights ... [It] will depend on the number of interests and sects; and this may be presumed to depend on the extent of the country and the number of people comprehended under the same government." The great virtue of federalism lies in its ability to bring together under one national government a wider range of interests and opinion—the principle Madison discussed in Federalist Paper no. 10—at the same time as it divides public authority between the federal and state governments. "[A] double security arises to the rights of the people. The different governments will control each other at the same time that each will be controlled by itself."

All of the Federalist Papers, including nos. 10 and 51, may be read at http://www.yale.edu/lawweb/avalon/federal/fed.htm.

divided into different interests not by their difference of size, but principally from their having or not having slaves."[3] The gulf between the openly abolitionist delegates, who were certainly a minority, and the uncompromising refusal of states such as Georgia and South Carolina to even consider agreeing to the new Constitution if abolition were to be the price was too wide to be bridged. Most delegates, even those who disliked slavery in principle, were prepared to tolerate its continuation in order to get agreement on the Constitution. Thus, "the distinguishing feature of the [Constitution] when it came to slavery was its evasiveness," observes historian Joseph Ellis.[4] The founders simply put off the day of reckoning.

But they did not put it off entirely. Two sections of the Constitution are pertinent to slavery, although the actual word is not used. The first is Section 2 and involves the apportionment to each state of seats in the House of Representatives. Delegates from the slave-holding states did not want any sort of citizenship rights to be conferred on slaves, but they wanted to be able to count them as persons in order to get as much representation in Congress as possible. Slaves constituted a large portion of the populations of the southern states (according to the 1790 Census, Maryland's percentage of slaves was 32%; Virginia had 39%; Kentucky, 17%; North Carolina, 26%; South Carolina, 43%; Georgia, 35%). There was, therefore, quite a lot at stake in terms of representation. The final compromise was that non-free persons would count as three-fifths of free persons. The other oblique reference to slavery is in Section 9, which denied Congress the ability to prohibit the importation of slaves before 1808, although it did allow imported slaves to be taxed at a rate of up to $10 each.

It may seem, therefore, that the fine democratic principles expounded in the Declaration of Independence were sacrificed on the altar of political expediency at Philadelphia in order to cut a deal. At one level this is undeniable, but there are two arguments that may at least soften this harsh judgment. One is that the racism countenanced by the American Constitution was not very different from the practice in the colonies of Great Britain, France, and Spain. Slavery was not abolished in these colonies until 1834, 1848, and 1879, respectively. This may not sound very convincing.

A bit stronger, perhaps, is the argument that the liberal democratic values embodied in the Declaration of Independence, the Constitution, and the Bill of Rights generated what would prove to be an irresistible momentum in the direction of equality. Achieving at least formal equality for blacks was slowed by the economic and cultural interests that had developed around plantation slavery since the first importation of slaves at Jamestown, Virginia in 1619 and also by the fact that the slave proportion of southern states actually increased in the first half of the nineteenth century. However, the anomaly of slavery in a society that both thought of itself and presented itself to the world as one whose twin pillars were liberty and equality eventually became untenable.

The Bill of Rights

The omission of a bill of rights from the Constitution was soon rectified. The fact that one was not included in the first place was due to the founders' expectation that the new federal government's powers would be few in number and limited in scope. Most state constitutions already included bills of rights, and the state governments were expected to matter more in the affairs of citizens and commerce than the new national government. However, the lack of a bill of rights applying to the federal government became a major issue in some of the state ratification conventions, and

What Is Covered by the Bill of Rights?

RIGHT	PROTECTION
Free speech	First Amendment
Freedom of religion	First Amendment
Freedom of assembly and association	First Amendment
Freedom from arbitrary arrest	Fifth Amendment
Freedom from unreasonable search and seizure	Fourth Amendment
The right to own a gun	Second Amendment
The right to a fair trial, trial by jury, etc.	Sixth and Seventh Amendments
The right not to be subjected to cruel or unusual punishment	Eighth Amendment
Separation of church and state	First Amendment

The right to privacy is not explicitly mentioned in the Bill of Rights, although many jurists and legal philosophers argue that it is implicit in the very concept of civil liberties.

advocates of the Constitution agreed that the new national Congress would immediately act to pass such a bill.

The first ten amendments to the American Constitution, known as the Bill of Rights, were ratified by the state legislatures in 1791. They applied only to the new national government. This remained the case until 1925 when the Supreme Court ruling in *Gitlow v. New York* extended the authority of the Bill of Rights to all governments in the United States.

In keeping with the preoccupation with liberty that prevailed at the time, the Bill of Rights is concerned to guarantee the rights of individuals against interference from government actions. It is not about equality rights. Amendments to the Constitution dealing with civil rights and equality, particularly the 13th, 14th, 15th, and 19th Amendments (see Appendix 3) were passed much later. The matters covered by the Bill of Rights are indicated in the box above.

The Supreme Court's Role in Establishing the Authority of the Federal Government

Today it goes without saying that the national government is the supreme level of government under the American Constitution. This was anything but a foregone conclusion when the Constitution was agreed to. Indeed, given the Anti-Federalists' strong mistrust of centralized power and the very limited size and scope of the national government's activities, it seemed far more probable that the Constitution would evolve as a comparatively decentralized arrangement between the states and Washington. One of the factors that helped tip the balance in the direction of a strong central government was the Supreme Court. Under Chief Justice John Marshall (1801-35) the Court handed down a number of rulings that had the dual effects of establishing its own authority as the final word on the Constitution and the federal government's superiority over the states.

The first of these decisions came in *Marbury v. Madison* (1803), a case involving a law passed by Congress in 1789 that assigned a particular jurisdiction to the Supreme Court. Chief Justice Marshall declared that the jurisdiction and authority of the Supreme Court, as is also true of the other branches of government, are established by the Constitution and not by laws passed by the legislature. This was the first time the Supreme Court had struck down a law passed by Congress, but in doing so it was not taking the side of those who believed that states' rights should trump federal powers. The clash was really between two competing visions of the Constitution at a point in time when its authority and interpretation were still very uncertain. On the one hand were those who believed that the legislature ought to be the superior branch of government. On the other were those, including Chief Justice Marshall, who insisted that the Constitution must take precedence over acts of Congress and, if the Court determined that Congress's actions violated the Constitution, then it was obligated by that document to declare such actions void. Thus, Marshall and the Court were defending the principle of constitutional supremacy over the competing notion that the will of the people, as expressed through laws passed by their representatives, must supersede all other considerations. Marshall believed the latter position to be contrary to the true spirit of what had been agreed to in Philadelphia and a threat to the separation of powers and the notion of limited government.

Marshall's Federalist sympathies were clear in many of the decisions he wrote in the years after *Marbury v. Madison*. In what is probably the most famous of these cases, *M'Culloch v. Maryland* (1819), he upheld an act of Congress that chartered a bank against a state challenge that no such authority is stated in the Constitution. Many specific legislative actions are not mentioned in the Constitution, Marshall observed, nor would such an exhaustive menu of powers be possible or even desirable. The court relied on a broad interpretation of the "necessary and proper" clause in Section 8 of the Constitution as the basis for ruling that, "Let the end be legitimate, let it be within the scope of the constitution, and all means which are appropriated, which are plainly adapted to that end ... are constitutional." This was

Chief Justice Marshall Expounds the Doctrine of Constitutional Supremacy

In the following excerpt from *Marbury v. Madison*, 5 U.S. 137, Chief Justice Marshall responds to those who argued that the Supreme Court had no business striking down laws on the grounds that they were in violation of the Constitution.

This doctrine would subvert the very foundation of all written constitutions. It would declare that an act which, according to the principles and theory of our government, is entirely void, is yet, in practice, completely obligatory. It would declare that if the legislature shall do what is expressly forbidden, such act, notwithstanding the express prohibition, is in reality effectual. It would be giving to the legislature a practical and real omnipotence with the same breath which professes to restrict their powers within nar-row limits. It is prescribing limits and declaring that those limits may be passed at pleasure.

That it thus reduces to nothing what we have deemed the greatest improvement on political institutions, a written constitution, would of itself be sufficient, in America, where written constitutions have been viewed with so much reverence, for rejecting the construction....

Thus, the particular phraseology of the constitution of the United States confirms and strengthens the principle, supposed to be essential to all written constitutions, that a law repugnant to the constitution is void, and that courts, as well as other departments, are bound by that instrument.

already a great victory for those who believed in a strong national government. But Marshall went further, arguing that the government of the United States, "is the government of all; its powers are delegated by all; it represents all, and acts for all." The authority of the national government, he declared, "proceeds directly from the people," a claim that was challenged by those who saw the young national government and the Constitution that empowered it as the creation of sovereign states. Although limited to the powers assigned to it by the Constitution, "The government of the United States ... is supreme" (*M'Culloch v. Maryland*, 17 U.S. 316 [1819]).

Marshall repeated this view of national supremacy in subsequent rulings, notably in *Cohens v. Virginia* (1821) and *Gibbons v. Ogden* (1824). In *Cohens v. Virginia* he stated that "the American people are one ... America has chosen to be, in many respects, and to many purposes, a nation.... The people have declared that in the exercise of all the powers given [to the national government] it is supreme" (*Cohens v. Virginia*, 19 U.S. 2649 [1824]). In *Gibbons v. Ogden* (22 U.S. 1 [1824]), Marshall made clear his belief that the defenders of states' rights, who wanted the powers of the national government to be few and narrow and who rejected the principle of national supremacy, were willfully misinterpreting the meaning of the Constitution and subverting the will of the American people. His argument against a narrow, literal interpretation of the Constitution and in favor of a broad understanding based on the central principles of that document adapted to evolving circumstances is the first great expression of what has come to be known as the philosophy of judicial activism.

The Secessionist Challenge

The states existed before the United States was formed, and even among those who supported the ratification of the Constitution most did not share Chief Justice Marshall's centralist vision. The Anti-Federalists believed that the states retained their essential sovereignty in those matters not clearly assigned to Congress by the new Constitution. A rather extreme expression of this view was put forth by two of New York's delegates to the constitutional convention who refused to sign the document. "[W]e were of the opinion," they said, "that the leading features of every amendment [to the Articles of Confederation] ought to be the preservation of the individual states in their uncontrolled constitutional rights."[5]

States' rights quickly became the rallying call of those who mistrusted the Federalist vision of the Constitution and the doctrine of national supremacy expounded by the Marshall court. No less a figure than Thomas Jefferson argued the case for states' rights over national supremacy in the Virginia Resolutions, December 24, 1798. The Virginia state assembly passed resolutions authored by Jefferson declaring "that it views the powers of the Federal Government as resulting from the compact to which the states are parties, as limited by the plain sense and intention of the instrument constituting that compact; [and] as no further valid than ... authorized by the grants enumerated in that compact." In other words, it was up to state legislatures to decide whether a law or action of the federal government fell within the constitutional powers of Congress.

An even more extreme form of this doctrine of state sovereignty was expressed by the Kentucky legislature. In resolutions passed in 1799, it put forward what became known as the *doctrine of nullification*. According to this doctrine, a state legislature that determined a federal law to be unconstitutional was, as the representative body of a sovereign state, within its rights in nullifying such a law within that state.

All of the states from Maryland north objected to the extreme states' rights vision of the Constitution expressed by the Virginia and Kentucky legislatures. Over time the rift between the northern and southern states grew wider as a result of the slavery issue. Slavery had been outlawed in most of the northern states by the time the Constitution was ratified and soon after

Dred Scott and the Struggle over Slavery

The question is simply this: Can a negro, whose ancestors were imported into this country, and sold as slaves, become a member of the political community formed and brought into existence by the Constitution of the United States, and as such become entitled to all the rights, and privileges, and immunities, guaranteed by that instrument to the citizen?

... We think they are not, and that they are not included, and were not intended to be included, under the word "citizens" in the Constitution, and can, therefore, claim none of the rights and privileges which that instrument provides for and secures to citizens of the United States. On the contrary, they were at that time considered as a subordinate and inferior class of beings, who had been subjugated by the dominant race, and whether emancipated or not, yet remained subject to their authority, and had no rights or privileges but such as those who held the power and the government might choose to grant them ...

... [Moreover] the right of property in a slave is distinctly and expressly affirmed in the Constitution. The right to traffic in it, like an ordinary article of merchandise and property, was guaranteed to the citizens of the United States, in every State that might desire it, for twenty years. And the Government in express terms is pledged to protect it in all future time, if the slave escapes from his owner.... And no word can be found in the Constitution which gives Congress a greater power over slave property, or which entitles property of that kind to less protection than property of any other description. The only power conferred is the power coupled with the duty of guarding and protecting the owner in his rights.

Excerpts from Dred Scott v. Sandford, *60 U.S. 393 (1857).*

in the others. But in the South matters were quite different. The addition of vast new territories after the end of the war with Mexico in 1848 made the question of whether they would be slave or free even more contentious than it had been previously. In 1850 Congress passed a series of resolutions stating that "slavery does not exist by law, and is not likely to be introduced into any of the territory acquired by the United States from the republic of Mexico,"[6] but leaving unresolved the matter of whether these territories and the new states that would be created in them could permit slavery. The Compromise of 1850, as this is known, was not seen as much of a compromise by the southern states. Their reaction to the resolutions passed by Congress was summed up in this declaration: "*Resolved*, that the slaveholding States cannot and will not submit to the enactment of any law imposing onerous conditions or restraints upon the rights of masters to remove with their property into the territories of the United States" and that "this controversy should be ended, either by a recognition of the constitutional rights of the Southern people, or by an equitable partition of the territories."[7]

With its larger population and therefore more votes in the House of Representatives, and given the strong likelihood that most of the new states being created in the west would choose to ban slavery, the southern states saw that abolitionist pressure would continue to mount. One of the few "victories" they enjoyed during these years came in the Supreme Court's decision in *Dred Scott v. Sandford* (1857). The Court ruled that slaves were not citizens but property, not unlike other forms of property, and that the mere fact that this property—in this particular case, the slave known as Dred Scott—finds himself in a state where slavery is not permitted does not diminish his owner's property rights.

The Dred Scott ruling was hailed in the South and by and large reviled in the North. The issue of slavery had driven the two regions of the country further and further apart, as Lincoln acknowledged in his 1858 debates with Senator Stephen Douglas of Illinois. "Has anything ever threatened the existence of this Union save and except this very institution of slavery?," Lincoln asked his listeners. "What has ever threatened our liberty and prosperity, save and except this institution of slavery? If this is true, how do you propose to improve the condition of things by enlarging slavery—by spreading it [to territories and new states]?"[8]

By this point the secessionist tide was unstoppable. In his last annual address to Congress, President James Buchanan gave his opinion that if southern states wished to secede from the Union, there were no constitutional grounds and no acceptable way to stop them. The Constitution, he said, does not give Congress the power to make war against any state. Moreover, "our Union rests upon public opinion, and can never be cemented by the blood of its citizens shed in civil war. If it cannot live in the affections of the people, it must one day perish." Buchanan blamed the North for bringing the country to the brink of secession: "The long-continued and intemperate interference of the Northern people with the question of slavery in the Southern States has at length produced its natural effects."[9]

Buchanan's successor, Abraham Lincoln, thought differently. His vision of the Constitution was that the union, being the creation of the American people, not a contract between sovereign state governments, and extending all the way back to the Articles of Confederation voted by the Continental Congress in 1774, was indivisible. In his first inaugural address Lincoln said,

> Plainly, the central idea of secession is the essence of anarchy. A majority held in restraint by constitutional checks and limitations, and always changing easily with deliberate changes of popular opinions and sentiments, is the only true sovereign of a free people.

Whoever rejects it does, of necessity, fly to anarchy or to despotism. Unanimity is impossible; the rule of a minority, as a permanent arrangement, is wholly inadmissible; so that, rejecting the majority principle, anarchy or despotism in some form is all that is left.

The Union forces defeated the Confederates after four years of civil war and at the cost of over 600,000 lives. Slavery was made unconstitutional by the Thirteenth Amendment (1865), and the Fourteenth (1868) and Fifteenth (1870) Amendments extended the equal protection of the laws and voting rights to all citizens (although not to women, whose voting rights were not guaranteed until 1920). If any further proof was needed that constitutional theories of state sovereignty were effectively finished, this was supplied by the Fourteenth Amendment: in declaring that "No State shall make laws" depriving persons of their liberties and civil rights and establishing in the Constitution a definition of citizenship, it protected the rights of citizens from intrusions by all governments, federal and state. Previously the protections for rights and freedoms in the Constitution had applied only to the laws and actions of the federal government. This was an important step in consolidating both the authority of the Constitution and the vision that those such as Justice Marshall and President Lincoln had expounded.

Federalism

When the form of government appropriate to the United States was being discussed, first under the Articles of Confederation and then under the American Constitution, it was virtually certain that it would have to recognize two levels of government authority. Some of the colonial territories and their governments had already been in existence for several generations. There was such a thing as a Virginian or Pennsylvanian identity at the time of independence, but whatever American identity existed was rather weak. Moreover, there was enormous mistrust of a new central government and a reluctance among most to assign it more powers than thought absolutely necessary to manage the common commercial affairs, defense, and foreign relations of the states.

Federalism, which divides constitutional authority between national and regional governments, was inevitable. But in drafting a federal constitution the founders had little to draw upon. Confederal forms of government had existed in Switzerland, the German Empire, and the Low Countries (what are now Belgium and the Netherlands), and in each case the powers assigned to the confederal government were very similar to those assigned to the federal government in the United States. But the American case was different from its predecessors, Tocqueville observed, in two crucial respects: "In America, the subjects of the Union are not states, but private citizens ... The old confederate governments presided over communities, but that of the [United States] presides over individuals. Its force is not borrowed, but self-derived; and it is served by its own civil and military officers, its own army, and its own courts of justice."[10] In other words, a citizen of Massachusetts was also and directly a citizen of the United States, without his relationship to the federal government depending on and being mediated by his or her state government. This is an important difference between a confederal association of states and a federal form of government.

The second vital way in which the American federal system differed was cultural. The communities brought into association with one another under previous confederal arrangements, as in the case of Switzerland and the Low Countries, spoke different languages, practiced different religions, and had different histories. But in the United States these differences were comparatively small or non-existent. "I do not know of any European nation, however small," wrote Tocqueville, "that does not present less uniformity in its different provinces than the American people ... The distance from Maine to Georgia is about one thousand miles, but the difference between the civilization of Maine and Georgia is slighter than between the habits of Normandy and those of Brittany."[11]

Sharing the same language, customs, religious traditions, and social norms was a factor that, Tocqueville correctly points out, contributed to a sense of national citizenship and helped diminish the pull of state loyalties, at least over time. Confirmation of Tocqueville's argument is provided by the case of Canada, where the decision to adopt a federal constitution was made in 1867. One of Canada's founding provinces, Quebec, had and retains a francophone majority. From the first years of Canadian federalism, Quebec has had a decentralizing influence on the development of federal-provincial relations, and it is the only province that has seriously threatened to secede from the Canadian union.

The list of powers assigned by the American Constitution to Congress is comparatively short—much briefer than Canada's, for example—and the Tenth Amendment states that "powers not delegated to the United States by the Constitution, nor prohibited by it to the States, are reserved to the States respectively, or to the people." Despite this, the federal government appears able to involve itself in almost any policy field, from matters that are obviously national in their significance, such as foreign policy, banking, and commerce, to such local matters as school lunch programs and the design requirements for public transit vehicles in towns and cities. The history of American federalism has been marked by a dramatic increase in the power of Washington *vis-à-vis* the state governments. There has been some resistance and even some reversals, but the overall trend has been toward a centralized model of federalism.

One of the factors contributing to this trend involves court decisions on the federal government's powers. As the American economy rapidly industrialized in the late nineteenth and early twentieth centuries, the pressures on governments to regulate a growing range of economic matters, from working conditions to anti-competitive business practices, increased sharply. Businesses were quick to challenge these forms of regulation, leading to a theory of the constitutional division of powers known as *dual federalism.* According to this doctrine, both the federal and state governments were sovereign and equal as long as each was acting in accordance with powers assigned to it under the Constitution. Dual federalism proved to be impractical because of the difficulty—sometimes the impossibility—of separating and isolating the various activities in what the courts called the "stream of commerce." For example, a grain elevator in Iowa stores corn, most of which is destined for mills in other states where it will be ground into flour with the aid of machines manufactured out of state, then shipped to distributors and finally to retailers in Iowa and in other states, as well as to markets abroad. The grain elevator company is incorporated in Iowa, and all of its employees live in a rural area of that state. Should Congress be permitted to pass laws that regulate the hours of work or safety conditions of these employees, or should this be a state matter?

By the early twentieth century, the Supreme Court effectively gave up trying to determine a line between intra- and inter-state commerce: it was all part of the larger stream of commerce. But there was considerable reluctance among judges, as among most other elites in American society, to accept the more intrusive economic role for the federal government that was proposed by President Franklin Delano Roosevelt and passed by Congress in the 1930s. This changed with the Supreme Court's five to four ruling in *United States v. Darby* (1937), upholding the constitutionality of the *National Labor Relations Act.* The more muscular role for the federal government that the courts now appeared to sanction was reinforced by the high levels of spending and federal government planning during World War II. By the end of the war, the federal government's dominance in matters of economic regulation was no longer seriously contested.

The power of Washington *vis-à-vis* the states has also been reinforced by court rulings and congressional actions on civil rights. The desegregation ruling in *Brown v. Topeka* (see Chapter 8) was resisted by southern states that revived the notion of states' rights. "We regard the decision of the Supreme Court in the school cases as clear abuse of judicial power," declared 96 southern congressmen in a jointly signed protest. "It climaxes a trend in the Federal judiciary toward undertaking to legislate ... and to encroach upon the reserved rights of the states and the people."[12] The federal government had to send troops to Little Rock, Arkansas to enforce compliance with the Court's ruling.

In 1964 Congress passed the *Civil Rights Act*, enabling Washington to impose numerous obligations—known as *federal mandates* in the jargon of American federalism—on state and local governments. Sometimes Congress would provide money to help pay for the costs of compliance with these civil rights mandates, but often it would not, leading many state and local officials to complain. In 1985 the Supreme Court ruled in *Garcia v. San Antonio Metropolitan Transit Authority* that the Constitution imposes almost no limits on the ability of the federal government to act in ways that interfere with state powers. Although there has been a bit of backtracking on this ruling (the 1995 *Lopez* decision found that Congress went too far when, by using its commerce power, it attempted to regulate the permissible distance between a school and a gun vendor), anyone who looks to the courts to defend states' rights against federal powers is likely to be disappointed.

Another factor that has tipped the federal-state balance decisively in the direction of Washington has been the proliferation of federal programs of financial aid to state and local governments and the growing dependence of these recipient governments on federal dollars. These programs are called *grants-in-aid* and go back to the *Morill Act* (1862), which established land grant colleges and imposed certain standards that states had to meet to receive such a grant. Their number has grown from a mere handful before 1900 to over 800 as of 2006. As Figure 5.1 shows, this growth has occurred in two main spurts. The first was in the 1960s, when the number of federal aid programs quadrupled and their value increased from about $7 billion to $24 billion, and the second occurred after 1990, a period that has seen almost a doubling in the number of such programs and an increase in federal spending from $135 billion to $436 billion.

Spending on grants-in-aid accounted for less than 1% of all federal spending in 1900, 7.6% in 1960, and 16.1% by 2007. The purposes of this spending have also changed. Until the 1960s, transportation (spending on roads and bridges) and income security programs accounted for about

70% to 80% of all grants-in-aid. The shift toward increased social spending through federal grants accelerated through the 1960s and 1970s, and today health programs alone account for close to half of all federal outlays to state and local governments (see Figure 5.2).

FIGURE 5.1:   NUMBER OF FEDERAL AID PROGRAMS TO THE STATES, 1900–2006

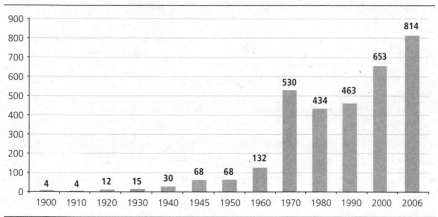

Source: Chris Edwards, "Federal Aid to the States: Historical Cause of Government Growth and Bureaucracy," Policy Analysis 593 (22 May 2007). Adapted from Figure 2.

The financial dependence of the state and local governments that receive these grants has diminished their independence. Chris Edwards of the Cato Institute goes so far as to say that "As federal aid has increased, [state] governors have become less like chief executives and more like regional deputies for the federal government."[13] The federal Advisory Committee on Intergovernmental Relations, commenting on the 1980s when there were far fewer grants-in-aid programs and state financial dependence on them was less than it has been in recent years, already concluded that these grants had transformed the states into "administrative units of the national government."[14]

The explosion of federal grants in the 1960s was generated in large measure by a growing confidence in the ability of government, especially the national government, to identify national needs and address them through appropriate policies and spending. "The national government is best placed," said long-time Democratic Senator Edmund Muskie, "to have a broad view of the national interest, to identify national priorities, and to see to it that they are met."[15] Muskie was a liberal politician, but conservatives have been almost as enthusiastic in their support of grants-in-aid. The reason has to do with credit-taking in politics and the lobbying of state and local governments.

FIGURE 5.2:   THE CHANGING PURPOSES OF FEDERAL GRANTS TO STATE
AND LOCAL GOVERNMENTS

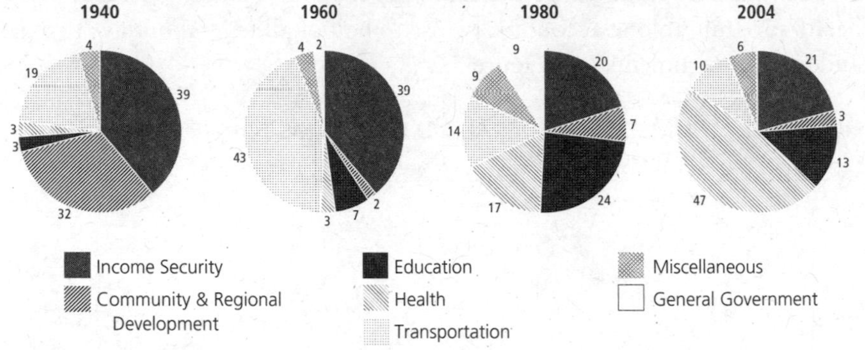

Source: Based on data reported in United States, The Budget for Fiscal Year 2006, Historical Tables, Table 12.2.

Whether it is a school lunch program in Detroit or a bridge in Utah, federal politicians generally are keen to take credit for spending that provides identifiable benefits to their constituents and for which media opportunities exist. Chris Edwards explains, "Spending on aid programs rewards the egos of politicians. They get lauded for their noble public service, get toasted at gala dinners, and get building and highways named in their honor ... Most legislators become advocates of programs rather than neutral referees who judge the merits of programs against the costs to taxpayers."[16] This motivation cuts across party and ideological lines. Given the relatively low level of party discipline in American politics, there are great incentives for individual lawmakers to behave as political entrepreneurs, seeking out and capitalizing on opportunities to provide benefits to constituents and in the process improve their ability to raise campaign money and win votes.

This entrepreneurship is encouraged by the enormous federal grants lobby that has emerged since the 1960s. The National Governors Association, the Council of State Governments, and the United States Conference of Mayors are among the large umbrella interest groups with permanent offices in Washington. But many states and cities maintain their own separate lobbying presence in the nation's capital. State governments have grant agencies whose function is to identify and extract as much money from the federal government as possible. And state and municipal governments often hire professional lobbying firms, some of which specialize in this particular form of influencing government.

Although state and local governments often complain that they do not receive their fair share of federal grants, they complain even more often and bitterly about what are known as *unfunded mandates*. These are rules that state or local governments are bound to comply with, but unlike grants-in-aid programs they are not accompanied by money. These unfunded mandates may be imposed by Congress, by the executive branch, or as a result of a court ruling. An example of the latter are the requirements regarding the necessary space per prison inmate in state penitentiaries that have resulted from judicial decrees. Complying with mandates can cost a government millions of dollars, and in some cases, according to state and local officials, there are more efficient ways of achieving the policy goal imposed on them by a federal mandate. This is what former New York Mayor Ed Koch was referring to in 1980 when he spoke of the "mandate millstone," a millstone that weighs much more today than it did when he complained about this burden.[17]

All of this adds up to a picture of federalism that the founders would have found unrecognizable and extremely troubling. Court rulings lowered the constitutional barriers that prevented Washington from involving itself in state and local matters. The behavior of entrepreneurial federal politicians looking to take credit for programs and projects and encouraged by a huge federal grants lobbying industry operating on behalf of state and local governments that have become increasingly dependent on federal dollars also created a centralized form of federalism that seems to mock the Tenth Amendment. Its declaration that powers not delegated to the American government are reserved to the states rings rather hollow alongside the reality of over 800 grants-in-aid programs, about $500 billion in federal grants to state and local governments, and countless mandates, funded and unfunded.

Amending the Constitution

If longevity is a measure of success, then the American Constitution must be judged one of the political world's success stories. Among written constitutions in operation today, it is the oldest. Part of the reason for this has been its adaptability to changing circumstances, adaptability that has been helped by the willingness of the courts to interpret and reinterpret its provisions in the light of the times. Another reason for the Constitution's durability has been that formal amendments, though neither frequent nor easy to achieve, have proven to be possible when a sufficiently great national consensus exists.

Constitutional amendments are not supposed to be commonplace occurrences, responding to the vicissitudes of public sentiment or transient conditions. As the basic law of the political system, a constitution is expected to outlast governments that come and go and to have a status and permanence above those of mere statute laws. Consequently, in all democracies the bar for changing the constitution is set higher than it is for simply passing or revising a law. A "super majority" is generally required, and under federal constitutions two levels of approval, one national and the other regional, is also required.

Article V of the American Constitution provides for a two-stage process of amendment. The first is the proposal stage; the second involves the process of ratification. Each of these stages includes two options:

- *Proposal.* This may be made through a resolution passed by a two-thirds majority in both the House of Representatives and the Senate *or* as a result of a resolution for constitutional amendment that has been passed by two-thirds of the state legislatures. Only the first proposal option has ever been used.

- *Ratification.* A proposal to amend the Constitution must be ratified by majorities in three-quarters of the state legislatures *or* by three-quarters of state conventions created especially for the purpose of ratification. The state convention model was used to ratify the constitutional agreement of 1787, but since then it has been used only once, when Prohibition was repealed in 1933.

Using these rules the Constitution has been amended on 18 occasions between 1791, when the first ten amendments were passed as a bloc, and 1971. Only one of these changes, the Eighteenth Amendment that established Prohibition, has been repealed, suggesting that for the most part amendments have been responses to a broadly shared consensus, such as that on the enfranchisement of women (1920), the limitation on presidential terms to two (1951), the ban on legal and administrative restrictions on the right to vote (1964), and extending the right to vote to 18-year-olds (1971).

The scope of agreement needed to bring about an amendment to the Constitution may be seen in two cases where the process did not succeed. The first case involves the Equal Rights Amendment (ERA), passed by Congress in 1972. The ERA stated that "Equality of rights under the law shall not be denied or abridged by the United States or by any state on account of sex." By 1975, 35 states had ratified the amendment. This fell three short of the 38 necessary. Finally, when the seven-year ratification deadline established by Congress passed—the Constitution does not prescribe a set period during which ratification must be achieved, but Congress has generally set such a deadline—the ERA died. (In fact, the demise of the ERA was much messier than this, involving some rescinded ratifications, an attempt to extend the seven-year deadline, and a successful court challenge to this proposed extension.)

The ERA proposal was divisive and some of the interests that mobilized in opposition to its ratification, including conservative religious groups, had significant popular support and access to the media. The second case—that of a proposed amendment that would make flag-burning and other forms of flag desecration a punishable offense—is rather different. This proposal has been around for decades, but in 2006 it almost achieved enough votes in Congress to move on to the ratification stage, where its chances of passage would have been better than even. The needed two-thirds threshold was reached in the House, 286 to 130, but it just fell short, 66 to 34, in the Senate. The proposal read, "The Congress shall have power to prohibit the physical desecration of the flag of the United States." This issue is much less divisive than that of the ERA, since the vast majority of Americans are opposed to desecration of the flag. Opposition to the amendment has come mainly from First Amendment groups, including the ACLU. Few members of Congress would have lost votes by supporting the proposed amendment, and yet it was opposed by roughly one-third of those federal lawmakers who voted. The nature of the proposed change to the Constitution, in particular that it seems to diminish the First Amendment's protection of free speech, caused many lawmakers to vote on the basis of their personal convictions rather than according to the public opinion polls.

Notes

1 Joseph Ellis, *Founding Brothers: The Revolutionary Generation* (New York: Vintage 2002) 3. The text for speeches by American presidents can be found at, for instance, the Presidential Speeches Archive, Miller Center of Public Affairs, http://www.millercenter.org.

2 James Madison, http://www.teachingamericanhistory.org.

3 Quoted in Ellis 91.

4 Ellis 115.

5 Letter of Robert Yates and John Lansing to the Governor of New York, 1787.

6 See http://www.teachingamericanhistory.org.

7 Nashville Convention, 10 June 1850.

8 Seventh Joint Debate, Alton, Illinois, 15 October 1858.

9   For this and other presidential speeches quoted below, see Presidential Speeches Archive, cited in note 1 above.

10   Tocqueville, *Democracy in America*, Book I.

11   Tocqueville, *Democracy in America*, Book I.

12   March 12, 1956.

13   Chris Edwards, "Federal Aid to the States," *Policy Analysis* 593 (22 May 2007): 22.

14   ACIR, "Federal Regulation of State and Local Governments: The Mixed Record of the 1980s" (July 1993), http://www.library.unt.edu/gpo/acir/browstitles.htm.

15   Muskie Archives, http://abacus.bates.edu/Library/aboutladd/departments/special/ajcr.

16   Edwards 20.

17   Ed Koch, "The Mandate Millstone," *Public Interest* 61 (Fall 1980).

CHAPTER SIX

Institutions of Government

How government operates and how policy is made in the United States reflect the principle of divided power that the founders wove through the Constitution. Consider the following three vignettes.

Vignette 1. On a typically hot and humid June day in Washington, DC, Professor X walks down Pennsylvania Avenue to Capitol Hill. His destination is the Sam Rayburn Building, named after a former speaker of the Senate. The professor is on his way to a 10:00 a.m. meeting of the Senate Committee on Homeland Security, scheduled to discuss a new electronic surveillance system being installed along stretches of the American-Mexican border. Arriving about 9:20 a.m., Professor X sees a long line of people waiting for the roughly 100 available seats; indeed, some people who arrive after him leave, knowing that there will not be enough room for everyone. The professor overhears the conversation of three other people who are dressed in very expensive suits. It is clear from their conversations that they are lobbyists, probably at the meeting in order to collect information for their clients.

Once the committee meeting begins, it is quickly evident that this is no sideshow. Seated behind the senators are staffers whose job is to provide committee members with the resources they need and the information they request. Several witnesses appear, including executives from companies that have contracts to provide the surveillance system, high-level bureaucrats from the Department of Homeland Security, and an engineer with expertise in the area of electronic surveillance systems. Although the Secretary of

Homeland Security is not there that day, cabinet officials regularly do appear before congressional committees.

Vignette 2. On April 18, 2007 the Supreme Court of the United States handed down a ruling that upheld the constitutionality of limits on certain abortion techniques. Several months earlier, when the Court began to hear oral arguments in the case, the National Organization for Women (NOW) and a number of other feminist groups had organized a rally in front of the Supreme Court building to oppose any change to *Roe v. Wade* (1973), the landmark ruling on abortion. Dozens of groups and individuals were allowed to submit *amicus curiae* (friends of the court) briefs in this highly controversial case. The Court's five-to-four ruling in favor of the legality of the restrictions on a procedure commonly referred to as partial birth abortion re-energized both pro- and anti-abortion groups who looked toward the 2008 presidential election as critical to their respective goals. The incoming president would be in a position to fill at least one Supreme Court vacancy during his or her term in office and thus, potentially, swing policy on abortion in one direction or the other. In the meantime, it was widely believed that the Court's 2007 decision would pave the way for state legislatures to impose greater restrictions on abortion, since the majority of the justices appeared to be sympathetic to such limits.

Vignette 3. On October 1, 2007 President George W. Bush met with his vice-president and some advisors at the White House before being transported in the presidential limousine to the State Department, where a few minutes after 10:00 a.m. he delivered a 20-minute speech entitled "Toward a New Global Approach to Climate Change and Energy Security." In the audience was Indonesia's Minister of the Environment, who would chair the December 2007 United Nations (UN) meeting on climate change, as well as the Executive Secretary of the UN Framework Convention on Climate Change and many other foreign officials. Some members of Congress were also present. President Bush outlined a plan for addressing climate change that relied largely on new technologies for generating energy. However, almost none of what he proposed domestically could be done without the cooperation of Congress, and his expressed goal of reaching a global consensus on climate change by 2009 faced serious international obstacles, notably from governments whose diagnosis of the causes of climate change and how they could be addressed were not the same as those of the Bush administration. The president's speech was widely covered and discussed in the media at home and abroad. In any event, another person would be in the

White House by the 2009 deadline proposed by UN Secretary-General Ban Ki-moon for a global agreement on climate change.

These three vignettes add up to only a partial picture of governance in the United States. What they are intended to show is that each of the three branches of the federal government has important powers and plays a crucial role in the process of governance. These powers and roles are different, but in some respects they are also overlapping and competing.

When the Constitution was written, the balance between the legislative, executive, and judicial branches of government was neither clear nor agreed upon. Some were mistrustful of placing significant powers in the hands of the president, while others thought that the failure to do so was one of the chief deficiencies of the Articles of Confederation and necessary for the better defense of the fledgling republic against external threats. But virtually everyone agreed that it was important to keep governmental power divided between the branches of government as the most effective guarantee of liberty.

In Federalist Paper no. 47 Madison shows that the principle of separate and distinct powers was violated in the constitutions and practices of all the state governments.[1] He did not believe that it was possible to create watertight barriers between the roles and powers of the three branches of government, and in Federalist Paper no. 51 he argues that the important thing is

---

Madison on the Division of Powers

One of the principal objections inculcated by the more respectable adversaries to the Constitution, is its supposed violation of the political maxim that legislative, executive, and judiciary departments ought to be separate and distinct. In the structure of the federal government, no regard, it is said, seems to have been paid to this essential precaution in favor of liberty ...

No political truth is certainly of greater intrinsic value, or is stamped with the authority of more enlightened patrons of liberty, than that on which the objection is founded. The accumulation of all powers, legislative, executive, and judiciary, in the same hands, whether of one, a few, or many, and whether hereditary, self-appointed, or elective, may justly be pronounced the very definition of tyranny. Were the federal Constitution, therefore, really chargeable with the accumulation of power, or with a mixture of powers, having a dangerous tendency to such an accumulation, no further arguments would be necessary to inspire a universal reprobation of the system....

[However], the charge cannot be supported....

Excerpts from Federalist Paper no. 47.

not to aim at an unattainable level of separation between the branches of government, but to give "those who administer each [branch] the necessary constitutional means and personal motives to resist encroachments of the others." Madison, along with everyone else, expected that Congress would be the preeminent branch of the federal government. By dividing Congress into two houses, each of whose members would be selected in a different way, and by giving the executive branch the power of veto over legislation, Madison believed that the danger of an excessive accumulation of power in the hands of the legislative branch would be prevented. Not all the founders agreed with him, but his observations on divided government found few dissenters.

A more widespread fear was that the executive branch might become too powerful and that the president might become a sort of king. In Federalist Paper no. 69 Alexander Hamilton attempts to answer these fears by pointing out the numerous ways in which the president is accountable to the people and the checks that Congress has when it comes to the exercise of his constitutional powers.

The office of President of the United States, inconsequential though it was, had existed under the Articles of Confederation. But a national judiciary did not. In Federalist Paper no. 78 Hamilton discusses the role that would be played by the judicial branch under the new Constitution. Like virtually everyone else at the time, he completely failed to anticipate the important and sometimes divisive role that the Supreme Court would quickly come to assume in the American system of government. "[F]rom the nature of its functions," Hamilton said of the judiciary, "it will always be the least dangerous to the political rights of the Constitution; because it will be least in a capacity to annoy or injure them." The executive branch, he observed, has the power to bestow honors and enforce the laws. The legislative branch is entrusted with making these laws and controls the public purse strings. "The judiciary, on the contrary, has no influence over either sword or the purse," Madison said, adding, "It may truly be said to have neither *force* nor *will,* but merely judgment." This power of mere judgment very soon upset the defenders of states' rights, who thought the Supreme Court too sympathetic to the idea of a strong central government, and the Supreme Court's "mere judgment" proved tremendously divisive in the Dred Scott slavery decision. Today we are used to the idea that court rulings may have major consequences for public policy. Madison's confident claim that "the supposed danger of judiciary encroachment on the legislative authority ... is in reality a phantom"[2] is not one with which most contemporary students of American government would agree.

Congress

For non-Americans, and even many Americans, one of the most difficult things to understand about governance in the United States is the power of Congress. Images on the nightly news and the headlines at one's website of choice focus on the president—what he has done and said, who he has met, and where he is. It is not surprising that people draw the conclusion that the president, like the prime minister in Canada or the UK or the president in France or Mexico, is "in charge." In fact, however, Congress must always be reckoned with, even when the president's party controls a majority in both houses. In no other democracy does the legislative branch enjoy as much independence from the executive branch as in the United States. Canadian Prime Minister Pierre Trudeau's characterization of members of Parliament in his country as "nobodies" would be hugely incorrect if made about members of Congress in the United States. They are "somebodies," and no president dares to forget this.

TABLE 6.1:   PROFILE OF MEMBERS OF 110th CONGRESS (2007–09)

	House		Senate	
ETHNICITY/GENDER	**NUMBER**	**%**	**NUMBER**	**%**
African Americans	41 (R-0; D-41)	9.4	1(R-0;D-1)	1
Hispanics	23 (R-3; D-20)	5.3	2(R-1;D-1)	2
Women	71 (R-21; D-50)	16.3	16(R-5;D-11)	16
LEADING OCCUPATIONS				
Law	162 (R-68; D-94)	37.2	59(R-27;D-32)	59
Business	166 (R-91; D-70)	38	27(R-18;D-9)	27
Public Service/Politics	174 (R-68; D-106)	40	32(R-13;D-19)	32
Education	88 (R-33; D-55)	20.2	14(R-6;D-8)	14
Agriculture	23 (R-15; D-8)	5.3	6(R-4;D-2)	6
Real Estate	36 (R-32; D-4)	8.3	3(R-2;D-1)	3
Medicine	13 (R-10; D-3)	3	3(R-3;D-0)	3
Journalism	0	0	8(R-4;D-4)	8
Law Enforcement	10 (R-3; D-7)	2.3	0	0
Labor	13 (R-6; D-7)	3	3(R-1;D-2)	3

Who are the Lawmakers?

The typical member of Congress is a white male whose professional background is in law, business or politics, and public service. This is true of both the House and the Senate, although representation in the House is more diverse. Table 6.1 shows the representation of blacks, Hispanics, and women in the 110th Congress (2007–09), as well as the leading occupations for members of the House and Senate.

Checks and Balances Between the Three Branches of Government

CHECKS ON THE PRESIDENT'S POWER

By Congress

- Has the power of presidential impeachment.
- Can override a presidential veto.
- Must confirm presidential appointments and consent to foreign treaties.
- May refuse to pass laws and budget measures favored by the White House.
- Can investigate executive branch actions and policies through committees of both the House of Representatives and Senate.
- Can propose a legislative agenda different from the president's.

By the courts

- Actions taken by the executive branch may be declared unlawful or unconstitutional by the courts.

By the voters

- Since the president serves a four-year term, he or she may be removed by voters after one term.

CHECKS ON CONGRESS'S POWER

By the president

- May veto bills passed by Congress.
- "Executive privilege," enables the president and others in the executive branch to withhold requested information in some circumstances.
- As the commander-in-chief of the armed forces (Article II, s.2) and despite the constitutional requirement that only Congress may issue a declaration of war, the president's freedom to launch and prosecute military actions is great.
- The president may "on extraordinary Occasions" (Article II, s.3) convene or adjourn either or both houses of the legislature.

By the courts

- Laws or parts of laws passed by Congress may be struck down as unconstitutional.

By the voters

- Voters may not re-elect members of the House of Representatives after their two-year terms and senators after their six-year terms.

CHECKS ON THE COURTS' POWERS

By the president

- All Supreme Court justices, the Chief Justice of the Supreme Court, and other judges of federal courts are nominated by the president.

By Congress

- All Supreme Court and other federal judicial nominations must be confirmed by the Senate.
- The number and structure of federal courts, below the Supreme Court, are determined by Congress (Article I, s.8 and Article III, s.1).
- Congress, along with the states, may amend the Constitution in order to overcome a Supreme Court ruling.

By voters

- Although federal judges are not elected and cannot be removed for unpopular decisions, there is a good deal of evidence that they are not indifferent to public opinion. The Supreme Court's declaration in the 1954 *Brown* [347 U.S. 483] desegregation ruling, to the effect that public opinion was unenlightened when the separate-but-equal doctrine was formulated in *Plessy v. Ferguson*, 1896 [163 U.S. 537], is a classic and dramatic illustration of this sensitivity.

Until fairly recently, women and minorities were virtually absent from leadership positions in Congress. This has changed, however, most significantly since the Democratic Party regained control of both houses of Congress in the 2006 elections. Nancy Pelosi (D) became the first female speaker of the House of Representatives, and eight congressional committees were chaired by women or blacks (six in the House and two in the Senate). Eight out of a combined 41 committee chairs may not sound like much, but this was roughly in line with the share of seats in Congress held by women and blacks.

Turnover in Congress is relatively low as may be seen in Table 6.2. Moreover, it is usually the case that new members are there because of the decision of an incumbent not to seek re-election and not because of an incumbent's defeat. The re-election rate for incumbent members of the House is usually over 90% and for senators about 80–90% in recent election cycles. Most House seats are fairly safe, due largely to the way state legislatures have drawn the boundary lines of the districts that members of the House represent: Democratic-controlled state legislatures attempt to draw district boundaries so as to favor candidates of their party, and Republican-controlled state legislatures attempt to give their party's candidates for Congress a similar advantage. This practice goes back at least to the time of Massachusetts Governor Elbridge Gerry, whose creative drawing of district boundary lines inspired the term *gerrymander*. Figure 6.1 shows why.

FIGURE 6.1:   THE GERRYMANDER

Senator Daniel Patrick Moynihan's Statement in Congress on When a President Should and Should Not Be Impeached

Removal of a sitting president by Congress under the Constitution involves two steps. The first requires that a majority in the House vote to approve articles of impeachment against the president. The second involves a trial in the Senate where conviction and removal of the president requires the agreement of a two-thirds majority of those voting. Only two presidents have been impeached, Andrew Johnson and Bill Clinton, but neither was convicted in the Senate. The House was preparing articles of impeachment against President Richard Nixon, but his resignation brought an end to the process.

In the following excerpts from a speech given by New York Senator Daniel Moynihan regarding President Clinton's impeachment, Moynihan explains why he believes this check on presidential behavior should be used in only rare and extreme circumstances.

Mr. Chief Justice, Senators, I speak to the matter of prudence. Charles L. Black, Jr. begins his masterful account, Impeachment: A Handbook, *with a warning: "Everyone must shrink from this most drastic of measures.... [t]his awful step."*

For it is just that. The drafters of the American Constitution had, from England and from Colonial government, fully formed models of what a legislature should be, what a judiciary should do. But nowhere on earth was there a nation with an elected head of an executive branch of government.

... Impeachment was to be the device whereby the Congress might counteract the "defect of better motives" in a President. But any such behavior needed to be massive and immediately threatening to the state for impeachment ever to go forward.

Otherwise a quadrennial election would serve to restitute wrongs.

... [T]he Framers clearly intended that a President should be removed only for offenses "against the United States." It may also be concluded that the addition of the words "high Crimes and Misdemeanors" was intended to extend the impeachment power of Congress so as to reach "great and dangerous offences," in [George] Mason's phrase. The question now before the Senate is whether the acts that form the basis for the Articles of Impeachment against President Clinton rise to the level of "high Crimes and Misdemeanors." Which is to say, "great and dangerous offences" against the United States.

Over the course of 1998, as we proceeded through various revelations, thence to Impeachment and so on to this trial at the outset of 1999, I found myself asking whether the assorted charges, even if proven, would rise to the standard of "great and dangerous offences" against the United States. More than one commentator observed that we are dealing with "low crimes."

... We are an indispensable nation and we have to protect the Presidency as an institution. You could very readily destabilize the Presidency, move to a randomness. That's an institution that has to be stable, not in dispute. Absent that, do not doubt that you could degrade the Republic quickly.

This could happen if the President were removed from office for less than the "great and dangerous offences" contemplated by the Framers.

From the Congressional Record, February 12, 1999.

A modern variation of the gerrymander involves the majority-minority district, which is one whose boundaries have been drawn in such a way as to maximize the percentage of minority citizens, usually black, residing within the district. Minority candidates are more likely to be elected in such districts than in ones that are predominantly white. Figure 6.2 shows the contours of a majority-minority district in North Carolina, the 12th Congressional District. The majority-minority district is, of course, a form of affirmative action intended to increase the representation of blacks and Hispanics in Congress. It could not occur in France, where the law forbids the collection of information on the race, ethnic origins, or religion of citizens.

TABLE 6.2:   RATES OF INCUMBENCY, 1979–1994

Country	N (no. of elections)	Incumbency return rate (mean) %	Incumbency return rate (st. dev.)	Turnover per year %
United States	8	84.9	6.14	7.51
Australia	6	80.0	5.99	7.87
West Germany	3	78.7	3.60	5.77
Ireland	6	76.1	6.45	9.30
United Kingdom	4	75.7	1.51	5.58
Japan	6	74.9	6.29	7.77
Denmark	6	74.6	5.67	10.22
Sweden	6	74.1	3.77	8.63
New Zealand	5	72.5	7.74	9.17
Malta	3	71.5	5.49	5.55
Belgium	4	69.5	5.43	9.45
Iceland	4	66.4	8.27	10.47
Finland	4	65.0	2.97	9.03
Luxembourg	4	64.7	7.69	7.03
Italy	4	64.5	6.89	8.97
Greece	6	64.4	15.05	13.43
Switzerland	4	64.3	3.66	8.94
Israel	4	63.8	1.58	9.6
Netherlands	5	63.7	10.87	10.68
Austria	4	61.4	7.66	10.29
Norway	4	60.7	4.73	9.85
France	3	57.7	0.58	9.76
Spain	4	56.0	10.30	12.36
Portugal	5	54.8	8.84	19.10
Canada	4	53.1	21.25	13.01
AVERAGE		**67.7**		**9.56**

Source: Richard Matland and Donley Studlar, "Determinants of Legislative Turnover: A Cross-National Analysis," British Journal of Political Science 34 (2004): 93, Table 1; used with permission.

The Work of Congress

The president may get most of the headlines, but Congress is where much of the action is. Indeed, until the New Deal reforms proposed by the administration of Franklin Delano Roosevelt in the 1930s, presidents tended to be

Leadership Positions in the 110th Congress

HOUSE OF REPRESENTATIVES

Speaker of the House, Nancy Pelosi (D-California)
Elected by members of the party that controls the House, the speaker plays a key role in setting the legislative agenda and determining who will become chairs of House committees, including the conference committees that negotiate the final version of bills with members of the Senate. Under the Presidential Succession Act, 1947, the speaker is second in line after the vice-president to become president.

Party Floor Leaders, Steny Hoyer (D-Maryland) and John Boehner (R-Ohio)
The majority leader is the second highest official in the House, after the speaker. His or her role is to take care of much of the House scheduling and planning work that was looked after by the speaker's office when the House was smaller, when there was less government business, and when the speaker's role as a nationally prominent voice of the party was less important than it is today. The majority leader is also expected to fulfill informal duties having to do with developing and communicating the party's position on issues that are before the House. The minority leader performs similar functions for his or her party.

Whips, James Clyburn (D-South Carolina) and Roy Blunt (R-Missouri)
As in all legislatures, the congressional whips are responsible for mobilizing House members of their respective parties on important votes. The whip is a key liaison person between the party's leadership and its caucus in the House and is responsible for ensuring that members are present on the floor for close votes.

SENATE

Majority Leader, Harry Reid (D-Nevada)
Chosen by the members of the party with a majority in the Senate, the majority leader is seen as a key spokesperson for the party on the issues before Congress and schedules the legislative agenda in the Senate. One of the main sources of the majority leader's influence is his or her right of first recognition. This means that if several senators wish to be recognized to speak, the majority leader has the right to be called upon first, thus enabling him or her to introduce motions or amendments before other senators have the chance. Lyndon Johnson, a powerful majority leader in the 1950s, described the influence of the position as relying on the power of persuasion.

Minority Leader, Mitch McConnell (R-Kentucky)
The selection and functions of the minority leader are similar to those of the majority leader, who acts as a spokesperson for his or her party. The two party leaders in the Senate usually work closely in order to coordinate activities.

Whips, Richard Durbin (D-Illinois) and Trent Lott (R-Mississippi)
The functions of the Senate whips are similar to those of their counterparts in the House and no less challenging, given the tradition of senators' independent behavior and the fact that at some points a number of senators may seldom be in the Capitol as they travel the country pursuing presidential ambitions.

President and President Pro Tempore, Richard Cheney (R-Vice-President) and Robert Byrd (D-West Virginia)
The only Senate leadership position specified by the Constitution is that of its president. This position is filled by the vice-president of the United States, although the Constitution states that he may not vote except in the event of a tie. The vice-president's functions as presiding officer in the Senate are actually carried out by the president pro tempore, who is a sitting member of the Senate.

The current holders of all congressional leadership positions may be found at http://www.house.gov/house/orgs_pub_hse_ldr_www.shtml and http://www.senate.gov/pagelayout/senators/a_three_sections_with_teasers/leadership.htm.

mainly reactive when it came to domestic policy, legislative initiatives coming from and the domestic agenda being determined mainly by Congress. This is no longer the case. Every president is expected to set forth his or her domestic agenda, including laws and budget measures that will have to be passed by Congress. But Congress also has its own agenda—or agendas—and even when the president's party controls both houses, there is no guarantee that his or her legislative preferences will trump those of the legislature.

At the heart of the American congressional system is the fact that any member of Congress may introduce legislation. In the 109th Congress (2005–07), 6,540 bills were introduced in the House alone, about 1,000 more than the average for the previous several congresses. Most of these were, in the end, unsuccessful, but unlike the bill introduction process in most democratic legislatures, the American model is relatively decentralized. The president and members of his cabinet cannot be sitting members of Congress, and so they are dependent on like-minded members of the House and Senate to introduce bills and other public measures that they wish to see enacted. While much of the business of Congress is taken up with measures that have originated in the executive branch, it also spends a lot of time dealing with bills or investigations that have originated in the legislative branch and which may be opposed by the president.

FIGURE 6.2:   DRAWING MAJORITY/MINORITY DISTRICTS

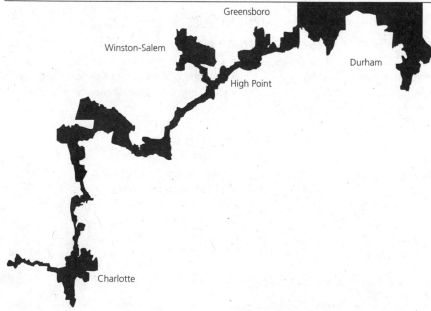

In some democracies the legislature is a place where lawmakers talk—the *parler* in the word *parliament*—and vote on public matters, but they do not make the law in other than a rather formal way. These legislatures are law-passing rather than law-making bodies. In democracies like Canada and the UK, for example, the prime minister and cabinet set the legislative agenda, and during periods of majority government they rarely experience much difficulty getting their legislative and budget priorities passed in the form in which they were introduced. Even in parliamentary systems where coalition governments are typical, as in Germany and Italy, the role of the legislature in hammering out what laws are passed in what form tends to be very secondary to that of the leaders of the coalition parties. Important matters can and do often take place on the floor of the legislature and in committee, but it is rare for an important bill sponsored by the government to be significantly changed as it passes through the legislative mill. And it is even rarer that such a bill originates with members of the legislature who are not also members of the government.

On a very superficial level one might draw the same conclusion about Congress. The political conversation so often seems to revolve around the White House and the president's agenda and preferences. Visitors to

Congress's Resources and Workload, 109th Congress

HOUSE RESOURCES
- Committee staff: 1,363
- Average office staff per member: 20-30*
- General Accounting Office (GAO) and Congressional Budget Office (CBO) provide support in congressional oversight of the executive branch

HOUSE WORKLOAD
- Days in session: 242
- Average hours per day: 7.9
- Public measures introduced: 6,540
- Public measures passed: 770
- Public laws enacted: 482

SENATE RESOURCES
- Committee staff: 1,000
- Average office staff per senator: 45-55*
- GAO and CBO provide support as in the House

SENATE WORKLOAD
- Days in session: 138
- Average hours per day: 7.4
- Public laws passed: 248
- Treaties ratified: 14
- Nominations confirmed: 29,603

*This does not include unpaid student interns, of whom an office may have more than a dozen at any point in time.

Source: Data reported by Don Wolfensberger, Director, "The Congress Project," http://www.wilsoncenter.org; and "20-year Comparison of Senate Legislative Activity," Senate Daily Digest, Office of the Secretary, Senate of the United States.

the House or Senate might be underwhelmed by what they see. "Your Congress is very strange," said a Russian visitor in the early twentieth century. "A man gets up to speak; he says nothing; nobody listens; and when he sits down everyone gets up to disagree."[3] But this Russian visitor was observing the wrong things and looking in the wrong places. Instead of sitting in the visitors' gallery, he should have sat in on committee meetings. If he could have been a party to the communications and negotiations that go on between key leaders in Congress and the White House and within the congressional caucuses of the political parties, he would have come away much wiser about how law-making, not just law-passing, works in Congress.

The formal process of moving a bill from its introduction in Congress to the president's desk for his signature or veto is shown in Figure 6.3. In Figure 6.4 the *informal* law-making process—what former congressman Lee Hamilton calls "how a bill really becomes law"[4]—is shown. These two representations of the law-making process, formal and informal, are not contradictory or inconsistent. The steps outlined in Figure 6.4 are indeed those that have to be followed in the legislative process. The messiness of the actual process of moving from an idea to a law, and all that needs to be achieved and overcome along the way, is better illustrated in Figure 6.4.

FIGURE 6.3:   FROM BILL TO LAW: THE FORMAL STEPS

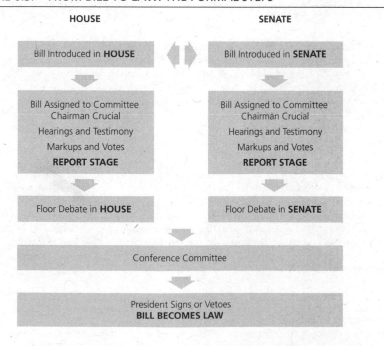

FIGURE 6.4:   HOW A BILL *REALLY* BECOMES A LAW

Stage 1: **The Idea**	The idea at the core of any legislative proposal may originate in many places. It may come from organized interests, public opinion, expert opinion, the White House, reaction to a specific event or condition, or the thoughts of a particular member of Congress. Usually it will be the product of some combination of these factors.
Stage 2: **Deciding how to Frame the Idea as a Bill: Expanding the Conversation**	Any member who wishes to introduce a bill must be mindful that he or she is only one of 435 members in the House or 100 members in the Senate. Each member represents a different set of interests and has his or her own ideas of what sorts of policies should be passed by Congress. The reactions of at least some of them should be anticipated and their ideas and preferences taken into account—especially those of committee and sub-committee chairs, party leaders, and key individual members, particularly those who are skilled at attracting media attention. Likewise, the anticipated reactions and views of the White House and agencies in the executive branch that stand to be affected by a member's proposal should be taken into account. Interest groups will also be consulted, and the precise wording of a bill will often be influenced by their input.
Stage 3: **Navigating a Bill Through Congress**	A bill that has reached the hearings and testimony stage is already exceptional. But its successful passage is far from guaranteed. The multiple conversations referred to at Stage 1 and 2 above continue as the bill moves through the crucial committee stage where amendments will be proposed by other members. The dilemma for the bill's sponsor is described by former congressman Lee Hamilton: "[A]ltering the proposal to accommodate skeptics might broaden its appeal, but compromising too much could alienate core supporters." The reactions of affected interest groups, campaign contributors, and voters must be gauged at each step of this process. The member must constantly be aware of how many votes the bill has in its form at any point in time and whether the president is likely to veto it or sign it into law.
Stage 4: **The Need to Reach Agreement with the Other House**	Before it reaches the president's desk, a bill must be passed in identical form by the House and the Senate. Reaching such an agreement is seldom easy. "The two houses are different in their culture, their makeup, their outlook, and their procedures," observes Don Wolfensberger. "[T]the House tends to be more local, more parochial, more attuned to public opinion and sentiments than the Senate. It reacts more quickly to popular anger and discontent." The conversation between the bill's supporters in the House and in the Senate must begin well before the conference stage, otherwise the likelihood of resolving differences may be small.
Stage 5: **The Idea Becomes Law**	Bills that reach the president's desk are usually signed into law. In many cases the original idea for the bill may have come from the executive branch or at least been supported by the president. Neither Congress nor the president likes the idea of a veto showdown, but it sometimes happens that their preferences are so different or a bill has acquired so much additional baggage as it moves through the process that the president vetoes the bill. In more normal circumstances, however, the conversations and negotiations that will have taken place between Congress and the White House from Stage 1 through Stage 4 will prevent matters from reaching this impasse.

Source: Adapted from, and quotations from, former Congressman Lee Hamilton, "How a Bill Really Becomes Law," http://congress.indiana.edu/radio_commentaries/how_bill_really_becomes_law.php.

In addition to its law-making activities, another crucial function of Congress is oversight of the executive branch. This is carried out in large measure through the committee system. Calling witnesses and hearing expert testimony provide committees with the opportunity to scrutinize and criticize government programs, spending, and operations. Some committees, such as the Senate Subcommittee on Federal Financial Management, Government Information, and International Security, have government oversight and the identification of waste, abuse, and fraud as their chief function. Committees may also decide to carry out special investigations into a particular issue, program, or agency of government. The important thing is that committees have the freedom to launch such investigations and frequently do.

Individual members of Congress may also engage in "lone ranger" oversight, making it their mission to bring attention to wasteful spending, inefficiency, or malfeasance in government operations. There is always a market for stories about government mismanagement and corruption, and members know that one of the most effective ways to capture some media coverage in a highly competitive market is to be a crusader on the side of exposing such behavior.

Congress's oversight function is supported by the General Accounting Office (GAO) and the Congressional Budget Office (CBO). The GAO was created in 1921 when the *Budget and Accounting Act* passed that year required the president to submit an annual budget to Congress. This had the effect of increasing the president's power in the budget-making process, and so to ensure that Congress had some capacity to monitor this expanded executive function the GAO was created with a broad mandate to investigate federal spending. The GAO performs ongoing auditing and evaluation of government spending under the direction of the Comptroller General, but it also carries out special evaluations based on requests from Congress.

Although the *Budget and Accounting Act* requires that the president formulate an annual budget that is submitted to Congress, members of the legislative branch have never relinquished what they see as their constitutional authority over matters of spending and taxation. This struggle between Congress and the president over control of the budget came to a head in 1974 when Congress reacted to President Nixon's refusal to spend money on programs as authorized by Congress—a practice known as the impoundment of funds—by passing the *Congressional Budget Act, 1974*. The act was intended to limit the president's use of impoundment and also to create a process whereby the legislature could develop its own budget priorities independent of the executive branch. But the main and enduring impact of the act was the creation of the Congressional Budget Office which was, in the words of Democratic Senator

Edmund Muskie, expected to "provide Congress with the kind of analysis it needs to work on an equal footing with the executive branch."[5] Like the GAO, the CBO represents Congress's attempt to re-establish balance in the system of checks and balances between itself and the executive branch.

Leaving aside some of those who study it and many of those who work within it, Congress's performance as a law-making body usually receives a poor report card. The American people, while usually expressing very positive feelings about their member of the House or their senators, generally think of Congress as an inefficient and even corrupt institution. Foreign observers tend to be no kinder in their assessments. The lack of party discipline in Congress, the practice of freighting legislation with *earmarks*, provisions that have nothing to do with the bill's central purpose but everything to do with "buying" the support of the members who proposed them, and the paralysis that results when the two houses of Congress or Congress and the president cannot resolve their differences over legislation or budget matters—a situation knows as *gridlock*—leave them shaking their heads.

Party unity in Congress is comparatively low, and it is also true that disagreement between Congress and the White House is not uncommon. During

One of Canada's Foremost Constitutionalists on the Alleged Dysfunctions of the Separation of Powers Model

A President ... may have a coherent program to present to Congress, and may get Senators and Representatives to introduce the bills he or she wants passed. But each house can add to each of the bills, or take things out of them, or reject them outright, and what emerges from the tussle may bear little or no resemblance to what the President wanted. The majority in either house may have a coherent program on this or that subject; but the other house can add to it, or take things out of it, or throw the whole thing out; and again, what (if anything) emerges may bear little or no resemblance to the original. Even if the two houses agree on something, the President can, and often does, veto the bill....

So when an election comes the President, the Senator, the Representative, reproached with not having carried out his or her promises can always say: "Don't blame me! I sent the bill to Congress, and the Senate (or the Representatives, or both) threw it out, or mangled it beyond recognition;" "I introduced the bill I'd promised in the Senate, but the House of Representatives threw it out or reduced it to shreds and tatters (or the President vetoed it);" "I introduced my bill in the House of Representatives, but the Senate rejected it or made mincemeat of it (or the President vetoed it). Don't blame me!"

So it ends up that nobody—not the President, not the Senators, not the Representatives—can be held really responsible for anything done or not done. Everybody concerned can honestly and legitimately say, "Don't blame me!"

Excerpts from Senator Eugene Forsey, How Canadians Govern Themselves, http://www.parl.gc.ca.

the Bill Clinton and George W. Bush presidencies both the Republican and Democratic parties in Congress became more unified, signifying the increased (but not unprecedented) level of partisan polarization that existed during those years. Many commentators have ascribed this increased polarization to the character and values of these two presidents, each of whom generated a good deal of enmity from members of the opposing party. In fact, however, part of the explanation lies in the fact that the United States was very close to a 50/50 country during those years—about as many people voting Democrat as Republican—and the margins separating the parties in both the House and Senate were relatively narrow. The intensity of the competition between the parties, where a very small movement of seats from one party to another would make the difference in who would control Congress, may be as important in explaining the increase in party voting as the ideology and character of party leaders.

During George W. Bush's second term the level of disagreement between the president and Congress, one of the dysfunctions of the American model according to its critics, reached the lowest level since the Congressional Quarterly began to keep track of such matters in 1953. Figure 6.5 shows the percentage of votes in the House where a majority of members supported the president on issues where he took a clear position. Most presidents do better early in their term than later, and it also appears that among those who serve two terms, their success in Congress falls off somewhat in the second term. The reasons for this will be discussed later in the chapter.

FIGURE 6.5: PRESIDENTIAL SUPPORT SCORES, 1953–2006 (average score for Congress by year)

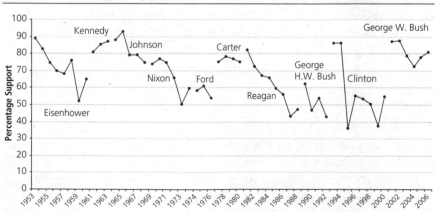

Note: Presidential support scores are based on those roll call votes in Congress on which the President has taken a position and on which a majority of members support that position.

The President

A member of the House represents those in his or her district (on average about 600,000 people) and a senator represents his or her state. Of course members of Congress may and often do think of themselves as representatives of broader constituencies and of interests and ideas that extend beyond their particular district or state. Nevertheless, the tug of local interests is always there. The president, however, is elected nationally by the American people and therefore represents the largest possible constituency. His perspective on an issue and, indeed, what issues he believes are worthy of his time will often be different from those of members of Congress. At the same time, however, the president needs the support of a majority in Congress in order to get anything done. He cannot count on party discipline, assuming that his party controls Congress, nor can he expect members of the legislative branch to automatically defer to his stature as the only nationally elected official in the country. Instead, the president must rely on leadership.

The Constitution says almost nothing about the president's policy-making role. Instead, it specifies that he or she must be a natural-born citizen of the United States who is at least 35-years-old and stipulates the term of office (four years), how the president will be chosen (i.e., the electoral college), the line and process of succession in the event that the president dies in office or for some other reason cannot carry out his duties, and the oath that he or she must take on assuming office. The Constitution declares that the "executive power shall be vested in a President of the United States" and goes on in Article II, Section 1 to specify some of these executive powers. They include the president's role as commander-in-chief of the armed forces and head of the federal civil service; the authority to make treaties; the power to nominate individuals to ambassadorial, judicial, and thousands of civil service positions; and the duty to receive ambassadors (and therefore acknowledge or reject the legitimacy of a particular regime) and to grant reprieves and pardons. The president, declares the Constitution, "shall take care that the laws be faithfully executed." There is no suggestion in any of this, however, that the president will involve himself in setting the policy agenda, proposing particular laws, setting a budget for the federal government, or otherwise *making*—as opposed to simply *executing*—policy.

But in fact the president is deeply and constantly involved in the policy-making process and is expected by everyone, including members of Congress, to perform this role. In addition to being the commander-in-chief, a role assigned to the president by the Constitution, he or she has a number

A Typical Day for Senator "X"

The following is an actual senator's schedule for a fairly typical Tuesday during the autumn of 2007.

7:30 AM DEPART HOME You will be driving.

8:00 AM–9:00 AM FYI: BIPARTISAN BREAKFAST RE: FARM BILL W/SENATORS "Y" AND "Z"—S-120, The Capitol

9:50 AM PARTICIPATE IN PERMANENT INTERNET ACCESS TAX BAN PRESS CONFERENCE—Pre-Meeting, S-230, The Capitol, Press Conference, Senate Radio/TV Gallery, S-325 9:50 am: Meet Senators McConnell ... (more)

10:00 AM COMMERCE COMM HEARING ON THE TRANSPORTATION SECURITY ADMINSTRATION and "Progress on H.R. 1, Implementing the Recommendations of the 9/11 Commission Act of 2007"—253 Russell Building

10:00 AM HOMELAND SECURITY AND GOVERNMENTAL AFFAIRS COMMITTEE HEARING "One Year Later: A Progress Report on the SAFE Port Act"—342 Dirksen POC WITNESS LIST: Panel I—STEWART A. BAKER, Assistant Secretary for Policy, U.S. Department of Homeland Security ... (more)

10:30 AM STAFF MEETS W/EASTER SEAL REPRESENTATIVES FROM THE SENATOR'S STATE—111 Russell You have agreed to speak at the Easter Seal annual meeting on Tuesday, November 27.

11:00 AM STOP BY CENTER FOR STRATEGIC AND INTERNATIONAL STUDIES TASK FORCE ON HIV/AIDS—432 Russell POC: Stop by and make 5-10 minute remarks. 11:30 am: Senator Feingold will speak.

11:30 AM MEET W/CHRIS MOORE, HOLDERNESS, HUGO CHAVEZ DOCUMENTARY FILMMAKER—111 Russell POC: OTHER ATTENDEE: Co-Director Magee Mcilvaine

11:45 AM FYI: FOREIGN RELATIONS TOP SECRET BRIEFING: GULF SECURITY DIALOGUE—S-407

12:00 PM ATTEND WHIP MEETING HOSTED BY SENATOR LOTT—S-208, The Capitol

12:30 PM–2:00 PM REPUBLICAN POLICY COMMITTEE LUNCH—S-207, The Capitol

2:00 PM MEET W/LOWELL MCADAMS, CEO VERIZON WIRELESS, AND SENATOR DEMINT

3:00 PM FYI: STAFF MEETS WITH RISK AND INSURANCE MANAGEMENT SOCIETY MEMBERS—111 Russell ATTENDEES: Representatives from Major League Baseball, UPS, Sun Microsystems ... (more)

3:15 PM MEET W/STEPHEN NORTHRUP, VICE PRESIDENT, AND JERRY STEFFL, DIRECTOR, WELLPOINT—111 Russell Introductory meeting. Wellpoint is the largest insurer in the US and ... (more)

4:00 PM ATTEND COFFEE W/WALID JUMBLATT, MEMBER OF THE LEBANESE PARLIAMENT AND THE HEAD OF THE PROGRESSIVE SOCIALIST PARTY IN LEBANON, HOSTED BY CONGRESSMAN RAHALL—1334 Longworth

6:00 PM–9:00 PM FYI: XM RADIO LAUNCH PARTY FOR P.O.T.U.S.(Presidents of the United States) '08 W/LEWIS BLACK—1401 K Street, N.W., Washington

Reprinted with permission.

of informal roles that are no less important despite not being explicitly set down in the Constitution. They include the following.

Lawmaker

When Woodrow Wilson was elected president he announced his intention to spend considerable time on Capitol Hill in order to be closely involved in the law-making process. As a foremost student of American government and a former president of Princeton University, Wilson was as conversant as anyone with the American Constitution and the separation of powers doctrine. But the powers of the presidency had already been enlarged by his predecessors, particularly under Theodore Roosevelt, and so Wilson's bold announcement that he planned to set up shop in the President's Room of the Senate seemed just another step in the direction of the president becoming a de facto lawmaker-in-chief.

Today it is taken for granted that the White House will be involved in the law-making process long before a bill gets in sight of the president's desk. Indeed, it is common for major legislative initiatives to originate in the White House, although these origins are far from a guarantee that a bill will experience smooth passage through the congressional mill. During the presidency

"Wilson Innovations Excite Washington"

Washington, February 27—Official Washington is greatly stirred by the reported inclination of Governor Wilson to visit the Capitol frequently after he is President and use the President's room there for consultations with Senators and Representatives. Such a departure will be in line with the practice Mr. Wilson has followed as Governor of New Jersey in going to the very doors of the legislative chambers to press bills in which he was interested. The possibility has occasioned much secret alarm and considerable open opposition at both ends of the Capitol today....

The President's room is for ordinary purposes a part of the Senate lobby.... The use of this room for informal conferences between the President and members of Congress would enable a freer interchange between the legislative and executive branches of the Government than has existed since the Government was founded.

Democratic Congressmen, many of whom are warm supporters of Gov. Wilson, have of recent years condemned what they called the growing usurpation, and the growing influence of the White House upon legislation. Now that Mr. Wilson is credited with planning a more direct influence on legislation than even President Roosevelt attempted, a few continue to criticize the tendency, while others comment guardedly or vaguely that the President will be welcome at the Capitol ... "The President will be pretty busy at the other end of the avenue," said [Democratic Senator] James O'Gorman with a smile, "but he will always be welcome when he can come."

Excerpts from the New York Times, *27 February 1913.*

of George W. Bush, the *Patriot Act*, introduced after 9/11, was an example of a bill that was drafted in the executive branch and that received quick passage only 43 days after the events that prompted it. President Bush's plan for reform of the social security system, the centerpiece of his legislative agenda immediately after his re-election in 2004, experienced a very different fate. Despite an enormous public relations offensive intended to move public opinion in the direction of Bush's proposal to allow for voluntary personal accounts, whereby social security contributors could choose to invest some part of their mandatory contributions into a private sector bond and stock fund, this initiative eventually died.

Often times, however, it is impossible to say that a particular bill "originated" in the executive or legislative branch. It is commonly the case that bills represent responses to circumstances on which both the White House and congressional lawmakers hold views, and multiple bills may be proposed to address the same issue. The version of the bill that is ultimately discussed and amended in congressional committees, debated and voted upon on the floors of the House and Senate, and whose House and Senate versions have been reconciled in conference before being sent to the president will usually contain the DNA of both branches of government.

In his book, *The Presidency as a Separated System*, Charles O. Jones examined 28 major laws passed between 1948 and 1990. He found that 21 originated in the White House and only seven in Congress. But in terms of each branch's influence on the final legislative product, Jones argues that the president was dominant in six cases, Congress in seven; there was a balance between the branches with the president being very active in five cases; and in the remaining 10 laws there was what he characterizes as a true balance of influence between the executive and legislative branches.[6]

When the White House's preferences for a law have been disregarded by congressional lawmakers, the possibility of a presidential veto increases. Table 6.3 shows the number of bills vetoed by presidents between 1789 and 2008, as well as the number of vetoes overridden by Congress. It may be seen that whether the president's party controls Congress is not a decisive factor determining the frequency with which the veto is used. Democratic President Jimmy Carter served while his party had majorities in both the House and Senate, yet he used the veto much more often on a pro-rated basis than Democratic President Bill Clinton, who faced a Republican majority in the House for six of his eight years in office. Presidential vetoes are very difficult to overturn, so the threat of one usually operates as an influential trump card that the White House may use during the give-and-take of negotiations with Congress over a particular piece of legislation.

TABLE 6.3:   SUMMARY OF BILLS VETOED, 1789–2008*

President	Regular Vetoes	Pocket Vetoes	Total Vetoes	Vetoes Overridden
George Washington	2		2	
John Adams			0	
Thomas Jefferson			0	
James Madison	5	2	7	
James Monroe	1		1	
John Q. Adams			0	
Andrew Jackson	5	7	12	
Martin Van Buren		1	1	
W.H. Harrison			0	
John Tyler	6	4	10	1
James K. Polk	2	1	3	
Zachary Taylor			0	
Millard Fillmore			0	
Franklin Pierce	9		9	5
James Buchanan	4	3	7	
Abraham Lincoln	2	5	7	
Andrew Johnson	21	8	29	15
Ulysses S. Grant	45	48	93	4
Rutherford B. Hayes	12	1	13	1
James A. Garfield			0	
Chester A. Arthur	4	8	12	1
Grover Cleveland	304	110	414	2
Benjamin Harrison	19	25	44	1
Grover Cleveland	42	128	170	5
William McKinley	6	36	42	
Theodore Roosevelt	42	40	82	1
William H. Taft	30	9	39	1
Woodrow Wilson	33	11	44	6
Warren G. Harding	5	1	6	
Calvin Coolidge	20	30	50	4
Herbert Hoover	21	16	37	3
Franklin D. Roosevelt	372	263	635	9
Harry S. Truman	180	70	250	12
Dwight D. Eisenhower	73	108	181	2
John F. Kennedy	12	9	21	
Lyndon B. Johnson	16	14	30	
Richard M. Nixon	26	17	43	7
Gerald R. Ford	48	18	66	12
Jimmy Carter	13	18	31	2
Ronald Reagan	39	39	78	9
George H. W. Bush	29	15	44	1
William J. Clinton	36	1	37	2
George W. Bush	9	1	10	2
TOTAL	**1493**	**1067**	**2560**	**108**

*As of the end of May, 2008.

Political Leader

Every President has to inspire the confidence of the people. Every President has to become a leader, and to be a leader he must attract people who are willing to follow him. Every President has to develop a moral underpinning to his power, or he soon discovers that he has no power at all.—Lyndon Baines Johnson[7]

President Johnson certainly knew what he was talking about. During the first two years of his presidency he had support scores in Congress that were among the highest ever recorded (see Figure 6.5). By the time he decided not to seek re-election, after his crushing loss in the 1968 New Hampshire primary, his ability to command support for his ideas and policies had fallen very low. Although he still was on the winning side of most votes in Congress, the public had turned against the war in Vietnam, and Johnson's moral authority to lead the country had hit bottom.

Leadership involves a bundle of attributes that are difficult to measure. Moreover, the personal qualities that are associated with successful leadership may change over time and vary depending on circumstances. Television has elevated the importance of being telegenic and having communication skills appropriate to this medium. The circumstances in which decisions are taken are also crucial. It is probably no accident that virtually every list of "best presidents" compiled by historians and other experts is dominated by wartime presidents. Bill Clinton, despite his exceptional popularity while in office, lamented that circumstances did not give him an opportunity to demonstrate the sort of greatness that Americans associate with such presidents as Washington, Jefferson, Lincoln, Theodore Roosevelt, Woodrow Wilson, and Franklin Delano Roosevelt.

In the previous section we saw that the president must be able to persuade a majority in Congress to support his budget and legislative preferences. The president's ability to do so is increased if he or she is perceived to have widespread support among voters. Public approval ratings of the president's performance generally drop off during his or her term, after an initial "honeymoon" period with voters. The fact that most presidents have seen their support scores in Congress decline as their term went on (see Figure 6.5) is probably related to members' tendency to see the president as weaker in public support. One needs to be careful, however. Bill Clinton experienced relatively low success scores in Congress at the same time as his public approval ratings were very high, especially during his second term. But generally speaking, and the partisan composition of Congress aside, a president who is perceived by members of Congress to have strong support with the public will be better able to move his or her agenda through the congressional mill.

The American people look to the president for leadership, and in an age of 24/7 cable news channels and an insatiable media demand for stories that involve the president, there is no way that he or she can avoid being the focal point for much of the hopes, aspirations, disappointments, and grievances of the public. Not that the president is likely to want to avoid the spotlight. An ongoing study of presidential personality, character, and leadership by two psychiatrists finds that recent presidents are much more extraverted—needing to and enjoying calling attention to themselves—than their predecessors tended to be.[8]

Being perceived as the embodiment of ideas and values that are right for the times, at least in the eyes of a majority of voters, is the secret of popularity. This is not, historians will be quick to note, the same as successful leadership. During President Truman's second term, as the Korean War came to an inconclusive stalemate between Cold War rivals, his approval ratings were among the lowest ever recorded. History has, however, vindicated Truman's leadership as he generally is ranked among the leading 10–12 presidents by polls of experts. Few presidents have been as divisive as Lincoln was in his time, yet he usually is ranked first by such polls for reasons that are obvious with the benefit of hindsight.

In the time frame measured by election results and job approval ratings, the president's ability to connect with voters is crucial to successful leadership. This ability is in part a function of an individual president's communication skills—what he says and how and where he says it—but also to events that may be beyond his control. For example, it is well known that a president's public approval ratings and the election chances of the candidate of the party that controls the White House are directly correlated with the state of the economy. Better economic performance tends to produce more favorable public opinion. But only the economically illiterate believe that all that goes well or badly with the economy should be laid at the president's doorstep. Nevertheless, the public's evaluation of leadership will be influenced by popular perceptions of the state of the economy.

"Perceptions" is the key word. Richard Brody argues that, "Public evaluations of the president are linked most closely to the ratio of good results [reported in the media] minus bad results divided by all results news (good, bad and neutral)." Moreover, a new piece of information regarding the president's performance is evaluated by the public against the backdrop of assessments that have already been formulated on the basis of past information. If the accumulated information on presidential performance is mainly negative, this reduces the impact of a "good news" story because it is incongruent with this popular negative assessment. Stories reported earlier in a president's term, Brody argues, tend to have a larger impact on public assessments of his leadership than those reported later because there is less accumulated information about the president's performance against which the public absorbs this early information.[9]

Brody's argument directs our attention toward those who select, frame, write, and produce stories and images related to presidential performance. The White House controls some of these, such as the president's weekly radio broadcasts (but who listens to these?) and orchestrated events, speeches, and press conferences intended to show the president's performance in a good light. But most of what the mass public reads, hears, and sees about presidential performance is generated by media organs that the White House does not control.

Some presidents, however, have seemed capable of withstanding a preponderance of negative media coverage of their performance. This was true of Ronald Reagan during the barrage of criticism that occurred over the Iran-Contra scandal during his second term and also of Bill Clinton, whose public approval ratings stayed high during the saturation media coverage of the Lewinsky scandal. Such leaders are sometimes referred to as "Teflon Presidents," to whom nothing negative sticks. There are several possible explanations for this. One, suggested in Brody's model, is that an accumulation of positive information related to the president's performance and leadership earlier in his presidency enables him to survive even a fairly heavy barrage of negative stories later on. A second explanation is that some presidents have that "royal jelly" or personal charisma that insulates them in the public mind from stories that would likely prove damaging to the popular assessment of other leaders. A third is that not all news stories are equally helpful or damaging to a president's public approval ratings. The economy— strong during the periods when Reagan and Clinton received their heaviest onslaught of negative media coverage—may have more of an impact than stories about scandal. When stories of scandal are difficult for most people to understand or are found to be uninteresting by the mass public, their ability to damage a president's popularity may be less. For example, the story of White House involvement in the "outing" of CIA agent Valerie Palme, whose husband Joe Wilson had written a 2003 *New York Times* article casting strong doubt on some of the evidence used by the Bush administration in its public justification for overthrowing the Saddam Hussein regime, generated enormous and sustained interest among those who read the *New York Times* and the *Washington Post* and who listen to National Public Radio. Most Americans, however, were not paying much attention to what was a highly complicated story that riveted the "chattering classes" for a couple of years.

As the leader of his or her party, a president also performs roles of more special concern to party activists. These people are more interested in politics than most citizens and also tend to be more ideological, in the sense of being conscious of the beliefs and outcomes that they wish to be expressed by their leader and implemented through his or her actions in office. Many thousands of these activists will be needed as volunteers in presidential election campaigns. In order to motivate them, their presidential candidate must be perceived as someone likely to advance their issue agenda. This can be problematic given the divisions that exist within each party. A socially conservative Republican who opposes *Roe v. Wade* on abortion and believes that many social services are best provided through faith-based organizations such as churches will motivate like-minded party members. He or she is unlikely to be embraced with much enthusiasm by fiscal conservatives or libertarians who expect a Republican presidential candidate to focus on downsizing government and leaving people free to make their own choices. On the Democratic side, a president or presidential aspirant generally faces the challenge of appealing to the left wing of the party—much of the Democratic Party's activist base occupies this ideological space—or crafting

Leadership and the Public Assessment of Presidential Candidates in 2004

The 2004 presidential election that saw George W. Bush re-elected was in large measure determined by the public's assessment of the two candidates as leaders in a post-9/11 world. This was how the Republican campaign attempted to frame the choice facing voters, as one between an incumbent president who had reacted forcefully by attacking the Taliban in Afghanistan after 9/11 and who through the War on Terror made national security and preventing another attack on American soil his chief priority. The main source of vulnerability in this narrative of presidential leadership involved the decision to go to war in Iraq. This was framed as part of the larger War on Terror, suggesting a link between the threat that al-Qaeda posed to America and that represented by Saddam Hussein.

American public opinion, more so than in Canada or Europe, took very seriously the danger of future terrorist attacks. A May 2004 survey, for example, found that 53% of Americans compared to only 14% of Canadians believed it was "very likely" that their country would be the victim of a terror-

ist attack in the coming year.[10] The candidate who was best able to convince voters that the issue was central to their decision on who to vote for and, moreover, that he was best able to provide effective leadership on this issue would have an important advantage. The Bush campaign attempted to sow seeds of doubt among voters about John Kerry's abilities as a leader, describing him as a "flip-flopper" on the issues, including the issue of war in Iraq. The Kerry campaign attempted to generate doubts about the leadership of President Bush, arguing that the war in Iraq was not linked to the terrorist attacks of 9/11 and the War on Terror and that the invasion of Iraq had become and would continue to be a sort of Vietnam quagmire for the United States.

In the end, voters made their decisions based on many different considerations. There is little doubt, however, that perceptions of the respective candidates' ability to lead on national security issues was important for many and that more of them gave the advantage to George W. Bush than to John Kerry on this issue.

a message that is more likely to be preferred by centrist Democrats. In both parties, effective leadership of the activist base requires a fine sense of balance and the ability to appeal to the main ideological factions who provide the foot soldiers needed for a successful campaign. Ronald Reagan was able to do this, as was Bill Clinton. George Herbert Walker Bush, mistrusted by socially conservative activists in his party, was not.

The president's role as party leader also involves the ability to raise money for the party and its candidates. No one is a bigger draw on the fundraising circuit than the president. Even when his public approval numbers are low, he is still more likely to fill a room with donors willing to pay $1,000 a plate (sometimes much more) to hear him give a speech after an unmemorable meal. As fundraiser-in-chief, the president is expected to spend some part of his time attending national party functions and events for particular candidates where the central purpose is to raise money for future campaigns. The fundraising function of the president has occasionally gone beyond the limits of what most people believe to be ethical, as when the Lincoln Bedroom of the White House was essentially rented for a donation of $100,000 a night to President Clinton's "guests."[11]

Chief Diplomat

Every president has a Secretary of State, numerous ambassadors including an Ambassador to the United Nations, a corps of professional foreign service officers, and, occasionally, specially appointed envoys assigned to represent the administration on particular issues. Most negotiations with other states are carried out on behalf of the president by his or her representatives. Presidents vary in terms of their interest and knowledge of and direct involvement in foreign affairs, but no president can remain disengaged from these matters.

Part of the reason for direct presidential involvement in diplomatic affairs is that the heads of state and government of other countries will expect to deal with their American counterpart, even if this involves a brief telephone conversation or a photo opportunity such as a signing ceremony or statements delivered in the Rose Garden of the White House. The President of Liberia, no less than the President of Russia, expects to meet with the President of the United States if the occasion is an official state visit, a bilateral or multilateral summit, or the signing of a treaty. Moreover, the populations of Liberia and Russia, respectively, think of the American president as the person whose ideas and authority matter in international affairs. The intricacies of the American system of divided government and the influence of particular congressional committees and members is often, even usually, lost on foreign populations and even on their leaders.

The American people also look to the president for leadership on foreign policy matters, particularly during times of uncertainty and crisis. Presidential disengagement is not an option, although the investment of time and style of presidential management of foreign affairs varies considerably. Jimmy Carter was deeply and directly involved in foreign policy-making and diplomacy. His days at the White House began early in meetings with his National Security Advisor, Zbigniew Brezinski. Carter involved himself directly in the American-mediated peace talks between Egypt and Israel that culminated in the Camp David Accord, certainly the high point of an otherwise problem-ridden presidency. Ronald Reagan, on the other hand, tended to delegate the management of foreign affairs and to take a less direct interest in these matters most of the time. Reagan's personal negotiation with Soviet President Mikhail Gorbachev on strategic arms reduction was, however, an important exception to his usual practice of delegation.

Presidents often have backgrounds that include little professional involvement in foreign affairs. Since World War II, Presidents Truman, Johnson, Carter, Reagan, Clinton, and George W. Bush all came from such backgrounds, although aspects of Carter's and Clinton's educations made their presidential interest in foreign affairs unsurprising. Some presidents, including George W. Bush, came to power promising to spend more time on domestic affairs and less on the rest of the world than their predecessor. But given America's role in the world, no president, even if his or her initial level of interest and lack of knowledge of foreign affairs are low, can avoid assuming the role of chief diplomat for his or her country and spending considerable time on foreign affairs leadership.

Assessing Presidential Performance

Probably more than people in most societies, Americans like to rank order and quantify everything from who is the richest—*Forbes* magazine's annual ranking of the world's richest people is always eagerly awaited—to more subjective matters such as the 100 best movies of the twentieth century—*Citizen Kane* came in at number one, according to the American Film Institute's ranking.[12] Other peoples also attempt to rank such difficult to measure attributes as greatness, significance, and success. But in no other country is the evaluation of presidential performance and greatness the cottage industry that it is in the United States. Rating the performance of presidents from Washington to the present day began with Arthur Schlesinger's assessments for *Life Magazine* in 1962. His son, Arthur Schlesinger Jr., replicated his father's work in his 1997 article, "Rating the Presidents: Washington to Clinton."[13] This prompted a spate of additional studies, in part because some critics challenged the Schlesingers' rankings on the grounds not only that there was a liberal bias in the selection of the historians whose views were polled but also because the subject of what makes for a great or lousy president is one that interests many people and excites much impassioned argument.

There is, in fact, a large measure of agreement between most of these assessments when it comes to who deserves to be in the "top 10." Table 6.4 compares the lists of the 10 greatest presidents according to three polls that end with Bill Clinton's presidency.

Surveys like these ask the experts doing the assessing of presidential leadership to score presidents according to a number of separate leadership criteria. The C-SPAN survey, for instance, used the following leadership categories:

- Public persuasion
- Moral authority
- Relations with Congress
- Crisis leadership
- International relations
- Vision/setting an agenda
- Economic management
- Administrative skills
- Pursued equal justice for all
- Performance within the context of his times

Bill Clinton, one of the more popular of recent presidents, ranks in the top 10 on economic management and pursuing equal justice for all, but he receives mediocre or even very low scores on most other attributes of presidential leadership (he ranked last on moral authority). Lyndon Baines Johnson, on the other hand, exited his presidency on a very unpopular note, but history's assessment of him has tended to improve over time, based on the high rankings that he gets on his relations with Congress, vision for the country, and pursuing equal justice for all. Evidently, popularity in one's time is not necessarily the same thing as history's verdict on a president's leadership and performance.

TABLE 6.4:   THE TOP 10 PRESIDENTS: THE RESULTS OF THREE EXPERT
SURVEYS

	1997 Schlesinger Survey	2000 Federalist Society/ Wall Street Journal Survey	2000 C-SPAN Survey
1.	Abraham Lincoln	George Washington	Abraham Lincoln
2.	George Washington	Abraham Lincoln	Franklin D. Roosevelt
3.	Franklin D. Roosevelt	Franklin D. Roosevelt	George Washington
4.	Thomas Jefferson	Thomas Jefferson	Theodore Roosevelt
5.	Theodore Roosevelt	Theodore Roosevelt	Harry S. Truman
6.	Woodrow Wilson	Andrew Jackson	Woodrow Wilson
7.	Harry S. Truman	Harry S. Truman	Thomas Jefferson
8.	James Polk	Ronald Reagan	John F. Kennedy
9.	Dwight D. Eisenhower	Dwight D. Eisenhower	Dwight D. Eisenhower
10.	John Adams	James Polk	Lyndon B. Johnson

Sources: Arthur M. Schlesinger Jr., "Rating the Presidents": Washington to Clinton," Political Science Quarterly 11,2 (Summer 1997): 179–90; http://www.fed-soc.org/docLib/20070308_pressurvey.pdf; http://www.americanpresidents.org; used with permission.

The Judicial Branch

For three days in 1991 the Supreme Court of the United States attracted a television audience larger than some of the soap operas that were aired at the same time. A combination of sex and race transformed what had been rather quiet and uneventful Senate confirmation hearings on the nomination of Clarence Thomas to the Supreme Court into a televised spectacle with enough allegations of scandal to interest even those who did not normally follow politics. Clarence Thomas was a black United States Court of Appeals judge nominated by President George H.W. Bush to fill the vacancy left by the retirement of the first black Supreme Court Justice, Thurgood Marshall. Just before the Senate judiciary committee was to vote on Thomas's nomination, Anita Hill, a law school professor and former assistant to Thomas, came forward with allegations that he had sexually harassed her several years earlier. She accused him of lewd and suggestive behavior, including talking dirty to her. Asked why she had waited so long to go public with her claims, Professor Hill said that Thomas's authority as her workplace superior and the fact that her subsequent career prospects could be influenced by his recommendations led her to keep quiet about what had gone on. But with Judge Thomas being nominated to sit on the country's highest court, she felt that the stakes were too high to remain silent any longer.

Professor Hill's critics suggested that the timing of her allegations had more to do with blocking the appointment of an ideologically conservative judge than with improper behavior in the workplace. Over three days of televised testimony the Senate Judiciary Committee heard accusations from Professor Hill and denials from Judge Thomas. The American public was riveted by the "he said, she said" nature of a story worthy of the sensational tabloid press. In the end, however, Thomas's nomination was narrowly confirmed by a vote of 52 to 48 on the floor of the Senate.

High court nominations occasionally generate some controversy in other countries, although it is usually limited to legal and political circles and perhaps followed by some part of the politically attentive public. This is not because the stakes are lower in the choice of top judges in these other countries. In Canada, for example, the Supreme Court has an influence on policy that is no less than in the United States. But public controversy over judicial appointments in Canada has been rare, and it was not until 2006 that legislative committee hearings on a Supreme Court nomination were permitted. And in other democracies too, fears have been expressed over what some charge is a trend toward American-style judicial activism.

The United States is exceptional, however, in the degree to which its judiciary has long played a major role in shaping public policy through its interpretation of the Constitution. "I am unaware," observed Tocqueville, "that any nation of the globe has hitherto organized a judicial power in the same manner as the Americans.... A more imposing judicial power was never constituted by any people."[14] For this reason, and because the process whereby federal judges are nominated and confirmed is more transparent than in other countries, appointments to the American Supreme Court, and occasionally to some federal appellate courts, are sometimes highly controversial.

Such controversy is nothing new. Only six years after the Constitution was ratified, George Washington's nomination of John Rutledge to the Supreme Court was rejected by the Senate. Roughly 20% of presidential nominations to America's highest court have been rejected by the Senate. All that was new in the case of the Clarence Thomas confirmation process was the presence of television cameras to broadcast the dogfight between the White House and the Senate into the living rooms of Americans. Televised confirmation proceedings began in 1982, but some confirmation fights in the pre-television era were as bitter and hard fought as that of Clarence Thomas. President Woodrow Wilson's 1916 nomination of Louis Brandeis, who was an outspoken advocate of "social jurisprudence" whereby judges would take social and economic circumstances into account in their interpretation of the Constitution, was such a case. Brandeis's nomination was even opposed by the American Bar Association, but after a hard fight in the Senate Judiciary Committee he was confirmed by a comfortable margin on the floor of the Senate.

The Brandeis confirmation, according to some, represented a shift away from partisan reasons for rejecting presidential nominees to ideological ones. Since Brandeis, but particularly over the last half century, whether a nominee favors an *activist* or an *originalist* interpretation of the Constitution has become the key issue for senators. In fact, however, many earlier Senate rejections of presidential nominations to the Supreme Court were based on whether a nominee was thought to be a supporter of states' rights. And in at least one case, that of Jeremiah Black, nominated by President James Buchanan in 1861, Senate rejection was based on the nominee's opposition to the abolition of slavery. These too were ideological issues, every bit as much as where a judicial nominee stands on abortion rights or affirmative action is today.

The Work of the Court

The Supreme Court of the United States has nine justices, although this number is not prescribed by the Constitution. The first Supreme Court under Chief Justice John Jay had only six, but the number has been fixed by Congress at nine since 1869.

Each year the Supreme Court receives roughly 8,000 petitions from the decisions of appellate courts, about two-thirds of these involving requests for review of a federal district court ruling. These petitions take the form of a *writ of certiorari*, from the Latin *certiorari volumnus*, meaning "we wish to be informed." The Court grants certiorari in about 150 cases per year, representing slightly less than 2% of all petitions. Clearly, the selection of cases is crucial. In deciding which cases to hear, the justices are assisted by law clerks who are recent graduates from the leading law schools or junior lawyers with the country's most prestigious law firms. Each of the justices chooses four clerks per annual term who, among other roles, assist in the determination of the cases that raise constitutional and legal issues weighty enough to warrant the Court's attention.

If four justices agree that a case warrants review, it is then scheduled as part of the Court's business. This is called the "Rule of Four." The justices meet in conference and discuss the cases that they think worthy of the Court's attention and a vote is taken to determine those that will go forward. Former Chief Justice William Rehnquist described the justices' selection criteria as "a rather subjective decision, made up in part of intuition

Judicial Activism, Original Intent, and the Litmus Test for Supreme Court Nominees

When a person's name is mentioned as a potential Supreme Court nominee, the first question asked about him or her is not, "Does this person have a distinguished record in the law?" or "Is he or she an individual of character?" Instead, it tends to be, "Where does this person stand on *Roe v. Wade*, or the *Patriot Act*, or on affirmative action?" Issues like these, generally involving the interpretation of civil liberties and civil rights, are considered to be ideological litmus tests that will help predict how a nominee is likely to behave on the court. Particularly since President Reagan's 1987 nomination of conservative legal scholar Robert Bork, rejected by a Democratic Senate, questions about a nominee's views on these issues and whether he or she considers a ruling like *Roe v. Wade* to be settled precedent—it is, said current Chief Justice and George W. Bush appointee John Roberts during his 2005 confirmation hearings—are standard. Nominees almost always refuse to answer the many questions they get from senators about how they might rule on a particular issue or in a specific set of circumstances. Presidents have expectations, of course, for how their nominees will decide ideologically divisive cases, but they are sometimes surprised.

Broadly speaking, Republican presidents have tended to prefer nominees who appear to lean toward an interpretation of the Constitution that emphasizes its actual words and simple meaning, as well as the intentions of those who drafted it, while Democratic presidents are more likely to favor nominees who believe that constitutional interpretation should involve the application of the general principles found in the Constitution to changing social and economic conditions. The first approach is referred to as *originalism* or *strict constructionism* and the second as *judicial activism*.

The arguments in favor of the originalist approach are as follows:

- Judges are not elected and are not democratically accountable to the people, although the president and Congress are. The courts should not, therefore, go beyond the straightforward interpretation of what the Constitution actually says.
- The democratic process is sidestepped when individuals and groups go to court in an attempt to achieve a decision that they are unlikely to get from Congress or as a result of electoral politics.
- Activist judges tend to be liberal judges whose views are not those of the general public. "The will of the people is replaced by the personal predilections and political biases of a handful of judges," says Republican advisor Karl Rove, expressing a common complaint of conservatives about what they see as the liberal elitism of activist judges.[15]
- Judicial activism violates the principle of separation of powers because it essentially results in non-elected judges legislating from the bench.

The arguments in favor of judicial activism are quite different:

- The Constitution is a living document and needs to be interpreted in light of changing social and economic circumstances and evolving political values. The survival of the Constitution for so long may be credited, in part, to the readiness of judges to adapt its words and principles to changing times.
- While money may buy privileged access to politicians and the airwaves, it is less likely to determine whose issues and arguments get before a court. Public interest groups— such as the ACLU, the NAACP, and the Sierra

Club—and lawyers who do pro bono work on behalf of litigants unable to achieve their goals in Congress or through elections promote democracy by providing greater access to the governmental process.

- Judges of the Supreme Court are more likely than elected politicians to decide issues in ways that are just. They do not have to raise funds for their re-election or listen to lobbyists, and tenure in office during good behavior gives them an independence from the vagaries of public opinion that no elected official enjoys. Consequently, they are more likely to worry about what is right than what is politically most expedient.

More than the members of other segments of America's political elite, Supreme Court judges tend to come from very similar educational backgrounds. Of the 16 justices on the Court between 1986 and 2007, nine had law degrees from Harvard. Another three graduated from Yale, two from Stanford, and one each from Columbia, Northwestern, and Howard University. The preponderance of Ivy League graduates is clear. A typical career pattern leading to the Supreme Court involves legal studies at an elite university; some time in private practice with a prestigious law firm or a clerkship with a Supreme Court justice or other federal court judge; some public service, often with the Justice Department; and appointment as a federal court judge. Although over one-third of Supreme Court justices over the life of the court were not judges prior to their appointment, this seems to have become more rare. All of the members of the Court in 2008 had judicial experience prior to their selection.

---

and in part of legal judgment."[16] Subjectivity aside, Rehnquist states that the existence of significant differences in the way a case has been decided by lower courts is a factor that increases the likelihood that the Supreme Court will grant certiorari.

Before cases are heard, the parties to the cases submit legal briefs to the Court; it is also common for *amicus briefs*—arguments submitted by organizations or individuals who are not direct parties to the case—to be accepted by the Court. Not all cases are accepted for full court deliberation, including oral arguments in the courtroom. For those that are, each side in a case is allowed only 30 minutes to present its oral arguments before the justices. Lawyers' presentations are typically followed by hard questioning from at least some of the judges. And although an hour of oral arguments and some time for the justices' questions may not sound like much, particularly if some important and controversial constitutional principle is at stake, this is nevertheless a crucial stage in the process whereby justices make up their minds. "Oral argument is the absolute indispensable ingredient of appellate advocacy," observed Justice William Brennan (1956-90), one of the most influential justices in the history of the Supreme Court. "Often my whole notion of what a case is about crystallizes at oral argument. This happens even though I read the briefs before oral argument."[17]

Justices of the Supreme Court meet on Wednesdays and Fridays to vote on the cases that they have heard that week. If the Chief Justice is in the majority for a particular ruling, it is his responsibility to decide who will write the decision. The senior justice on the minority side will determine who will write the minority's dissent. Individual justices may choose to include their own opinions, either in support of the majority or against it, but only the majority opinion has official standing as the decision of the court. Dissenting and individual opinions can, however, sometimes, prove influential in future litigation.

Although their law clerks are not present at the voting stage, their role and potential influence are significant before and after the justices reach their decisions. The law clerks carry out essential research before cases are selected for review and are heavily involved in necessary research and even opinion drafting after the justices have voted and a decision has to be written. Some students of the Court argue that the influence of the law clerks is excessive, although there is little beyond anecdotal information on the subject. One recent attempt to measure the impact of law clerks on the votes of justices suggests that it may be about one-third as great as the ideology of the individual judges. "[This] suggests that, at a minimum," conclude Todd Peppers and Christopher Zorn, "the justices rely heavily upon their clerks as sounding boards and advisors in deciding how to vote on the merits of cases."[18]

Ideology and the Supreme Court

In 1937 Justice Owen Roberts, who had been part of a five-member majority ruling against the constitutionality of Franklin Delano Roosevelt's New Deal legislation, dramatically shifted to the other side. This has been called the "switch in time that saved nine," because Roosevelt had made clear that increasing the size of the Supreme Court and nominating justices favorable to his New Deal reforms was a possible solution to the log jam that the Court's rulings produced. Roberts immediately became one of the most famous Supreme Court justices to have changed his judicial ideology from what it was when he was appointed. He is not alone, however. Harry Blackmun, appointed by Republican President Richard Nixon, is considered probably the most dramatic case of ideological change during his 24 years on the Court, shifting from being one of its most conservative to one of its most liberal members. John Paul Stevens, appointed by Republican President Gerald Ford in 1975, is today as liberal as any justice on the Court.

There is no guarantee that the predicted ideological leanings and judicial voting behavior of an appointee to the Supreme Court will turn out to be his or her actual leanings and behavior. However, in selecting a nominee the president and members of both parties are very aware of how they think

A Year in the Life of the Supreme Court

The 2005–06 term saw personnel changes on the highest court for the first time since President Clinton's appointment of Stephen Breyer in 1994. President George W. Bush appointed John Roberts to replace the deceased William Rehnquist as Chief Justice, followed by the appointment of Samuel Alito, who replaced retired Justice Sandra O'Connor. Court watchers expected that the narrow conservative majority on the court would be reinforced by these appointments, although neither Roberts nor Alito generated the sort of ideological fight during Senate confirmation hearings that had been seen in the case of the 1987 Robert Bork (rejected) and 1991 Clarence Thomas (confirmed) nominations.

In fact, the Court appeared less divided during 2005–06 than it had for quite some time. About half of its decisions were unanimous, and another quarter involved at least six-judge majorities. Fewer than one-quarter of the Court's rulings were decided by one vote. However, on some controversial matters—environmental law, the executive branch's war powers, free speech rights of public servants, and the Fourth Amendment's exclusionary rule on evidence unconstitutionally obtained—the Court was divided.

Supreme Court rulings on the Bill of Rights and the Fourteenth Amendment tend to grab the headlines. But during any term the Court rules on a much broader range of questions, including anti-trust law (i.e., competition policy), civil law procedure, federalism, the powers of the executive branch, and other matters. This was true during the 2005–06 term. Among the Court's important rulings were the following:

Death penalty. In *Brown v. Sanders* and *Kansas v. March*, both five to four rulings, the Court upheld the constitutionality of state laws against challenges that would have made it more difficult, in some circumstances, to impose the death penalty.

Election law. In *Randall v. Sorrell*, the Court struck down a Vermont law that limited the amounts donors could give to state parties and candidates and the amounts that those running for state office may spend.

Environmental law. In two five to four rulings, the Court favored a narrow reading of the federal government's authority to regulate wetlands under the 1972 *Clean Water Act*. The reasoning, however, and in particular Justice Kennedy's opinion, seemed to leave the door open to further litigation in support of federal regulation of wetlands.

Free speech. In *Garcetti v. Ceballos*, a divided Court upheld the constitutionality of limits on the free speech rights of public servants, distinguishing between "official" and "private" speech.

Police powers. In three cases involving the Fourth Amendment, the Court limited warrantless police searches in one but supported police powers in another. In the third, a five to four Court ruled that failure to knock and announce themselves before entering a defendant's home is not grounds for excluding evidence in cases where the police have a valid search warrant.

War powers. In probably the most discussed decision of the 2005–06 term, the Court decided that the president lacked the authority to try Guantanamo Bay prisoners through military commissions. The Court did not rule that their detention was illegal; rather, it held that the process used to try them needed to be changed.

the nominee will rule on politically divisive issues. So too are groups and organizations such as the ACLU, the NAACP, the National Organization for Women, the Heritage Foundation, Right to Life, and the Federalist Society as well as individual opinion-leaders, including journalists, editors, and political commentators. They all contribute to a web of ideological expectations that are held for a nominee before he or she has said a word during Senate confirmation hearings.

FIGURE 6.6:   JUSTICES' IDEOLOGY AND THEIR ACTUAL VOTING BEHAVIOR
              ON THE SUPREME COURT

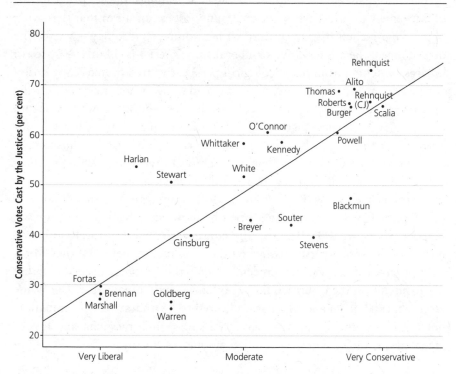

Note: The line represents a prediction of the justices' votes based on their ideology. The closer a point to the line, the stronger the association between the justice's ideology and the justice's votes. Justices above the line voted more conservatively than predicted; justices below the line voted more liberally than predicted.

Source: Lee Epstein, et al., "Ideological Drift Among Supreme Court Justices: Who, When, and How Important?" Northwestern University Law Review 101,4 (2007): 10; used with permission.

Figure 6.6 shows the relationship between newspaper editors' predictions for a Supreme Court appointee's ideological behavior and the appointee's actual voting record on the Court. The straight line indicates predicted behavior, so the further a particular justice is from the line the less his or her actual behavior matches the prediction of newspaper editors. Most justices behave pretty much as they were predicted to, but the fit between expectations and behavior is not tight in every case. Based on a separate study of 16 justices who served at least 10 years and whose full terms on the Court fell between 1937 and 1993—a period that included a dramatic shift in public opinion and policy on civil rights—Lee Epstein and her colleagues found that seven of them remained consistent in their ideological leanings over their years on the Court. Nine changed their leanings, becoming significantly more liberal or conservative, or crossing the ideological divide.[19]

The fact that some drift in the ideological leanings and voting behavior of Supreme Court justices is not uncommon does not mean that the rather obsessive pre-confirmation concern with a nominee's ideology—whether he or she meets the conservative or liberal litmus test—is pointless. Cases of justices switching from one ideological perspective to a dramatically different one are still quite rare. And leaving aside how a nominee rules during his or her years on the Court, selecting a justice who is believed to fit into a particular ideological pigeon hole is politically important. It is a way for a president to keep faith with his base by selecting a justice whose views are believed to reflect those of the party activists and voters whose support helped elect him and who may be needed for re-election.

President George W. Bush discovered the importance of this dimension of Supreme Court appointments when he nominated his longtime advisor, Harriet Miers, in 2005. The socially conservative base of the Republican Party and its spokespersons attacked the nomination, believing that Miers did not have the conservative credentials they thought were needed and that her behavior on the Court would not be sufficiently predictable. The White House backed down and Miers was allowed to "withdraw" her nomination, but not before the president experienced some embarrassment and loss of face with people he normally counted among his friends.

Notes

1 The Federalist Papers can be found at http://www.yale.edu/lawweb/avalon/federal/fed.htm. Quotes here and below are taken from this source.

2 *Federalist No. 81.*

3 Recounted in Don Wolfensberger, "The Politics and Processes of Congress," 8 April 2004. See "Congress Project," http://www.wilsoncenter.org.

4 See http://congress.indiana.edu/radio/commentaries/how_bill_really_becomes_law.php.

5 Edmund Muskie, 21 June 1974, htttp://www.cbo.gov/aboutcbo/introcbo.pdf.

6 Charles O. Jones, *The Presidency as a Separated System*, 2nd ed. (Washington, DC: Brookings Institution Press, 2005) 256–57.

7   Lyndon Baines Johnson, *The Vantage Point: Perspectives of the Presidency, 1963–1969* (New York: Holt, Rinehart and Winston, 1971) 450.

8   Steve Rubenzer and Thomas Faschingbaeur, "The Personality and the Presidency Project," http://www.testingthepresidents.com.

9   Richard A. Brody, "Public Evaluations and Expectations," in James Streling, ed., *Problems and Prospects for Presidential Leadership: The Decade Ahead* (Lanham, MD: University Press of America, 1983).

10 Woodrow Wilson Centre, 2005, http://www.wilsoncenter.org/topics/pubs/threats.pdf.

11 "Lincoln Bedroom Guests Gave $5.4 Million," 26 February 1997, http://edition.cnn.com/ALLPOLITICS/1997/02/26/Clinton.Lincoln/.

12 See http://www.forbes.com/lists and http://www.afi.com.

13 Arthur Schlesinger Jr., "Rating the Presidents: Washington to Clinton," *Political Science Quarterly* 179 (1997).

14 Tocqueville, *Democracy in America*, Book I.

15 Karl Rove, "Address to the Federalist Society," Washington, DC, 10 November 2005.

16 William Rehnquist, *The Supreme Court: How It Was, How It Is* (New York: William Morrow, 1987).

17 Quoted in Joan Biskupic and Elder Witt, *The Supreme Court at Work*, 2nd ed. (Washington, DC: Congressional Quarterly Books, 1997) 243.

18 Todd Peppers and Christopher Zorn, "Law Clerk Influences on Supreme Court Decision Making," 5 March 2007, http://www.uga.edu/pol-sci/home/zorn_paper.pdf.

19 Lee Epstein *et al.*, "Do Political Preferences Change? A Longitudinal Study of US Supreme Court Justices," August 1998, http://epstein.law.northwestern.edu/research/prefchange.html.

PHOTOS (LEFT TO RIGHT)

1. Mother African Methodist Episcopal Zion Church, Harlem. Churches have long been focal points for civic participation in the black community.
2. The "New Deal Coalition" that ensured Democratic control of Congress for a half century from the 1930s emerged during the presidency of Franklin Delano Roosevelt. Image courtesy of the National Archives and Records Administration.
3. The Latino segment of the electorate has been called the "Sleeping Giant" of American politics. As the Latino population increases, both parties have tried to find ways to attract their votes.
4. Although it is frequently argued that the golden rule of politics applies in America—i.e., those with the gold rule—others argue that the power of money is sometimes exaggerated.
5. One of the cherished images of American politics is of town hall democracy, where people come together to manage their common affairs. It continues to operate in some communities across the United States, although state-wide and national politics are necessarily more impersonal.

PART FOUR

Participation and Power

CHAPTER SEVEN

Civic Participation

Introduction

Almost nine out of ten eligible French voters showed up on voting day in April 2007 to cast their ballots for either Nicolas Sarkozy or Ségolène Royal. Unlike France's neighbors Germany, Belgium, and Italy, the law did not require that citizens vote so this impressive level of voter turnout was not produced by the fear of fines for not voting. Nor was it the result of a proportional representation electoral system, a system whose supporters often claim generates higher voter turnout than winner-take-all systems. Instead, it was generated by the enthusiasm of millions of French citizens who perceived the two rivals for the presidency as representing distinct ideological directions for France and whose willingness to spend part of a sunny spring day in line at a polling station was motivated by their desire to make a difference in the outcome.

In 2004 Americans faced a choice that was, arguably, no less momentous than the one facing the French in 2007. Indeed, in the eyes of non-Americans in countries throughout the world, the choice between the Republican President George W. Bush and his Democrat opponent John Kerry was nothing less than a choice between two very different paths for America's role in the world. It is possible that the stakes were perceived as higher by non-Americans than Americans. However, the circumstances of the 2004 election, particularly the war in Iraq, and the fact that the contenders for the presidency appeared to represent very different points on the American political spectrum ensured that Americans too believed that the outcome of the 2004 presidential election was important. In the end, however, fewer than six out of ten eligible voters cast their ballots. Four years later, despite the charisma of Barack Obama and a Democratic campaign that mobilized millions of volunteers, voter turnout was only marginally higher at about 61%.

Measured against the standards of recent decades, the 2004 turnout rate was actually quite good. In most presidential elections almost half of all Americans eligible to vote in presidential elections do not. Voter turnout is even lower during off-year elections when control of Congress is at stake. And things just get worse if one looks at the percentage of Americans who vote in state and municipal elections and on the hundreds of referendum questions—ranging from whether voters are willing to approve a tax increase to pay for new schools to their preferences on stem-cell research—that are asked in any election year. Non-Americans, as well as Americans, often point to these low voter turnout rates—much lower than in many democracies—as proof that American democracy is in rough shape. Apathy, alienation, marginalization, and discrimination are among the reasons given by critics for the failure of so many Americans to exercise their most basic and important democratic right.

TABLE 7.1:   VOTER TURNOUT IN NATIONAL ELECTIONS FOR SELECTED DEMOCRACIES, 1945–2000*

Rank	Country	Turnout as Percentage of Voting Age Population
1	Italy (14)	92.5
2	New Zealand (18)	86.2
3	Belgium (17)	84.9
4	Netherlands (15)	84.8
5	Australia (21)	84.4
6	Denmark (22)	83.6
7	Sweden (17)	83.3
8	Germany (13)	80.6
9	Israel (14)	80.0
10	Norway (14)	79.5
11	Finland (15)	79.0
12	Spain (7)	77.0
13	Ireland (16)	74.9
14	United Kingdom (15)	74.9
15	Japan (21)	69.0
16	Canada (17)	68.4
17	France (15)	67.3
18	Luxembourg (12)	64.1
19	Switzerland (13)	49.3
20	USA (26)	48.3

* Number of elections shown in parentheses.

Source: Adapted from Institute for Democracy and Electoral Assistance, http://www.idea.int.

As Table 7.1 shows, voter turnout in American presidential elections is lower than in the presidential and parliamentary elections of most other affluent democracies. Apologists offer several explanations for this, some of which are more plausible than others.

Higher costs associated with voter registration in the United States. In some countries, such as the UK and Australia, citizens are required by law to register as voters, and once on the list of eligible voters they remain there. In Canada a person of voting age need only check a box when submitting his or her tax return in order to get on the roll of voters. Indeed, in most democracies the list of eligible voters is maintained on a continually updated basis by the state. This is not true in the United States where the onus to register as an eligible voter is on individual Americans. In fact, however, the burden is not as great as is sometimes portrayed. Since the 1993 enactment of the *National Voter Registration Act*, voting age citizens are given the option of checking a box when they renew their driver's license, thereby registering them to vote. And in the lead-up to an election it is common for party volunteers to be at malls, on street corners, and even at churches, where they offer to help fill out the undemanding paperwork that registration involves.

But despite the fact that there are many opportunities to register to vote, a large segment of the voting age population does not bother to register. Some say that this is due to psychological factors (apathy, alienation, cynicism, etc.) that, in turn, may be linked to socio-economic circumstances and race or ethnic group membership. But others argue that structural factors, including the personal costs associated with becoming a registered voter, explain most of the difference between turnout rates in the United States and other democracies.

Americans have more opportunities to vote and are faced with more choices than are citizens elsewhere. An eligible voter in Toronto will probably be provided with three or four occasions to vote during a four-year period. This will include a federal, provincial, and municipal election. In the case of each of the federal and provincial elections, the voter will be given the opportunity to make a single choice: which candidate for the legislature does he or she prefer? Municipal elections provide more opportunities for choice, typically including the mayor, members of council and school boards, and a few other local officials. Altogether, this Torontonian will probably have the opportunity to cast 10–12 votes during a four-year period, most of them for local office-holders.

In San Diego or Boston, however, a registered voter may have three or even four times as many voting opportunities during the same period, on everything from who should become president (and before that, who a party's candidate for the president should be) to who should be the local sheriff. Figure 7.1 shows a fairly typical ballot that an American voter would have been given in the 2004 election. Ballots in local and state elections are sometimes even longer and more complex, often including long and, for some voters, bewildering referendum questions on policy issues and whether taxes should be raised or the government should be allowed to borrow money to finance a particular capital project. To put it simply, Americans do a lot more electing than do citizens in most other democracies.

Some argue that part of the explanation for lower voter turnout in the United States may be the fact that Americans are always going to polls—or

FIGURE 7.1:   THE OREGON BALLOT

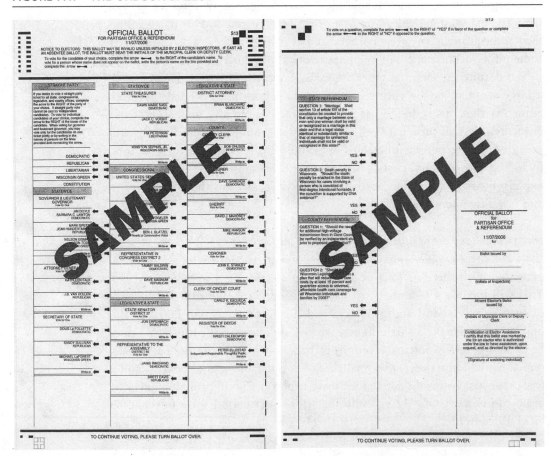

at least being given the chance to go—and so the opportunity and act of voting become less special than if they occur more rarely. Moreover, the personal cost of acquiring information pertaining to many of the officers and issues that Americans are able to vote for is certainly greater than what a voter experiences when the election involves only one level of government and a decision about a single public office.

No amount of spin can transform a voter turnout of 50% or less in a presidential election into something stellar. However, the reality is that civic participation in the United States is far healthier and more widespread than voter turnout numbers suggest. Voting is only one of many forms of citizen engagement, albeit an important one. When Alexis de Tocqueville visited the United States almost two centuries ago, he was struck by the number and vitality of voluntary organizations through which citizens came together to achieve shared purposes without relying on government to do this for them. "As soon as several of the inhabitants of the United States have taken up an opinion or a feeling which they wish to promote in the world," he wrote, "they look out for mutual assistance; and as soon as they have found one another out, they combine. From that moment they are no longer isolated men, but a power seen from afar, whose actions serve for an example and whose language is listened to."[1] These voluntary associations of like-minded individuals were, Tocqueville argued, critically important and influential forms of civic engagement in America.

Turning out with others on a Saturday to clean up litter in one's neighborhood, working unpaid hours for a charity bingo to finance local youth sports teams or a shelter for battered women, signing a petition, and participating in the activities of associations from the Boy Scouts to the Rotary Club are, one might argue, forms of civic participation that are at least as demanding as voting. They are, moreover, forms of participation that Americans have engaged in more often than their counterparts in other democracies. This continues to be the case. Americans may be less likely to vote than Germans or Australians—countries where voting is required by law—or even the French, but they are more likely to sign petitions, give money to private charities, and participate directly alongside their fellow citizens in the management of their common affairs.[2]

Tocqueville thought that the tendency of Americans to join voluntary organizations and the dense associational life of the country were at the heart of American democracy. And so it has troubled some observers that in recent years this tendency has seemed to be in decline. This argument was made famous by Robert Putnam in his book *Bowling Alone*.[3] In it he describes what he calls the "strange disappearance of civic America," the

America that Tocqueville wrote about and which persisted, Putnam argues, until the 1970s. Since then, he says, Americans have become much less likely to join community groups from parent-teachers associations to bowling leagues. The associational tissue that long compensated for the individualistic tendencies in American life, making citizens aware of their connection to others and dependence on them, has been frayed by cultural and social forces. Key among these, Putnam argues, is television and the ensemble of media that have the effect of privatizing our leisure time. Americans still go bowling, he says, but increasingly they bowl alone.

Putnam's thesis about what he claims to be the erosion of American democracy's civic underpinnings received the ultimate political compliment when Presidents Bill Clinton and George W. Bush invited him to the White House to talk about his views on the decline of social capital in America and how it could be reversed. But political scientists have been divided in their assessment of Putnam's thesis. There are two questions here. First, is Putnam correct in claiming that civic engagement in America is in decline? Second, does it matter?

On the first question, the evidence is mixed but certainly not overwhelmingly in support of Putnam's argument. The data reported in *Bowling Alone* shows a sharp drop in the percentage of adult Americans who belong to unions, regularly attend PTA meetings, and are active in their communities through church organizations. On his website, Putnam notes that over the last 25 years in the United States there has been a 58% decline in the attendance at club meetings, a 43% decline in family dinners, and a 35% decline in having friends over for dinner.[4] But some forms of civic engagement seem to have remained steady: levels of volunteerism, according to most studies, have remained fairly constant and charitable giving has actually increased.[5]

There is, of course, the possibility that political and non-political forms of civic participation have been declining among certain groups in American societies, particularly among the poor and racial or other minorities. Indeed, there is quite a lot of research suggesting that participation rates are highly correlated with levels of income and education which, in turn, are linked to one's sense of political efficacy and level of interest. This relationship is displayed in Figure 7.2.

In fact, however, the relationship between ethnicity and race, on the one hand, and civic engagement on the other is neither as straightforward nor as strong as generally believed. Greg Markus and his colleagues have examined the forms and levels of civic participation in lower income, predominantly black communities in various parts of the United States. Along with virtually everyone who has studied political participation in America, Markus notes that those with high incomes and more education are more actively engaged. The participation gap is particularly great between those with very low incomes and those occupying the upper 10–20% of rungs on the income ladder. The conventional explanation has two parts.

FIGURE 7.2:   WHAT LEADS TO CIVIC PARTICIPATION?

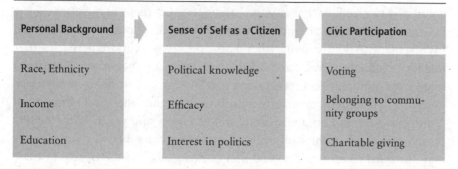

Personal Background		Sense of Self as a Citizen		Civic Participation
Race, Ethnicity		Political knowledge		Voting
Income		Efficacy		Belonging to community groups
Education		Interest in politics		Charitable giving

First, those with more education and higher incomes—these two attributes are highly correlated in the United States as in all developed societies—are more likely than those toward the lower end of these scales to be interested in politics and believe that they can make a difference in what happens— what social scientists call political efficacy. In recent years, surveys have shown that a majority of Americans agree with the statement, "People like me don't have a say in what the government does," but college graduates and those with comparatively high incomes (40%) are much less likely to agree than those with only a high school education (62%) or who fall into the bottom two-thirds of income households (57%).[6]

Secondly, parties, candidates, fundraisers, and interest groups are more likely to target and contact people who have higher levels of education and income. This is undeniably true. Recent American National Election Studies (ANES) surveys show that the likelihood of being contacted by party activists to register and vote during an election year is twice as great for those who have graduated from university compared to high school dropouts. As Markus observes, "That participating inequalities have increased at the same time that income inequalities have ballooned is surely more than coincidental."[7]

However, electoral forms of civic involvement are, Markus acknowledges, only part of the story. Voting, contributing money to a campaign, attending a campaign meeting or rally, wearing a candidate's button, or putting his or her sign on your lawn are all forms of electoral participation. When asked if they had engaged in two or more of these activities in the past four years, the vast majority of respondents in a survey of 14 American cities (total N = 5626) said no. At the higher end were citizens in Portland, Seattle, and Madison, where about one-quarter of respondents claimed to have done at least two of these activities, but in some cities, including Philadelphia and Phoenix, the percentage was not much more than 1 in 10.

The other form of civic involvement includes activities that are not directly connected to elections, parties, and candidates. Levels of non-electoral civic involvement, Markus found, were roughly twice as high as for electoral involvement. Asked whether they had done two or more activities that included contacting an elected official, attending a public meeting on some matter of community concern, taking part in a protest or demonstration, or doing any work for a community organization, slightly more than four out of ten respondents in Portland, Seattle, and Madison said yes. Even at the low participation end of this sample of 14 American cities, between one-quarter and one-third of respondents said they had engaged in at least two of these forms of non-electoral participation during the preceding four years.

The biggest surprise, however, was West Side Chicago. This is an urban community where about one-third of households have incomes below the government's official poverty line, only one in ten residents has graduated from university, and the level of trust in others was the lowest among the urban communities in Markus's study and was less than half the level found in a high trust community like Madison. Despite all of this, the level of non-electoral civic involvement was found to be as high in West Side Chicago as in much more affluent, educated, and trusting Portland, Seattle, and Madison. The electoral civic involvement of West Side Chicagoans was only marginally lower than among the citizens of these other communities. "In fact," says Markus, "after controlling statistically for the effects of education, income and age, this Chicago West Side is easily the most active place in our study on both the non-electoral and electoral participation indexes."[8] What is the explanation for this?

The answer appears to be organizations or, more precisely, the presence of community-based and usually faith-based organizations. Chicago's West Side has an extensive and longstanding network of faith-based organizations that serve to mobilize civic engagement around such issues as policing and racial profiling, education, lending practices, the cost of housing, economic opportunities, and other matters that have obvious policy implications. Moreover, churches were found to be important sites for the direct discussions of political issues. This has long been true of predominantly black churches in the United States. Marginalized and underrepresented in the structures of economic and political power, the churches of black America have provided a disproportionate share of the community's leaders.

So it appears that, in some American communities at least, low levels of education, income, and social trust do not produce low levels of civic involvement. The extent to which the findings from predominantly minority West Side Chicago may be generalized to other low income, low education urban settings, such as Detroit, St. Louis, and Washington, DC, or to poorer rural communities is not clear. It may be that West Side Chicago is, for historical reasons, rather special. Nevertheless, this case demonstrates that the determinants of civic engagement are more complicated than the usual explanation, portrayed in Figure 7.2, suggests.

Charitable Giving

Giving money to an organization or cause whose activities are meant to improve opportunities or living standards for the disadvantaged, protect the environment, promote athletic or artistic endeavors, or finance some other activity whose benefits are expected to be enjoyed by others is a form of civic engagement. Americans do more of this than do the citizens of any democracy. Figure 7.3 shows charitable giving as a percentage of GDP for the United States and several other countries. The data confirm what has long been known: the United States is a nation of givers.

FIGURE 7.3: CHARITABLE GIVING IN SELECTED COUNTRIES (percentage of GDP)

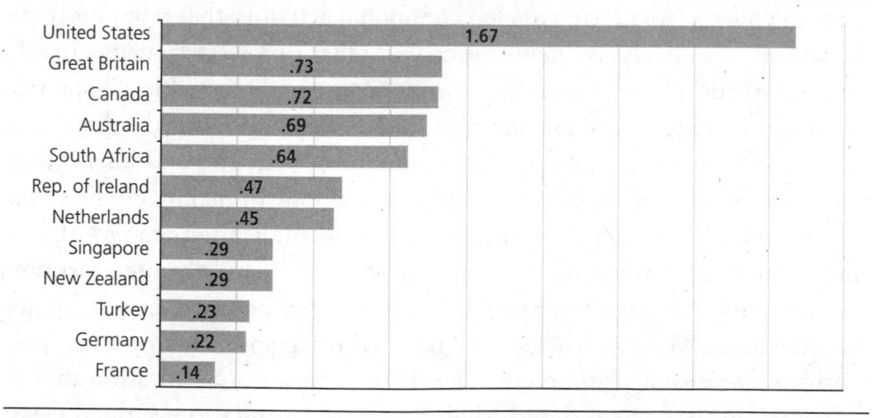

Source: Charities Aid Foundation, International Comparison of Charitable Giving, http://www.cafonline.org.

There is, of course, the possibility that the comparatively high level of giving by Americans is not what it may seem to be. Instead of being due to private generosity and sentiments related to caring and sharing, it could be due to the comparatively lower level of social and cultural spending by American governments combined with generous tax breaks that reduce the cost of such private giving. This is the critical interpretation offered by those who see higher levels of personal charitable giving in the United States as a consequence of the inadequacy of the public sector and, in particular, the feebleness of its welfare state. Americans give more than other citizens because they are taxed at levels too low to pay for services and activities that, in other countries, are financed mainly or exclusively by the state. Taxation policy encourages individuals to believe that the financing of such things as a new medical school, shelters for battered women, or community broadcasting ought to be largely a private matter, depending on the choices and generosity of individuals rather than on public policy.

A second critical interpretation of high levels of charitable giving in the United States is that they conceal enormous inequalities between those who give and those who do not. The wealthy, it is said, account for a disproportionate share of all charitable and philanthropic giving, and, moreover, they prefer to finance university buildings, symphonies, theater companies, and other high-profile causes rather than food banks and summer camps for inner-city kids.

It is difficult to determine the degree to which institutional factors—what some would call welfare state impoverishment combined with the American tax code's more generous breaks for private giving—account for the higher levels of charitable donation in the United States. But even if we assume that institutional factors are more important, we still need to ask why Americans seem to prefer a model of financing communal activities that relies more on the choices of individuals than is the case in other rich Western democracies. In other words, the individualism of Americans, as discussed in Chapter 2, is almost certainly a fundamental part of the explanation for the American model for financing a whole range of communal activities and institutions that, under the European model, are financed wholly or mainly by the state.

The second criticism of charitable giving in the United States—that a small and wealthy minority accounts for most of it, and they tend to prefer university buildings and art to the needs of the poor—does not square with the facts. Wealthy benefactors and their often spectacular acts of philanthropy receive attention; consider, for instance the $30 billion that is managed through the Bill and Melinda Gates Foundation. Nonetheless, Americans of average means give often and, compared to counterparts in other Western countries, more generously. As much as one-third, by some estimate, of this giving is through churches and religious organizations.

The religious impetus associated with much of charitable giving in the United States is an indication of American exceptionalism. In the largely secularized democracies of Western Europe, churches and religious organizations have come to play only a minor role in financing and providing social services. In the United States too, most of these services are provided by state agencies and funded with taxpayer dollars, but the private sector's involvement, mainly through religious organizations, is much more extensive than elsewhere. An important form of civic engagement for many Americans is through their faith community and religious organizations. Indeed religion, not income, education, or even political ideology, is the key determinant of whether one gives to charity and how generously. Arthur Brooks demonstrates that secular Americans are considerably less likely than their religious fellow citizens to engage in virtually all forms of charitable activity from giving money to volunteering their time and even donating blood.[9] Moreover, and perhaps most surprisingly, religious Americans are more likely than their secular counterparts to give to all sorts of charitable organizations, religious *and* secular. The explanation for this, Brooks says, has largely to do with the different ways that religion and secular citizens view the role of government.

FIGURE 7.4:   RELIGION AND COMMUNITARIAN BEHAVIOR

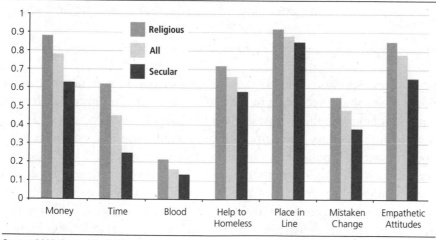

Source: 2002 General Social Survey.

Brooks's findings shed light on the "two Americas" thesis discussed in Chapter 2. Brooks argues that the real fault line in American culture and politics is between those who are religious (whom he defines as those who attend a house of worship regularly or, among those who do not, those who say they spend a lot of time worrying about their spiritual life) and those

Churches and Civic Engagement: Does Faith-based Activity Deserve to be Called Civic Engagement?

The First Baptist Church of Atlanta (http://www.fba.org) is one of an estimated 320,000 houses of worship across the United States. It has a mixed race congregation of several thousand members. For many of these people, the church and its activities are the focus for their involvement in the community. The forms that this involvement takes are numerous and include the following:

- free aerobics classes for women;
- "Branches," a performing ministry of the church's Dramatic Arts Department, which presents "quality drama in the church and in behalf of the church";
- "Single Life Ministry," which supports activities for single mothers;
- vacation Bible school for younger children and "Beach Camp" for teenagers;
- clothing, furniture, and household items provided to missionaries;

- Christian counseling for individuals, couples, and families; and
- extensive missionary activities abroad.

First Baptist Church of Atlanta is larger than most American churches, but the range of its involvement in social and cultural activities is far from exceptional. Many of these activities could be carried out by the state, and in Western European democracies they are without, of course, the faith message that is an essential part of these activities when this church or any other religious organization in America delivers them.

Would you say that the religious component of these activities makes them something other than civic engagement? Are such activities less important forms of citizen participation in their communities than voting, talking about politics, and attending political meetings?

---

who are secular (those who say they have no religion or who never attend a house of worship). According to the Social Capital Community Benchmark Survey,[10] about one-third of Americans fall into the first category and one-quarter in the second. The particular faith community that one belongs to does not matter, Brooks finds; rather, it is the fact of practicing one's religion regularly or thinking often about spiritual matters that makes the difference in one's volunteer activity and charitable giving. As Figure 7.4 shows, religious Americans are more likely to display communitarian behavior and attitudes than other Americans, and they do so in ways that are not limited to the members and activities of their particular faith community.

Rites of Civism and Community

For millions of American school children the day begins with the Pledge of Allegiance and the singing of the national anthem. Virtually every sporting event from high school basketball and American football to professional auto racing and baseball begins with the singing of the Star-Spangled Banner, often accompanied by a military color guard of soldiers proudly displaying the flag. Not only do Americans, unlike many if not most people in France and Belgium, know the words of their national anthem—which is not terribly surprising, given that they have heard it everyday at school—more significantly, many of them sing along when the anthem is played.

Prayer used to be an important part of the rites of civism and community engaged in by Americans in their public spaces and still is in some places. Prayer circles, in which players kneel together while the coach or team captain leads them in prayer before or after a school sporting event, are common throughout the United States, if more so in the South than the North.

Traveling through the United States, one is struck by the ubiquity of the flag. Not only is it displayed on every public building, it frequently is flown in front of corporate offices, gas stations, stores, restaurants, and private homes. And it does not stop there. The flag or some attribute of it have long been one of the staple images used in advertising. It adorns car bumpers, shirts, and baseball caps. The flag even has a nickname, "Old Glory," and has been immortalized in song and poetry.

These are all signs of civism in American life. Viewed from the outside, they may appear to be symptoms of what Tocqueville felt was the excessive and often irritating patriotism of Americans. Some read a more sinister meaning into these daily calls for citizens to declare publicly their loyalty to "the Republic and the values for which it stands." An Israeli couple whose four children were attending American schools for a year described the singing of the anthem and the reciting of the Pledge of Allegiance as "brainwashing."[11] The American writer and social critic Susan Sontag has criticized the flag as representing patriarchy, oppression, and imperial aggression.[12] In the weeks after 9/11, the Berkeley city council prohibited the city's fire trucks from flying American flags, believing that the public proliferation of this symbol was militaristic and no better than the dictum "My country, right or wrong."

The widespread and, by some lights, vulgar abuse of civic symbols like the flag, images of presidents and the White House, and holidays like Independence Day and President's Day to sell everything from divorce services to automobiles, tends to be seen as a particularly egregious case of emptying civic values and symbols of their authentic meaning and harnessing them for mere commercial ends. It is, in fact, difficult to find much that is dignified in an actor dressed to look like Abraham Lincoln extolling television viewers to rush on down to Honest Abe's President's Day blow-out sale on kitchen appliances. However, like the daily recital of the Pledge of

The Pledge of Allegiance: Its History and Controversy

I pledge allegiance to the flag of the United States of America and to the Republic for which it stands, one Nation under God, indivisible, with liberty and justice for all.

The Pledge of Allegiance was written by Baptist minister Francis Bellamy in 1892. The original version did not include the words "under God," which were added by an act of Congress in 1954 during the Cold War, at a time when many Americans believed that the values and institutions they cherished were threatened by "godless communism." Adding the reference to God made clear that religious faith was integral to the American ethos and way of life.

Controversy over the pledge began even before the words were changed, when members of the Jehovah's Witness religion challenged the requirement that their children be required to salute the flag and recite the pledge in public schools. In *West Virginia State Board of Education v. Barnette*, the Supreme Court ruled in their favor. This ruling has since been upheld by a federal district court in a 2006 case that successfully changed a Florida law that required students to stand during recital of the pledge.

A different challenge involves the question of whether the words "under God" in a pledge that has been sanctioned by Congress violates the separation of church and state required by the First Amendment. An atheist father brought suit on behalf of his daughter and won in a 2005 federal district court ruling. However, on appeal to the Supreme Court, it was decided that he did not have standing to bring the case, and so the lower court ruling was overturned. The thorny issue of whether the words of the pledge involve an unconstitutional mixing of church and state has not, therefore, been decided.

Allegiance at the local public school, the prayer said at the beginning of the day's business in the state legislature, and the flag flown atop the roof of the corner gas station, these are ways of reaffirming the shared values of America. They are all rites and symbols of civism, the meta-language (that is, a language that does not necessarily rely on words) through which Americans establish and re-establish their connections with one another and with previous generations.

There is, however, something puzzling in the sheer number and frequency of these reminders of civic pride and national identity. Theories of nationalism generally conclude that nationalist sentiment is a reaction to the awareness of difference, often sharpened by feelings of insecurity, exploitation, or subordination by a more powerful group or external threats. But there can be few countries in the world that, over the last century, have been less threatened territorially or culturally than the United States. Moreover, Americans are generally thought to be quite secure in their sense of who they are and in the superiority of the "American way." Indeed a 2003 survey showed that 96% of Americans believed that foreigners, if given a chance, would leave their homeland for America.[13] Why all these public affirmations and reaffirmations of the civic faith if it faces no serious rivals, at least in the hearts and minds of most Americans?

The solution to this puzzle may lie in the narrative that Americans have constructed about themselves and their history. It is a narrative that has long been linked to a belief in its special destiny. "The eyes of all people are upon us," said John Winthrop, the first governor of Massachusetts Bay Colony. Winthrop wrote these words 400 years ago. When he did, he and other colonial leaders were very conscious of the Old World's regard.

Today, however, the outward and continuous expression of civic pride and reaffirmation of an idealized America are indifferent to the world's opinion and in no way a reaction to the perceptions and actions of others. The sense of special destiny that Winthrop spoke of has been transformed over time into an unshakeable conviction that America and America's story are central to the modern history of mankind. The ubiquity of the flag, the anthem, the portraits, and the mythologies associated with the greatest presidents and all the other civism that one observes in the United States are essential to the interpretative narrative that Americans tell themselves about themselves. They are part of an idealized notion of America and are properly understood as an expression of and a way of maintaining community in a country whose nationalism is based on civic ideals rather than ethnicity or religion.

Notes

1 Tocqueville, *Democracy in America*, Book II.

2 Russel J. Dalton, "Citizenship Norms and Political Participation in America: The Good News is ... The Bad News Is Wrong," Occasional Papers Series, Center for Democracy and Society, Georgetown University, October 2006.

3 Robert Putman, *Bowling Alone: The Collapse and Revival of American Community* (New York: Simon and Schuster, 2000).

4 Robert Putnam, http://www.bowlingalone.com.

5 Based on data reported annually by Independent Sector, "Charitable Giving: September 11th and Beyond, 2004, http://www.independentsector.org.

6 Gregory Markus, "Civic Participation in American Cities," Report of the Civic Engagement Study, Institute for Social Research, University of Michigan (February 2002) 4, citing 1996 ANES. The statistics in the following paragraphs come from this source.

7 Markus 3.

8 Markus 13.

9 Arthur Brooks, *Who Really Cares? The Surprising Truth about Truly Compassionate Conservatism* (New York: Basic Books, 2006).

10 Social Capital Community Benchmark Survey, http://www.sfsv.org/community survey/.

11 Personal communication, 10 July 2007.

12 David Burge, "Pacifists, Dictators Rally for Peace," Cybercast News Service, 5 October 2001, http://www.cnsnews.com.

13 BBC-ICM, "What the World Thinks of America," June 2003, http://www.bbc.co.uk/2/shared/spl/hi/programmes/wtwta/poll/htmil/default.stm.

CHAPTER EIGHT

Equality

Equality is one of the two pillars of the ideal America. But the Declaration of Independence—"all men are created equal, that they are endowed by their Creator with certain unalienable Rights, that among these are Life, Liberty, and the pursuit of Happiness,"—has never been understood by Americans to mean that they should have roughly equal portions of the things that people value. "Endowed by their creator with equal political and legal rights and an equal right to pursue their dreams, *and possibly fail to achieve them*" would be closer to the reality of what most Americans expect when it comes to equality. Karl Marx's famous aphorism, "From each according to his abilities; to each according to his needs," has no positive resonance in the United States. Indeed, it would seem to most to be an absolutely un-American sentiment.

Tocqueville was struck by what he saw as the unparalleled degree of equality in the social conditions of Americans. In arriving at this assessment he was not unaware of the circumstances of black slaves, but like most of his Western contemporaries he was quite ready to overlook the glaring denial to blacks of the rights and conditions thought proper for the white population. Eventually this double standard would be widely seen in America and abroad as racist hypocrisy that undermined the Declaration of Independence's fine words about equality.

Race has been at the heart of political controversy over equality in America since before the Revolutionary War, when the Quakers in particular advocated the abolition of slavery. It remains *the* American dilemma, the title of Gunnar Myrdal's classic 1942 treatise on race relations in the United States.[1] Even slavery, abolished by the Thirteenth Amendment to the

Alexis de Tocqueville on Inequality Between the Races

Three races, naturally distinct, and, I might also say, hostile to each other, are discoverable [in America] at the first glance. Almost insurmountable barriers had been raised between them by education and law, as well as by their origin and outward characteristics, but fortune has brought them together on the same soil, where, although they are mixed, they do not amalgamate, and each race fulfills its destiny apart.

Among these widely differing families of men, the first that attracts attention, the superior intelligence, in power, and in enjoyment, is the white or European race ... below him appear the Negro and the Indians. These two unhappy races have nothing in common, neither birth, nor features, nor language, nor habits. Their only resemblance lies in their misfortunes. Both of them occupy an inferior position in the country they inhabit, both suffer from tyranny, and if their wrongs are not the same, they originate from the same authors.

From Tocqueville, Democracy in America, *Book I, Chapter 18.*

American Constitution, continues to influence American politics and race relations in important ways. Groups such as the NAACP and the Urban League advocate reparations paid to black Americans for the servitude experienced by their ancestors. After leaving office, former President Bill Clinton visited Africa and apologized on behalf of the American people— not in any official capacity as he was no longer president—for his country's role in the slave trade. The language of the slave era still surfaces in America, in rap music, black poetry, and even in political conversation. The famous black singer Harry Belafonte described Colin Powell, who at the time was Secretary of State, as a "house n----r," a term that goes back to plantation slavery. When Illinois senator Barack Obama decided to run for the Democratic presidential nomination, a major controversy ensued in the African American community over whether he was "black enough"; Jesse Jackson and some other prominent leaders in the black community suggesting that he "acted white" on some issues involving race. Obama's father, who was black, had moved to Hawaii from Kenya in 1960, and so his family could not claim any direct connection to the experience of slavery in America. In the eyes of some, this made him insufficiently black to be considered an authentic black American candidate for the presidency.

In more recent times, particularly since the 1980s, the debate on equality in America has acquired another important dimension. This involves inequalities in wealth and whether the nature, scale, and causes of these inequalities undermine American democracy. John Edwards, a candidate for the Democratic presidential nomination in 2004 and again in 2008, broke ranks with most mainstream American politicians in talking about what he called the "two Americas": one affluent and able to afford for itself and its children the opportunity to achieve the American dream and the other struggling to get by, without health insurance and without the ability to pay for the post-secondary education that would enable them and their children to get on the ladder that leads to a middle-class lifestyle. The American way of providing healthcare and post-secondary education are routinely singled out by critics, at home and abroad, as two of the major sources of inequality in America.

A third dimension involves immigration, especially illegal immigration to the United States, mainly by Hispanics from Mexico and other countries of Central America, and their treatment. They pick crops from California to Florida, they work on construction sites from Utah to Maryland, they clean hotel rooms everywhere in the United States, and they often clean and take care of the children of affluent Americans and even their political leaders (Bill Clinton's nomination of Zoe Baird for the post of attorney general and George W. Bush's nomination of Bernard Kerik as secretary of Homeland Security were both withdrawn when it came to light that each had employed illegal immigrants as domestic workers). Their children go to American schools, and they fill the emergency rooms at hospitals in places like Tucson and Houston. The presence of millions of illegal Hispanic immigrants has challenged Americans' image of their country and raised enormously controversial issues over whether and when rights extended to Americans should be given to those who have entered the country illegally.

A fourth dimension is sexual equality. At the same time as some were asking whether Barack Obama was "black enough" to be considered a genuinely black candidate for the Democratic presidential nomination, there were those who asked whether Hillary Clinton was "woman enough" to win the presidency. The question was not whether Americans would vote for a woman—although some expressed doubts on this score—but whether the image that Hillary Clinton projected to many voters was too cold, harsh, and unfeminine to make her an acceptable candidate. This, according to some, reflected a sexist double standard in the sorts of attributes considered positive or negative for political candidates. And it was simply one of the many ways, feminists charged, in which women continued to be discriminated against in America.

Race

The statistics on racial inequality appear bleak. In 2006 in the United States, the rate of poverty was 24.2% among black households (alone or in combination) compared to 10.3% for white (alone); the average income of a black family was only about 60% of what its white counterpart earned. Although blacks account for only about 12% of the population of the United States, they comprise roughly 40% of the prison population and over one-third of those executed for capital offenses. Rates of obesity, heart disease, and violent death are all higher among blacks than whites. Although well-represented among music performers, comedians, and professional basketball and football players, blacks are underrepresented among engineers, accountants, school teachers and business managers. Blacks tend overwhelmingly to live in predominantly black neighborhoods and to send their children to predominantly black schools. White Americans are far more likely than black Americans to believe that policing and the justice system are color blind. In light of all this, the title of Andrew Hacker's bestselling *Two Nations: Black and White, Separate, Hostile, Unequal*[2] seems pretty close to the mark.

But there is another perspective. Between 1967 and 1997, according to various publications of the Bureau of Labor Statistics, the gap between the earnings of black and white women decreased from 78.7% to 94.6% and for black males from 57.2% of what white males earned to 69.3%. The percentage of black Americans with at least a bachelor's degree increased from 3.5% in 1960 to 14.3% in 2000 (compared to an increase of 8.1% to 26.1% for whites). A black American has held every major cabinet post in the federal government, and Illinois Senator Barack Obama became the first black president in 2009. Blacks have been mayors of many of America's largest cities, including Los Angeles, Atlanta, Chicago, Detroit, Houston and Boston. Upscale neighborhoods like Cascade Heights outside of Atlanta, where the luxurious houses routinely have several bedrooms and bathrooms and are priced well beyond the means of an average American household, are almost entirely black. This seems far from the picture of black America that one would have drawn during the period of civil rights marches in the 1960s.

Both of these images are accurate, each emphasizing very different aspects of the conditions of black America. Part of the problem with discussions of race in America is that the conversation takes place against a backdrop of mistrust, sentiments of guilt, anger, and political correctness.[3] An example of how these often confusing and repressed sentiments can shape the conversation on race in America is found in the box opposite.

White and black Americans often perceive the world in very different ways, and the level of trust between the two races is sometimes very low. There is a persistent gap between whites and blacks when asked whether blacks are treated the same as whites in one's community. The gap is nar-

"Harold, call me"

Harold Ford was a black Democratic congressman from Tennessee running for re-election in 2006. The race was a fairly tight one in an election year when every seat in Congress mattered in terms of which party would control the legislative branch.

Several weeks before Election Day, Ford's opponent, Bob Corker, and the Republican National Committee ran a television commercial that became the talk of the nation. In it a playful blonde says, "I met Harold at a Playboy party." The ad's closing segment returns to the apparent Playboy bunny, who says, "Harold, call me," and winks lasciviously.

Charges of racism were immediately made against Ford's opponent. His ad attempted, Democrats said, to use white fears about and objection to interracial sex to mobilize voters against Ford. Nonsense, responded the ad's creators and sponsors. The fact that the woman in the ad was white was sheer coincidence. Most Playboy bunnies are white and a disproportionate number of them are blonde. The selection of a person with such traits merely conformed to the image that most viewers would have of such a person. And, after all, Ford never denied having attended a Playboy club. Those who read racism and fears concerning interracial sex into the ad were, defenders countered, revealing more about their own racist mindset than anything else.

rower than it was several decades ago, but it is still very wide. Asked whether black children have the same chance as white children to get a good education, whites and blacks are as skeptical as they were during the civil rights era (see Figure 8.1). Blacks are more likely than whites to believe that black Americans experience discrimination on account of race in virtually all circumstances but especially in their dealings with the police, at work, and when shopping.[4]

Various studies have suggested, however, that the perception of racial discrimination among black Americans is much greater than their actual experience of it. A 2000 survey for ABC News found that black respondents were much more likely to agree that blacks were discriminated against by taxi drivers, sales clerks in expensive stores, and by the police than they were to have been the victims of such discrimination themselves.[5] Although blacks were more than twice as likely as whites to agree that the police are more likely to pull over black motorists (75% to 33%), the percentage of blacks and whites saying that they personally had been pulled over was virtually identical (55% to 53%).[6] Periodic Gallup polls have confirmed the existence of a considerable gap between black Americans' perception of the extent of discrimination and the degree to which their white fellow citizens believe such race-based discrimination continues to exist.[7] At the same time, however, reliable data show very clearly that the arrest rate for blacks is higher—much higher in many cases—than for whites for almost all crimes. Various studies have shown that the sentences received by black offenders tend to be longer and that the death penalty is three to four times more likely to be imposed on blacks than on whites who have committed similar crimes.[8] Blacks comprise more than half of all persons arrested for robbery, murder, and manslaughter and over one-third of those arrested for such offenses as prostitution, rape, possession of weapons, drug possession and trafficking, and automobile theft. In 1930 blacks accounted for slightly more than one in five Americans behind bars. Today the percentage is closer to two out of five. A black male between the ages of 18 and 24, living in such major American cities as Houston, Detroit, or Washington, DC, is more likely to be in jail or out on probation than in college. There is, in short, abundant evidence to suggest that black Americans are far more likely than whites to commit crime and do time. But is some part of this difference due to race discrimination?

FIGURE 8.1:   DO BLACK CHILDREN HAVE SAME CHANCE AS WHITE CHILDREN TO GET A GOOD EDUCATION IN OWN COMMUNITY, 1962–2001 (% saying yes)

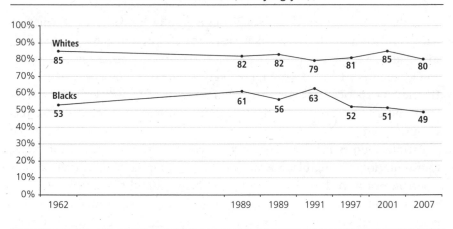

Source: Adapted from Pew Research Center for the People and the Press, The Pew Forum on Religion and Public Life, "Pragmatic Americans Liberal and Conservative on Social Issues," survey released 3 August 2006.

Most serious analysts will concede that it is, as reflected in racist decisions by police officers, prosecutors, judges, and juries. The real debate is over how important a factor discrimination is in explaining this difference between whites and blacks. Discrimination is, in any case, not just or even primarily due to personal bigotry. Economic and family circumstances are more important than personal bigotry in explaining black/white differences in crime rates. Culture is another factor that some argue to be an important cause.

The economic explanation is, however, the most popular. It begins from the empirically verifiable premise that poorer people are more likely than more affluent ones to commit at least certain sorts of crimes (not necessarily white-collar crimes like tax fraud, insider trading, and workplace embezzlement). Black Americans tend to have lower incomes than white Americans and are about three times more likely than whites to fall below the poverty line (see Figure 8.2). But when race is controlled for, it remains the case that poor blacks are more likely than similarly poor whites to be convicted of crimes. This could be due, of course, to discriminatory behavior by those in the justice system, from police officers making arrests to juries determining guilt or innocence, but it is unlikely that the scale of the difference can be explained by this alone.

FIGURE 8.2:   INCOME DISTRIBUTIONS FOR WHITE AND BLACK FAMILIES, 2004

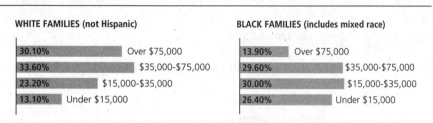

WHITE FAMILIES (not Hispanic)

30.10%	Over $75,000
33.60%	$35,000-$75,000
23.20%	$15,000-$35,000
13.10%	Under $15,000

BLACK FAMILIES (includes mixed race)

13.90%	Over $75,000
29.60%	$35,000-$75,000
30.00%	$15,000-$35,000
26.40%	Under $15,000

Source: Adapted from Gallup Poll Social Audit, "Black-White Relations in the United States, 2001 Update," July 2001, http://media.gallup.com/GPTB/specialReports/sr010711.PDF.

An important part of the explanation for this difference may involve family structure. Black males are far more likely than their white counterparts to be raised without the presence of a father. Daniel Patrick Moynihan, one-time senator from New York State, warned of the potential consequences of this in his 1965 study entitled, *The Negro Family: The Case for National Action.* "[A] community that allows a large number of men to grow up in broken families," he argued, "dominated by women, never acquiring any stable relationship to male authority, never acquiring any set of rational expectations about the future—that community asks for and gets chaos. Crime, violence, unrest, disorder—most particularly the furious, unrestrained lashing out at the whole social structure—that is not only to be expected; it is very near to inevitable. And it is richly deserved."[9] Moynihan's assessment was roundly criticized at the time as racist. Over time, however, it has come to be accepted that family structure has an important impact on such outcomes as the likelihood of finishing school, future employment and income prospects, and the probability of criminal behavior. Some experts argue that it is the lower incomes of single-parent families, usually headed by women, that explain these outcomes. Others maintain that family structure has an independent effect and that it may be even stronger than the effect of income.

Leaving aside the important question of whether income or family structure matters more in explaining the higher rates of crime among black Americans, the data on family structure are disturbing. About 20% of white households are headed by women compared to about 60% of black households. Most of these families are headed by a mother, but it is often the case that they are headed by the children's grandmother or that she and the mother live under the same roof. The reason for this dramatic difference between whites and blacks is not that blacks are more likely than whites to divorce. It is, rather, the much higher rate of births outside of marriage among black women, about three times the rate for whites, that is the cause.[10] Figure 8.3 shows the out-of-marriage birthrates for various racial and ethnic groups in the United States.

FIGURE 8.3:   OUT-OF-MARRIAGE BIRTHS, VARIOUS RACIAL AND ETHNIC GROUPS, 2003

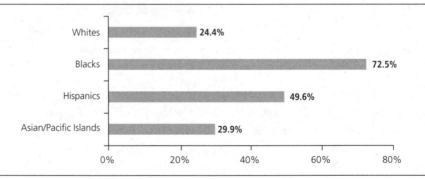

Source: National Center for Health Statistics, http://www.cdc.gov.

Culture is the most contested part of the explanation for race differences in the crime rate. Rap music, for instance, often contains misogynist and violent lyrics, glorifying the "gangsta" lifestyle and portraying the police as the enemy. Hip-hop music videos are sometimes accused of reinforcing a black culture whose role models are all about sex and glamour. This is, however, a charge that can and is made about much popular culture, white and black. Nevertheless, some argue that the work ethic, education and studying, and

Bill Cosby on What Holds Black Americans Back

Ladies and gentlemen, [civil rights leaders]—they opened the doors, they gave us the right, and today ... in our cities and public schools we have 50 percent drop outs. In our own neighborhood, we have men in prison. No longer is a person embarrassed because they're pregnant without a husband ...

Ladies and gentlemen, the lower economic and lower middle economic people are not holding their end in this deal. In the neighborhood that most of us grew up in, parenting is not going on. In the old days, you couldn't hooky school because every drawn shade was an eye. And before your mother got off the bus and to the house, she knew exactly where you had gone, who had gone into the house, and where you got whatever you had and where you got it from. Parents don't know that today.

Brown v. Board of Education is no longer the white person's problem.... Just forget telling your child to go to the Peace Corps. It's right around the corner. It's standing on the corner. It can't speak English. It doesn't want to speak English. I can't even talk the way these people talk. "Why you ain't where you is go, ra."... Everybody knows it's important to speak English except these knuckleheads. You can't land a plane with, "Why you ain't ..." You can't be a doctor with that kind of crap coming out of your mouth.

Excerpts from Bill Cosby's address to the NAACP on the occasion of the fiftieth anniversary of Brown v. Board of Education, *17 May 2004, Chicago.*

the values and lifestyle of the middle-class, predominantly white society are rejected by a significant portion of black youth as being alien to authentic black American culture. Fear of being thought by others as "acting white" operates, according to the prominent black comedian Bill Cosby, to keep blacks within a ghetto of their own making

The response to Cosby's criticism is that centuries of discrimination at the hands of whites have generated pathological and self-destructive behavior among blacks. The common use of the "N-word" among African Americans in addressing one another and in black popular culture is sometimes argued to be a symptom of self-hatred that finds expression in the banalization of a word whose original significance, as Andrew Hacker observes, "implie[d] a creature so debased and degraded, that such a person must represent a lower level of humanity." Hacker places the responsibility for a subculture that seems to tolerate and even glorify violence on white America. "It is white America that has made being black so disconsolate an estate," he says. "Legal slavery may be in the past, but segregation and subordination have been allowed to persist. Even today, America imposes a stigma on every black child at birth."[11] At the same time, it should be acknowledged that many black Americans, if not most of their spokespersons, seem to agree with Cosby. A 2007 survey conducted by the Pew Research Center and the Press reported that 53% of black Americans agreed that blacks who do not get ahead are mainly responsible for their own condition, versus 30% who said this was due to discrimination.[12]

The persistence of segregation, more than half a century after *Brown v. Board of Education* declared that laws permitting or even requiring racial segregation were unconstitutional, is beyond question. The preceding discussion suggests that the segregation may be to some degree cultural, black America tending to have different values from white America. This difference should not be exaggerated, however. Rap, hip-hop music, fashions, and ways of speaking that are considered "urban"—code for black in America—are immensely popular across American society. The vast majority of Americans, white and black, say that they approve of interracial marriage, a dramatic shift from a generation ago. Cultural racial segregation, to the extent that it exists, is chiefly between a relatively small portion of the black underclass and the rest of society. Historically black colleges like Howard, Spellman, and Morehouse and Black Studies programs, which by their nature are built

From Separate but Equal to Separate is not Equal

Court decisions have played an important role in the political struggle for civil rights in the United States. Two of the landmark rulings on laws enforcing racial segregation are *Plessy v. Ferguson, 1896* and *Brown v. Topeka, 1954*. The decisions are as different as night and day.

In the *Plessy* case, an 1890 Louisiana law that prohibited blacks from riding in railway cars reserved for whites was upheld by the Supreme Court. The plaintiff claimed that his right to equality under the law, guaranteed by the Fourteenth Amendment, was thereby violated. A majority on the court ruled that this was not the case. Here is what they said:

The object of the [Fourteenth] amendment was undoubtedly to enforce the absolute equality of the two races before the law, but in the nature of things it could not have been intended to abolish distinctions based upon color, or to enforce social, as distinguished from political, equality, or a commingling of the two races upon terms unsatisfactory to either. Laws permitting, and even requiring their separation in places where they are liable to be brought into

contact do not necessarily imply the inferiority of either race to the other....

... Legislation is powerless to eradicate racial instincts or to abolish distinctions based upon physical differences, and the attempt to do so can only result in accentuating the difficulties of the present situation. If the civil and political rights of both races be equal, one cannot be inferior to the other civilly or politically. If one race be inferior to the other socially, the Constitution of the United States cannot put them upon the same plane.

It is usual to cite the *Plessy* ruling as an illustration of the hypocrisy of American democracy during that era. But were Americans alone? Even if no law in Canada prohibited a black person from sitting alongside a white person on a train from Toronto to Montreal, would he have done so (especially a black male next to a white female)? Where blacks and whites lived near each other in French, British, Belgian, or Portuguese colonies, did they eat in the same restaurants and did their children attend the same schools? The answer is no.

Moreover, there was a dissenting opinion in the *Plessy* case, just as a segment of American public opinion did not concur with the separate but equal principle set forth in that decision. Justice Harlan spoke for this minority point of view:

If laws of like character should be enacted in the several states of the Union, the effect would be in the highest degree mischievous. Slavery as an institution tolerated by law would, it is true, have disappeared from our country, but there would remain a power in the states, by sinister legislation, to interfere with the full enjoyment of the blessings of freedom ... and to place in a condition of legal inferiority a large body of American citizens....

The times caught up to Justice Harlan in 1954 when the case of *Brown v. Topeka* came before the Supreme Court. This time the circumstances involved a Kansas law that banned black students from all-white schools. The NAACP brought the case on behalf of an 11-year-old girl by the name of Linda Brown. Although Jim Crow laws enforcing racial segregation were still common across the United States and even where they did not exist the actual mixing of blacks and whites in schools, neighborhoods, and other public and private places was uncommon, public opinion had changed from what it was when *Plessy* was decided. The American military had been racially integrated under President Truman in the 1940s. The black civil rights movement, supported by some northern politicians and opinion leaders, became more active in bringing the issue of racial inequality to the public's attention. Public opinion, at least in the North, gradually became more accepting of the idea of integration.

Speaking for a unanimous court, Chief Justice Earl Warren was categorical in overturning the separate-but-equal rule that had been established in *Plessy*. "In approaching this problem," he said, "we cannot turn the clock back to 1868, when the [Fourteenth] Amendment was adopted, or even to 1896, when

Plessy v. Ferguson was written. We must consider public education in the light of its full development and its present place in American life throughout the Nation. Only in this way can it be determined if segregation in public schools deprives these plaintiffs of the equal protection of the laws."

The Court had no doubt that in matters of education, "Separate educational facilities are inherently unequal." Relying on evidence from social psychology that was submitted to the Court, Chief Justice Warren expounded on what he and his colleagues saw as the broader effects of educational segregation:

To separate [students] from others of similar age and qualifications solely because of their race generates a feeling of inferiority as to their status in the community that may affect their hearts and minds in a way unlikely ever to be undone.... The impact is greater when it has the sanction of the law, for the policy of separating the races is usually interpreted as denoting the inferiority of the negro group. A sense of inferiority affects the motivation of a child to learn. Segregation with the sanction of the law, therefore, has a tendency to [retard] the educational and mental development of negro children and to deprive them of some of the benefits they would received in a racially integrated school system. Whatever may have been the extent of psychological knowledge at the time of Plessy v. Ferguson, *this finding is amply supported by modern authority.*

The confidence that the Court expressed in the benefits for blacks of being taught in classrooms alongside whites is no longer shared by all educational psychologists. Some argue that all-black schools may actually improve the learning experience for black students. Historically black colleges in the United States have experienced a revival over the last couple of decades, due partly to this belief that an all-black educational setting may carry advantages in terms of learning and self-esteem.[13]

on the concept of a separate black identity, emphasize the separateness and otherness of blacks and may also be thought to perpetuate a sort of cultural segregation.

America's Underclass

Poverty in America is disproportionately black. And at the bottom end of the poverty scale is a particularly impoverished segment of the population that has become associated in the minds of many, at home and abroad, with black America. It is the underclass. The existence and characteristics of the underclass, although not the term itself, were brought to the world's attention in Daniel Patrick Moynihan's 1965 report, *The Negro Family: The Case for National Action*. William Julius Wilson, one of the foremost scholars of black poverty in the United States, describes the underclass this way:

> [It is] that heterogeneous grouping of families and individuals who are outside the mainstream of the American occupational system. [It includes] individuals who lack training and skills and either experience long-term unemployment or are not members of the labor force, individuals who are engaged in street crime and other forms of aberrant behavior, and families that experience long-term spells of poverty and/or welfare dependency.[14]

Statistically speaking, the underclass is disproportionately black, although it contains significant numbers of whites and Hispanics. Although the actual size of the underclass is a subject of disagreement, depending on the particular definition of this group, it is usually placed at between 2 and 3 million Americans. But the image of the underclass in popular culture and that is often communicated by politicians and others who frame the conversation on race and poverty frequently suggests that it is much larger. Indeed, if Hollywood films were one's only source of information, a person might well conclude that black Americans are far more likely to be part of the underclass than the middle class.[15]

But it is the continuing physical segregation of the races in America that is most striking (although it should be said that the extent of this segregation is probably no greater than in France or Britain). This segregation is no longer, of course, the result of laws and public policies. Indeed, the court-ordered school busing programs that began in the 1960s and various forms of affirmative action in college admissions, public employment and the awarding of public contracts are policies that have aimed at increasing the integration of the races. This has not been without some success. Police forces, fire departments, and the civil service of many cities, states, and the federal government, particularly in Washington, DC, are more racially integrated than they were before the 1964 passage of the *Civil Rights Act*.[16] But in terms of where blacks and whites live, where their children go to school, and even with whom they pray, a sort of de facto segregation reigns.

A city such as metropolitan Detroit represents the extreme end of racial segregation in housing. In 1960 about 29% of Detroit's population of 1,670,144 was black. In 2000, 82% of its much diminished population of 951,270 was black. On the other hand, Grosse Pointe, situated on the northern edge of Detroit and one of the most affluent communities in the United States, is 94% white and only 2.5% black. Bloomfield Hills, another edge city just outside of Detroit, is highly affluent and 84% white and only 7% black. The dramatic transition from Detroit to Grosse Pointe always amazes those who experience it for the first time. The liquor stores, barred windows, and boarded-up buildings of Detroit suddenly are replaced at the city line by the clean prosperity and even opulence of Grosse Pointe. It was at this border that National Guard troops in tanks had their guns pointed toward Detroit during the riots in the summer of 1967.

Detroit is not alone when it comes to racial segregation, although it is at the high end of the scale. Chicago, New York, Philadelphia, St. Louis, Miami, Cleveland, and Newark all have very high rates of urban segregation. The good news is that in most of these metropolitan areas, and in the country as a whole, the level of residential segregation of whites from blacks has fallen. Table 8.1 shows what demographers call the *dissimilarity index*. It signifies the percentage of members of one race who would have to move in order for an area to have even numbers of residents from both races. A high number therefore signifies a high level of residential segregation and a low number a more racially integrated urban area. The data shows that the index of dissimilarity for blacks from whites declined from 73.9 in 1980 to 65.2 in 2000; moreover, racial integration actually increased in 240 of the 255 metropolitan areas covered by the American census.

Racial segregation in housing patterns tends to produce racially segregated schools. But although there has been some measurable decline in residential segregation, this has not been true of racial segregation in American schools. In most states the percentage of white students in a school attended by the average black student actually declined between 1980 and 2003.[17] Table 8.2 shows the states in which black/white segregation was highest in 2003–04. To take one state as an example, 86% of black students in New

York attend a school where the majority of students belong to the black minority. Fully 61% of New York State's black students attend a school where 90% to 100% of all students are non-white. The average black student in this state attends a school whose student population is only 18% white.

TABLE 8.1:   SEGREGATION IN METROPOLITAN AREAS, 1980–2000

Measure	Blacks From Whites	Hispanics From Whites	Asians From Whites
Index of Dissimilarity			
1980	73.9	51.0	41.8
1990	68.9	50.7	41.9
2000	65.2	51.6	42.2
Average Percentage Change in the Decade			
1980 to 1990	-5.8	0.7	1.9
1990 to 2000	-4.6	4.9	2.1
Number of Metropolises, by the Direction of Change			
1980 to 2000			
Index of segregation was higher in 2000 than in 1980	15	124	69
Index of segregation was lower in 2000 than in 1980	240	86	47

Source: Adapted from John R. Logan, Brian J. Stults, and Reynolds Farley, "Segregation of Minorities in the Metropolis: Two Decades of Change," Demography 41,1 (February 2004): 6.

Martin Luther King, Jr. once described 10:00 a.m. on Sunday as America's most segregated hour. He meant by this that blacks generally attended all-black churches and whites attended churches where the congregation was either entirely white or contained only a smattering of non-white members. This continues to be the case, due, in large measure, to the fact that blacks and whites tend to live in separate neighborhoods and most church-goers attend a church close to home. The style of preaching, the music, and the nature of the interaction between the pastor and the congregation are all quite different. The more dynamic and engaged gospel style is much more common among black churches, although many predominantly white Evangelical churches also favor a style of preaching and worshipper engagement that resembles that of black gospel churches.

TABLE 8.2:   MOST SEGREGATED STATES FOR BLACK STUDENTS, 2003–2004

Rank	% Black in Majority-Minority Schools		% Black in 90–100% Minority Schools		% Black Exposure to White	
1	California	87	New York	61	New York	18
2	New York	86	Illinois	60	Illinois	19
3	Illinois	82	Michigan	60	Michigan	22
4	Maryland	81	Maryland	53	California	22
5	Michigan	79	New Jersey	49	Maryland	23
6	Texas	78	Pennsylvania	47	New Jersey	25
7	New Jersey	77	Alabama	46	Mississippi	26
8	Louisiana	77	Wisconsin	45	Louisiana	27
9	Mississippi	76	Mississippi	45	Texas	27
10	Georgia	73	Louisiana	41	Wisconsin	29
11	Wisconsin	72	Missouri	41	Pennsylvania	30
12	Connecticut	72	Ohio	38	Georgia	30
13	Pennsylvania	72	California	38	Alabama	30
14	Ohio	71	Texas	38	Hawaii	32
15	Alabama	70	Georgia	37	Ohio	32
16	Arkansas	69	Florida	32	Connecticut	32
17	Nevada	69	Connecticut	31	Missouri	33
18	Massachusetts	67	Massachusetts	26	Florida	34
19	Florida	67	Indiana	23	Arkansas	36
20	Missouri	67	Arkansas	23	Nevada	38

Source: Adapted from Gary Orfield and Chunmei Lee, "Racial Transformation and the Changing Nature of Segregation," The Civil Rights Project, Harvard University (January 2006): 26, Table 11.

Affirmative Action

In order to speed up the pace of racial integration, legislatures in the United States have, since the 1960s, instituted various policies whose goal has been to increase the representation of blacks in universities, the public sector workforce, and in the suppliers of goods and services to governments and their agencies. Such policies are usually referred to as *affirmative action*. Those who oppose them are more likely to call such policies preferential treatment or reverse discrimination. Their advocates will sometimes describe these policies as compensatory redress for past injustice. Whatever label is used to describe them, affirmative action policies involve identifying people according to some ascribed trait such as race (sex and ethnicity followed race as attributes used in some affirmative action programs) and making decisions about people in part on the basis of this attribute.

Americans have been quite ambivalent about affirmative action, an ambivalence reflected in judicial rulings on the constitutionality of using race or any other ascriptive criterion as a basis for treating persons differently. Based on a review of polling data from 1972 through 1990, sociologist Seymour Martin Lipset concluded that the conflicted views of Americans toward affirmative action reflected the struggle in the American creed between values of egalitarianism and individualism. "Americans distinguish compensatory action from preferential treatment," he observed. "Few object to the former, which helps disadvantaged people improve their qualifications by special training and community development. But most object to the latter, in which standards of admission or employment are lowered for disadvantaged people."[18] The ambivalence that Lipset describes continues to show up in polling data on affirmative action. Table 8.3 shows that when such policies are framed as compensation for past injustices (Part A), they tend to enjoy widespread support. But when they are characterized as preferential treatment for the members of some groups over others (Part B), they are overwhelmingly rejected. The conflicted nature of Americans' views on affirmative action is even more evident from Figure 8.4. Part A seems to show pretty solid support for university admissions policies that aim to increase the representation of minorities. But Part B, where the same policy is framed differently, suggests that most Americans, including members of minority groups, prefer a solely merit-based admissions policy.

TABLE 8.3:   VARIED RESPONSES TO AFFIRMATIVE ACTION

Part A: In order to overcome past discrimination, do you favor or oppose affirmative action programs ...
... designed to help blacks, women, and other minorities get better jobs and education?

Favor 63	Oppose 29	DK/Ref 8

... which give special preferences to qualified blacks, women, and other minorities in hiring and education?

Favor 57	Oppose 35	DK/Ref 8

Part B: We should make every possible effort to improve the position of blacks and other minorities, even if it means giving them preferential treatment.*

Agree 24	Disagree 72	DK/Ref 4

* Asked in July 2002.

Source: "Conflicted views of affirmative action," The Pew Center for the People and the Press, 14 May 2003; reprinted with permission.

FIGURE 8.4:   PUBLIC AMBIVALENCE TOWARD AFFIRMATIVE ACTION IN
                       UNIVERSITY ADMISSIONS

Part A: All in all, do you think affirmative action programs designed to increase the number of
black and minority students on college campuses are a good or bad thing?

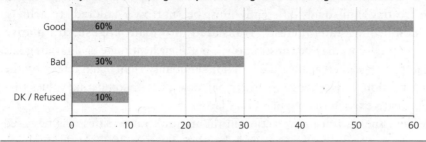

Source: "Conflicted views of affirmative action," The Pew Center for the People and the Press, 14 May 2003.

Part B: Which comes closer to your view about evaluating students for admission into a college
or university: applicants should be admitted solely on the basis of merit, even if that results in
few minority students being admitted (or) an applicant's racial and ethnic background should be
considered to help promote diversity on college campuses, even if that means admitting some
minority students who otherwise would not be admitted?

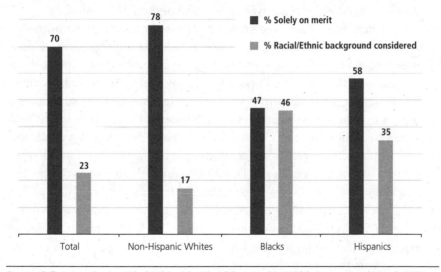

Source: Gallup News Service, "Black-White Educational Opportunities Widely Seen as Equal," 2 July 2005.

The ambivalence of the American public when it comes to affirmative action is mirrored in court rulings on whether such programs violate the Fourteenth Amendment's guarantee of equal protection under the law. In *Bakke v. the Regents of the University of California*, 438 U.S. 265 (1978), a white male who was denied admission to the medical school at UCLA challenged the constitutionality of the school's admissions policy on the grounds that it recognized race as a criterion for admission and that many black applicants with lower test scores than his were admitted. The Supreme Court upheld this affirmative action policy, ruling that race could be used as an admissions criterion but that the use of group membership as a basis for treating individuals differently must be "narrowly tailored" to achieve a "compelling state interest." Translated into plain English, affirmative action programs may be constitutional, but their legitimate egalitarian goals need to be weighed against the individual equality rights guaranteed by the Constitution. This is the same tricky balancing act of competing values that appears to exist in the population at large.

The issue of affirmative action in the nation's universities was revisited in a pair of Supreme Court rulings handed down in 2003, both involving the University of Michigan. Several of the justices who heard these cases had been appointed by Republican presidents, and there was a belief among some that this could result in *Bakke* being overturned. But in fact the spirit of that earlier decision was upheld, and the court, although divided, showed a sensitivity to the balancing act between individual rights and fair treatment for disadvantaged groups that was also found in the *Bakke* ruling.

The Michigan cases involved challenges brought against the admissions policy of the law school, *Grutter v. Bollinger*, and the undergraduate admissions policy, *Gratz v. Bollinger*. In the *Grutter* case, the court upheld by a five to four vote the law school's policy of giving preference to some African Americans and ethnic minorities with lower test scores than some white applicants, a policy that the university defended on the grounds that it was instituted to achieve diversity in the student body and that this condition was relevant to the university's educational goals. "We expect that 25 years from now," wrote Justice Sandra Day O'Connor, "the use of racial preferences will no longer be necessary to further the interest approved today." But in the *Gratz* case, the court decided six to three that the university's point system, which awarded 20 admission points to black, Hispanic, and Native American applicants, did not meet the test of being "narrowly tailored" to meet the diversity goals of the university.

Class

"The rich, the poor and the growing gap between them." This leader from a 2006 article that appeared in *The Economist*[19] expresses the conventional wisdom on class inequality in America. "Rags to rags, riches to riches," was the conclusion of a 2007 article in the influential monthly, *The Atlantic*.[20]

The Image of America as Racist: Fact or Fiction?

... [T]hough America has made progress, the goal of a race-irrelevant society remains distant [and] is perhaps unattainable. Middle-income blacks will sometimes feel that race explains why they are less likely to be judged as individuals and more likely to be judged as affirmative-action symbols; for lower-income blacks, especially young ones, race can explain to them why they have not done as well as they would like; both middle- and lower-income blacks may think that any police officer who stops them is engaging in unjustified racial profiling. True or false, these beliefs remind us that, as W.E.B. Dubois put it, blacks feel a "two-ness": they are American and they are black, and so have "two souls, two thoughts, two unreconciled strivings, two warring ideals in one dark body."

The progress that America has made in the treatment of racial and ethnic groups ought to be a source of self-congratulation. But there is very little self-congratulation going on. When I was doing research on the politics of black Americans during the 1950s, race wasn't generally a topic of conversation, even though there was much that cried out for debate. At the time, blacks found themselves residentially segregated, economically deprived, and politically manipulated to a far greater extent than they do now. These days, when things are so much better, we sometimes talk about race as if the nation were stuck in a dark period of unbridled racism.... In [black leader] Al Sharpton's word, "confrontation works," and so confrontation continues.

Excerpts from James Q. Wilson, "Race in America," http://www.manhattan-institute.org/turningintellect/book/pdfs/chapter3/pdf.

"Maybe it's time to stop calling America 'the land of opportunity,'" says the author of that article, Clive Crook, a sentiment that is a virtual heresy to those who believe in the American dream. But even some politicians, from both the right and the left, have questioned whether the dream has moved beyond the reach of many Americans. Some blame globalization and what they see as greedy corporations outsourcing the livelihoods and prospects of American workers. Others blame illegal immigration, which they claim has had a depressing effect on wages.

The facts on the distribution of income and wealth in the United States are not as clear as headlines and hand-wringing over the growing gap between the rich and the poor suggest. Inequality is greater than it was a generation ago, and it is also greater than in any other advanced industrialized democracy. Beyond these facts, however, the picture is somewhat murkier. Figure 8.5 shows the national income share for the top-earning one-thousandth of families in the United States, the UK, and France. By 2000, over 7% of all income was accounted for by the richest one-thousandth of all families, a significant increase since the 1960s, when the proportion was only about 2%. But it is no higher than the share that went to a small fraction of all families during the first few decades of the twentieth century. The figure shows relatively higher levels of income inequality for all three countries until World War II, followed by a period of reduced inequality between the 1940s and 1980s. Since then inequality in the United States has spiked, reaching levels not seen since before the stock market crash of 1929. Inequality has increased more modestly in the UK, while in France the share of national income going to the richest households appears to have remained fairly stable for two generations.

FIGURE 8.5:   TOP 0.1 PER CENT INCOME SHARES IN THE UNITED STATES, FRANCE, AND THE UNITED KINGDOM, 1913–1998

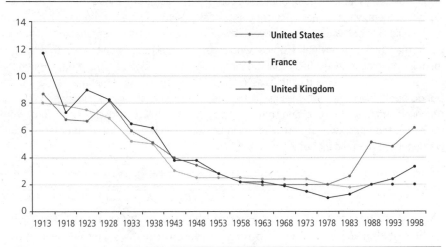

Source: Adapted from Thomas Piketty and Emmanuel Saez, "Income Inequality in the United States, 1913–2002," November 2004, Figure 12, http://elsa.berkeley.edu/~saez/pikettysaezOUP04US.pdf.

If instead of looking at the income share of the top one-thousandth of families we focus on the leading 10% of households, the picture is fundamentally the same. The top 10% accounted for between about 40 and 47% of income from 1920 to 1940. This dropped sharply to between 32 and 35% from World War II until the late 1980s. Since then there has been a steady increase in inequality, the wealthiest 10% of households accounting for about 42% of income by 2002. But if we look at the distribution of wealth instead of income, the picture is rather different. The share of the nation's wealth held by the richest one-thousandth of families has, by some calculations, remained pretty stable since the middle of the twentieth century.

Another way of looking at the long-term trend in economic inequality is to compare the rates and direction of change in real incomes for the wealthiest tax-filers and the rest of American society. This is done in Figure 8.6. The data show that the relative well-being of the bottom 99% of tax-filers compared to the top 1% improved from World War II until the 1970s. Since then the top 1% of tax-filers have improved their position *vis-à-vis* the bottom 99%. The apparent stagnation in real incomes since the 1970s for the bottom 99% of tax-filers is, however, rather misleading. Some estimates suggest that real incomes for this bottom 99% in fact grew by about 40% from 1973 to 2002, and that the incomes of the richest 1% also grew more sharply than shown in this figure, but that the relative gains of the richest 1% outpaced those of the bottom 99%.

FIGURE 8.6:   AVERAGE REAL INCOME OF BOTTOM 99 PER CENT AND TOP 1
               PER CENT IN THE UNITED STATES, 1917–2002

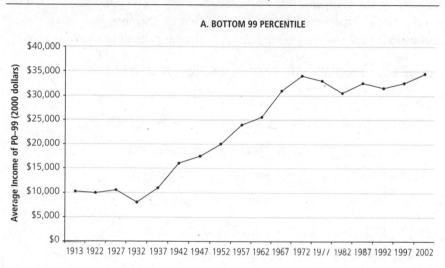

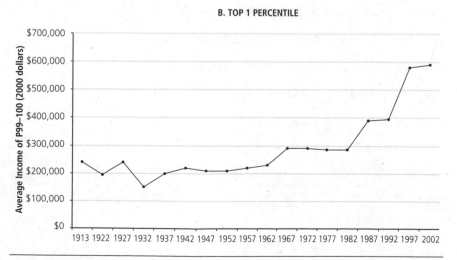

Source: Adapted from Piketty and Saez, Figure 12.

Compared to other wealthy democracies, the distribution of income in the United States is more unequal. Economists use what are called *Gini coefficients* as a measure of the distribution of income in a society. A value of 1.0 indicates that all income is controlled by one person or household, while a value of 0.0 would indicate that all persons or households have the same income. Figure 8.7 shows that the measure of inequality is considerably greater in the United States than in most other countries. In fact, it is closer to the level of inequality observed in some developing countries such as Brazil and Mexico than to the levels found in some Scandinavian and northern European societies. The outlier status of the United States is also reflected in the compensation of those who run its companies compared to the pay of their workers. Table 8.4 shows that the gap between what bosses and workers earn in the United States is far wider than elsewhere.

FIGURE 8.7:   INCOME DISTRIBUTION, GINI COEFFICIENT* (2000 or most recent year)

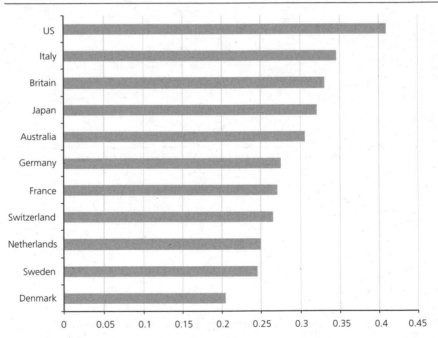

*0=Perfect equality of income, 1=Perfect inequality of income.

Sources: *National Survey of Family Income and Expenditure; OECD; World Bank*, The Economist, *17 June 2006: 48.*

TABLE 8.4:   CEO COMPENSATION AND PAY OF PRODUCTION WORKERS IN MANUFACTURING, 2001 (US$)

Country	CEO/Worker Pay Ratio	Country Rank by Ratio
US	44	1
Australia	33	2
France	32	3
UK	31	4
Sweden	21	5
Canada	21	6
Germany	17	7
Japan	16	8

Source: Adapted from Lars Osberg and Timothy Smeeding, "'Fair' Inequality? An International Comparison of Attitudes to Pay Differentials," Russell Sage Foundation, Occasional Papers (21 June 2005): 31.

Given the foregoing numbers, one might assume that economic inequality would be one of the prominent fault lines in American politics. But, as Alan Wolfe observes, "If anything is a truism in American politics, it is that people do not care about income inequality."[21] In fact, this is only partly true. Class envy—even the sentiment of belonging to a class whose economic interests are opposed to those of another—do not run very deep in the United States. People are much more likely to admire the wealth of a Bill Gates or Oprah Winfrey than want to confiscate it through wealth taxes or some other means. Ladd and Bowman's observation that "Americans tolerate great differences in wealth if they believe that opportunity is broadly present,"[22] is undeniably true. By and large, Americans believe that these opportunities are widespread and available to those who wish to pursue them. As we saw in Chapter 4, Americans are less likely than the citizens of other rich democracies to blame circumstances beyond the control of the individual for his or her material failure.

This does not mean, however, that Americans will tolerate any level of economic inequality. Table 8.5 shows the averages for the United States and several other countries in what individuals say should be the ratio between what earners at the top and bottom of the income ladder make. The average of 9.68 for American respondents—meaning, on average, a top level of pay that is just a bit under ten times what earners at the bottom make—is not as great as in Japan, France, the UK, and Canada. Compared to Scandinavian populations, Americans seem to be much more tolerant of a wider earnings gap, but the same may be said for almost all countries. Earlier cross-national surveys found that Americans seemed to be significantly more tolerant of pay gaps than were the citizens of other countries.[23] This no longer appears to be the case. The diminished tolerance of wide earnings gaps has not, how-ever, found its way into the mainstream of American politics. "A chicken in every pot" and "A car in every garage" are slogans that have resonated with American voters over the years, but "Make the rich pay" sets few hearts rac-ing (except those of the rich!).

TABLE 8.5:   DISTRIBUTIONS OF SHOULD-EARN RATIONS ACROSS COUNTRIES, 1999

Country	Mean Max/Min Ratio	Country Rank by Mean Max/Min Ratio
Japan	12.347	1
France	11.615	2
United Kingdom	10.945	3
Canada	10.156	4
United States	9.680	5
Northern Ireland	8.097	6
Austria	8.050	7
New Zealand	7.982	8
Israel	7.750	9
Portugal	7.722	10
Germany	7.553	11
Australia	6.110	12
Sweden	4.018	13
Norway	3.206	14
Spain	3.313	15

Source: Adapted from Lars Osberg and Timothy Smeeding, "'Fair' Inequality? An International Comparison of Attitudes to Pay Differentials," Russell Sage Foundation, Occasional Papers (21 June 2005): 31.

Given that roughly 40 million Americans live below the poverty line (as of 2005), the fact that the gap between the rich and poor has not been more effectively exploited in American politics may seem surprising. There are three main reasons for this. First, the value system of Americans, which tends to emphasize individual self-reliance and the belief in the opportunity of all to succeed in life, is widespread. Those with lower incomes are about as likely as citizens with higher incomes to believe that "People should take more responsibility to provide for themselves"—the percentages agreeing for the lower, middle, and upper thirds of income earners were 21, 18, and 20%, respectively, in the 2000 World Values Survey.

Second, it is important to realize that being poor in the United States, as in other affluent countries, is a relative matter. Most who are considered poor by the standards generally used to measure this condition, such as the Census Bureau's definition of poverty, do not experience the grinding and even life-threatening conditions of those who are poor in developing countries. Indeed, the standard measures of poverty define that condition relative to the average level of income and purchasing power. The box below lists several attributes of America's poor, according to various government sources.

A third factor involves the often overlooked fact of income mobility.

Putting "Poor" in Perspective

- 46% of all poor households own their own homes. The average home owned by persons classified as "poor" by the Census Bureau is a three-bedroom house with one and one-half bathrooms, a garage, and a porch or patio.
- 76% of poor households have air conditioning. Thirty years ago only 36% of the entire American population had air conditioning in their homes.
- Only 6% of poor households are overcrowded, using the Census Bureau's definition of overcrowding.

- The average poor American has more living space than the average person living in Paris, London, Vienna, Athens, and many other European cities.
- Almost three-quarters of poor households own a car, and 30% own two or more cars.
- 97% of poor households have a color television, over half own two or more color televisions, 78% own a VCR or DVD player, and 62% have cable or satellite TV reception.

Adapted from data reported in Robert Rector, "Understanding Poverty and Economic Inequality in the United States," Heritage Foundation (15 September 2004): 4–5.

Many of those who are counted among America's poor by the census are there temporarily. They may be students living on their own, or young people who have just entered the workforce, or older Americans whose incomes were once higher and have now fallen to a level below the poverty line. Some of these elderly Americans are genuinely poor, but some have wealth, particularly a home that is paid for and savings of various sorts, that are not taken into account in the measurement of income used to determine whether one is poor. The popular image of poverty as a persistent condition into which one is born and from which one is unlikely to escape describes the lives of millions of Americans, but not nearly all of those who income demographers and social critics describe as poor.

Exactly what share of the population is stuck in a rut of intergenerational poverty is difficult to determine. Those who study such matters are far from agreement. Nonetheless, Americans believe that theirs is still the society of upward socio-economic mobility, par excellence. Asked whether, compared to European countries, moving up the social ladder in the United States was harder or easier, 46% said easier and only 13% harder (26% said it was the same and 15% gave no answer). This 2005 survey in *Time Magazine* also found that only 16% of Americans said that their current class position was lower than when they were growing up (45% said higher and 38% said it was the same), and a considerably greater share of respondents, 34%, said that it was "somewhat likely" that they would eventually become wealthy compared to 22% who said that it was "not at all likely." The percentage of Americans who agreed that it is possible to "start out poor, work hard, and become rich" increased from just under 60% in 1983 to about 80% in 2005.[24]

For millions of people the expectation of greater opportunities and upward mobility for themselves and their children was, and continues to be, the chief reason they immigrated to the United States. In the case of Mexicans, this expectation is usually met. But what about Britons or Canadians who might be thinking of moving to the United States? Some recent studies suggest that whatever upward mobility advantage the United States may have had over other affluent democracies no longer exists. Figure 8.8 shows that a very poor family in Canada, Denmark, or France is likely to move out of poverty more quickly than one in the United States. Moreover, some studies show that parental income is a better predictor of whether one will be rich or poor in the United States than in Canada and several European countries.[25]

In all societies education is one of the key factors determining a person's likelihood of getting on and climbing the socio-economic ladder. "There is a particular fear," observes the influential newspaper, *The Economist*, "about the engine of American meritocracy, its education system. Only 3% of students at top colleges come from the poorest quarter of the population."[26] This is, in fact, a usual part of the indictment of income or class inequality in America: only the rich can afford to go to university and this perpetuates class inequality.

There are actually two questions here. First, is post-secondary education in the United States comparatively inaccessible? Is it less open than, say, the university systems of Canada or Germany? Second, does it matter that most Americans cannot afford to send their children to Harvard or Yale, instead having to settle for Bowling Green State University or Michigan State?

Most people, including many Americans, are surprised by the answers. The share of the main university-age population, 18–24 years, attending university in the United States is about as large or even larger than such

FIGURE 8.8:   INCOME MOBILITY ACROSS GENERATIONS

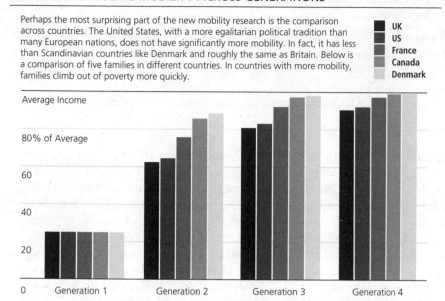

Perhaps the most surprising part of the new mobility research is the comparison across countries. The United States, with a more egalitarian political tradition than many European nations, does not have significantly more mobility. In fact, it has less than Scandinavian countries like Denmark and roughly the same as Britain. Below is a comparison of five families in different countries. In countries with more mobility, families climb out of poverty more quickly.

- UK
- US
- France
- Canada
- Denmark

Source: Miles Corak, Statistics Canada, reproduced in David Leonhardt and Ben Werschkul, "Class Matters: A Special Section," New York Times, 15 May 2005; reprinted with permission from Statistics Canada.

countries as Canada, France, Germany, the Netherlands, and Sweden. In some of those countries students pay no or only nominal university tuition fees. Roughly 40% of Americans between the ages of 25 and 64 have post-secondary degrees, compared to 45% in Canada, 38% in Japan, 29% in the UK, 25% in Germany, 24% in France, and only 11% in Italy.[27] Most of these graduates and those currently attending America's thousands of public and private universities and colleges are educated at state institutions, such as Florida State University and the University of Texas, or at non-elite private schools such as Wabash College and the University of the South. Tuition at such institutions is high by European standards, but apparently millions of Americans manage to afford what everyone who studies class knows is an investment in what is likely to be a higher stream of earnings throughout one's working life.

The second claim—that those who can afford to attend the expensive elite schools will occupy the highest status and most remunerative rungs on America's socio-economic ladder, leaving the graduates of state institutions behind—is simply untrue. A 1999 study by Alan Krueger and Stacy Berg Dale did what no one had bothered to do previously, namely, look at the jobs and earnings of graduates from elite and non-elite schools. Their conclusion was, "*that* you go to college is more important than *where* you go."[28] Comparing students with similar grades and admission scores, some of whom went to what are considered top schools and others who went to lesser ranked institutions, they found that twenty years after graduation the incomes of those from the two streams were about the same.

Do You Need Harvard to Succeed?

Beyond the [statistical data], there is abundant anecdotal evidence that any of a wide range of colleges can equip its graduates for success. Consider the United States Senate. This most exclusive of clubs currently lists twenty-six members with undergraduate degrees from the Got-Get-Ins—a disproportionately good showing considering the small percentage of students who graduate from these schools. But the diversity of Senate backgrounds is even more striking. Fully half of US senators are graduates of public universities, and many went to "states"—among them Chico State, Colorado State, Iowa State, Kansas State, Louisiana State, Michigan State, North Carolina State, Ohio State, Oklahoma State, Oregon State, Penn State, San Jose State, South Dakota State, Utah State, and Washington State. Or consider the CEOs of the top ten Fortune 500 corporations: only four went to elite schools. H. Lee Scott Jr., of Wal-Mart, the world's largest corporation, is a graduate of Pittsburg State, in Pittsburg, Kansas.... Steven Spielberg was rejected by the prestigious film schools at USC and UCLA; he attended Cal State Long Beach, and seems to have done all right for himself. Roger Straus, of Farrar, Straus & Giroux, one of the most influential people in postwar American letters ... was a graduate of the University of Missouri. "[Students] have been led to believe that if you go to X school, then Y will result, and this just isn't true," says Judith Shapiro, the president of Barnard. "It's good to attend a good college, but there are many good colleges. Getting into Princeton or Barnard just isn't a life-or-death matter."

Excerpts from Greg Easterbrook, "Who Needs Harvard?," The Atlantic Monthly (October 2004).

Immigrants: Legal and Illegal

No country has been a greater magnet for immigration than the United States. Figure 8.9 shows the historical trend in immigration between 1800 and 2000. Although the rate of intake waxed and waned, what is most striking are the sheer numbers of those who left their home countries to settle in the United States, roughly 70 million between 1820 and 2004. This counts only legal immigrants, those whose entry into the country has been documented. At the present time there are roughly 25 million legal immigrants in the United States. By some calculations the number of illegal immigrants is almost as large, estimates ranging between eight and 20 million with about 12 million (and perhaps one million more each year) being the most commonly accepted number.

FIGURE 8.9:   IMMIGRATION TO THE UNITED STATES, 1820–2000

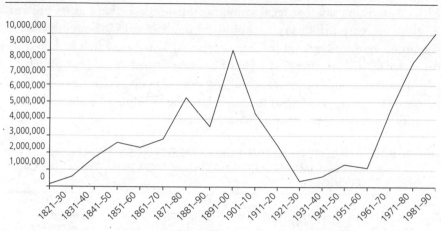

Source: United States Immigration and Naturalization Service.

Americans will often say "we are all immigrants." This statement expresses the fact that for most Americans their roots in the United States may go back no more than four or five generations and more than one out of ten was actually born outside the country. But new immigrants and particular groups of immigrants have not always been viewed positively. The wave of Irish who fled the Potato Famine in the late 1840s and settled in the United States were widely seen as a barely absorbable element, as was later true of the millions of eastern and southern Europeans who immigrated in the late 1800s and early 1900s. Chinese immigrants who were recruited to build the railways in the west and to work in the mines were denied citizenship rights under the *Chinese Exclusion Act* of 1882, and many were sent back to China after years of working in the United States. Japanese-Americans, many of whom had lived in the United States for three or four decades and most of whom were American citizens, fell under a cloud of suspicion during World War II and had their property and freedom taken away when they were placed in wartime internment camps. More recently a cloud of suspicion has hung over Muslim and Arab Americans in the wake of 9/11. But the most controversial and politically important aspect of immigration in recent years has involved illegal immigration from the countries of Central and South America.

It is important to note at the outset that although Americans are ambivalent toward immigration, a majority believe that legal immigration has been good for the country throughout its history and that legal immigration has helped rather than hurt the American economy (see Figure 8.10). More Americans say that legal immigration should be kept at its present level or increased than say it should be decreased (55% saying that it should be increased or kept the same versus 41% who say that it should be decreased).[29] This is often lost sight of or even denied in the heat of debate over visa restrictions on people coming from particular countries, claims of ethnic or religious profiling at the border, or the building of walls and other security measures at the frontier with Mexico.

FIGURE 8.10: PER CENT OF NATIVE-BORN AMERICANS SAYING LEGAL/ ILLEGAL IMMIGRATION HAS HELPED OR HURT THE AMERICAN ECONOMY

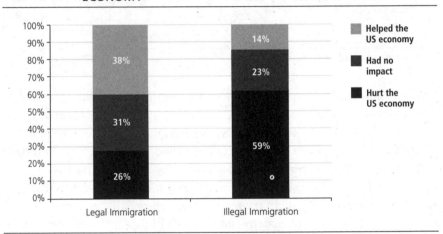

Source: Reprinted with permission from NPR/Kaiser/KennedySchool Immigration Survey (4 August 2004), http://www.npr.org/news/specials/polls/2004/immigration/.

Most Americans are opposed to illegal immigration. Indeed, it is likely that the focus on illegal immigration in the public conversation has had some spillover effect, depressing the overall level of support for immigration. And it is certain that the attacks of 9/11 resulted in at least a temporary increase in popular hostility toward immigration, although some surveys suggest that this abated within a few years.[30]

The history of most immigrant groups has been characterized by fairly rapid integration into American society, members of the second or third generation attending university at rates and earning incomes similar to or even higher than the national averages. Some groups have done very well, including people of Armenian, Korean, Asian Indian, and Chinese ancestry. Hispanics, today the largest and fastest growing ethnic group in the United States, have comprised the majority of legal and illegal immigrants over the last few decades. Although their education and income levels tend to lag behind those of most Americans, this is not unusual for first-generation immigrants. Data shows that the second generation has closed the gap considerably, although the education and income levels of Hispanics born in the United States are still below national averages.[31]

At the same time, however, the presence of a large population of illegal immigrants, the vast majority of whom are Hispanic, has generated enormous controversy. In California, home to the largest concentrations of legal and illegal Hispanic immigrants, ballot measures have passed that attempted to deny social benefits to illegal immigrants (Proposition 187, subsequently challenged in the courts and ultimately ruled unconstitutional) and ending bilingualism in public schools (Proposition 227). A 2006 national survey by the Pew Research Center found that 70% of Americans agreed that illegal immigrants should be denied local social services, but 71% said that the children of illegal immigrants should be allowed to attend public schools.[32] Talk radio programs across much of the United States, but especially in the west, have given enormous coverage to the issue in recent years, most of it very hostile toward illegal immigration and any legislative proposal that would regularize the status of those who entered the country illegally, as occurred when illegal immigrants were granted amnesty in 1986. "On no issue are elites and ordinary Americans further apart than on immigration," observes Francis Fukuyama.[33] Elites tend to be more sympathetic, or at least accommodating, toward illegal immigrants whereas the general public tends to see those who are in the United States illegally as competition for jobs, a factor that depresses wages and a threat to American culture. Some of the complex ethical and equality issues in this debate are described in the box on the next page.

Women

The year 2008 was an exceptional one for women in American politics. Hillary Rodham Clinton was almost chosen as the Democratic Party's presidential candidate. Another Democrat, Nancy Pelosi (California), was Speaker of the House of Representatives, a position of considerable influence in the congressional system of government. Several other leadership positions, including two Senate committee chairs and three committee chairs in the House, were held by women. Altogether there were 16 women in the Senate and 70 in the House, representing 16.3% of all seats in the 110th Congress. Almost one-quarter of all state lawmakers (1,733 of 7,382) and nine of the 50 state governors were women. There were female mayors in

Perspectives on Illegal Immigration: A Conversation

ANGELICA SALAS (Coalition for Humane Immigrant Rights, Los Angeles): We have a fundamental belief that an individual has inalienable human rights and that those rights are not diminished once they cross a border. There is a belief by the general populace that the undocumented do not have rights. So because of that situation you have employers who are more than willing to pay individuals less than minimum wage, but unfortunately we see people who are not paid at all.

GONZALEZ (PBS Interviewer): Ira Mehlman, with the Federation for American Immigration Reform, says the US needs to be more concerned about upholding its immigration laws than protecting undocumented workers.

IRA MEHLMAN (Federation for American Immigration Reform): The United States has an obligation to enforce the laws of this country—all the laws of this country—not just the ones that people want to obey. Why should anybody obey our immigration laws when there's clear evidence that if you come here illegally, nobody is going to do anything about it? And, in fact, you're going to have advocates here who are going to say, "Let's legalize these people once they get here, let's reward them for having broken the law."

GONZALEZ: Some people of faith believe the country needs to show immigrants hospitality, even those who are here illegally.

RABBI MARC DWORKIN (Leo Baeck Temple): The first thing we have to do is not to deny people basic human and civil rights. So I would say this concept of welcoming, of hospitality even, certainly not exploitation of the stranger, is very essential to religious thought.

VICTOR DAVIS HANSON (Author, *Mexifornia*): You and I welcome people into our home. Do we welcome 500 people into our home? It's a question of the limitations of time and space.

GONZALEZ: Victor Davis Hanson is a fifth-generation California grower, an author, and social commentator. He says lax enforcement of immigration laws has permitted more people to come in than the United States can assimilate.

Mr. HANSON: The American tradition is that the immigrants come legally, they go through English immersion, a cultural immersion, and the second generation is clearly better off than the first. For so many people who come here so quickly and without knowing English, and illegally, we've overwhelmed the powers that we used to rely on to assimilate.

GONZALEZ: Hanson lives in California's agricultural heartland, the San Joaquin Valley, a region whose economy benefits from undocumented workers like Geraldo Reyes.

GERALDO REYES (undocumented worker, through translator): We pick all the crops. And immigrants that are documented, you don't see them here in the fields working, inhaling dirt. They think we're bad, but without us, who is going to do it?

GONZALEZ: Hanson, who advocates stricter border enforcement, says those who favor relaxing immigration laws fail to recognize the moral consequences of their position.

Mr. HANSON: They are the immoralists, so to speak, because they depend on cheap labor to do what they do not want to do. They've allowed apartheid communities to spring up in California where the people who cut their lawns, clean their pools, paint their house are here illegally from Mexico, and yet their own children will never go to school with those kids, they'll never shop at the same store, they'll never wonder where they work. It's almost as if they come in from Mars, parachute down, work eight hours, then out of sight, out of mind.

GONZALEZ: Illegal immigrants themselves are becoming increasingly vocal. In October, thousands converged on New York demanding legal status and safer workplace conditions. In Congress, legislators are once again considering bills long sidelined by the 9/11 attacks that would grant guest worker visas to hundreds of thousands of people now in the United States illegally. Immigrant rights advocates say such benefits are long overdue, considering what undocumented workers contribute to the nation's economy.

Ms. SALAS: It is morally suspect when you're receiving the work of all immigrants that you really do benefit from cheaper products and just overall the service that immigrants give, but then not to see these individuals as humans, not to see them as people with families, with needs, with aspirations, hopes and dreams. That is incorrect.

Mr. MEHLMAN: The social costs of illegal immigration are enormous. It's estimated that it costs about $7.5 billion (2003) in the US every year to educate illegal alien children in our public schools. And so we are taking enormous resources that could be used to provide a higher quality of education for a lot of other kids in this country and spending it on illegal immigrants.

GONZALEZ: Others would say these immigrants must be educated so they can be part of the work force of the future. As the national debate continues over the burdens and benefits of illegal immigration, some people of faith say that compassion should govern policy.

Excerpts from the transcript of the PBS program, "Religion & Ethics," 14 November 2003; printed with permission.

197 (17.3%) of the 1,137 American cities with populations over 30,000. The Secretary of State, Condoleezza Rice, was a woman, as were the secretaries of Transportation, Education, and Labor, as well as the US Trade Representative (a cabinet-level post).

However, the vast majority of elected and non-elected offices in American government at all levels were still held by men. Measured against the benchmark of history, 2008 was a high-water mark for female representation. Measured against the levels of female representation in some European democracies or against a strict proportional standard of how many women should hold office, this performance looked much less impressive.

It was, however, better than that of France, Italy, and Japan and about as good as in the UK and Canada. The representation of women in American politics only looks feeble compared to the Nordic and a handful of other democracies, almost all of which have in common a proportional representation electoral system. Under such a system the selection of party candidates for the legislature is determined by each party's leadership. The greater the share of the popular vote received by a party, the greater the number of candidates from its rank-ordered list will be elected to the legislature. The effect of a proportional representation system on the likelihood of women being nominated as candidates and ultimately elected to office is explained by Alan Siaroff:

> ... [I]n a PR system a party can go so far as to institute quotas, as was first done on a broad basis in Norway. If a party fails to nominate many women this is much more visible to the average voter than in single-member systems. Finally, since the success of new, smaller parties is much greater in a PR system, if the traditional parties do not nominate many women, both the reality of, and the threat of, forming a new women's party are far greater than in a single-member system, where such a party probably would not win any seats. Such a women's party was set up in Iceland in the 1980s, and the threat of women in the Swedish Social Democratic Party to do likewise in the 1990s led to the formal adoption of quotas by that party.[34]

The United States has a single-member, simple plurality electoral system, which uses primary elections to select the parties' candidates for public office in a way that diminishes the influence of the party leadership on candidate selection and does not allow for even the consideration of gender quotas in the fielding of candidates. Of course the fact that every one of the countries that has at least one-third greater representation of women in its national legislature than the United States has a political culture in which leftist values have been historically strong[35] also helps to explain this difference.

The representation of women in executive positions in the American government is significantly greater than their representation at the legislative level. Siaroff found that one-quarter of federal cabinet positions were held by women in 1998, a percentage exceeded by only eight of the 27 democracies that he examined. In 2007 the 21-person cabinet of George W. Bush included five women. This was less female representation than in the French cabinet of Nicolas Sarkozy (seven of 15) but it was a higher percentage than in the Canadian government of Stephen Harper (seven of 31) and about the same as in Gordon Brown's cabinet in the UK (six of 22). The fact that members of the president's cabinet may not be elected members of the legislative branch—most parliamentary democracies have a tradition of selecting cabinet ministers from the legislature—has the effect of increasing the pool of women who may be nominated to cabinet posts.

Economically, the status of women in the United States is comparable to that in most other democracies. Table 8.7 shows that the United States falls in the middle of the pack among affluent democracies in terms of both its HDI ranking (8th) and its gender-related development ranking (8th). In

TABLE 8.6:   RANKINGS OF WOMEN IN PARLIAMENT AND CABINET (after last national elections to the end of 1998)

	Women in Parliament	%		Women in Cabinet	%
1.	Sweden	42.7	1.	Sweden	50.0
2.	Denmark	37.4	2.	Norway	47.4
3.	Norway	36.4	3.	Denmark	38.1
4.	Netherlands	36.0	4.	Finland	37.5
5.	Finland	33.5	5.	France	35.7
6.	Germany	30.9	6.	Germany	31.25
7.	New Zealand	29.2	7.	Netherlands	26.7
8.	Austria	26.8	7.	Spain	26.7
9.	Iceland	25.4	9.	Austria	25.0
10.	Spain	24.6	9.	**United States**	**25.0**
11.	Australia	22.3	11.	United Kingdom	22.7
12.	Switzerland	21.0	12.	Canada	21.4
13.	Canada	20.6	13.	Liechtenstein	20.0
14.	Luxembourg	20.0	14.	Luxembourg	16.7
15.	United Kingdom	17.8	14.	Portugal	16.7
16.	Portugal	13.0	16.	Italy	14.3
17.	Belgium	12.0	16.	Switzerland	14.3
18.	Ireland	12.0	18.	Belgium	13.3
19.	**United States**	**11.7**	18.	Ireland	13.3
20.	Italy	11.1	20.	Greece	10.5
21.	France	10.9	21.	Iceland	10.0
22.	Malta	9.2	22.	South Korea	8.7
23.	Israel	7.5	23.	Cyprus	7.7
24.	Greece	6.3	23.	Malta	7.7
25.	Cyprus	5.4	25.	Australia	5.9
26.	Japan	4.6	26.	New Zealand	5.0
27.	Liechtenstein	4.0	27.	Israel	0.0
28.	South Korea	2.0	27.	Japan	0.0

Source: Adapted from International Political Science Review 21(2): 2000, Table 1.

12 of the 21 countries included in this table the average earned incomes of females compared to males is higher than in the United States, although only marginally so in five of these national cases. But in one respect the United States tops the table. According to the UN's data the percentage of females among legislators, senior officials, and managers—a measure that is used to infer women's participation in decision-making and power over economic

resources—is higher in the United States at 42% than in any of these other countries. The fact that only ten women are included in the Fortune 500 list of CEOs for 2006 (up one from the previous year's list), or that only 11 women crack the Forbes 400 list of wealthiest Americans (2004) might seem cause for skepticism about this high ranking. On the other hand, how well do women in these other countries fare on measures of leading CEOs and wealthiest persons?

TABLE 8.7:   VARIOUS MEASURES OF FEMALE ECONOMIC EQUALITY COMPARED TO MALES, RANKINGS FOR TOP 21 COUNTRIES ON THE UN HUMAN DEVELOPMENT INDEX, 2004

Countries Ranked by HDI Score (Gender-related development ranking in parentheses)		
	Female Earned Income as % of Male[*]	Female Percentage of Leadership Positions[†]
1 Norway (1)	75%	29%
2 Iceland (2)	71%	29%
3 Australia (3)	70%	37%
4 Ireland (4)	51%	29%
5 Sweden (5)	81%	31%
6 Canada (7)	63%	36%
7 Japan (13)	44%	10%
8 United States (8)	62%	42%
9 Switzerland (10)	61%	27%
10 Netherlands (9)	63%	26%
11 Finland (1)	71%	28%
12 Luxembourg (6)	49%	—
13 Belgium (12)	63%	30%
14 Austria (17)	44%	28%
15 Denmark (15)	73%	25%
16 France (14)	64%	—
17 Italy (18)	46%	21%
18 United Kingdom (16)	65%	33%
19 Spain (19)	50%	32%
20 New Zealand (20)	70%	36%
21 Germany (21)	58%	35%

* This figure takes no account of the different rates of full- and part-time work between men and women. † Women's share of positions defined according to the International Standard Classification of Occupations (ISCO-88) to include legislators, senior government officials, traditional chiefs and heads of villages, senior officials of special-interest organizations, corporate managers, directors and chief executives, production and operations department managers, and other department and general managers.

Source: United Nations, Human Development Report, 2006; http://hdr.undp.org/en/reports/global/hdr2006/.

Women's rights in the United States continue to be linked to the issue of abortion to a degree that is exceptional among Western democracies. The pro-choice leanings of former New York mayor Rudy Giuliani and Mitt Romney's acceptance of liberal access to abortion when he was governor of Massachusetts were obstacles that each had to deal with in their fight to become the 2008 Republican candidate for president. John McCain, who eventually won the Republican nomination, also had to respond to mistrust from the pro-life movement, on the grounds that he stated in 1999 that he did not support overturning *Roe v. Wade* (1973). Opposition to that landmark Supreme Court decision on abortion is an important litmus test for social conservatives in selecting a candidate.

The percentage of pregnancies terminated by an abortion in the United States is about the same as in most affluent democracies, at between 20 to 25%. Although access to abortion varies across parts of the country, court decisions have established one clear rule: a woman has a constitutional right to abort her pregnancy, based on the right to privacy that judges have inferred to be guaranteed by the Constitution. This right is not, however, absolute and unrestricted.

But despite the fact that the core of *Roe v. Wade* has remained solid since 1973, every presidential nominee for the Supreme Court and the cabinet post of Attorney-General can count on being grilled during Senate confirmation hearings on his or her views on this landmark abortion decision. This is partly because several abortion rulings since *Roe v. Wade* appear to some to have whittled away at the basic right to abort a pregnancy guaranteed by that decision. The reality of subsequent court rulings is, however, rather mixed:

- *1976, Planned Parenthood of Central Missouri v. Danforth*, 428 U.S. 52. This ruling struck down a state law requiring the consent of spouses or the parents of minors for an abortion.
- *1979, Bellotti v. Baird*, 443 U.S. 622. This challenge to a Massachusetts law that required minors to get the consent of their parents before an abortion procedure was approved was struck down as unconstitutional.
- *1980, Maher v. Roe*, 432 U.S. 464. This was one of three cases decided at the same time on public funding for abortion. The court ruled that state limits on Medicaid funding for abortions were constitutional on the ground that they simply had the effect of encouraging childbirth over abortion

Roe v. Wade, 1973

The Constitution does not explicitly mention any right of privacy. In a line of decisions, however ... the Court has recognized that a right of personal privacy, or a guarantee of certain areas or zones of privacy, does exist under the Constitution....

This right of privacy, whether it be founded in the Fourteenth Amendment's concept of personal liberty and restrictions upon state action, as we feel it is, or, as the District Court determined, in the Ninth Amendment's reservation of rights to the people, is broad enough to encompass a woman's decision whether or not to terminate her pregnancy. The detriment that the State would impose upon the pregnant woman by denying this choice altogether is apparent. Specific and direct harm medically diagnosable even in early pregnancy may be involved. Maternity, or additional offspring, may force upon the woman a distressful life and future. Psychological harm may be imminent. Mental and physical health may be taxed by child care. There is also the distress, for all concerned, associated with the unwanted child, and there is the problem of bringing a child into a family already unable, psychologically and otherwise, to care for it. In other cases, as in this one, the additional difficulties and continuing stigma of unwed motherhood may be involved. All these are factors the woman and her responsible physician necessarily will consider in consultation.

On the basis of elements such as these, appellant and some amici [briefs] argue that the woman's right is absolute and that she is entitled to terminate her pregnancy at whatever time, in whatever way, and for whatever reason she alone chooses. With this we do not agree. Appellant's arguments that Texas either has no valid interest at all in regulating the abortion decision, or no interest strong enough to support any limitation upon the woman's sole determination, are unpersuasive. The Court's decisions recognizing a right of privacy also acknowl-

edge that some state regulation in areas protected by that right is appropriate. As noted above, a State may properly assert important interests in safeguarding health, in maintaining medical standards, and in protecting potential life. At some point in pregnancy, these respective interests become sufficiently compelling to sustain regulation of the factors that govern the abortion decision. The privacy right involved, therefore, cannot be said to be absolute. In fact, it is not clear to us that the claim asserted by some amici that one has an unlimited right to do with one's body as one pleases bears a close relationship to the right of privacy previously articulated in the Court's decisions. The Court has refused to recognize an unlimited right of this kind in the past. *Jacobson v. Massachusetts*, 197 U.S. 11 (1905) (vaccination); *Buck v. Bell*, 274 U.S. 200 (1927) (sterilization).

We, therefore, conclude that the right of personal privacy includes the abortion decision, but that this right is not unqualified and must be considered against important state interests in regulation....

(a) For the stage prior to approximately the end of the first trimester, the abortion decision and its effectuation must be left to the medical judgment of the pregnant woman's attending physician.

(b) For the stage subsequent to approximately the end of the first trimester, [the] State, in promoting its interest in the health of the mother, may, if it chooses, regulate the abortion procedure in ways that are reasonably related to maternal health.

(c) For the stage subsequent to viability, the State in promoting its interest in the potentiality of human life may, if it chooses, regulate, and even proscribe, abortion except where it is necessary, in appropriate medical judgment, for the preservation of the life or health of the mother.

Excerpts from Roe v. Wade *(1973).*

but that they did not unduly limit a woman's constitutional right to an abortion. This ruling was handed down before the ideological composition of the Supreme Court began to shift in a conservative direction because of appointments by Reagan and George H.W. Bush.

- *1983, City of Akron v. Akron Center for Reproductive Health*, 462 U.S. 416. The Court once again reaffirmed that laws requiring the consent of parents before a minor could abort a pregnancy were unconstitutional. It also struck down legislated requirements that abortions after the first trimester of a pregnancy be carried out in a hospital and that fetuses be disposed of in a "humane" manner.
- *1983, Planned Parenthood v. Ashcroft*, 462 U.S. 476. Once again, the Court struck down a state law that required the consent of either a minor's parents or a judge before an abortion could be performed.
- *1986, Thornburgh v. American College of Obstetricians and Gynecologists*, 476 U.S. 747. A Pennsylvania law that required women requesting an abortion to first hear a state-approved speech intended to discourage the procedure was struck down in a five to four ruling.
- *1989, Webster v. Reproductive Health Services*, 492 U.S. 490. A divided court, five to four, upheld a Missouri state ban on the use of public employees and facilities for abortions.
- *1991, Rust v. Sullivan*, 500 U.S. 173. The Court upheld a law passed by Congress that prohibited abortion counseling at family planning clinics that received federal funds. This was another five to four decision, demonstrating yet again the very divided character of the Supreme Court.
- *1992, Planned Parenthood v. Casey*, 505 U.S. 833. Widely seen by pro-choice advocates as the biggest blow to *Roe v. Wade*, this five to four ruling upheld a Pennsylvania state law that required minors to receive written consent from at least one parent before an abortion procedure and also upheld the law's 24-hour waiting period before an abortion could be performed.
- *2000, Stenberg v. Carhart*, 530 U.S. 914. A divided court on abortion was by now routine. But this time the five to four vote gave comfort to pro-choice advocates. The Court

struck down a Nebraska state law that banned partial-birth abortions (i.e., late pregnancy abortions that kill the fetus by collapsing its skull once it has passed through the vagina).

- *2007, Gonzales v. Carhart,* 550 U.S. 124. In 2003 Congress passed and the president signed into law the *Partial-Birth Abortion Ban Act* that made illegal the procedure that was challenged in the 2000 case of *Stenberg v. Carhart*. This time, however, the opponents of partial-birth abortion were successful. The federal ban was upheld by a five to four vote. Justice Kennedy spoke for the majority in saying that the ban "does not have the effect of imposing an unconstitutional burden on the abortion right." But Justice Ginsburg, who was part of the dissenting minority, argued that the court's ruling, "cannot be understood as anything other than an effort to chip away a right declared again and again by this court, and with increasing comprehension of its centrality to women's lives."

As this long string of decisions by a sharply divided court shows, the abortion issue continues to be a very contentious one in American politics. Legislative attempts to place various sorts of limits on the basic right established in *Roe v. Wade* are immediately responded to with legal challenges in the courts. In recognition of the courts' critical role in determining abortion law, both pro-choice and pro-life forces devote their energies to what they see as key election races. Pro-life groups were galvanized by the candidacy of George W. Bush in 2000 and 2004, expecting—correctly as it turned out—that he would be in a position to fill vacancies on a Supreme Court that had been leaning by a five to four margin toward their opponents. Pro-choice groups also were motivated by the high stakes represented by judicial appointments. The Senate's constitutional authority in the confirmation of presidential appointments to federal courts ensures that groups on both sides of the abortion issue target close Senate races and even primary elections, the ultimate goal being the selection of judges sympathetic to their side's position.

Notes

1 Gunnar Myrdal, *An American Dilemma: The Negro Problem and Modern Democracy* (New York: Harper and Brothers Publishers. 1944).

2 Andrew Hacker, *Two Nations: Black and White, Separate, Hostile, Unequal* (New York: Balantine, 1992).

3 Hacker, Chap. 4.

4 Gallup Poll Social Audit, "Black-White Relations in US, 2001 Update," 10 July 2001, http://www.gallup.com.

5 See http://abcnews.go.com/images/pdf/810Race.pdf.

6 ABCNEWS Poll on Racial Discrimination, http://www.abcnews.go.com.onair/2020/2020_000217_abcpoll_races.html.

7 Gallup Poll, "Social Audit on Black/White Relations in the United States, 1997 and 2001," http://www.gallup.com.

8 Summarized at http://www.aclu.org, "Race and the Death Penalty," 26 February 2003.

9 Daniel Patrick Moynihan, *The Negro Family: The Case for National Action* (Washington, DC: Department of Labor, 1965).

10 National Center for Health Statistics, http://www.cdc.gov/nchs/.

11 Hacker 61, 218.

12 http://www.pewsocialtrends.org.

13 Walter R. Allen, Edgar G. Epps, and Nasha Z. Haniff (eds.), *College in Black and White* (Albany, NY: State University of New York Press, 1991).

14 William Julius Irving, *The Truly Disadvantaged: The Inner City, the Underclass, and Public Policy* (Chicago: University of Chicago Press, 1987) 8.

15 See the interview with William Julius Wilson, "The two nations of black America," at *Frontline*, http://www.pbs.org/wgbh/pages/frontline/shows/race/interviews/wilson.html.

16 A good summary of major provisions of the *Civil Rights Act* may be found at http://usinfo.state.gov.usa/infousa/fact/democrac/39.htm.

17 "Racial Transformation and the Changing Nature of Segregation," The Civil Rights Project (January 2006), http://www.civilrightsproject.ucla.edu; 18, Table 8.

18 Seymour Martin Lipset, "Equal Chances versus Equal Results," *The Annals of the American Academy* 523 (September 1992) 68.

19 *The Economist*, 17 June 2006: 28–30.

20 Clive Crook, "Rags to Rags, Riches to Riches," *The Atlantic*, June 2007.

21 Alan Wolfe, "The New Politics of Inequality," *The New York Times*, 27 September 1999: A27.

22 Everett Carl Ladd and Karyn H. Bowman, *Attitudes Toward Economic Inequality* (Washington, DC: American Enterprise Institute, 1998) 3.

23 See Tables A1 and A2 in the Appendix: Lars Osberg and Timothy Smeeding, "Fair Inequality? An International Comparison of Attitudes to Pay Differentials," Russell Sage Foundation, 21 June 2005, http://www.russellsage.org.

24 All of these figures are from *The New York Times Magazine*, "Class Matters: A Special Section," 2005, http://www.nytimes.com/pages/national/class/index.html.

25 Miles Corak (ed.), *Generational Income Mobility in North America and Europe* (Cambridge, UK: Cambridge University Press, 2005).

26 "Inequality and the American Dream," *The Economist*, 17 June 2006: 13.

27 National Center for Education Statistics, *Comparative Indicators of Education in the United States and Other G-8 Countries: 2006* (Washington, DC: Department of Education, August 2007) 49, Figure 17a.

28   Alan Krueger and Stacy Berg Dale, as quoted in Greg Easterbrook, "Who Needs Harvard?," *The Atlantic Monthly* (October 2004).

29   NPR/Kennedy School/Kaiser Immigration Survey, 2004, http://www.npr.org/news/specials/polls/2004/immigration/.

30   NPR/Kennedy School/Kaiser Immigration Survey, 2004.

31   Pew Hispanic Center, http://www.pewhispanic.org.

32   Reported at NPR, "Illegal Immigration Divides Americans, Poll Says," 30 March 2006.

33   Francis Fukuyama, "Identity Crisis: Why We Shouldn't Worry about Mexican Immigration," *Slate*, 4 June 2004.

34   Alan Siaroff, "Women's Representation in Legislatures," *International Political Science Review* 21 (2000): 203.

35   As measured by the Esping-Anderson scale of welfare state socialism, in Gosta Esping-Anderson, *Politics Against Markets* (Cambridge, MA: Princeton University Press, 1985).

CHAPTER NINE

Parties and Elections

Election campaigns never stop in the United States. This used to be said half in jest when the business of raising money, advertising, and running in first a primary and then a general election stretched over an ever longer period. Now, however, it is the literal truth. The 2004 re-election of George W. Bush was barely confirmed when speculation began regarding who were the favorites to capture the White House in 2008.

The media has an insatiable hunger for stories in a 24-hour per day, seven days per week news and entertainment environment, in which the competition for audience share and the advertising dollars this represents is a large part of the explanation for the unrelenting coverage of who's up and who's down, even years before the actual election date. So too is the enormous cost of running for many public offices in America, requiring that candidates develop a campaign organization and begin raising money very early. Finally, the method by which the parties' candidates are chosen can require considerable spending long before the general election campaign. Indeed, winning their party's nomination can be the most expensive phase of some candidates' run for office.

The American Two-Party System

Many of the founders had serious misgivings about political parties, associating them with division and strife. Madison expressed the sentiment of most of the founders when he warned against the danger of "factions," a category that included political parties. No less a figure than George Washington spoke out against parties in his 1796 farewell address. Parties, he said, "serve to organize faction, to give it an artificial and extraordinary force; to put, in the place of the delegated will of the nation the will of a party, often a small but artful and enterprising minority of the community; and, according to the alternate triumphs of different parties, to make the public administration the mirror of the ill-concerted and incongruous projects of faction, rather than the organ of consistent and wholesome plans digested by common counsels and modified by mutual interests."[1]

It is not surprising that parties were viewed so negatively. There was, first of all, little experience with competitive political parties at the time. They were largely unknown in the colonial legislatures, although opposing coalitions certainly existed. What did not exist, however, was a system in which one group controlled the government and another opposed it.[2] Moreover, although the United States existed, the American people did not, except in the weakest sense. New Yorkers and South Carolinians now shared a constitution and a common citizenship, but a widespread and deep sense of national identity—the sentiment of being American—would take generations to develop. The founders understandably feared that if politics were to be organized on party lines, then this might reinforce the fault-lines that existed in the fledgling American republic. Division, they believed, could be ill-afforded at a time when the country had no real friends among the great powers of Europe, three of whom had colonial possessions on the borders of the United States.

But parties emerged nevertheless. The Federalists, who advocated a much stronger national government and its supremacy over the states in such important matters as trade and commerce, and the Anti-federalists, the original defenders of states' rights who were suspicious of the power of the national government, were the first parties in American politics. They emerged even before the ink was dry on the Constitution. Today's Democratic Party traces its roots back to Thomas Jefferson and the Anti-federalists, although Jefferson's followers called themselves Republicans. Today's Republican Party did not emerge until the mid-1800s and did not hold power nationally until the Civil War. Since then, the Republican and Democratic parties have dominated the American political scene, with third parties and independent candidates only rarely having an influence on election outcomes. However, although their impact at the polls has generally been slight, some argue that third parties have sometimes had a significant effect on the policies and directions of the major parties. For example, George Wallace, a disgruntled former Democratic governor of Alabama, led the American Independent Party in the 1968 election. He won about 15% of the popular vote in the presidential election and carried five states in the South. Some analysts believe that the Republican Party's "southern strategy" of focusing on socially conservative voters in the South was a reaction to Wallace's obvious appeal in this part of the country. Third parties, such as Ross Perot's Reform Party, have occasionally provided a sort of safety valve to let off steam from segments of the electorate who were dissatisfied with the major political parties. Perot won about 20% of the presidential vote in 1992 but did not carry a single state.[3]

Unlike the party systems of most other Western democracies, the American two-party system has never been significantly divided on class lines. After the Civil War, a farmer in a state from the defeated Confederacy was very likely to vote Democrat, as was his wealthy plantation owner neighbor and the owner of the store where both families bought their groceries. In the North, however, a farmer was more likely to vote Republican, as was the local banker. The issue of slavery emerged as a clear line between the parties in the 1860 election. For most of the remainder of the nineteenth century, the two parties were associated in the public mind with the position each had taken on the slavery question, northerners voting overwhelmingly for the Republican Party and southerners for the Democrats.

The presidential election of 1896 is generally considered to be a *realignment election*, one in which significant and durable change took place in the parties' bases of voter support. The Republican Party under its candidate William McKinley came to be seen as the party of industry, business interests, sound money, protectionism, the cities, and the North. Under William Jennings Bryan's leadership, the Democratic Party stood for the interests of the southern and midwestern farm states, and for rural America versus urban America. Bryan's fiery rhetoric mixed agrarian populism with Christian fundamentalism (see his portrayal in the classic American play, "Inherit the Wind?") in a message that was about Everyman versus the Establishment. An important economic issue now divided the parties.

Republicans dominated national politics for most of the next few decades, with the exception of the first several years of Woodrow Wilson's presidency, until the realignment election of 1932. The onset of the Great Depression created enormous dissatisfaction among voters. Segments of the electorate that had given strong support to the Republican Party over the previous few decades swung into the Democratic fold. They included urban workers, blacks, and Jews. Combined with the "Solid South," whose support of the party had not wavered, this became the *New Deal coalition* that swept Franklin Delano Roosevelt into the White House and gave the Democrats firm control over both houses of Congress in the 1932 elections. Although the Democratic Party occasionally lost the presidency to the Republicans in the years between 1932 and 1980, they seldom lost control over Congress, controlling both houses during 44 of these 48 years.

The most recent party realignment has occurred more gradually than those of 1860, 1896, and 1932. It began in 1980 when Ronald Reagan captured the White House for the Republican Party and has been marked by three main features. One is the softening of support for the Democratic Party among some elements of the New Deal coalition. Although black voters have remained stalwartly Democratic, the support of Catholics, blue-collar workers, and, to a much lesser degree, Jewish voters is not as solid as in the past. Second, and perhaps most strikingly, the once solidly Democratic South has shifted to the Republican Party. Third, the center of the American political spectrum shifted after 1980 as both parties became more conservative. Bill Clinton, the most successful Democratic politician of his generation, was less liberal than every Democratic candidate for the presidency after John F. Kennedy. Clinton's signing into law of the *Welfare Reform Act, 1996*, ending the Aid to Families with Dependent Children program that had been brought in under Franklin Delano Roosevelt in the 1930s, was a step that no Democratic president before him would have considered. This conservative tilt has meant that both parties engage in a competition for an increasingly large segment of the electorate that responds favorably to either fiscally or socially conservative messages and policies.

The election of Barack Obama in 2008 and increased Democratic majorities in both the House and Senate led some to question whether the post-1980 period was truly a realignment in voter behavior and party support or whether the 2008 election might even mark the beginning of yet another realignment, this time in a liberal-Democratic direction. But it is not at all clear that the Democratic wave in 2008, already presaged by the party's congressional and state gains in 2006, signified a tilt away from conservatism and toward liberalism. Obama's campaign was very much in the centrist tradition of recent American politics and many of the Democratic gains in Congress in 2006 and 2008 were won by socially conservative candidates. In opting for a message of change and hope in 2008, and rejecting what was widely seen as failed management of the economy by the Bush administration, it was not at all clear that American voters were shifting their allegiances in more profound and enduring ways. Time will tell.

Are Two Parties Too Few?

The United States, along with the other Anglo-American democracies, has a single member/simple plurality electoral system. Candidates compete to represent a particular state or district. The latter is the equivalent of what is called a constituency or riding in the Commonwealth democracies. It is not necessary for a candidate to receive a majority of the popular vote in order to win the election. More votes than any other candidate receives—a plurality—are sufficient. Such a system tends to reduce, rather than enlarge, the number of political parties that are seen by voters as serious options. Indeed, it tends to produce a two-party system. British politics has been dominated by two parties for most of the last century; this is also true of Australia. Even New Zealand, which adopted a form of proportional representation in 1996, continues to have a party system dominated by two main competitors, which between them usually account for about 80% of the popular vote. In the case of Canada, the Liberal and Conservative parties have been the dominant parties in that country's history, although third parties have had a long and important presence.

In no country, however, have two political parties so dominated the political scene as in the United States. In all of the other Anglo-American democracies minor parties have played a significant role in national and sometimes sub-national politics, winning a respectable share of the popular vote, sometimes holding the balance of power during a minority government situation, capturing power in regional legislatures, or influencing the policies of the two major parties by championing policies that become popular with voters. Not so in the United States. Figure 9.1 shows the percentage of the popular vote cast for candidates of the Republican and Democratic parties in congressional elections between 1932 and 2006. The dominance of the two parties has been only slightly less in presidential elections. Independent or third-party candidates for the White House have occasionally made their presence felt, receiving a share of the popular vote ranging from Green Party leader Ralph Nader's 2.7% in 2000 to independent candidate Ross Perot's 19% in 1992.

Critics at home and abroad have sometimes argued that two parties are too few to represent the vast range of interests that exist in American society. By discouraging the emergence of serious third-party candidates, the American electoral system, they charge, denies an adequate voice to interests and values that would be represented in a multi-party system. A second criticism of the two-party system is that the Republican and Democratic parties are far more similar than different when it comes to crucial issues, particularly on matters of corporate power, the environment, and national security. The two-party system is, according to critics like Ralph Nader, really a one-party system masquerading as competition.

FIGURE 9.1:   TWO-PARTY DOMINANCE OF AMERICAN NATIONAL ELECTIONS, 1930–2006 (percentage of House votes for each party)

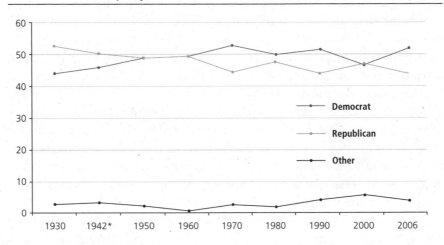

*Official records of the popular vote for members of the House of Representatives were kept in a slightly different form in 1940, so 1942 has been used instead.

Source: Congress of the United States, Congressional Election Statistics, various years.

Neither of these criticisms is well founded. The claim that two parties are incapable of representing the range of interests and values that exist in America's pluralistic society overlooks two important facts. First, each party is, in fact, a broad coalition of interests and values that often cohabit uneasily. This may be demonstrated in a couple of ways. If we look inside each party's share of the electorate, we find a disparate collection of voters. Social conservatives in the suburbs and rural areas of Georgia prefer Republican candidates, but so do affluent small-business conservatives and highly educated libertarians. The "typical" Republican voter in Michigan, New York, or Connecticut is significantly different from his or her counterpart in Mississippi or Tennessee. The same is true of the Democratic Party. The party continues to be preferred by several groups that were part of the New Deal coalition, notably blacks, union members, and Jews, and is also the preferred party of women and Hispanics. It outpolls the Republican Party in a university town like Ann Arbor, Michigan or Northampton, Massachusetts, as well as in industrial cities with large black populations like Detroit and Cleveland, but it does so on the strength of votes cast by citizens who are quite different in terms of values, socio-economic status, and group membership.

The heterogeneous character of each of the parties may also be seen in the behavior of their elected officials. The *National Journal* is a public affairs media group that publishes an annual rating of each member of Congress's record on economic, social, and foreign policy matters that come to a vote in the House or Senate. The rating is a measure of the degree to which a lawmaker's voting record fits a liberal or conservative pattern. As may be seen from the selection of members of Congress on the following page, the voting behavior and ideological leanings of lawmakers *within the same party* can be wide-ranging.

Few Democratic members of the House or Senate voted in a conservative direction more often than a liberal one, and likewise few Republicans voted in a liberal direction more often than a conservative one. Some did, however, including Nebraska's Democratic Senator Ben Nelson—more often conservative than liberal on social issues, and only marginally more liberal than

---

Ralph Nader Argues Against What He Calls the Phony Choice Between the Two Parties

The following is a segment of an interview between Green Party presidential candidate, Ralph Nader, and Sam Donaldson of ABC's "This Week," broadcast October 29, 2000.

DONALDSON: You've said it doesn't matter to you who is the president of the United States, Bush or Gore.

NADER: Because it's the permanent corporate government that's running the show here. What do you think 22,000 corporate lobbyists every day and 9,000 corporate PACs do? The two parties are becoming increasingly insignificant that way, and you can see they're morphing more and more, on more and more issues, into one corporate party.

DONALDSON: All right, let's look at some of the differences ... Bush would offer private investment accounts on Social Security to some extent; Gore would not. Bush would lower taxes for everyone; Gore would not. Bush favors a voucher-type option in education: Gore does not. Linguistic [differences]?

NADER: You think they're going to make the decisions? AARP is going to make the decision on Social Security, the retired people's lobby, and the corporate lobbies are going to make the other decisions. ... We look at Washington as having been hijacked, just the way Senator McCain said. Politicians, in order to get re-elected, raise tons of money from these corporate interests, and in return they sell our government to the highest bidder. That's the overriding issue in this election. Are the people going to run this country? Or are the corporations going to run this country?

National Journal Ratings for Selected Members of the House of Representatives, 2004

DEMOCRATS (A HIGHER NUMBER INDICATES A MORE LIBERAL VOTING RECORD)			REPUBLICANS (A HIGHER NUMBER REPRESENTS A MORE CONSERVATIVE VOTING RECORD)		
Jane Harman (D), California's 36th District			Nancy Johnson (R), Connecticut's 5th District		
Economic	67	33	Economic	47	53
Social	71	29	Social	59	41
Foreign	74	26	Foreign	49	51
Bill Delahunt (D), Massachusetts' 10th District			Vernon Elders (R), Michigan's 3rd District		
Economic	94	6	Economic	44	56
Social	83	17	Social	49	51
Foreign	96	4	Foreign	54	46
Ben Chandler (D), Kentucky's 6th District			Joe Wilson (R), South Carolina's 2nd District		
Economic	70	30	Economic	100	
Social	51	49	Social	20	80
Foreign	52	48	Foreign	32	68
Jim Marshall (D), Georgia's 3rd District			Chris Chocola (R), Indiana's 2nd District		
Economic	57	43	Economic	10	90
Social	47	53	Social	21	79
Foreign	54	46	Foreign	4	93

Source: Data from http://www.nationaljournal.com/voteratings/.

conservative on economic and foreign policy matters—and Rhode Island's Republican Senator Lincoln Chafee—more often liberal than conservative on economic and social matters, and marginally more conservative on foreign policy. A much larger number split their votes fairly evenly, say 60/40, between liberal and conservative tendencies. Even in the case of the most liberal of Democratic lawmakers and the most conservative of Republican ones, Senator Edward Kennedy (D) of Massachusetts and Senator Jim De Mint (R) of South Carolina, their voting behavior in Congress is not uniformly in one ideological direction. Most members, as the cases in the box above illustrate, have divided ideological leanings, depending on the issue and the circumstances. And each party's congressional caucus includes a broad range of ideological tendencies, Democrats within a predominantly left-of-center band and Republicans distributed mainly right-of-center.

It is quite wrong, therefore, to think of the Democratic and Republican Parties as each representing a fairly cohesive set of interests and configuration of values. Each is a broad coalition of diverse interests, values, and ideological tendencies. The argument that this diversity would be better represented through a greater number of political parties may be correct; it overlooks, however, the crucial fact that the variety that exists within the parties finds expression in the behavior of elected officials. The priorities and voting behavior of a socially conservative Democratic lawmaker from the South will be quite different from a Democratic lawmaker elected to represent South Chicago or South Central Los Angeles. The Republican Party in Connecticut is strikingly different in its ideological leanings from that party's Utah or Alabama organization. The American political system

Informal Congressional Caucuses, 110th Congress (2008)

CAUCUS TYPE	HOUSE	SENATE	BICAMERAL	TOTALS
Constituency	50	10	18	78
1. Industry	(15)	(4)	(7)	(26)
2. Geographic	(12)	(2)	(4)	(18)
3. Demographic	(23)	(4)	(7)	(34)
4. Party	6	1	3	10
5. Personal Interest	40	4	17	61
TOTALS	96	15	38	149

1. The industry constituency caucuses include not only manufacturing and service industries, but such industries as agriculture and tourism.

2. The geographic constituency caucuses include not only states and regions, but common geographic characteristics such as borders or coasts.

3. The demographic constituency caucuses include those based on characteristics of race, ethnicity, age, gender, occupation, and population density (e.g., rural, urban).

4. The party constituency caucuses refer to those formed within one of the two parties that are not part of the formal party organizations in the Congress.

5. The personal interest constituency caucuses are those that do not necessarily or obviously fall within one of the above.

The classification system used here is that of the author of this document and not of the Yellow Book. *The designations are at times subjective and arbitrary because some caucuses could just as easily fit under another category.*

Compiled and classified by Donald R. Wolfensberger, Woodrow Wilson Center, Washington, DC.

allows these *intra*-party differences to be expressed in two main ways: first is the comparative lack of party discipline in the national and state legislatures; second is the highly decentralized way in which candidates for the political parties are chosen.

The fact that a member of Congress feels freer to vote against the preferences of the party leadership than does his or her counterpart in Canada, France, or the UK gives this lawmaker the opportunity to respond more directly to the preferences and demands of his or her constituents. The penalties that exist for what in these other countries would be considered maverick legislator behavior are weaker or non-existent in the United States. A Canadian member of Parliament (MP) who votes against his or her party line on an important bill might expect to be ejected from party caucus or have his or her nomination as the party's candidate rejected by the party leader at the next election; at a minimum, the MP will have seriously compromised his or her chances of moving up within the party. None of these penalties apply to lawmakers in the United States.

In some ways the existence of multiple caucuses within Congress operates as the broad equivalent of a multi-party system in terms of providing organization and expression to a diversity of interests and ideas that could not be represented by two disciplined political parties. There are close to

Open and Closed Primaries

The selection of candidates through primaries has not eliminated the influence of the party establishment on who become their standard-bearers at election time, but it has diminished their influence significantly. The key to becoming the party's candidate for office involves, first, the ability to raise enough money to campaign effectively and, second, the capacity to mobilize enough voters to turn out on primary election day. The blessing of the party leadership is not required; indeed, it is sometimes an advantage to position oneself as an "outsider," opposed by and unbeholden to the "establishment." The result of this system is that many lawmakers feel no sense of dependence on or debt to the party. They feel free and even obliged to represent the views and interests of those whose votes and dollars won them the party's nomination and then election to the legislature.

States set their own rules regarding primary elections and the result is a hodge-podge of different systems across the United States. The basic difference, however, is between *open* and *closed* primaries. In open primaries, voters may vote in the primary of either party, regardless of whether they are registered voters of that party. In a closed primary only registered voters of the party may vote in its primary elections. Currently about twice as many states have closed primaries as have open ones. The system is made even more complicated by the fact that some states, like New Hampshire, allow independent (i.e., non-registered) voters to decide on election day the party primary in which they will vote.

200 informal caucuses in the House and Senate combined. Some of these involve groups of lawmakers with common interests from only one of the parties, but others, such as the Congressional Automotive Caucus and the Congressional Hispanic Congress, are bipartisan. Caucuses are often more important than the views of the party leadership in influencing the way in which lawmakers vote on issues that come before the legislature.

The comparative independence that characterizes the behavior of American legislators would not exist were it not for the decentralized method through which the parties' candidates for office are chosen. Until the early twentieth century the so-called party machines and bosses exercised tight control over who would be the party's candidates in general elections. That changed in the early 1900s when the parties began to use primary elections to select their candidates for public office. Primaries are elections between individuals who wish to be a party's candidate for public office. The rules governing them are established by the state organizations of each political party, including who may vote in them, what a person needs to do in order to get on the ballot, and campaign finance restrictions.

The Three Ms of Election Campaigns: Money, Media, Mobilization

Money

When Hillary Rodham Clinton ran for a Senate seat in New York in 2000, she was challenged by Republican congressman Rick Lazio. The race stayed close until election day approached, and then Clinton pulled away to win by a comfortable margin of 55% to 43%. Her campaign spent $41.5 million, or about $11.20 for every vote she received. Clinton's opponent spent $40.6 million, making this one of the most expensive congressional races on record. In the Canadian general election that same year, total campaign spending by all of the five main political parties came to roughly US$25 million, considerably less than the combined spending of Clinton and Lazio in what was only one of hundreds of election races in the 2000 American election cycle. "The best democracy that money can buy" is the conclusion of many critics of the role that money plays in American elections.

This adage seemed to be confirmed by the 2008 elections. Senator Barack Obama's decision to decline public funding enabled him to raise and spend private money without restriction. The roughly $640 million he raised exceeded by far all previous spending records. Obama's campaign spent about $10 for every vote he received on election day. The average cost of winning a House race in 2008 was nearly $1.1 million and just under $6.5 million for a Senate seat.

The amount of money spent on campaigning for office in America is extraordinary by the standards of other democracies, but charges that the amounts are somehow "obscene" or that wealthy interests are able to buy election results should not be accepted uncritically. An estimated $911.8 million was spent on marketing congressional candidates in the 2004 election cycle. Three fast food chains combined—McDonald's, Wendy's, and Burger King—spent just about the same amount on advertising in the United States that same year. Most people would agree that decisions on who will govern are probably more important than the choice of a Happy Meal at McDonald's or a Kid's Meal at Burger King. Looked at from this perspective, the amounts spent on informing voters about candidates may not seem quite so outrageous.

Some will say that whether what is being advertised is hamburgers or a candidate for public office, the problem is not the amount of money spent. It is, rather, the fact that this money is spent by self-interested parties that are not interested in providing consumer/voters with objective and relevant information but merely wish to persuade people to buy product X or vote for candidate Y. In countries like France and Germany, where the law prohibits candidates and political parties from advertising on television or radio, voters nevertheless have access to plenty of information about the parties and their candidates. Far more than in the United States, they depend on the media for this information. Some believe that this is preferable because the media will be a more objective source of the sort of information that will enable voters to make rational decisions on election day.

There are, of course, several debatable and possibly dubious premises embedded in this argument. The first is the claimed objectivity of the media. Those who construct and interpret political news tend to have systematic biases in one ideological direction or another. In the United States studies have shown repeatedly that those in the national media tend to be left of the general population, although some are more favorable to conservative points of view. Thus, the liberal tilt of the *New York Times* and the *Washington Post* is offset by the more right-of-center slant of the *Wall Street Journal* and the *Washington Times*. In television and radio, too, the more conservative coverage of Fox News exists alongside the more liberal perspective provided by CNN. The radio talk shows that discuss politics and that have the largest national audiences are virtually all conservative. The Internet, including the blogosphere, is a sort of Wild West of ideological perspectives. It is, therefore, rather naïve to accept claims of media objectivity, although it may be fair to say that, taken as a whole, the media provide a range and depth of information and a spectrum of interpretation that surpass what voters would have if they relied exclusively on what parties and their candidates say about themselves and their opponents.

The point is that voters do not have to make this choice. The tsunami of campaign ads and other information unleashed by parties and candidates, not to mention other organizations who spend money on campaign advertising in order to influence election outcomes, is only part of a tidal wave of images, information, and interpretation that washes over American voters during campaigns. Critics seem to assume that voters, or at least the less intelligent and more gullible among them, are more likely to be influenced by information provided by the self-interested parties and candidates than by media coverage. They tend to be particularly harsh in their judgment of negative or attack ads, finding these to be particularly deficient in truth and dependent on appeals to irrational impulses and emotion.

There is, in fact, little evidence to support the claim that television spot ads paid for by a candidate have a greater impact on voter choice than other sources of campaign information. Sometimes they do, and criticism of campaign advertising is based largely on those memorable cases where a particular ad or series of ads appeared to have a significant impact on poll numbers. The claim that negative ads are particularly mendacious and manipulative turns out to be even more dubious. As we will see later in this chapter, some recent work that examines the nature and impact of negative advertising concludes that they are no more untruthful than other ads and that more educated and engaged voters are, against expectations, more likely to be influenced by these allegedly irrational appeals than are other voters.

Most democracies have moved away from reliance on private contributions to finance election campaigns to a public financing model. Parties and candidates receive, according to a formula established by law, public subsidies that may be spent on advertising (to the extent and in the forms that are allowed) and other activities during election campaigns. Private contributions to parties and candidates are strictly limited, and spending on campaign advertising by organizations and individuals other than political parties and their candidates is either prohibited, as in France, or severely limited, as in Canada.

The reasoning behind the public financing model is that this frees parties and candidates from dependence on private donors and thus reduces the potential for deep-pocketed special interests to influence public policy. Although the American model permits private contributions, it also imposes certain limits on their size and includes public subsidies for candidates who

Election Finance Rules

The laws governing election finances for candidates and parties are complex. A good place for straightforward explanations of these rules may be found at http://www.opensecrets.org, a website of the Center for Responsive Politics. The rules on Political Action Committees, contribution limits, and matching funds are explained below.

Political Action Committee (PAC): A political committee that raises and spends money to elect or defeat candidates. Most PACs represent businesses, such as the Microsoft PAC; labor unions, such as the Teamsters PAC; or ideological interests, such as the EMILY's List PAC[4] or the National Rifle Association PAC. An organization's PAC will solicit money from the group's employees or members and make contributions in the name of the PAC to candidates and political parties. Individuals contributing to a PAC may also contribute directly to candidates and political parties, even those also supported by the PAC. A PAC can give $5,000 to a candidate per election (primary, general, or special) and up to $15,000 annually to a national political party. PACs may receive up to $5,000 each from individuals, other PACs, and party committees per year. A PAC must register with the Federal Election Commission within ten days of its formation, providing the name and address of the PAC, its treasurer, and any affiliated organizations.

Contribution Limits: The rules governing how much an individual or PAC can contribute to a federal candidate or party committee. Limits apply to contributions of hard money, which is used to influence the election or defeat of a federal candidate. Unlimited contributions, also called soft money, were once allowed to the national political parties but are now banned by the *Bipartisan Campaign Reform Act* (2002). Contributions to state and local candidates and party committees to be used exclusively to elect state and local candidates are subject to state con-

tribution limits. Under federal law, an individual may contribute:

- $2,000 to a candidate per election (primary and general)
- $25,000 to a political party per year
- $5,000 to a PAC per year
- $95,000 per election cycle to candidates, parties, and PACs, combined.

A PAC may contribute:

- $5,000 to a candidate per election (primary and general)
- $15,000 to a political party per year
- $5,000 to another PAC per year.

Matching Funds: Public funds available to a presidential candidate to help bankroll his or her primary campaign. The Presidential Election Campaign Fund matches up to $250 of each individual contribution to help candidates defray the cost of their primary campaign. (Contributions from PACs are not matched.) To receive matching funds, candidates must meet certain threshold requirements showing sufficient public support. Candidates also must agree to a number of restrictions, including spending limits during the primary campaign that are set by law and adjusted for inflation. The primary spending limit for the 2004 presidential election was about $45 million. In 2000, George W. Bush became the first major candidate to opt out of the matching fund system, a decision that allowed him to spend several times more than his opponent, Al Gore. Bush again refused matching funds for the 2004 election, as did Democratic candidates Howard Dean and John Kerry. In 2008 Barack Obama chose to refuse public money during both the primaries and the general election campaign and went on to raise about $640 million dollars and outspend his opponent, John McCain, by about a 2 to 1 ratio. McCain's campaign accepted public funding and the spending limits that this imposes.

meet certain conditions. It does not establish limits on how much a candidate or party may spend—such limits have been ruled by the Supreme Court to be violations of the First Amendment guarantee of free speech—and it permits election spending by groups other than parties and candidates.

Unlike the money raised by parties and candidates, there are no legal limits set on the amounts that may be contributed by a group or individual to an organization that is registered under section 527 of the Internal Revenue Code and that spends this money on issue ads that do not explicitly endorse or oppose any party or candidacy. A single individual donor, billionaire George Soros, spent $27 million on such ads in an effort to defeat George W. Bush in 2004. Attempts to regulate this sort of spending, notably through the *Bipartisan Campaign Reform Act* (2002), have been unsuccessful. The goal of that law was to ban *soft money* contributions to parties and candidates and also to prohibit special interest groups from spending money on issue ads that support or oppose a specific candidate within 60 days of a general election or 30 days of a primary election. Soft money refers to contributions that are not supposed to be spent in ways that directly promote the election or defeat of a particular candidate or party. In theory, at least, such contributions, the amounts of which were at one time unlimited, were to be used for so-called "party-building" activities like voter registration drives. In fact, however, soft money was used largely to pay for issue ads that were thinly veiled efforts to influence voter behavior. Soft money contributions were banned by the *Bipartisan Campaign Reform Act*, but huge amounts of money have continued to be spent by advocacy groups on issue ads. The 2007 Supreme Court decision in *Federal Election Commission v. Wisconsin Right to Life* ruled that these ads constituted protected speech under the First Amendment.

Some who defend the amounts of private money contributed to parties and candidates and spent directly by 527 committees on issue ads point out that money is contributed and spent by many groups, often on different sides of the same issue. This is certainly true. The shooting match of paid ads that took place in 2004 between MoveOn.org (anti-Bush) and Swiftboat Veterans for Peace (anti-Kerry) was a good illustration of lots of money being spent on both sides of the partisan and ideological divide. Moreover, it is wrong to assume that pro-business and ideologically conservative groups will always outspend their opponents. Realtors, property developers, trial lawyers, and oil and gas associations will always give more money to candidates and parties than environmental and human rights groups. Nevertheless, a tremendous amount of non-business money finds its way into American election campaigns.

The enormous potential for tapping these sources of revenue was first shown during Vermont Governor Howard Dean's run for the Democratic Party's presidential nomination in 2004. Before his campaign came to an abrupt end following his poor showing in the Iowa caucuses and his widely broadcast and somewhat crazy-sounding scream to supporters (this may be seen and heard at YouTube and many other websites), Dean's campaign had raised about $60 million through its website, mainly in contributions of under $100. Leading up to the 2008 primary season, Republican Ron Paul raised over $4 million through Internet contributions on a single day, 6 November 2007, establishing what was at the time a one-day record for this sort of fundraising. But the presidential campaign of Barack Obama dispelled any remaining doubts about the Internet as a fundraising tool. In September 2008 alone his campaign received Internet contributions totaling $100 million, representing about two-thirds of all the money raised by his campaign that month. A considerable portion of this money was contributed using prepaid credit cards, so that the source of these Internet contributions could not be traced.

The bottom line is this: there is more private money in American election campaigns, with fewer legal restrictions on how much is spent, how and by whom, than in other democracies. Whether this is a good or a bad thing is

---

Limiting Issue Ad Spending by Interest Groups in the United States and Canada: Two Perspectives from Two Supreme Courts

HARPER V. CANADA, 2004: ISSUE ADS MAY BE CONTROLLED TO PROTECT CANADIAN DEMOCRACY

In the absence of spending limits, it is possible for the affluent or a number of persons pooling their resources and acting in concert to dominate the political discourse, depriving their opponents of a reasonable opportunity to speak and be heard, and undermining the voter's ability to be adequately informed of all views. Equality in the political discourse is thus necessary for meaningful participation in the electoral process and ultimately enhances the right to vote. This right, therefore, does not guarantee unimpeded and unlimited electoral debate or expression. Spending limits, however, must be carefully tailored to ensure that candidates, political parties, and third parties are able to convey their

information to the voter; if overly restrictive, they may undermine the informational component of the right to vote. Here, s. 350 does not interfere with the right of each citizen to play a meaningful role in the electoral process....

While the right to political expression lies at the core of the guarantee of free expression and warrants a high degree of constitutional protection, there is nevertheless a danger that political advertising may manipulate or oppress the voter. Parliament had to balance the rights and privileges of all the participants in the electoral process....

Third party advertising expense limits are rationally connected to [these] objectives. They prevent those who have access to significant financial resources, and are able to purchase unlimited amount of advertising, to dominate the electoral discourse to the detriment of others; they create a balance between the financial resources of each candidate or political party; and they advance the perception that the electoral process is substantively fair as it provides for a reasonable degree of equality between citizens who wish to participate in that process. Second, s. 350 minimally impairs the right to free expression. Parties may freely spend money or advertise to make their views known or to persuade others.

FEDERAL ELECTORAL COMMISSION V. WISCONSIN RIGHT TO LIFE, 2007: LIMITS ON ISSUE ADS THREATEN THE FIRST AMENDMENT RIGHTS THAT ARE FUNDAMENTAL TO DEMOCRACY

... Appellants are wrong in arguing that WRTL has the burden of demonstrating that s. 203 [of the *Bipartisan Campaign Reform Act*] is unconstitutional. Because s.203 burdens political speech, it is subject to strict scrutiny ... under which the Government must prove that applying BCRA to WRTL's ads furthers a compelling governmental interest and is narrowly tailored to achieve that interest....

... Because WRTL's ads may reasonably be interpreted as something other than an appeal to vote for or against a specific candidate, they are not the functional equivalent of express advocacy.... To safeguard freedom of speech on public issues, the proper standard for an as-applied challenge to BCRA s.203 must be objective, focusing on the communication's substance rather than on amorphous considerations of intent and effect. It must entail minimal if any discovery, to allow parties to resolve disputes quickly without chilling speech through the threat of burdensome litigation. And it must eschew "the open-ended rough-and-tumble of factors," which "invit[es] complex argument in a trial court and a virtually inevitable appeal." In short, it must give the benefit of any doubt to protecting rather than stifling speech. In light of these considerations, a court should find that an ad is the functional equivalent of express advocacy only if the ad is susceptible of no reasonable interpretation other than as an appeal to vote for or against a specific candidate. WRTL's three ads are plainly not the functional equivalent of express advocacy under this test. First, their content is consistent with that of a genuine issue ad: They focus and take a position on a legislative issue and exhort the public to adopt that position and to contact public officials with respect to the matter. Second, their content lacks indicia of express advocacy: They do not mention an election, candidacy, political party, or challenger; and they take no position on a candidate's character, qualifications, or fitness for office.

... Although the Court has long recognized "the governmental interest in preventing corruption and the appearance of corruption" in election campaigns, it has invoked this interest as a reason for upholding contribution limits and suggested that it might also justify limits on electioneering expenditures posing the same dangers as large contributions ... But to justify regulation of WRTL's ads, this interest must be stretched yet another step to ads that are not the functional equivalent of express advocacy. Issue ads like WRTL's are not equivalent to contributions, and the corruption interest cannot justify regulating them. A second possible compelling interest lies in addressing "the corrosive and distorting effects of immense aggregations of wealth that are accumulated with the help of the corporate form and that have little or no correlation to the public's support for the corporation's political ideas." [The Supreme Court has] held that this interest justifies regulating the "functional equivalent" of campaign speech. This interest cannot be extended further to apply to genuine issue ads like WRTL's because doing so would call into question this Court's holdings that the corporate identity of a speaker does not strip corporations of all free speech rights.

Source: Harper v. Canada *(Attorney General), 2004 SCC 33, [2004] 1 S.C.R. 827;* Federal Election Commission v. Wisconsin Right to Life, *551 U.S. (2007).*

in the eyes of the beholder. What is certain, however, is that it is a model that accords with the greater market orientation of Americans and their belief that freedom of expression includes the freedom to spend their money as they wish. They are, therefore, less receptive than Canadians or Swedes to arguments that the financial playing field needs to be leveled and private money banned or strictly regulated in order to ensure that democracy operates as it should.

Media

George Allen was an American senator from Virginia running for re-election in 2006. His campaign had lots of money, and he was widely considered to be a serious contender for the 2008 Republican presidential nomination. Then, Allen was videotaped at an outdoor rally referring to a heckler as "Macaca"—a reference to the heckler's dark skin (a macaque is a monkey native to Southeast Asia, and the word is considered a racial slur). Had the video footage been shown only on the television news the damage done by the episode might have faded after a week or so, as other new stories pushed it aside. However, it was immediately posted on YouTube where it became one of the most popular postings for a number of weeks, attracting several hundred thousand "hits." The YouTube video increased the reach and duration of what might otherwise have been an embarrassing but survivable gaffe. Combined with some other missteps on the campaign trail, it was instrumental in causing Allen's unexpected defeat.

The impact of the Internet on American election campaigns is still in its early, evolving stages, but already its influence is important and growing. When Hillary Rodham Clinton, John Edwards, and Barack Obama launched their candidacies for the Democratic presidential nomination two years before the actual election date, all three did so using very slick productions posted at their respective websites. These postings generated an enormous amount of secondary coverage in the so-called Old Media of television news broadcasts and print, where the use of the Internet in a political campaign was discussed as if it were still a novelty and somehow not quite as legitimate as an interview on "Larry King Live" or an op-ed piece in the *New York Times*. The truth is, however, that the Internet's role in campaigning—an activity that never takes a vacation in the US—had already been well established by 2004 and shows every sign of growing rapidly in importance.

In discussing the role of the media in American election campaigns, it is useful to distinguish between what are sometimes called Old and New

Media. Old Media encompass the historically dominant television broadcast networks and print journalism; New Media include websites and blogs on the Internet as well as cable television news and talk radio. The distinction is mainly a chronological one: Old Media came first and dominated the scene until the early 1990s when CNN established itself as the television network of record during the 1991 Gulf War. Between the Republican Party's loss of the White House in 1992 and its capture of both houses of Congress in 1994 for the first time in over 40 years, conservative talk radio was the focal point for opposition to the Clinton administration and talk show host Rush Limbaugh was its general. "America held hostage" was the rallying cry that began Limbaugh's daily program, listened to by an estimated 15–20 million people each day, an audience that is not so far from the combined daily audience of about 26 million for the three Old Media television news broadcasts (ABC, CBS, and NBC). The emergence of Fox cable news in the late 1990s as a rival to CNN was yet another step in loosening the traditional dominance of Old Media. Not only were audience shares for the news and public affairs programming of ABC, CBS, and NBC in decline, newspaper readership was also waning (with at least one important exception: the *Wall Street Journal* continued to attract a faithful readership and remained so profitable that Rupert Murdoch's Newscorp bought it in 2007).

The next stage in the decentralization of the media occurred with the explosive growth in access to and reliance on the Internet for information of all sorts, including politics. Virtually all candidates for national office had websites by the 2000 election cycle, but these tended to be little more than cyber-locations where information on the candidate and party could be accessed. By 2004, however, the possibilities of the Internet became apparent. As mentioned earlier, the Howard Dean campaign showed that a candidate's website could be an extraordinarily effective vehicle for raising campaign funds. The liberal, anti-Bush website, MoveOn.org, was at the forefront of a new wave of campaign websites that used video and text to oppose the candidacies of some and support those of others. Blogs came into their own in American politics, on both sides of the political spectrum. They are the Internet equivalent of ongoing op-eds with the important difference that, unlike their print and television counterparts, blogs may be highly interactive, allowing those who read them to respond immediately and for the blogger to react to his or her readers in a manner that is essentially an unfolding conversation. Bloggers have also proven to be effective fact-checkers and investigators, performing roles that used to be monopolized by Old Media journalists. Text messages delivered to millions of voters via their cellphones were an important form of political communication in 2008, used most

effectively by the Obama campaign. It may be some time before the influence of the Internet surpasses that of Old Media in election campaigns, but
the impact of the New Media is well summarized by Michael Barone: "You
might have been able to cover the 1980 presidential campaign in five rooms.
But you could not cover the 2004 presidential campaign in 100 rooms. The
political media have moved from centralized command-and-control toward
a more decentralized networking model."[5]

One of the important ways in which television, including the older broadcast networks, remains very influential in election campaigns is through
political ads that are paid for by parties, candidates, and 527 committees.
Roughly $2 billion was spent on television political ads in the 2006 mid-
term election campaign, and total spending on all campaign advertising
in the 2008 elections is estimated to have been about $2.5 billion.[6] Media
spending is the single largest budget item in national campaigns, accounting
for about half of all expenditures in a presidential campaign, and most of
that media spending is accounted for by television ads.

Political advertising on television has become an important branch of
marketing science, as parties and candidates attempt to maximize the political returns from their media spending. Although presidential campaigns
will purchase some advertising time on national networks, most political ad
buying is carefully targeted at particular regional markets and even demographic segments of these markets.

The actual ads tend to be short, usually no more than 30 seconds (advertising time on television is typically sold in 15-, 30-, and 60-second blocks).
Over the years the amount of television coverage of candidates seen speaking in their own words has declined dramatically, from about 42 seconds
in 1968 to 7.3 seconds in 2000,[7] replaced by journalists and commentators
summarizing and interpreting their words. Television ads and other paid
uses of mass media represent a means through which parties and candidates
can seek to communicate directly with voters instead of relying on others
to do this for them. The television spot ad, first used in the 1992 presidential election, has become one of the main sources of information about the
policies and performance of candidates and parties. The results have been,
according to the conventional wisdom, disastrous for American democracy.

Neil Postman argues that the seductions of language are trivial compared
to the persuasive and manipulative powers of image-based media. This is
because images are more likely than language to be used to evoke, and to be
effective in evoking, visceral, emotional responses in their subjects. Speaking
of Ronald Reagan, widely acknowledged to have been one of the most effective television communicators. Postman says,

With Reagan, the issue was not whether the content of his televised statements was true or even plausible. The question was, "Do you like that image on the screen? Do you trust it? Is it sincere to you?" The effectiveness of such a televised image lies outside of the realm of logic and reason, conventionally understood, and in the realm of aesthetics.[8]

Postman's concerns are echoed by others. "It really doesn't matter what a politician says anymore," says Mark Crispin Miller. "It's not even necessary for a politician to be lucid. If they look right, if they have the right golden glow and use the right buzzwords ... then that politician can succeed and I think it has to do with the power of the image." But are American voters really so gullible, ill-informed, or downright stupid that they are incapable of recognizing the phoniness, artifice, and attempted manipulation that characterizes much of televised political communication, particularly spot ads? "The frightening thing," says Miller, "is that just recognizing the artificiality of something does not ensure immunity to that thing. Simply knowing that

Targeting Key Markets through Political Advertising

Advertising in the 2004 campaign has been—and will likely continue to be—narrowly targeted to the most competitive states and districts in the country. In fact, despite record television advertising, nearly 60 per cent of Americans live in areas where no presidential campaign TV commercials have been broadcast since the end of the primary season on March 4 [until June]....

While Democrats outspent Republicans almost across the board, the data show that Bush, Kerry, and interest group ads have been focused on the same groups of voters. Geographically, four of the top six media markets for advertising in the presidential race have been in Ohio, with Missouri markets seeing the third and sixth highest concentrations of advertising. Both sides targeted females more than males and older over younger viewers.

The oldest segment of viewers, those over 55, saw far more ads than viewers aged 25–54. Younger viewers, those under 25, have seen, by far, the fewest presidential campaign TV ads....

Both campaigns heavily favored local news in their media buying. Local news accounted for over 40 per cent of each presidential campaign's TV advertising. Morning network shows, such as *The Today Show* and *Good Morning America*, comprised another 11 per cent of ad buys. Following these two categories, the campaigns spent more of their money on syndicated daytime talkers—*The Oprah Winfrey Show*, *Dr. Phil*, and *Regis & Kelly*. Access programming, the shows following local news and before primetime, were next, with syndicated shows like *Wheel of Fortune* and *Jeopardy!* proving popular.

Excerpts from Ken Goldstein, "Political Advertising in 2004," Department of Political Science Newsletter, University of Michigan (Fall 2004): 10–11.

you are an object of propaganda is not enough to armor one against the appeals of propaganda."[9]

Political advertising by parties and candidates has never been about impartiality and objective truth-telling. Moreover, it would be quite wrong to imagine that the art of manipulation only began with television. The earliest election ads, going back to the vicious American presidential race between Thomas Jefferson and John Adams in 1800, were full of distortions and lies of a magnitude that would embarrass today's most loyal party stalwart. What has changed, however, is that the visual imagery that is at the heart of contemporary political communications works its persuasion in ways different from print-based communications and, according to some, in ways more difficult to hold to account. Much of modern political communication, including television ads, is intended to convey a sensation rather than provide information. It targets sentiments and emotions instead of reason and rationality. There is nothing wrong with feelings, of course. We buy all sorts of things because of the good feelings that we get from wearing clothes that everyone can see come from Lacoste or drinking a beer that says to us and others, "This is the sort of person I am." But whether voters should "buy" parties and their candidates on the basis of image and evoked feelings, neglecting to worry very much about whether the reality of the product coincides with the elusive claims used to market it, is what worries critics.

The manipulative quality of the vast majority of television campaign ads is an inevitable consequence of the nature and economics of the medium, which requires that a story be told in 15–30 seconds. If a company is selling mouthwash or toothpaste, it does this through images suggesting that you will be rejected if you do not use the product (fear, insecurity) and accepted if you do (hope, love). If what is being sold is a political party or a candidate, the formula is essentially identical and dictated in large measure by the fact that the story must be told quickly.

An expertly crafted and timely television spot ad that is viewed by a large segment of the electorate—the size of which may be increased through a controversial ad being replayed on television news programs or viewed online via news websites or web links in blogs—can be very effective in making associations between feelings and parties or candidates. Two of the best known illustrations of this phenomenon are the "Daisy" ad from Lyndon Johnson's 1964 presidential campaign and the "Willie Horton" ad from George Bush Sr.'s 1988 campaign. The "Daisy" ad very effectively made or reinforced the association of Johnson's opponent, Barry Goldwater, with the possibility of a nuclear Armageddon. The "Willy Horton" ad connected Bush's opponent, Massachusetts Governor Michael Dukakis, with leniency toward dangerous criminals, evoking race-related fears as well (Horton was black and had committed rape and murder while out on a weekend parole program that Governor Dukakis had signed into law). This ad is generally considered to be one of the more notorious examples of a genre of televised political ads known as negative advertising. There is an enormous literature on such advertising, the general conclusions of which are that negative ads are manipulative, target emotions, lack substance, rely on irrational appeals, and are most likely to sway less educated and more poorly informed voters.

In *Campaigning for Hearts and Minds: How Emotional Appeals in Political Ads Work*, Ted Brader examines these claims using empirical data collected from experiments conducted during an election for governor in Massachusetts. He concludes that, "contrary to conventional wisdom, heavy reliance on emotion does not necessarily entail an absence of logical argument, factual evidence, or policy discussion." He goes on to say that "Emotions are an essential part of our reasoning and social decision-making faculties ... and are therefore not manipulative or illegitimate. Attempts to elicit enthusiasm or fear [through ads] may help politicians motivate and inform otherwise apathetic citizens." Contrary to the widely accepted belief that negative ads work best on uninformed voters, Brader finds that "the most knowledgeable or "sophisticated" citizens are also the most responsive to emotional appeals."[10]

The Use of Emotions in Televised Political Ads

Political ads, like product commercials, usually contain more than words. They are full of pictures, sound, and music....The music and images accomplish something more precise than merely enhancing the pleasure of the viewing experience. They make the ad compelling, by eliciting specific emotions and, in doing so, change the way viewers respond to the message of the ad.

... Attempts to elicit fear or anxiety, through harsh images and tense music, lend negative ads the capacities to redirect the attention of viewer and persuade unbelievers. After exposure to fear ads,

citizens experience greater uncertainty about their political choices and are more likely to change their political preferences and vote choice.... As a result, these appeals exhibit the greatest persuasive power on the opponent's base of support. Fear ads also motivate citizens to contact campaigns for more information and turn their attention towards news sources that hold greater potential for addressing the alleged reason for anxiety. Finally, fear appeals can strengthen belief in the importance of voting and stimulate greater involvement in elections among some citizens ...

Excerpts from Ted Brader, Campaigning for Hearts and Minds.

A different defense of television spot ads comes from Kathleen Hall Jamieson, one of the foremost experts on political advertising in America. "If I had a choice between watching what you typically see in news about campaigns and typical ads, I would watch the typical ad," says Jamieson, "And I'd watch it back to back, so I'd watch both candidates' advertising because in the give and take of advertising you're likely to get more policy content than you are in the typical newscast."[11] News coverage tends to focus much of the time on the horse race aspects of a campaign—who's up, who's down, what the polls say, etc.—whereas ads will often provide viewers with content regarding the issues, the candidate's stand, the alleged shortcomings of his or her opponent, and other information that most voters should find useful in deciding who to vote for.

Readers may arrive at their own judgments regarding the qualities of political ads in American elections by viewing the hundreds that are archived at The Living Room Candidate website, which includes a selection of ads from every presidential election since 1952.[12] Most of these are ads paid for by the Republican and Democratic parties. However, some of the most effective ads in recent election cycles have been paid for by interest groups. A personal selection of some of what I consider to be the most effective ads used in American presidential campaigns since the 1960s is found in the box below.

Mobilization

A message that resonates with enough voters and the money to communicate it to them are crucial steps in a successful campaign. But they are not enough. Every campaign requires volunteers and most, except contests for local office in small communities, will have some paid staff. A campaign also

My "Top Ten" Televised Political Ads

Literally thousands upon thousands of spot ads have been produced and broadcast since the first televised campaign ad aired in the 1952 presidential campaign. In choosing my personal "top 10" I have limited my selection to presidential campaign ads sponsored by the two main political parties. All of these may be viewed at http://livingroomcandidate.movingimage. us. Select your own "Top Ten" list and think about what you think makes for an effective ad.

1. **1964 (Democrat), The "Daisy" ad.** This is a classic negative ad that never directly mentions the name of its target, Republican presidential candidate Barry Goldwater. The ad relies on fear, juxtaposing a scene of innocence—a young girl plucking the petals of a daisy—with a very scary image of nuclear Armaggedon.

2. **1964 (Republican), "Ronald Reagan defends Goldwater."** This ad uses the authority of a third party, in this case the well-known actor Ronald Reagan, to rebut claims made against Barry Goldwater. The use of someone who is respected because of his or her expertise, stature, or celebrity to promote a candidate is a longstanding device in campaign advertising. This particular ad is a short version of a much longer televised speech that Reagan gave on behalf of Goldwater. The ad and the speech did nothing to save Goldwater from a crushing defeat, but they did help propel Reagan into office as governor of California in 1966.

3. **1984 (Republican), "It's morning again in America."** Turn the volume down and just watch the images on screen. Or try to ignore the narrator and just listen to the music. You might imagine that insurance or a financial security policy is being advertised. In fact, however, this positive ad was for the re-election of President Reagan. It uses the principle of retrospective voting (see later in chapter), asking viewers "Why would we ever want to return to where we were less than four short years ago?"

4. **1988 (Republican), "The revolving door."** This negative ad portrays the Democratic presidential candidate, Massachusetts Governor Michael Dukakis, as soft on crime. The visuals are in black and white and the music is ominous, commonly used devices in this type of ad.

5. **1988 (Republican), "Willie Horton."** One of the most talked-about negative ads of all time, this one starts with candidate contrast, portraying Dukakis as soft and Republican candidate George Bush Sr. as hard on crime. It then quickly shifts to a weekend prison pass program signed into law by Governor Dukakis and the story of Willie Horton, who committed murder and rape while out on one of these weekend passes. Willie Horton was black and the use of his image led to claims that the Republican campaign was deliberately exploiting racial fears through this ad.

6. **1992 (Democrat), "Journey."** This beautifully crafted one-minute ad provides a biography of Democratic presidential candidate Bill Clinton from his birth in Hope, Arkansas to the ad's closing promise to "Bring hope back to the American dream."

7. **1992 (Democrat), "Leaders."** This positive ad for the Clinton-Gore ticket focuses on Bill Clinton's accomplishments as governor of Arkansas and his promises for the future. Its message—"Clinton-Gore: For people, for a change"—taps a deep populist stream in American political culture.

8. **1996 (Democrat), "The Next Century."** In this positive ad President Clinton is shown looking presidential, sitting at his desk in the Oval Office and looking out over the Mall toward the Washington Monument. His record of accomplishments is featured, and the ad ends with the optimistic, forward-looking message, "Building a bridge to the 21st century."

9. **2000 (Republican), "Really."** A kitchen that could be in anyone's home is the scene for this negative ad that shows Democratic candidate Al Gore apparently taking contradictory positions on issues and making claims ("I took the initiative in creating the Internet") that caused many Americans to question his credibility.

10. **2004 (Republican), "Windsurfing."** Playing baseball or football, or being seen hunting, can be a positive image for a candidate. But it is a fair bet that no candidate will be caught windsurfing after Democratic candidate John Kerry's afternoon on the gentle waves of San Francisco Bay was used against him. The image of Kerry as a "flip-flopper" on the issues was reinforced by this ad through video editing and narration that appeared to show him on opposite sides of the same issues. The ad concludes, "John Kerry: Whichever way the wind blows."

needs an effective strategy for getting its voters registered and to the polls on election day. The 2004 election campaign showed just how crucial organization and voter mobilization are to a successful campaign.

Voter registration and turnout in that election increased significantly for both parties, reversing a trend of declining participation that began in the 1960s. About 18 million more citizens voted than in 2000, an increase of about 17%, although the size of the voting age population increased by only 9.4% over those four years. The closeness of the 2000 race, in which Al Gore's share of the popular vote was only 0.6% greater than George W. Bush's, and some key states, including Ohio and Florida, were nearly dead heats, signaled to the parties the importance of mobilizing their supporters. Under the direction of strategist Karl Rove, the Republican Party aimed to increase voter turnout among Evangelicals, the most loyal part of its base. The Democrats focused on mobilizing black voters, Hispanics in certain cities, voters in university towns, and unionized workers. The means used to achieve this mobilization involved a combination of greater investment in traditional methods—volunteers manning phone banks and going door to door as well as voter registration at churches and malls—and newer methods such as using websites and carefully targeted direct mail and email messages to segments of the electorate considered to be particularly crucial.

All this begins with party activists. Those who are motivated to devote their time to working on an election campaign tend to be more interested in and knowledgeable about politics than typical citizens; they also differ from others of their party's supporters, being more ideological and holding issue positions that are more extreme. In the case of the Republican Party, this means that activists tend to be more conservative than the mainstream of that party's electoral support, while Democratic activists tend to be to the left of their party's voter base. Activists are much more likely than other citizens to participate in the party caucuses or vote in the primaries that determine who will be their party's candidate for office, from president down to city councilor. Turnout rates in presidential caucuses and primaries tend to be quite low—although the very close and highly publicized race between Hillary Clinton and Barack Obama in the 2008 Democratic primaries generated record turnout levels—so the characteristics of those who actually vote in these contests are crucial. Turnout rates for several state primaries and the Iowa caucuses in 2000, when the presidential nomination for both parties was open and therefore turnout in the primaries for the party controlling the White House would not be depressed by the fact of an incumbent running for re-nomination, and for 2008, a very exceptional year, are shown in Table 9.1.

TABLE 9.1:   SELECTED PRIMARY/CAUCUS TURNOUT RATES, 2000 AND 2008

State	VEP* Turnout Rate 2000	VEP* Turnout Rate 2008
Iowa Caucus	6.8%	16.3%
New Hampshire	44.4%	52.5%
South Carolina	20.2%	30.4%
Tennessee	11.3%	26.4%
California	40.3%	41.7%
Connecticut	15.6%	19.8%
Georgia	17.7%	32.7%

*Voter-eligible population.

Source: "Presidential primary Turnout Rates," United States Elections Project, http://elections.gmu.edu/Voter_
Turnout_2004_Primaries.htm and http://elections.gmu.edu/Voter_Turnout_2008_Primaries.htm.

With the exception of New Hampshire and California, the turnout rates are quite low. New Hampshire's higher rate may be explained in large part by the fact that it has been, historically, the first of the primaries and by virtue of this has attracted a degree of attention by the parties, their candidates and the media far out of proportion to the state's weight in the *electoral college* and the state's rather unrepresentative population. In the lead-up to the 2008 presidential primaries, some candidates began to visit the Granite State on a regular basis as early as 2006, and serious candidates already had state organizing committees in place. California's much higher than average turnout is due largely to the fact that it is the most delegate-rich of the states. A candidate from either party would have a very difficult time winning his or her party's nomination without winning in California. For this reason the campaigns tend to invest a lot of time and resources in the California primaries, which, being historically the first of the big state primaries, receives enormous national media attention.

In the case of the Iowa caucuses, the 6.8% turnout in 2000 represented a total of about 145,000 citizens, out of an eligible voting population of 2,121,836. They determined who would be seen as the "winners" and "losers" and who would then be perceived to have momentum or problems heading into the New Hampshire primaries. The caucus model for selecting delegates to a party's presidential nominating convention is about as close to populist direct democracy as one finds in the United States today. Those who attend state caucus meetings are registered members of their political party, a self-selection filter that ensures they will not be typical of the broader population. They meet at designated locations such as school gymnasiums, church halls, or community centers across the state on an appointed day and listen to speeches made by candidates and their representatives. Over a couple of hours there

The Electoral College

Few institutions appear to fit more uncomfortably with American ideals of democracy than that used to select the president of the United States. This became apparent in 2000 when Democrat Al Gore received about half a million more votes than Republican George W. Bush but won fewer delegates in the electoral college. Many Americans appeared surprised to learn that their Constitution does not automatically award the presidency to the candidate who wins the most votes. Loud calls for reform were heard, and a flurry of proposals were introduced in Congress. A few years later the issue of electoral college reform had fallen off the radar screen.

The electoral college is a body of representatives from each of the 50 states and the District of Columbia, whose sole purpose is to cast votes to determine who becomes president. Each state has a number of electors equal to its number of senators (two) plus members in the House of Representatives. Thus California, with 52 members in the House, has 54 electors. A small population state like Alaska or Wyoming has only one representative in the House and therefore has three electors. The District of Columbia has three (see the Twenty-third Amendment).

The Constitution declares that each state may determine the method by which electors are chosen. In each state the process is the same. Parties name a slate of electors (in California, for example, the state Republican Party will name 54 people, as will the state Democratic Party) shortly after the presidential and vice-presidential candidates of the party have been chosen. The position of elector carries no stipend and is generally an honorific reward to those who have served the party long and faithfully.

When citizens enter the polling booth they have the impression that they are voting directly for a party's presidential and vice-presidential candidates whose names appear on the ballot. But legally speaking they are not. They are actually voting for that party's slate of electors from their state, although the names of these electors are not on the ballot and in most cases would not be recognized by most voters. In 1952 the Supreme Court held that electors cannot be constitutionally required to vote for the candidates to whom they are pledged. However, in over 200 years there have been only a handful of cases where an elector has failed to vote as expected. The political and ethical pressure on electors to respect their pledge to a particular party's candidate is sufficient to ensure that such maverick behavior is rare.

In every state except Maine and Nebraska the presidential candidate who wins the greatest share of the popular vote wins all of that state's votes in the electoral college. Maine and Nebraska divide their electoral college votes between the parties' candidates according to a proportional formula.

The electoral college encourages presidential candidates to campaign regionally. Think of it this way. If election for president were decided simply on the basis of the nationwide popular vote, no candidate would ever spend any time in Nebraska and possibly not even in Connecticut. But when the prize for coming in first in a particular state is all of that state's votes in the electoral college, candidates will invest a good deal of campaign time and resources in closely contested states where the marginal return on this investment appears worthwhile. This explains why in the 2008 presidential race both Barack Obama and John McCain spent much more time in Ohio, Pennsylvania, and Florida, where the race was perceived to be competitive, than in California, New York, and Texas, each of which had more electors but where the outcome was a foregone conclusion.

This brings us back to 2000. It is possible that had that election not been decided by a Supreme Court ruling that stopped the recount process in Florida—a recount process, it has to be said, that had become so politicized as to make any suggestion of a fair and objective vote count almost farcical—the fact that the losing candidate received half a million more votes than the winner in the electoral college might not have caused such a furor. And in other democracies, including Canada and some of its provinces, it has occasionally happened that the party forming a government after an election was not the one that received the most votes. Nevertheless, many Americans were appalled that this could happen under their Constitution and were sympathetic to calls for reform. But reform requires that the Constitution be amended, not an easy process, and before long the economic slowdown that followed President Bush's election and then the terrorist attacks of 9/11 had most Americans thinking about other matters.

will be questions and discussion, and then those attending the caucuses move to the candidate they have decided to support and a tally is made of the votes for each candidate. It is a method of making political decision that nineteenth-century mid-westerners would have recognized as entirely normal but which seems rather anachronistic to many contemporary observers.

The perceived and actual importance of New Hampshire and Iowa, two states that together account for a rather minuscule percentage of the delegates needed to win a party's presidential nomination—seven and four votes, respectively—is due to the fact that they are at the front end of the process to select the parties' presidential nominees and so the national media pays attention to them. Without the media attention these would be thought of as minor league events in tiny states whose populations are, demographically, quite different from the national electorate. The practical importance of the Republican farmers and businesspeople and Democratic university students, professors, and union members in Iowa who attend the party caucuses is far greater than the state's size would seem to warrant. Likewise, the issues that concern New Hampshire's electorate—not necessarily ones that matter as much to Floridians, Texans, and Californians, whose chance to vote in primaries comes later—assume a significance far out of proportion to the state's size.

Party activists tend to pull the party and its choice of presidential candidate in the direction of the party's more extreme ideological elements. Sometimes the result is the selection of a candidate who is a disaster with voters. This was true of Republican Barry Goldwater in 1964, Democrat George McGovern in 1972, and Democrat Walter Mondale in 1984. In each of these cases the candidate chosen by the more activist elements of the party alienated too many of his own party's supporters. About one in five Republicans voted for Johnson over Goldwater, one in three Democratic voters chose Nixon over McGovern, and one in four Democrats preferred Reagan over Mondale.[13] Of course the perceived electability of a candidate is always a foremost concern for many party activists and particularly for party strategists. This concern is not always enough, however, to attenuate the tug of ideology exerted by party activists. Figure 9.2 compares the opinion of Republican and Democratic delegates to their respective presidential nominating conventions and those of registered voters of the two parties.

FIGURE 9.2:   ATTITUDES OF PARTY DELEGATES AND VOTERS, 2004

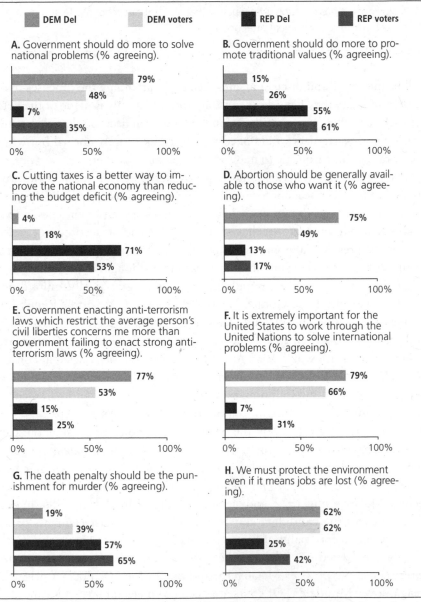

Source: Adapted from New York Times/CBS News Poll, 2004 Republican National Delegate Survey, August 2004.

The mobilization of thousands of party activist volunteers leading up to and during the primaries precedes an even greater mobilization campaign aimed at getting a candidate's supporters registered and to the polls on election day. This was once the task of local party machines whose wheels were greased by patronage. These have been replaced by extensive networks of grassroots activists who do door-to-door campaign literature drops, phone probable supporters, assist in getting voters registered, and drive voters to the polls.

The number of people involved in this effort to mobilize voters reached unprecedented levels in the 2004 campaign. It is estimated that the Bush-Cheney organization had the support of about 1.4 million volunteers. The Democratic National Committee placed its volunteer total at about 233,000, but even that represented an impressive army of party foot soldiers. This was particularly evident in closely contested states.

Most observers credit this increased emphasis on volunteers talking to or actually meeting voters with the jump in the turnout rate from 51% in 2000 to 61% in 2004. In Ohio and Florida, both closely contested states where the parties' volunteer networks were largest, voter turnout increased by 20% and 28%, respectively. The lesson appeared to be that low-tech social contact, aided by high-tech data collection on and targeting of those

---

Mobilizing the Republican Vote in 2004: Mixing Old and New Methods

The [2004] Bush campaign used connections—networks—to recruit volunteers and identify voters. The campaign built on existing connections—religious, occupational, voluntary—to establish contacts. If a Bush volunteer was a Hispanic accountant active in the Boy Scouts, the campaign would reach out through him to other Hispanics, accountants and their clients, and Boy Scout volunteers. Of course, the campaign put much effort into contacting people in religious groups—particularly Evangelical Christians, but also Catholics and Orthodox Jews. And the Bush campaign reached out to people with shared affinities who tend to be Republicans. The campaign consulting firms National Media and TargetPoint identified Republican-leaning groups—

Coors beer and bourbon drinkers, college football TV viewers, Fox News viewers, people with caller ID—and devised ways to connect with them. As Thomas Edsall and James Grimaldi wrote in the *Washington Post* after the election, "Surveys of people on these consumer data lists were then used to determine 'anger points' (late-term abortion, trial lawyers fees, estate taxes) that coincided with the Bush agenda for as many as 32 categories of voters, each identifiable by income, magazine subscriptions, favorite television shows, and other 'flags.' Merging this data, in turn, enabled those running direct-mail, precinct-walking, and phone-bank programs to target each voter with a tailored message."

Michael Barone, The Almanac of American Politics 2006, *22–23.*

most likely to vote for a party's candidate, paid high electoral dividends. The success of Howard Dean's 2000 primary campaign in mobilizing thousands of supporters and raising millions of dollars through his campaign website and the dominant role of television advertising in modern campaigns had somewhat obscured the potential of talk-to-your-neighbor as a strategy for increasing a party's vote. This was "rediscovered" in 2004.

The American Voter

For the better part of a generation the American electorate has been fairly evenly divided in its support of the two parties. During the half century prior to the 1980s, however, the electorate was predominantly Democratic. Although the Republican Party enjoyed considerable success in presidential elections, far more Americans thought of themselves as Democrats than Republicans between the New Deal and the election of Ronald Reagan, and

Mobilizing the Democratic Vote in 2008: Ground Troops and Cellphones

It is impossible to know exactly how many volunteers participated in Barack Obama's successful campaign for the presidency. Shortly before the Democratic convention that confirmed his nomination as the party's candidate, officials working for the campaign indicated that it already included about 2 million volunteers and that the number was expected to double or even triple by election day. The unprecedented amount of money raised by the Obama campaign enabled it to field the largest paid campaign staff ever seen in a presidential election. But it was the army of volunteers, many of them young voters who had never worked for a party or a candidate, that was the most remarkable and probably the most effective part of their candidate's effort to get supporters registered and to the polls on election day.

This huge advantage over rival John McCain was reinforced by what appeared to be the effective use of text messages by the Obama campaign. These messages were used as reminders for cellphone users to register to vote, help the campaign, and show up at the polls on election day. Studies by political scientists have shown that while direct contact at the door by a campaign volunteer is the most effective way of mobilizing a candidate's vote, text messages are not far behind and have the added advantage of being quite inexpensive. They are especially effective when they appear to be tailored to the receiver and when they are timely. And, unlike what are called "robo-calls"—automated telephone calls that include a recorded message—studies show that cellphone users are more likely to read their unsolicited text messages than people are to listen on the phone to what is obviously a recorded message.

Despite the enormous number of ground troops and the blitzkrieg of text messages, voter turnout in 2008 was only marginally higher than in 2004 at about 62%.

this was reflected in Democratic dominance of Congress and state legislatures. Figure 9.3 shows the percentage of the electorate who identified with the two parties between 1952 and 2004.

FIGURE 9.3: PARTY IDENTIFICATION, 1952–2004

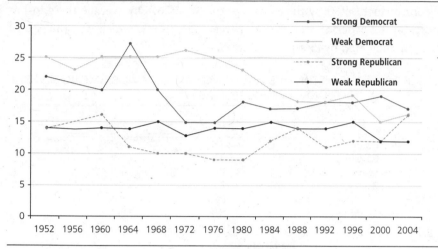

Source: Adapted from National Election Studies, http://www.electionstudies.org.

The electoral successes that the Democratic Party experienced during the half century after the New Deal of the 1930s were due to the party's strong support among voters in a coalition of groups: union members, Catholics, Jews, blacks, southerners, and low-income voters. Most analysts agree with Stanley and Niemi who after the 1992 election pronounced the coalition dead.[14] This obituary is, according to some, premature. In *The American Voter Revisited*, Lewis-Beck and his colleagues note that in four of the traditional New Deal coalition groups, the tendency to favor Democrats over Republicans remains strong. It has, however, weakened significantly among Catholics and dramatically among southern whites. Moreover, Hispanics and women have become important contributors to the Democratic Party's vote.[15]

The difference in the voting tendencies of men and women, a phenomenon known as the *gender gap*, may well have existed since women joined the electorate.[16] Survey data has existed on the phenomenon only since the 1950s. The first National Election Surveys showed that female voters preferred the Republicans, but since the 1960s the female portion of the electorate has favored the Democrats. The gender gap appeared to peak with Bill Clinton's re-election in 1996, a victory that was widely attributed to the votes of "soccer moms"—white suburban, married, middle-class mothers, typically driving a mini-van—who saw Clinton as the candidate of compassion and caring, linked to such issues as healthcare, education, and safety. The "soccer mom" explanation for the 1996 election result has been challenged by some,[17] but survey data indicate that 54% of women claimed to have voted for Clinton, versus only 43% of men. Women have been more likely than men to vote for the Democratic presidential candidate in every election since 1960, with the exception of 1976. On average the gap has been on the order of about seven percentage points, which was the size of the gap indicated by exit polls in 2008.

TABLE 9.2:   THE DISTINCTIVENESS OF VOTING BEHAVIOR AMONG SEVERAL SOCIAL GROUPINGS, 2000–2004*

	2000	2004
Union	+11*	+18
Catholics	+1	-1
Jewish	+39	+28
Blacks	+45	+50
Hispanic	+12	+18
Women	+9	+7

*Each entry indicates the difference in percentage Democratic presidential vote (of the two-party vote) between the group members and the non-group members. If the number is positive, that indicates the group was more Democratic than the non-group. If the number is negative, that indicates the group was less Democratic than the non-group.

Source: Lewis-Beck, et al., reprinted with permission.

The causes of the gender gap appear to lie in the tendency of men and women to have somewhat different values and priorities. To put it simply, women are more likely to care about issues linked to compassion—education, childcare, and health, for example—while men are more likely to care about issues related to force—matters such as national security, crime and community safety, and capital punishment. The Democratic Party is generally perceived by voters as stronger on compassion issues and the Republican Party on the force issues, leading some to characterize them as the "mommy" (Democratic) and "daddy" (Republican) parties.

The American electorate is also divided on class lines. The first National Election Surveys found that those who described themselves as working class were considerably more likely than those who saw themselves as middle class to vote Democratic.[18] This continues to be the case. Figure 9.5 shows that the Democratic Party presidential candidate did considerably better among working-class than middle-class identifiers in both 2000 and 2004. Unfortunately for the Democratic Party, Americans are much more likely to see themselves as middle than working class.

One of the fastest growing segments of American society over the last generation has been the Hispanic population. The 1960 census determined that 3.6% of the population was Hispanic, a category that includes people from Mexico, Puerto Rico, Cuba, and other Latin American countries. By the 2000 census they had become the largest ethnic/racial minority in the United Sates at 13.2% of the population compared to 12.9% for African Americans. The way in which this "sleeping giant" of the American electorate votes has been of great interest to both parties. As the debate on illegal immigration—most of it from Mexico and at an estimated rate of about 10,000 persons per week—roiled the waters of American politics in 2006–07, the Democratic Party was by and large supportive of a law that would effectively grant amnesty to the millions of illegal immigrants already in the United States. Some of these Democrats had large Hispanic populations in their districts and were very sensitive to the possibility of alienating current and future Hispanic voters by taking a hard line on illegal immigration. The Republican camp was more divided. Although the party's leadership, including President Bush, tended to support some sort of legislative compromise that would enable illegal immigrants to stay in the country and apply for American citizenship, many Republican members of Congress and lawmakers at the state level were strongly opposed. This was particularly true of Republican representatives in parts of the country such as California, Texas, Utah, and Colorado that had large illegal populations but who represented districts or states whose non-Hispanic majorities were very aware of the illegal immigration issue and strongly against any form of amnesty.

FIGURE 9.4:   REPUBLICAN PARTY IDENTIFIERS AMONG BLACKS AND
                SOUTHERN WHITES, 1952–2004

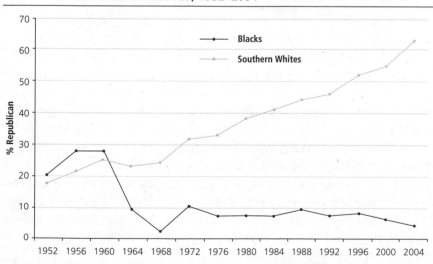

Source: Lewis-Beck, et al., reprinted with permission.

To this point the Hispanic vote has gone predominantly to the Democrats, as may be seen in Figure 9.6. Public opinion surveys show that Hispanics are likely to give the Democratic Party a more favorable rating than the Republican Party on almost all issues, despite the fact that their attitudes on such matters as abortion, same-sex marriage, and taxation are more conservative than those of the general population and closer to positions more commonly taken by Republicans than Democrats.[19]

FIGURE 9.5:   SUBJECTIVE SOCIAL CLASS AND PRESIDENTIAL VOTE, 2000 AND 2004

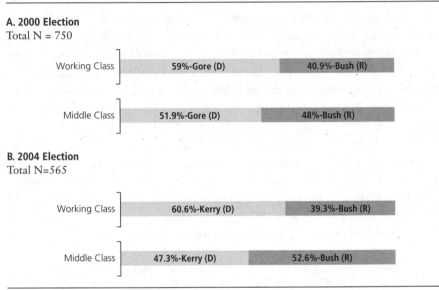

A. 2000 Election
Total N = 750

Working Class   59%-Gore (D)   40.9%-Bush (R)

Middle Class   51.9%-Gore (D)   48%-Bush (R)

B. 2004 Election
Total N=565

Working Class   60.6%-Kerry (D)   39.3%-Bush (R)

Middle Class   47.3%-Kerry (D)   52.6%-Bush (R)

Source: Lewis-Beck, et al., reprinted with permission.

There are, however, divisions in the Hispanic electorate. Those of Cuban origin have tended to favor the Republicans because of the party's harder line toward the Castro regime they fled. Mexicans and Puerto Ricans have tended to vote Democrat. Research has shown that the degree to which Hispanic voters identify principally with their ethnicity influences the likelihood that they will vote for the majority party of their group (this is also true for members of other social groups). To put it a bit differently, Hispanic voters who feel more integrated into the larger American community are more likely than those whose social interactions and identity are focused on their minority community to vote Republican.[20] This had led some to suggest that the Hispanic segment of the electorate, although presently mainly Democratic, might in time move into the Republican column. Some exit polls from the 2004 election suggested that Bush received about 45% of the Hispanic vote, a percentage that most commentators consider dubious.

Deep division among Republicans over illegal immigrants remains perhaps the main obstacle to the party making more significant and durable inroads with Hispanic voters. Nevertheless, illegal immigration was barely on the radar screen during the 2008 presidential election, and the positions of the candidates were, in any case, quite similar. Despite this, exit polls seemed to indicate that roughly two-thirds of Hispanic voters cast their ballots for Democratic candidate Obama and that even in Florida, where the Hispanic community is largely Cuban and has traditionally favored the Republican candidate, Obama outpolled McCain. The explanation for this may be that the bad economy affected lower income voters with more precarious employment—a category that includes Hispanics—more than Americans on the whole. Their shift toward the Democratic candidate may have been due chiefly to the economic issue that dominated the 2008 campaign.

FIGURE 9.6:   HISPANIC PRESIDENTIAL VOTE, 1948–2004 (cumulative)

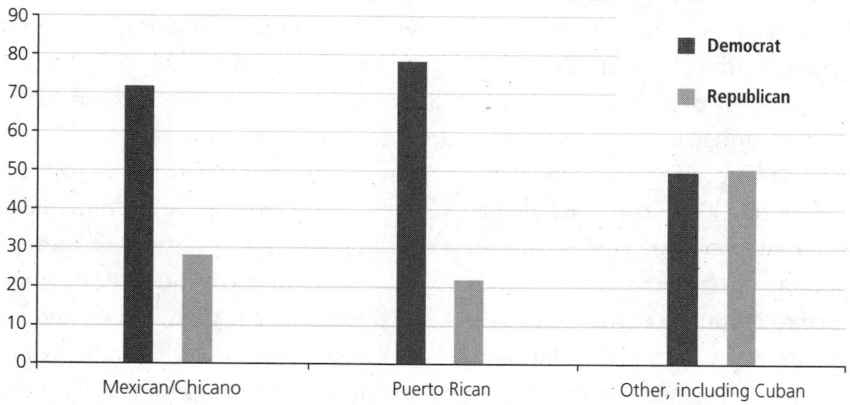

Source: Constructed from data available at the American National Election Study, http://www.electionstudies.org.

Voting and parties are two sides of the same coin. Parties and their candidates react to voters' priorities and preferences; voters, in turn, respond to the issues, positions, and images presented to them by those running for office. The interaction of voters and those who want their votes was famously expressed by Richard Nixon: "Run to the right in the primary, to the center in the general election." Substitute "left" for "right" in the case of

Democrats and this encapsulates one, if not *the* cardinal law of campaigning in America.

We already have seen that those who vote in primaries tend to be different in important ways from those whose votes a candidate will need to win a general election. They are more likely to be ideological purists, unwilling to compromise on values and policies and therefore to pull their party toward its more extreme edge. But there are not enough votes at the edge to win a general election, as the Democrats discovered when George McGovern was their candidate in 1972—thus Nixon's admonition to play to the center or what political scientists call the *median voter*. David King puts it this way:

> Rational parties and rational candidates should select positions near the median of their relevant voting constituencies. In the general election, this usually calls for staking out centrist positions. This formula is especially appealing in districts ... that have had a series of narrow wins and losses.[21]

But as King observes, candidates often seem to follow a different strategy, one that Samuel Huntington long ago argued would be most likely to deliver victory in a close race. Instead of aiming for the median voter, Huntington argued, candidates would try to mobilize "a high degree of support from a small number of interests [instead of] a relatively low degree of support from a large number of interests."[22] This does not mean ignoring the preferences of those voters in the center, some of whom will be needed for victory on election day. But as activist elements in the two parties have become more polarized over time (see Figure 9.7), candidates whose politics are centrist may have become fewer. Not only is it difficult for a candidate for public office to renounce entirely the values and positions that won him or her the primary election in favor of a blander centrist message, conviction probably will limit his or her movement toward the median voter. Combined with the fact that the groups for whom the candidate's convictions are the reason for their support are more likely to work for the candidate's election and turn out to vote on election day, a strategy of targeting the median voter may not be the one chosen by candidates in highly contested races.

In deciding who to vote for citizens are influenced by a number of factors. One of the most important is their assessment of how candidates for office have performed. This is the reward-punishment theory of voting described by V.O. Key. Voters assess a candidate and his or her party retrospectively, based on how they are seen to have performed in the recent past. The electorate is, Key argues, "an appraiser of past events, past performances, and past actions. It judges retrospectively; it commands prospectively only insofar as it expresses either approval or disapproval of that which has happened before."[23] There is considerable evidence in support of this theory of retrospective voting. Since 1948 there has been only one occasion when the candidate of the party controlling the White House won elections in a year when per capita real disposable income rose by less than 2%. That was Bill Clinton in 1996. Even more important than the actual state of the economy are voters' perceptions of its condition and how they and those around them have been faring. Table 9.3 shows that those who believe their personal financial situation has worsened tend to vote against the incumbent candidate. Those who feel their situation has improved are much more likely to vote for the candidate of the incumbent party.

FIGURE 9.7:   TRENDS IN THE POLITICAL IDEOLOGY OF STRONG PARTISANS*

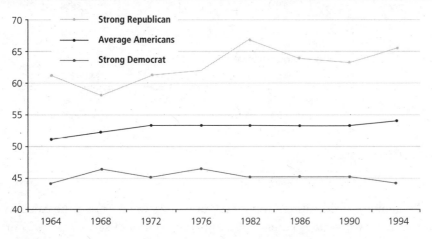

* A higher score on the vertical axis indicates greater conservatism.

Source: Adapted from David King, "Congress, Polarization, and Fidelity to the Median Voter," paper presented at the MIT Conference on Parties and Congress, 1997, p. 17.

Retrospective voting was almost certainly an enormous factor in Democrat Barack Obama's 2008 victory over Republican John McCain. As the candidate of the party controlling the White House, McCain had to struggle to disassociate himself from economic conditions that were perceived to be very bad and that were widely blamed on the Republican administration. Against all odds he appeared to be succeeding in this until the collapse of the Lehman Brothers investment bank about seven weeks before election day. This was followed by an avalanche of bad economic news that elevated the issue of the economy from the foremost issue in the campaign to almost the only issue on the minds of most voters. Although there was much journalistic musing about the impact of the respective campaigns, the influence of the candidates' respective vice-presidential picks (especially McCain's choice of Alaska Governor Sarah Palin), the performance of the candidates in the televised debates, and the role played by money in the campaign, voters' perceptions of who was to blame for what was widely seen as an economic mess surely had much more to do with the election outcome than any and perhaps all of these other factors.

TABLE 9.3:   RELATION OF PERSONAL FINANCIAL SITUATION TO THE PRESIDENTIAL VOTE, 2000 AND 2004

A. PERSONAL FINANCIAL SITUATION 2000 ELECTION		
	Worse	Same	Middle Class
Gore (I)*	45%	51%	56%
Bush (R)	55%	49%	44%
N	56	291	164

B. PERSONAL FINANCIAL SITUATION 2004 ELECTION		
	Worse	Same	Middle Class
Bush (I)*	28%	50%	64%
Kerry	72%	50%	36%
N	219	208	354

* (I) signifies the incumbent party.

Source: Lewis-Beck, et al., reprinted with permission.

Economic considerations are not the only ones to enter into the calculus of retrospective voting. Voters' assessments of national security, crime, or political corruption are among the issues that candidates often use to frame their opponent's record and on which voters arrive at assessments of the past performance of a candidate and a party. For example, the 2006 congressional elections saw Republican candidates punished across the board as a result of voters' assessment that the war in Iraq had gone badly (a Republican was in the White House) and that the Republicans in Congress were a corrupt bunch as shown by a number of scandals involving lobbyists (notably Jack Abramhoff) and also immoral behavior (revelations of Florida congressman Mark Foley's sexual approaches to young male pages in Congress were used by Democrats as part of a more general narrative about corruption in the Republican Party). Jimmy Carter's failure to win re-election in 1980 was certainly in large measure due to voters punishing him for a very weak economy, but their assessment of his performance was also influenced by his inability to free the 52 hostages who had been held in Iran for a year leading up to the election. Some of the most effective campaign ads are based on the premise that voters, or at least those who are not strong partisans, assess candidates and parties retrospectively.

Effective ads also seem to emphasize what students of campaigns call *valence issues*. These are issues where most everyone desires the same outcome. A healthy economy, safe communities, honest governance, and security against foreign threats are examples. A candidate will attempt to associate himself or herself with this outcome in order to be seen as the one most likely to contribute to the achievement of a goal that everyone supports. Or, in the negative version of a valence issue ad, there is an attempt to associate the other candidate or party with failure to attain the desired end.

Valence issues are often compared unfavorably to *position issues*, ones where the parties or candidates advocate different goals and government actions on some issue. Abortion, stem cell research, same-sex marriage, gun control, and the 2003 decision to go to war in Iraq are classic examples of position issues. The more favorable view that some commentators have of position issues is based on their belief that such issues require voters to make more informed and rational choices than is true of valence issues.[24] Valence issues are associated with 30-second television spot ads in which longer discursive explanations of why a particular position on an issue is best is impossible and where music and images substitute, according to critics, for the rational and unemotional discussion on which democracy depends.

But not everyone agrees. Some of the classic analyses of voter choice in the United States argue that valence issues and retrospective voting are quite rational, within the bounds of limited voter information, and that, in V.O. Key's words, "voters are not fools."[25] Thus, a television ad such as "It's Morning in America," dismissed by some as manipulative pap with no real informational content to help voters in making a rational choice about how to vote, in fact invites viewers to make a rational judgment on the performance of the ad's candidate. The ad is pure valence politics, but there is nothing irrational about people desiring the conditions that are portrayed in it. Whether the ad or any political communication misrepresents the facts, including the facts of a candidate's or party's performance, is another matter. The defenders of valence politics and the retrospective ads that rely on it take the position that people are the best judge of whether they feel safer, financially better off, or more optimistic about the future.

Notes

1   See http://millercenter.org/scripps/archive/speeches.

2   Arthur Schlesinger, ed., *History of U.S. Political Parties, Vol. 1* (New York: Chelsea, 1973) xxxiii.

3   J. David Gillespie, "Third Parties in American Politics: Rich History, Many Roles," interview, 30 August 2004, http://usa.usembassy.de/elections04/ef/08_gillespie.htm.

4   EMILY is an acronym for "Early Money Is Like Yeast" (it helps the dough rise). Founded in 1985, the organization is devoted to funding the election campaigns of women to various offices in the United States. See http://www.emilyslist.org/.

5   Michael Barone, *The Almanac of American Politics, 2006* (Washington, DC: National Journal Group, 2006) 36.

6   Campaign Media Analysis Group.

7   Center for Media and Public Affairs, "The Incredible Shrinking Sound Bite," Press Release, 28 September 2000.

8   Neil Postman, interview, Public Broadcasting System [PBS], *Consuming Images.* "The Public Mind" series, hosted by Bill Moyers, first broadcast in 1996.

9   Mark Crispin Miller, interview, Public Broadcasting System [PBS], *Consuming Images.* "The Public Mind" series, hosted by Bill Moyers, first broadcast in 1996.

10 Ted Brader, *Campaigning for Hearts and Minds* (Chicago, IL: University of Chicago Press, 2006) 183, 193.

11 Darla Crawford, "Television primary information source for most 2004 voters," http://www.usinfo.state.gov.

12 See http://livingroomcandidate.movingimage.us/.

13 See James Q. Wilson and John J. DiIulio Jr., *American Government* (New York: Houghton Mifflin Company, 2007) 254, Table 10.4, various polls.

14 H.W. Stanley, and R.G. Niemi, "The Demise of the New Deal Coalition: Partisanship and Group Support, 1952–1992," in H.F. Weisberg (ed.), *Democracy's Feast: Elections in America* (Chatham, NJ: Chatham House, 1995) 220–40.

15 Michael Lewis-Beck, William G. Jacoby, Helmut Norpoth, and Herbert F. Weisberg (eds.), *The American Voter Revisited* (Ann Arbor, MI: University of Michigan Press, 2009).

16 Carol Mueller, "The Gender Gap and Women's Political Influence," *The Annals of the American Academy of Political and Social Science* 515,1 (1991): 23–37.

17 Jack Citrin and Samantha Luks, "Revisiting Political Trust in an Angry Age," in John R. Hibbing *et al.*, eds. *What is it about Government that Americans Dislike?* (Cambridge: Cambridge University Press, 2001) 9–27.

18 Lewis-Beck 190.

19 See *New York Times*/CBS News Poll, reported in *New York Times* (3 August 2003): 14.

20 Lewis-Beck 33–34.

21 David C. King, "Political Party Competition and Fidelity to the Median Voter in the US Congress," JFK School of Government, Harvard University (15 February 2001) 9; ksghome.harvard.edu/~.dking.academic.ksg/Party_Competition_v1.pdf.

22 Samuel Huntington, "A Revised Theory of American Party Politics," *American Political Science Review* 54 (1950): 671.

23 V.O. Key, *The Responsible Electorate* (New York: Vintage, 1966).

24 Norman H. Nie, Sidney Verba, and John R. Petrocik, *The Changing American Voter: Enlarged Edition* (Cambridge, MA: Harvard University Press, 1980).

25 Key 8.

CHAPTER TEN

Who Rules America?

"The people reign in the American political world," said Tocqueville, "as the Deity does in the universe. They are the cause and the aim of all things; everything comes from them and everything is absorbed in them."[1] Sovereignty of the people was, he believed, no mere philosophical formula or political slogan in the United States. It was, rather, an accurate description of the inverted pyramid of American government, with the people at the top and public officials their faithful delegates. Tocqueville believed that there was no aristocracy or hereditary governing class in America and that the rapid circulation of wealth operated to prevent the concentration of economic power in few hands.

By the end of the nineteenth century, however, many Americans feared that the concentration of wealth that Tocqueville believed unlikely had arrived.[2] The rapid industrialization that occurred in the latter decades of that century was accompanied by the rise of fortunes never before seen in the United States. "Robber barons" was the colorful term coined to describe the new titans of American industry and finance. Their control over such crucial sectors of the economy as railroads, municipal services like electricity and streetcars, steel production, coal mining, banking, and oil generated the first wave of fear that American democracy was being subverted by an emerging plutocracy whose influence rested on control over the nation's wealth. At about the same time the rise of what came to be known as "party machines" in the major cities—Tammany Hall in New York being the most famous example—appeared to make a mockery of mass democracy and elections. The machines depended on their control over patronage and the spending of public money in order to elect and keep in power their favored candidates. Their methods were often unethical and even illegal, including intimidation, bribery, and violence.

Tocqueville's belief that the people were sovereign in America seemed to be undermined by this perversion of the processes and structures of democratic government, and critics of his judgments have been many and various. From William Jennings Bryan's famous 1896 "Cross of Gold" speech, castigating eastern commercial interests, to Ralph Nader's attacks on corporate power in contemporary America, the theme of the people versus the powerful—the economically powerful—has resonated throughout modern American politics. President Dwight Eisenhower gave the populist warning against the power of big business an added twist when he warned in his farewell address against the power of the "military-industrial complex" to bend the priorities and policies of government to their own ends.

America's long military engagement in Vietnam focused attention on another aspect of its power. The possibility of an American *imperium*, a new Rome maintained by fleets and troops around the world for purposes unrelated and even antithetical to democratic values, was raised by critics at home and abroad. The student demonstrations, street protests, and popular rejection of the Vietnam War reflected a widespread belief that power had been hijacked into the service of a Cold War agenda that was unconnected to the values and interests of the American people.

The 2003 invasion of Iraq and its aftermath were accompanied by similar fears. Indeed, characterizations of America as the new Rome have become commonplace since the break-up of the Soviet Union. The decision to invade Iraq, critics charged, would not have been taken had the levers of power in Washington not fallen into the hands of ideological conservatives with close ties to the oil industry and military contractors. Their answer to the perennial question "Who rules America?" was Exxon, Haliburton, and General Electric, an answer pretty much the same as that given by some critics during the Vietnam era.

The old fear that the wealthy would use their economic power to buy political access and influence has resurfaced with a vengeance in recent decades. A combination of increasing inequality in the distribution of income and other forms of wealth along with some egregious and spectacular cases of corporate greed and malfeasance are viewed by some as evidence of the corporate takeover of American society and politics. Ralph Nader, one of America's most prominent critics of big business since the 1960s, calls it the corporate welfare state. He is not alone. Before his death in 2006, the prominent economist John Kenneth Galbraith became increasingly pessimistic that the system of divided and countervailing power, traditionally relied on to check the influence of the wealthy and the big corporations, was up to the challenge in an era of globalized capital. Documentarist-activist Michael Moore targets inequality and corporate power in different ways in all of his films. The people versus the powerful is the story he tells, a story in the American tradition of Upton Sinclair's *The Jungle* (1906), John Steinbeck's *The Grapes of Wrath* (1939) and Howard Zinn's *A People's History of the United States* (1980).[3] And no less a figure than former President Jimmy Carter in his book, *Our Endangered Values: America's Moral Crisis*, blames the growth in corporate power and in the unequal distribution of wealth for undermining the fundamental values and processes of American democ-

Live Earth

On July 8, 2007, concerts and speeches took place in America and Europe at what were called Live Earth events. Robert F. Kennedy Jr., son of the assassinated Robert Kennedy and a well-known environmentalist, gave a speech at the Live Earth concert in Philadelphia. Here is some of what he said about power in America:

Now we've all heard the oil industry and the coal industry and their indentured servants in the political process telling us that global climate stability is a luxury that we can't afford. That we have to choose now between economic prosperity on the one hand and environmental protection on the other. And that is a false choice.

... Now you've heard today a lot of people say that there are many little things that you all can do today to avert climate change on your own. But I will tell you this, it is more important than buying compact fluorescent light bulbs or than buying a fuel efficient automobile. The most important thing you can do is to get involved in the political process and get rid of all of these rotten politicians that we have in Washington, DC. Who are nothing more than corporate toadies for companies like Exxon and

Southern Company, these villainous companies that consistently put their private financial interest ahead of American interests and ahead of the interests of all of humanity. This is treason and we need to start treating them now as traitors.

And they have their slick public relations firms and their phony think tanks in Washington, DC, and their crooked scientists who are lying to the American people day after day. And we have a press that has completely let down American democracy. That's giving us Anna Nicole Smith and Paris Hilton instead of the issues that we need to understand to make rational decisions in a democracy—like global warming.

And so I am going to tell you this, that the next time you see John Stossel or Glenn Beck or Rush Limbaugh or Sean Hannity—these flat-earthers, these corporate toadies, lying to you, lying to the American public, and telling you that global warming doesn't exist—you send an email to their advertisers and tell them that you are not going to buy their products anymore.

... And I will see all of you on the barricades!

racy.[4] About two-thirds of Americans, according to the World Values Survey (WVS) of 1990 and 2000, say that they believe the "country is run by a few big interests looking out for themselves." They are not, however, exceptional in this belief. Over half of Canadians agree that their country too is run by a few big interests, and the percentages agreeing in Spain, Switzerland, Australia, and New Zealand are about the same as in the United States.

At the same time, however, most Americans and most of those who comment on American politics are fairly sanguine about democracy's current condition and future prospects. According to the WVS, Americans are about as likely (nine out of ten) as people in other affluent democracies to agree with the proposition that "Democracy may have problems but it's better than any other form of government" and as likely as people in these other societies—more likely than in some—to say that they are "satisfied with the way democracy is developing" in their country, about two-thirds expressing satisfaction. They may tend to agree with humorist Will Rogers's aphorism that "Now and then an innocent man is sent to the legislature," and many believe that big business and other "special interests" are too powerful. But this cynicism exists alongside a firm confidence in the overall structures and processes of American democracy.

The Founders and the Question of Power

The issue of who should rule was very much on the minds of those who drafted the American Constitution. Indeed, it is fair to say that it preoccupied the founders. The circumstances that led the American colonists to revolt left them deeply mistrustful of unchecked power. The document that they agreed to at the Philadelphia Convention of 1787 created a system of checks and balances whose aim was to prevent the excessive concentration of political power in any branch of government. The scenario they feared and wished to prevent was less that of a sort of American version of George III emerging to tyrannize the American people—although there were some like Patrick Henry, who claimed to smell the rat of monarchy in the proposed Constitution—but that the people would use their superior numbers to run roughshod over minority rights, including the rights of property-holders. John Adams, who would become the second president of the United States, expressed the view of the majority of the founders when he wrote, "The rich have as clear a right to their liberty and property as the poor. It is essential to the protection of liberty that the rights of the rich be secured; if they are not, they will be robbed and become poor, and in their turn rob their robbers, and thus neither the liberty or property of any will be regarded."[5]

Despite fresh memories of despotism inflicted on the colonies under British rule, it was the unchecked power of the people that was seen by the founders as the main evil to be avoided. Everyone agreed that those who govern derive their right to do so from the people, but they were also, to varying degrees, skeptical about how far the people could be counted on to decide matters of policy in a wise and fair manner. There were those like Jefferson and Benjamin Franklin who had greater trust in the *vox populi*, but most of the leading men in the original 13 states agreed with John Adams's assessment that the people's hands should be kept at some distance from the levers of power, otherwise bad laws, injustices, and despotism would follow.

The question of power is dealt with by James Madison in Federalist no. 10. Madison starts by observing that every free society will give rise to factions or what contemporary readers would call special interests. Chief among these are those associated with the unequal distribution of property. One way of dealing with the conflict that arises from these divisions in society is, he observes, to eliminate its source. This would require that everyone have the same interests and opinions which, in turn, would require that individual freedom be extinguished. Such a solution is obviously undesirable, so the only practical course is to find methods that will limit the negative consequences that can arise from the existence of faction: "[T]he *causes* of faction cannot be removed and ... relief is only to be sought in the means of controlling its *effects*."[6]

The scenario of a like-minded majority using its superior numbers to deprive a minority or minorities of their rights and property is very clearly on Madison's mind. To reduce the risk of this happening, he makes a case for what he calls a republican form of government, which he distinguishes from a pure democracy. The language here sometimes gives rise to confusion. By democracy Madison meant what we might call a direct democracy in which citizens participate directly in the management of public affairs. A republic, his preferred model of government, kept the mass of the population at one remove from governmental power, which would be exercised by a small number of the people's representatives. This is a form of government—representative democracy—with which citizens in modern democracies are all familiar. Its advantage, Madison argued, lies in the fact that deliberations on public affairs and the balancing of competing ideas and interests are placed in the hands of "a chosen body of citizens, whose wisdom may best discern the true interest of their country and whose patriotism and love of justice will be least likely to sacrifice it to temporary or partial considerations."

Madison was still worried, however, that in a small country the range of interests would be narrower than in a larger one and that therefore it was possible that representatives might simply express the preferences of a like-minded majority without concern for the interests of those who are not part of this majority. The solution, he maintained, was to expand the size of the country to include as many and diverse interests as possible. "Extend the sphere," Madison writes, "and you take in a greater variety of parties and interests; you make it less probable that a majority of the whole will have a common motive to invade the rights of other citizens; or if such a motive exists, it will be more difficult for all who feel it to discover their own strength and to act in unison with each other." True to his skepticism about human nature, skepticism that he expresses quite clearly in Federalist no. 51, Madison was not willing to count on what he calls the "enlightened views and virtuous sentiments" of the people's chosen representatives. He believed that another layer of security to protect the interests and rights of minorities, including property-holders, was needed. That additional level of security, he argued, would be provided by a large political union that perforce would encompass a wide and diverse set of interests.

In his book, *An Economic Interpretation of the Constitution* (1913),[7] historian Charles Beard argues that the founders cared little for the democratic ideals expressed in the Declaration of Independence but much for the protection of the wealthy against the superior numbers of those who owned little or no property. As proof of this claim Beard trolls the record of the debates at the Philadelphia Convention, concluding that the checks and balances system was essentially about checking the power of the people and limiting democracy.

Beard's characterization of the founders' motives and aims is only partly correct. Subsequent scholarship has challenged his assertion that the founders were intent on creating a constitution that reflected and protected their own class interests.[8] But there is little room for doubt that most of the founders feared that the people could become too powerful and that their influence on legislation needed to be limited.

The Power of Public Opinion

> Those who invented this machinery of checks and balances were anxious not so much to develop public opinion as to resist and build up breakwaters against it. —Lord James Bryce[9]

Charles Beard on the Founders' Motives

... They were anxious above everything else to safeguard the rights of private property against any leveling tendencies on the part of the propertyless masses. Gouverneur Morris, in speaking on the problem of apportioning representatives, correctly stated the sound historical fact when he declared: "Life and liberty were generally said to be of more value than property. An accurate view of the matter would, nevertheless, prove that property was the main object of society.... If property, then, was the main object of government, certainly it ought to be one measure of the influence due to those who were to be affected by the government."

... [I]n support of the argument for a property qualification on voters, Madison urged: "In future times, a great majority of the people will not only be without land, but any other sort of property. These will either combine, under the influence of the common situation—in which case the rights of property and the public liberty will not be secure in their hands—or what is more probable, they will become the tools of opulence and ambition; in which case there will be equal danger on another side." Various projects for setting up class rule by the establishment of property qualifications for voters and officers were advanced in the convention, but they were defeated.

... Nevertheless, by the system of checks and balances placed in the government, the convention safeguarded the interests of property against attacks by majorities. The House of Representatives, Mr. Hamilton pointed out, "was so formed as to render it particularly the guardian of the poorer orders of citizens," while the Senate was to preserve the rights of property and the interests of the minority against the demands of the majority.

Charles Beard, American Government and Politics, *8th ed. (New York: Macmillan, 1939) 46–48.*

Whatever the intentions of the founders may have been, such astute observers of the nineteenth-century American political scene as Tocqueville and James Bryce concluded that the influence of the people on public affairs was quite extensive and operated through the force of public opinion. "It is in the examination of the exercise of thought in the United States," observed Tocqueville, "that we clearly perceive how far the power of the majority surpasses all the powers with which we are acquainted in Europe. Thought is an invisible and subtle power that mocks all the efforts of tyranny ... [A]s long as the majority is still undecided, discussion is carried on; but as soon as its decision is irrevocably pronounced, everyone is silent, and the friends as well as the opponents of the measure unite in assenting to its propriety."[10]

Bryce was no less impressed by the power of public opinion. "Towering over Presidents and State governors," he wrote, "over Congress and State legislatures, over conventions and the vast machinery of party, public opinion stands out, in the United States, as the great source of power, the master of servants who tremble before it."[11] Bryce gave three reasons for this:

1. First, the very checks and balances system that Madison and most of the founders expected would limit the power of the people actually increased it. No branch of government, Bryce argued, is strong enough to form, express, and give effect through its actions to public opinion. Consequently, public opinion develops and is expressed in American society at large: "It is expressed in voices everywhere. It rules as a pervading and impalpable power, like the ether which passes through all things."[12]

2. Second, and related to this, is the absence in the United States of a governing class. Bryce notes that public opinion in the Old World, including England, "has been substantially the opinion of the class which wears black coats and lives in good houses."[13] In America, however, no such governing class existed when Bryce made his observations. Nor was there any other elite associated with religion or the economy whose social standing was so pre-eminent that its views were capable of trickling down to and forming general public opinion.

3. This observation gave rise to Bryce's third reason: whereas public opinion in European societies was divided on class lines, in the United States public opinion cut across socio-economic differences and could truly be said to be the opinion of the whole nation. The fact that it was not tied to the interests of a particular class gave public opinion greater force as a governing power both because it appeared to all as the opinion of the people as a whole and, moreover, because of the sense of ownership of government that it gave to workers and bosses, property-holders and the property-less alike. In European societies, said Bryce, the public opinion that was listened to by those who governed was that of a privileged elite and thus reinforced existing class divisions. The democratic character of public opinion in America, by contrast, ensured that citizens across the socio-economic spectrum would recognize their voices and interests in the conduct of the government.

This description of public opinion and its impact on government will sound to some rather quaint and unconnected to the realities of contemporary American society. Indeed, every one of Bryce's three claims about public opinion has been challenged, in particular his argument that public opinion cuts across class lines at least on most issues. Survey data suggest, however, that class is not a significant predictor of attitudes that, logically at least, might be expected to depend on one's class. (If income is used instead of education, the range of variation in attitudes across income categories is no greater.) Figure 10.1 shows that there are only small and in some cases no variations between classes in attitudes on issues that might be expected to elicit significant differences of opinion between those who have more and those who have less. Not only is this true in the United States, it is also true in the other three democracies included. One might quibble with the measure of class used here, but formal education is known to be strongly correlated with occupation and income in all capitalist democracies. Perhaps the proper conclusion to draw is that public opinion largely cuts across class lines in the America that Bryce observed and continues to do so today. In this respect European democracies, where class divisions were historically quite wide, have come to resemble the United States.

FIGURE 10.1: CLASS AND ATTITUDE ON INDIVIDUALISM (United States, France, Britain, and Sweden, 2000)

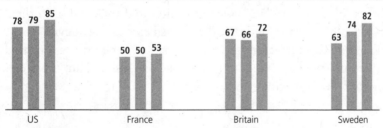

Some people feel they have completely free choice and control over their lives, while other people feel that what they do, has no real effect on what happens to them. (% saying "great deal," scores of 7–10 on a 10 point scale)
Note: Bars for each country represent level of education: left bars are the lower third, middle bars are the middle third, and right bars are the upper third.

Source: Adapted from World Values Survey.

Who Shapes Public Opinion?

Tocqueville and Bryce were both impressed by what they saw as the decentralized, diffuse, and democratic ways through which public opinion was formed in America. Newspaper editors, educators, politicians, and an educated and informed citizenry were among those who contributed to the national conversation. Neither of them thought that the business elite played much of a role in shaping the contours of the national conversation, much less the content of public opinion.

Today, however, it is commonplace to argue that public opinion is influenced by powerful elites and manipulated through the various institutions and processes through which citizens learn about their society. This already was the conclusion reached by Harold Laski, one of the most prominent British intellectuals of the first half of the twentieth century. In *The American Democracy*, he writes, "The environment out of which there emerges that intricate and half-conscious complex of emotions, sentiments, and convictions we call public opinion is always a weighted environment. The instruments which shape the minds of citizens are not freely at the disposal of anyone who wishes to operate them. They are controlled, for the most part, by men or bodies who can afford either to create or to employ them. And, for the most part, they are controlled by the vested interests which dwarf altogether the individual and leave him helpless...."[14]

Laski's argument that American public opinion had become captured and manipulated by elites has been echoed by many others. It is a claim that has become an important dividing line in the analysis of American politics, separating those who believe that power—including the power to determine what people think about and the values, beliefs, and opinions they hold—has drifted into the hands of corporate elites and those who do their bidding, versus those who think that the assessments of Tocqueville and Bryce are still essentially correct. As is so often the case when we set out to determine the truth of what appear to be mutually exclusive claims, the reality of the situation lies somewhere in between.

The Political Conversation: Whose Voices Get Listened to and Acted Upon?

To understand better the forces that influence the political conversation in America, it is useful to begin with political scientist E.E. Schattschneider's reminder that it is often what we do not see, hear, and think about that is most revealing of political power.[15] When a group is obliged to articulate its position and arguments and to spend time and money on trying to convince the public to share its views, this is an indication that its ability to achieve its goals has been challenged. It is a common error to assume that because a group spends a lot of money on political contributions, issue advertising, and lobbying that it is powerful. In fact, these activities may indicate that a group's interests and values are under siege and that to protect them from challenge the group is obliged to expend resources.

At the same time it would be plain silly to conclude from the facts that associations representing the oil and gas industries maintain permanent offices in Washington, DC and contributed $10.6 million to congressional candidates in the 2006 elections that the political influence of this sector is feeble. Nor should the fact that lawyers and law firms contributed $60 million to congressional candidates during that same election cycle and have a permanent lobbying presence in Washington through the American Trial Lawyers' Association and other interest groups be construed as signs of weakness. Powerful interests spend lots of money on various activities, including ones intended to shape public opinion on the issues that make a difference to their ability to achieve their goals.

Money can buy a multimillion dollar issue advertising campaign targeted at national opinion or it may finance a modest ad in the local newspaper intended to shape community views on some local issue. Money may also finance television and radio programming, print media, films, and other media whose message(s) those doing the spending find congenial. And if you think that this is too indirect a form of influence on the ideas, images, and arguments that reach the public, then consider that media outlets may be owned by corporate interests that, according to some critics, use them in order to push a particular ideological agenda.

Money can certainly buy access to the public conversation, more so in the United States than in virtually any other democracy. In some European democracies, including France and Germany, paid political advertising on television and radio is banned, as is campaign advertising by private organizations that might be construed as supporting or opposing a party or candidate. In the UK, the law regulates the permissible length of television ads—they must run for at least two minutes and 40 seconds and up to four minutes and 40 seconds—based on the apparent belief that longer ads are more likely to communicate information and address issues in less manipulative ways than the 15–30 second spot ads that are the norm in the United States. American courts have taken a dim view of legislative efforts to limit campaign spending on advertising on the grounds that this would violate the First Amendment's guarantee of free speech.

But money provides only a partial, simplistic, and misleading explanation for what gets talked about in American politics, whose voices are heard, and what people come to believe about the issues. Figure 10.2 represents the process leading to the formation of public awareness of and opinion on issues. The crucial stage in this process involves opinion leaders and the channels through which their ideas are communicated to the wider public. University professors of political science and sociology fall into this category, as do program producers and hosts for Fox broadcasting, radio talk show hosts like Rush Limbaugh, and journalists for the *New York Times*, to mention only a handful of opinion leaders. Their ideological leanings are not identical. The professors and *New York Times* journalists will tend to be more liberal than the average American. Rush Limbaugh and most of talk radio's most popular program hosts and the Fox network, are firmly on the conservative side of the American political spectrum. The thousands of interest and advocacy groups, think tanks, research institutes, corporations, unions, churches, and other organizations whose activities involve either mainly or incidentally, continuously or occasionally, an effort to influence public opinion represent a broad range of ideological points of view. Not all of them reflect or express the interests of the wealthy.

FIGURE 10.2: CONSTRUCTING PUBLIC OPINION: A SIMPLIFIED MODEL

ELITES	LINKAGE MECHANISMS	ELITE & MASS OPINION
Information / Image Generators	Structure & Nature of Info/ Image Communication System	Equality, Opportunity, Power
▪ Educators ▪ Opinion Leaders ▪ Politicians	▪ Media System ▪ Political System ▪ Education System	▪ Perceptions ▪ Sentiments ▪ Beliefs
INDEPENDENT VARIABLES*	INTERVENING VARIABLES*	DEPENDENT VARIABLES

* The feedback loop between the "Elites" and "Linkage Mechanisms" variable categories is intended to underline the fact that both of these may operate as independent variables. By labeling these linkage mechanisms as intervening variables I do not mean to suggest that the structures and processes included here may not also have a causal impact on elites, their selection, and value/belief formation.

Some argue, however, that the interests of the wealthy and ideas congenial to their interests are disproportionately represented in the American political conversation. At the same time those of the poor, the unorganized, and groups that experience discrimination are underrepresented. Although widely accepted, this claim is both hard to verify and almost certainly an overstatement. If a person gets all of his or her information about the world from a single source or from a narrow band of ideologically like-minded opinion leaders, and that source or those opinion leaders view the world in ways sympathetic to the interests of the wealthy, then this person is probably more apt to adopt or maintain a similar world view. But the universe of opinion leaders in the United States is quite diverse, despite being fre-

Think Tanks, Public Interest Groups, and the Political Conversation

Not only are there interest groups organized on all sides of virtually every issue in American politics, there are also organizations known as *think tanks* that generate and disseminate research and arguments in support of various policies. Some of them are nonpartisan and more or less centrist in their ideological orientation. Others, however, including many of those that are most successful in getting their ideas, research, and arguments discussed in the media and in policy-making circles, have a sharp ideological edge and are thought of as either liberal or conservative. The Children's Defense Fund, the Institute for Policy Studies, and the Progressive Policy Institute are examples of liberal think tanks. On the conservative side, the American Enterprise Institute, the Cato Institute, and the Heritage Foundation have been among the more prominent think tanks in recent years.

A rather different influence strategy is used by what are known as *public-interest law firms*. They rely on the courts, either by bringing suit on behalf of someone or group of persons alleged to have been harmed by a public policy or private behavior or by filing what is called an *amicus curiale* brief in support of someone's lawsuit. Public-interest law firms exist to advance a particular policy agenda. Among the well-known liberal ones are the American Civil Liberties Union, the Natural Resources Defense Council, and the Women's Legal Defense Fund. Important conservative ones include the Center for Individual Rights, the Mountain States Legal Foundation, and the Pacific Legal Foundation.

quently portrayed as ideologically conservative, particularly the media system. The ideological distance separating the political coverage and analysis of Adbusters and Mother Jones on the left from Rush Limbaugh's daily radio program or the Weekly Standard on the right, is enormous.[16]

Critics respond that what matters, however, are the opinion leaders, views, and ideas that most Americans hear, read, and watch. Analyses of the American media system typically have focused on the mainstream of that system for the very plausible reason that the views expressed in the major newspapers and magazines, television networks and radio programs, books and films are more likely than those at the margins of the media system to both reflect public opinion and influence it.

In recent years, however, the range of easily accessible information, images, and interpretation of everything from local to international affairs has broadened enormously, and the media system has become fragmented to an unprecedented degree. Old claims that the major television networks offer viewers a rather standardized, commercially driven window on the world or that conservative talk radio does the ideological bidding of the corporate elite[17] are quite simply much less relevant today than they were a generation ago. As shown in recent annual reports of the Project for Excellence in Journalism, "Americans are now news grazers sampling, through the course of the day, a varied media buffet. Categorizing people by education, region, or income or trying to imagine them as primarily newspaper readers, or consumers mostly of local TV news, is increasingly futile.... More than a third of Americans, some 36%, are regular consumers of four or more different kinds of news outlets—network news, local TV, newspapers, cable, radio, the Internet, and magazines."[18]

There is little doubt that the range of information, including coverage of public affairs, is broader and more easily accessible than ever. But even before the explosion in new media, claims that the media system was somehow controlled by the corporate elite tended to be exaggerated. French political scientist Pierre Gervais argues that the American system of countervailing power operates through the media, as it does through other institutions and processes in American society. "The media play this same role as an organism of community control over the powerful. Television programs such as '20/20' or 'Nightline' make their profits from denunciating the abuses of the powerful," writes Gervais. "[T]he media tap a constant stream of public opinion that is disposed to suspect the integrity of those who want to cheat and to subvert the accepted norms of behavior in society."[19]

Countervailing Power

The model of countervailing power that Gervais refers to above is able to recognize the obvious and often enormous inequalities that exist in the political influence of different interests while also recognizing that no group is so dominant as to be unchallenged and unchecked in pursuit of its particular aims. No one seriously argues that the American political playing field is level, but, as Gervais correctly observes, it is a playing field that includes more checks and counterweights to the powerful, including limits on the influence of powerful business interests, than some critics are willing to concede. These checks and counterweights have been more influential at certain points in American history than at others, but they have never been inconsequential.

Significant segments of the American population are dubious about the power of big business and favorable toward government regulation of business. These segments of public opinion represent a potential check on the power of business. In addition, many of those in America's education and media elites are skeptical of market values and more liberal in their political values than most Americans. Robert Lichter and others have shown that the media elite, particularly those in the national media, tend to hold more

Countervailing Power in American Politics

The close ties between big business and federal and state political elites and institutions should not lead one to conclude that the United States is a country controlled exclusively by the heads of major corporations. Counterweights exist, and they play a considerable role in the creation of an American environment that may at any moment generate major obstacles to business ambitions.

... All of these counterweights rest upon the fact that the population is much less convinced of the benefits of free enterprise than one might think by listening only to the political elites. Consumer associations and citizens interest groups have less weight than big business taken collectively, but no individual corporation, no matter how powerful, can permit itself to enter into open warfare with them. Above all, the ideological and ethical views of an overwhelming majority of Americans are, paradoxically, very far from those of the classical and neo-classical economists who, since Adam Smith, celebrate the efficiency of free markets and the collective benefits reaped from self-regarding behavior. The upshot of all this is a cultural atmosphere that is oddly schizophrenic, where talk about free markets and profit co-exist uneasily with an idealism that constantly questions these values.

Pierre Gervais, L'Avènement d'une superpuissance *(my translation).*

liberal views on both economic and social matters than do members of the general public.[20] This conclusion is supported by a 2004 survey carried out by the Pew Research Center.[21]

A second feature of countervailing power in American politics involves the fragmented character of business interests. When oil companies were reaping record profits from 2006 to 2008, at a time when the world price of a barrel reached $140, the casualties included American automobile manufacturers. Over the previous decade of comparatively low oil prices these automakers had come to rely increasingly on sports utility vehicles and light trucks—high profit-margin vehicles—at the expense of more fuel-efficient models. Their loss of domestic market share to such companies as Toyota and Honda accelerated when the world price of oil increased vertiginously. They became victims of their unwillingness to anticipate and adapt their product lines to compete with these foreign-based automakers. Clearly, the interests of "big oil" and those of the so-called Big Three (General Motors, Ford, and Chrysler) were not identical.

Conflicts like this, though not always on such a grand scale, have always existed in the American economy. The long-standing battle between free traders and protectionists spans two centuries of American history and was only won decisively by the advocates of trade liberalization in recent decades. The interests and lobbying efforts of insurance companies are often diametrically opposed to those of powerful professional groups like trial lawyers and medical doctors. Interest fragmentation reduces the likelihood that any single group will find that its interests and the demands that it makes on public policy are unchallenged.

Money is often believed to be the reason for the generally superior influence of business interests in American politics. Two points must be raised. First, business does not always win. Powerful business interests supported legislation that would have effectively granted amnesty to the estimated 12–15 million illegal immigrants living in the United States. Despite this and the support of a pro-business president, George W. Bush, the legislation was defeated in Congress in 2007.

TABLE 10.1:   TOP 20 DONORS, 1989–2006

Rank	Organization Name	Total	1989-2006 Dems	1989-2006 Repubs
1	American Fedn of State, County & Municipal Employees	$38,133,049	98%	1%
2	AT&T Inc	$36,992,735	44%	55%
3	National Assn of Realtors	$30,298,348	46%	52%
4	National Education Assn	$27,108,900	93%	6%
5	American Assn for Justice	$27,107,056	89%	9%
6	Intl Brotherhood of Electrical Workers	$25,779,741	97%	2%
7	Laborers Union	$25,018,639	91%	7%
8	Goldman Sachs	$24,902,461	61%	38%
9	Service Employees International Union	$24,675,343	95%	3%
10	Carpenters & Joiners Union	$24,422,870	89%	9%
11	American Medical Assn	$24,213,939	38%	61%
12	Teamsters Union	$24,172,339	92%	7%
13	Communications Workers of America	$24,119,624	99%	0%
14	United Auto Workers	$23,274,285	98%	0%
15	American Federation of Teachers	$23,151,968	98%	1%
16	FedEx Corp	$22,727,099	42%	57%
17	Altria Group	$22,380,050	26%	73%
18	Machinists & Aerospace Workers Union	$21,488,174	98%	0%
19	United Food & Commercial Workers Union	$21,180,159	98%	1%
20	Citigroup Inc	$20,999,996	48%	51%

Source: http://www.opensecrets.org.

Second, there is often money on all sides of an issue, and even when there is more money on one side than another, it should be kept in mind that money is simply one lever of political influence and is not always able to overcome opposition in the form of unfavorable public opinion, an unsympathetic judicial branch, or some other obstacle in its path. Some interests favor Republican candidates, others prefer Democrats, and yet others divide their financial support fairly evenly between the two parties. Table 10.1 shows the 20 largest political contributors in federal elections over the period 1989–2006. Over half of them are labor unions, five are corporations, and four are professional associations. If the list is extended, the proportion of major donors that are corporations, trade associations representing particular industries, or professional associations increases, but unions still account for about one-fifth of the 100 largest donors over this period. A handful of ideological groups—groups whose goals and membership are based on a particular set of values rather than the material interests of their members—also appear in the top 100, including Emily's List, Human Rights Campaign, and the National Committee for an Effective Congress.

TABLE 10.2:   TOP 25 INDUSTRIES GIVING TO MEMBERS OF CONGRESS, 2006

Rank	Industry	Total ($)	Dem %	Rep %	Top Recipient
1	Lawyers/Law Firms	59,963,678	62	36	Hillary Clinton
2	Retired	41,930,398	40	56	Hillary Clinton
3	Real Estate	35,283,779	42	53	Joe Lieberman
4	Health Professionals	32,494,209	36	62	Hillary Clinton
5	Securities/Invest	28,238,304	47	47	Joe Lieberman
6	Leadership/PACS	25,938,098	17	82	Rick Santorum
7	Insurance	21,262,375	36	62	Rick Santorum
8	Lobbyists	16,371,735	40	59	Rick Santorum
9	Commercial Banks	16,073,084	36	63	Hillary Clinton
10	Pharm/Health Prod	13,994,760	32	67	Rick Santorum
11	Misc Finance	13,590,823	40	55	Joe Lieberman
12	Electric Utilities	12,827,723	33	64	Rick Santorum
13	Business Services	12,144,982	49	48	Hillary Clinton
14	TV/Movies/Music	12,012,166	55	44	Hillary Clinton
15	Public Sector Unions	11,041,356	80	18	Steny H. Hoyer
16	Bldg Trade Unions	10,802,763	77	22	Harold E. Ford Jr.
17	Oil and Gas	10,619,176	19	81	Kay Bailey Hutchison
18	Transport Unions	9,947,924	75	24	James L. Oberstar
19	General Contractors	9,939,508	29	69	Robert Menendez
20	Computer/Internet	9,764,003	43	55	Maria Cantwell
21	Misc Business	9,356,478	41	56	Rick Santorum
22	Hospitals/Nurs Homes	9,292,364	42	57	Rick Santorum
23	Misc Mfg/Distrib	9,032,119	31	66	Joe Lieberman
24	Air Transport	8,922,608	34	65	Conrad Burns
25	Automotive	8,767,791	27	72	James M. Talent

Source: http://www.opensecrets.org.

Table 10.2 shows the 25 groups that gave the most to incumbents running for re-election to Congress in 2006. As in the case of the leading individual donors over the last several election cycles, one sees that money flows into the campaign process from many corners. Contributions from business and professional interests dominate this list, but union contributions and money from associations representing older and retired Americans, notably the American Association for Retired Persons, are also important.

Another way of demonstrating the fragmentation that exists in the money that finances elections in the United States is to look at group spending on a single issue. For example, pro-life anti-abortion groups donated about $5.3 million to congressional candidates during the election cycles between 1990 and 2006, compared to donations of about $14.5 million by pro-choice groups. Ideological/single issue groups range from ultra-conservative to ultra-liberal and have given a total of about $856 million to the two parties over this same period, favoring the Democratic Party in most election years (55% Democratic versus 45% Republican over the entire period).

527s and Other Advocacy Groups

The United States tax code recognizes a number of types of organizations that may raise and spend money on political activities, subject to certain restrictions. Failure to abide by these restrictions will cause a group to lose its tax status under the law and can result in fines. The following are the main such groups:

501(c) Groups: Nonprofit, tax-exempt groups organized under section 501(c) of the Internal Revenue Code that can engage in varying amounts of political activity, depending on the type of group. For example, 501(c)(3) groups operate for religious, charitable, scientific, or educational purposes. They are not supposed to engage in any political activities, though some voter registration activities are permitted. 501(c)(4) groups are commonly called "social welfare" organizations that may engage in political activities, as long as these activities do not become their primary purpose. Similar restrictions apply to Section 501(c)(5) labor and agricultural groups and to Section 501(c)(6) business leagues, chambers of commerce, real estate boards, and boards of trade.

527 Group: A tax-exempt group organized under section 527 of the Internal Revenue Code to raise money for political activities including voter mobilization efforts, issue advocacy, and the like. Currently, the Federal Election Commission only requires a 527 group to file regular disclosure reports if it is a political party or political action committee (PAC) that engages either in activities expressly advocating the election or defeat of a federal candidate or in electioneering communications. Otherwise, it must file either with the government of the state in which it is located or with the Internal Revenue Service. Many 527s run by special interest groups raise unlimited "soft money," which they use for voter mobilization and certain types of issue advocacy but not for efforts that expressly advocate the election or defeat of a federal candidate or amount to electioneering communications.

Political Action Committee (PAC): A political committee that raises and spends limited "hard" money contributions for the express purpose of electing or defeating candidates. See Chapter 9, page 256.

Source: http://www.opensecrets.org.

Much of the money spent during American election campaigns is used by groups to purchase time or space in the media, often in an advertising dogfight with other groups or candidates who are also spending money on a particular issue in an attempt to influence the outcome of an election. For example, in the 2004 presidential campaign, issue groups known as 527s—the section of the Internal Revenue Code under which they operate—spent large sums of money on issue advertising, the aim of which was to support or oppose a particular candidate. Moveon.org was the most prominent of these 527s on the pro-Democratic liberal side, spending $21.6 million on issue advertising. On the pro-Republican conservative side, Swiftboat Veterans for Truth spent $22.6 million challenging Democratic contender John Kerry's Vietnam War record and the truth of some of his claims. The Swiftboat ads were generally considered to have been quite effective, leading to the addition of a new verb to the American political lexicon: Kerry had been "swiftboated." The 527s also spend on advertising in an attempt to influence congressional races. In 2006 they spent a combined total of about $428 million, close to half of which was on congressional outcomes.[22] Table 10.3 shows the amounts spent by the ten highest-spending 527s in the 2004 election cycle.

TABLE 10.3: SPENDING BY THE LEADING 527 COMMITTEES, 2004

Committee	Expenditures
America Coming Together	$78,040,480
Joint Victory Campaign 2004	$72,588,053
Media Fund	$57,694,580
Service Employees International Union	$47,695,646
Progress for America	$35,631,378
Swiftboat Vets & POWs for Truth	$22,565,360
MoveOn.org	$21,565,803
College Republican National Cmte	$17,260,655
New Democrat Network	$12,524,063
Citizens for a Strong Senate	$10,228,515

Source: http://www.opensecrets.org.

The Governing Class in America

Already in the early months of 2007 the jockeying for the presidential nomination in each of the parties was a bare-knuckle affair. Commenting on the leading contenders among the Republican and Democratic hopefuls, one journalist remarked that they were all millionaires and that aspirations to reach the White House were limited to the rich. The 2000 and 2004 elections seemed to confirm this. In 2000 George W. Bush, millionaire son of a former president, faced the millionaire son of a long-time senator from Tennessee, Al Gore Jr., himself a senator from Tennessee. Then in 2004 Bush was challenged by John Kerry, husband of one of America's richest women, Theresa Heinz Kerry. It appeared to many that American politics had become a club for the wealthy.

This perception is wrong. Although the affluent are overrepresented in the American governing elite, entry into this group is still very fluid, particularly compared to many other democracies. Moreover, and despite the occasional talk of dynasties in American politics (as in the Bush or Kennedy dynasty), there is no governing class in the United States. This may partly be ascribed to the term limits and low salaries associated with many state and local offices, but a more important part of the explanation is that entry into the political elite, even at the highest levels, is comparatively open in the United States.

This openness is particularly apparent in local and state politics. In many states the job of a state legislator is a part-time one, the legislature sitting for only a small portion of the year. The pay is usually low. In Vermont, where the state's 150 lawmakers are in session for only about four months of every year and are paid under $600 per week, most members hold some other job. In 15 states, lawmakers are limited in the number of terms they may serve, ensuring a continuous circulation of new blood through the legislature. The composition of these state legislatures broadly mirrors that of the middle class from which members are drawn.

Even state governors, whose salaries are higher, are broadly middle class. Figure 10.3 shows that in 2006 about half of state governors came from working-class or farming families. Only one out of ten came from a wealthy family background. Moreover, the vast majority of governors had attended state universities or non-elite private ones, only about one out of four graduating from an elite school like Harvard, Stanford, or Yale. And some of these graduates were scholarship winners who made it into these elite schools by dint of intelligence and hard work, not because of a family able to pay the tuition bill. The main barriers to entry into this segment of the political elite involved sex and race. Most were males and all but one was white. Modest or even unpromising class circumstances were not, however, serious handicaps. Indeed, some of the personal biographies of the governors, including that of Ted Kulongoski of Oregon, orphaned at age four and raised by nuns in a Catholic boys' home, and Tennessee's Phil Bredesen, raised by a single mother on a bank teller's wages, read like classic Horatio Alger stories of pluck, perseverance, and hard work.

FIGURE 10.3: SELECTED BACKGROUND CHARACTERISTICS OF STATE GOVERNORS, 2006

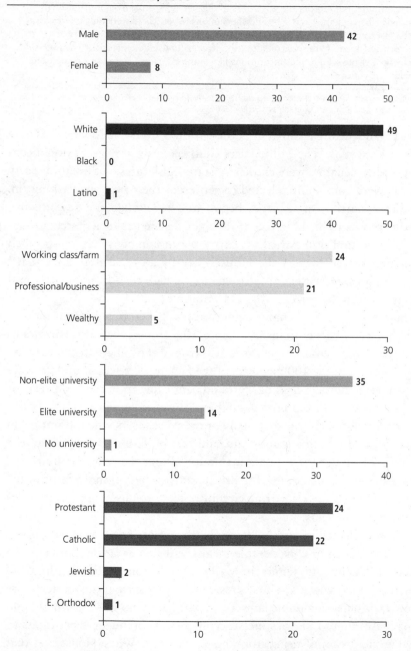

Note: Both the class and educational background categories required some discretionary judgments. For example, whether a governor whose family farmed 2,000 acres should be in the working class/farm category or the professional/business one is not obvious. Two thousand acres of cash crop land in South Dakota is not likely to represent the sort of family income and lifestyle that would be associated with this same acreage in California. If a governor's father or mother was a teacher then he or she was considered to have a professional background. But most of the governors in this category came from more affluent backgrounds where a parent was a businessperson or lawyer. There were only a few cases where the placement of a governor in one or the other category required this sort of discretionary judgment. In the case of education background, elite universities were considered to be Ivy League schools plus institutions like Stanford, Notre Dame or a recognized elite liberal arts college.

Source: Based on data for state governors provided in Michael Barone, ed., The Almanac of American Politics, 2006 *(Washington, DC: National Journal Group, 2006).*

Perhaps the picture is different at the national level. The American Senate was once known as "The Millionaires Club," a fairly apt description a century ago when senators were chosen by state legislatures, and wealthy party stalwarts were commonly selected to represent their state in Washington. (The direct election of senators began in 1913, when the Seventeenth Amendment was ratified.) In recent years the Senate has re-acquired a reputation as a bastion of the wealthy, partly because many senators—a much greater proportion than in the House—are by any reasonable standard wealthy persons. However, it is also due to the high cost of running for and winning a seat in the Senate (over $11 million in 2006).

In fact, however, the Senate remains accessible to people from modest and middle-class backgrounds. As Figure 10.4 shows, the main barriers to entry appear to be sex and race, as is also true of the gubernatorial elite. As of 2006 only 14 of the 100 members of the Senate were female and 95 were white. In terms of their class backgrounds, 45 came from working-class or farming families, 50 from professional and business families, and only five from rich families. It is true that many of the 95 senators who did not begin life rich became wealthy in adult life, and this probably contributes to the perception of the senate as unattainable for all but the rich. Two-thirds of senators attended state or non-elite private universities. In short, most of the members of the Senate came from circumstances broadly similar to those of middle-class Americans.

At the top of the political ladder is the president. The first several presidents were all men of considerable means, either plantation owners as in the case of Washington, Jefferson, Madison and Monroe, or wealthy businessmen or landowners. The first president to break from this pattern was Andrew Jackson, a small-time lawyer and war hero who was known as "Old Hickory." Abraham Lincoln's life story inspired subsequent generations to believe in the dream of rising from log cabin to the White House and that anyone may become president. This has been dismissed by many as a bit of mythology that serves the interests of powerful elites by encouraging average people to believe that opportunities in America, including a crack

FIGURE 10.4: BACKGROUND CHARACTERISTICS OF AMERICAN SENATORS, 2006

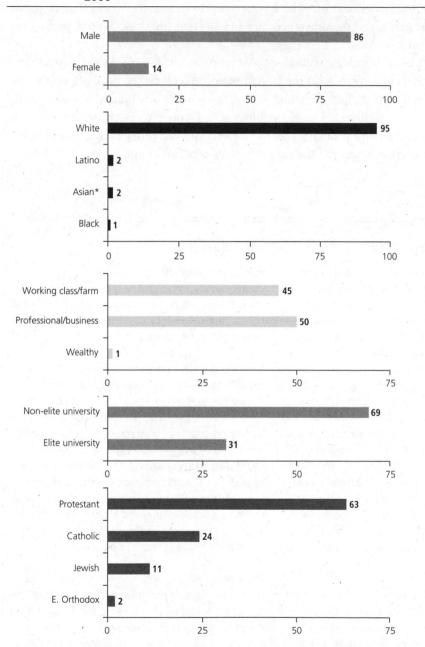

Source: Based on data on state governors provided in Michael Barone, ed., The Almanac of American Politics, 2006 *(Washington, DC: National Governal Group, 2006).*

at the brass ring, are open to all. However, an examination of the family circumstances of those who have been president since World War II shows that privileged circumstances are not needed for those who aspire to the White House.

The reasonable conclusion to draw from all this is that there is no governing class, as such, in the United States. Access to the pool of people running for office, including high office, is by no means limited to the wealthy and the privileged. The biographies of a George W. Bush or Al Gore may mislead us into believing that a self-perpetuating elite governs America, but the preponderance of the evidence disproves this claim.

Do Presidents Come from Privileged Backgrounds?

Harry S. Truman, the son of a farmer, was a small businessman before entering politics. Dwight Eisenhower was the son of an engineer and made his reputation in the military before becoming president. John F. Kennedy was, of course, the son of a wealthy man who made his fortune selling bootleg liquor during Prohibition. Lyndon Baines Johnson was the son of a South Texas dirt farmer and a graduate of San Marcos College. His successor, Richard Nixon, came from a similarly modest family: his father tried his hand at growing lemons in California then ran a gas station. Gerald Ford, who assumed the presidency after Nixon's resignation, came from a modest family in Grand Rapids, Michigan and as a college student managed to pay his way through university at Michigan and Yale law school by washing dishes and coaching sports teams. He was followed by Jimmy Carter, a peanut farmer and former submarine officer from Plains, Georgia.

After Carter's one term as president, Ronald Reagan occupied the White House. Reagan was the son of an alcoholic father and had nothing remotely resembling privilege in his background. He attended Eureka College, no one's idea of an elite college and it certainly was not when Reagan went there. Reagan's vice-president, George H.W. Bush, was elected president after him. Bush came from a wealthy family, but, it should be said, he enlisted in the military in World War II and became a decorated fighter pilot before locating in Texas and building a fortune in the oil business.

Bush lost the 1992 elections to a man who appeared to be the quintessential embodiment of the log house to White House dream, Bill Clinton. Clinton was born in a place called Hope, Arkansas— Hollywood could not have scripted it better—and was raised by a single working mother after his father died and his mother left his alcoholic, abusive stepfather. Clinton's successor, George W. Bush, is a son of favored circumstances. Barack Obama was raised by a single mother and his grandparents during most of his youth and managed to attend elite universities on the strength of scholarships.

The striking thing to note here is that only two of the 12 men to hold the office of president since 1945 have had a wealthy background. If one widens the pool to include those who ran against them and lost, as well as the leading contenders in the Republican and Democratic Party primaries, no evidence is found to support the claim that the road to the White House starts with a privileged upbringing.

Notes

1   Tocqueville, *Democracy in America*, Book I.

2   Tocqueville was aware of the possibility that a manufacturing elite could arise in the United States. See "How an Aristocracy May Be Created by Manufactures," in *Democracy in America*, Book II, Chapter 20.

3   Howard Zinn, *A People's History of the United States* (New York: HarperCollins, 1980).

4   Jimmy Carter, *Our Endangered Values: America's Moral Crisis*. New York, NY: Simon & Schuster, 2005.

5   In Henry Steele Commager, *Living Ideas in America* (New York: Harper and Brothers, 1951), 210.

6   See Appendix 2, this volume. Quotations below are from this source.

7   Charles Beard, *An Economic Interpretation of the Constitution* (1913; Edison, NJ: Transaction, 1998).

8   See, for example, Forrest McDonald, *We The People: The Economic Origins of the Constitution* (Chicago, IL: University of Chicago Press, 1958); Forrest McDonald, *Novus Ordo Seclorum: The Intellectual Origins of the Constitution* (Lawrence, KS: University Press of Kansas, 1985); and Robert E. Brown, *Charles Beard and the Constitution* (New York: Norton, 1956).

9   Lord James Bryce, *The American Commonwealth*, Vol. 2 (New York: Macmillan, 1920) 271.

10 Tocqueville, *Democracy in America*, Book I.

11 Bryce, 267.

12 Bryce, 271.

13 Bryce, 272.

14 Harold Laski, *The American Democracy* (New York, Viking Press: 1948) 617.

15 E.E. Schattschneider, *The Semi-Sovereign People* (New York: Holt, Rinehart and Winston, 1960).

16 See Adbusters, http://www.adbusters.org; Mother Jones, http://www.motherjones.org; and the Weekly Standard, http://www.weeklystandard.com.

17 This latter claim often seems to be made by people who have not paid sufficient attention to what is said on talk radio, because on some issues, such as illegal immigration, most conservative talk radio took a very critical position in opposition to big business, President George W. Bush, and most of the Republican establishment during the last years of the Bush administration.

18 Project for Excellence in Journalism, *The State of the News Media 2005: An Annual Report on American Journalism*, http://www.stateofthenewsmedia.org.

19 Pierre Gervais, *L'avènement d'une superpuissance* (Paris: Larousse, 2001); my translation.

20 S. Robert Lichter, Stanley Rothman, and Linda Richter, *The Media Elite: American's New Power Brokers* (Bethesda, MD: Adler and Adler, 1986).

21 Pew Research Center, "Bottom-Line Pressures Now Hurting Coverage, Journalists Say," Part IV on Values and the Press, 23 May 2004.

22 http://www.opensecrets.org.

PART FIVE

Foreign Policy

CHAPTER ELEVEN

America in the World

Introduction

When the American Constitution was adopted in 1789, the ability of the fledgling government to defend the country's borders was precarious. Compared to the great European powers of that era—Britain, France, and Spain—the United States had a rather unimpressive military. On the positive side of the ledger, however, were a couple of factors. One was geography. Separated from Europe by the Atlantic Ocean, Americans felt distant from the strife and centuries-old rivalries of the Old World and to some degree protected from military threat by this physical isolation—but only to some degree. The three European powers all had colonies in North America at the end of the eighteenth century, and, as much as some of the early leaders of the republic would have liked the United States to remain isolated from their quarrels and interests, the fact that they maintained outposts on America's doorstep meant that, at the very least, diplomatic relations with them were necessary.

It would take more than a century for the United States to achieve the status of a world power, with military capacities that spanned the earth's hemispheres. Along the way the American republic took some tentative but important steps in establishing a foreign policy that went beyond the avoidance of the "foreign entanglements" that George Washington had warned against in his farewell address. Among them were the War of 1812 with Britain, the development of the Monroe Doctrine, the Spanish-American War, and the doctrine of Manifest Destiny, as well as the acquisition of all of

the continental United States by the end of the nineteenth century. The isolation that Washington had counseled seemed a dim memory under President
Theodore Roosevelt (1901–09) when the Panama Canal was built, Spain
was expelled from the Philippines, and the United States naval fleet circled
the globe.

Today, the United States is the world's foremost military and economic
power and by far the leading exporter of cultural products—films, television programming, video games, music, fast food, and fashion—throughout
the world. Under President George W. Bush, American foreign policy took
a sharp turn toward greater intervention abroad. But debates in the United
States over the proper role for America in the world continue to reflect the
tension between isolationist and interventionist impulses, a tension that is
almost as old as the republic itself.

Idealism and America's Role in the World

From George Washington to the present day, American leaders have always
drawn on an idealistic language when explaining what they believed to be
the proper goals of American foreign policy and the country's relationship to
other countries. They have been, from the beginning, conscious of America's
role in the world, and their thinking about matters of diplomacy, trade, and
war and peace have been influenced by an idea of American exceptionalism that, in some ways, has remained largely unchanged since Washington's
time. At the heart of this idea is the belief, sometimes expressed in providential terms, that American democracy occupies a unique place in the world.
This has sometimes inclined America's leaders to prefer isolation in order to
protect the ideals and interests of the country from the corrupting influences
of foreign entanglements. At other times, the pendulum has swung toward
internationalism, based on the belief that the best security for American
ideas and interests lay in the spread of American democratic values and the
defeat of regimes and value systems opposed to American ideals. This internationalism has often been expressed in the language of duty, that is, the
duty of America to spread freedom and democracy and to defeat its enemies
wherever they may be.

There is, of course, no shortage of cases where the United States has
propped up autocratic regimes and even helped them defeat popular movements within their borders. There are also many cases where the United
States has come to the defense of democracies, as in World War II; helped
build democracies, as in postwar West Germany and Japan; and contributed

America's Duty to Spread Democracy

On a tall granite wall in the Woodrow Wilson Memorial Hallway in the Ronald Reagan Building in Washington, DC, these words from President Wilson's 1917 address to Congress, just before the entry of the United States into World War I, are inscribed:

It is a fearful thing to lead this great peaceful people into war, into the most terrible and disastrous of all wars, civilization itself seeming to be in the balance. But the right is more precious than peace, and we shall fight for the things which we have always carried nearest our hearts, for democracy, for the right of those who submit to authority to have a voice in their own governments, for the rights and liberties of small nations, for a universal dominion of right by such a concert of free peoples as shall bring peace and safety to all nations and make the world itself at last free. To such a task we dedicate our lives and our fortunes, everything that we are and everything that we have, with the pride of those who know that the day has come when America is privileged to spend her blood and her might for the principles that gave her birth and happiness and the peace which she has treasured. God helping her, she can do no other.

Almost a century later, President George W. Bush expressed his own idealistic vision for the spread of democratic institutions through the world and, in particular, the Middle East:

Source: http://millercenter.org/scripps/archive/speeches.

For a half century, Americans defended our own freedom by standing watch on distant borders. After the shipwreck of communism came years of relative quiet, years of repose, years of sabbatical—and then there came a day of fire. We have seen our vulnerability—and we have seen its deepest source. For as long as whole regions of the world simmer in resentment and tyranny—prone to ideologies that feed hatred and excuse murder—violence will gather, and multiply in destructive power, and cross the most defended borders, and raise a mortal threat. There is only one force of history that can break the reign of hatred and resentment, and expose the pretensions of tyrants, and reward the hopes of the decent and tolerant, and that is the force of human freedom.

We are led, by events and common sense, to one conclusion: The survival of liberty in our land increasingly depends on the success of liberty in other lands. The best hope for peace in our world is the expansion of freedom in all the world.

You may be dubious, if not about Wilson's democratic idealism then about the genuineness of President Bush's commitment to the spread of democracy. But the promotion of democracy has been, in fact, an important goal of American foreign policy under several presidents since Woodrow Wilson's time in the White House.

to the liberation of the formerly communist countries of Eastern Europe and several former Soviet republics, most of which have become democracies. In recent years American foreign policy has supported democratic forces in the Ukraine and Belarus in the face of opposition from Russia. The 2004–05 elections in Afghanistan and Iraq were showcased by the Bush administration as successes in its efforts to bring democracy to peoples and parts of the world that had known only autocracy and oppression.

Objections may be raised to every one of these examples. At the most basic level one might argue that even in what may appear to be the clearest case of defending democracy and human rights—participation in World War II on the Allied side against fascism in Germany and Japan—American intervention was motivated by economic self-interest and the Japanese attack on Pearl Harbor. But what reason is there to expect that a policy of promoting democracy should be disinterested and without the prospect of benefits for the country pursuing it? In arguing that democratization of the Middle East would be a good thing, the Bush administration clearly had in mind such factors as the security of energy supplies, undermining support for Islamic terrorism, and protecting Israel. Making life better for those who would live in these fledgling democracies was, in all likelihood, not at the top of the administration's list of priorities. That does not mean that the strategy of regime change in Iraq, followed by elections, was not influenced by the belief that a democratic regime would be less of a threat to American interests.

The Competing Pulls of Isolationism and Engagement

The principle of remaining apart from the affairs and conflicts of the rest of the world has a long history in the United States, being famously expressed in Washington's farewell address and echoed in Thomas Jefferson's equally famous first inaugural address. "The great rule of conduct for us in regard to foreign nations," declared Washington, "is, in extending our commercial relations to have with them as little political connection as possible."[1] This advice was based on a combination of America's self-interest, as Washington perceived it, and a romantic notion of America's unique place in the history of mankind. This combination of interest and idealism is evident in Washington's warning against allowing passion and permanent attachments to cloud judgment in foreign affairs:

> ... [N]othing is more essential than that permanent, inveterate antipathies against particular nations and passionate attachments for others should be excluded, and that in place of them just and amicable feelings toward all should be cultivated.

> The nation which indulges toward another an habitual hatred or an habitual fondness is in some degree a slave. It is a slave to its animosity or to its affection, either of which is sufficient to lead it astray from its duty and its interest.

Washington held steadfastly to these principles when he resisted the strong current of public opinion that clamored for an American alliance with revolutionary France and a declaration of war against England. As Tocqueville observes, it required the immense prestige of Washington to resist the passions that would have had the young republic take sides in this Old World struggle, but not even Washington's great stature could spare him from vicious public attacks.[2]

When Washington and his contemporaries turned their minds to international affairs and the dangers of foreign entanglements they quite naturally had Europe in mind. "Europe," said Washington, "has a set of primary interests which to us have none or a very remote relation." Jefferson made the same point in his first inaugural address (1801), where he observed that America was "Kindly separated by nature and a wide ocean from the exterminating havoc of one-quarter of the globe." In a letter to Baron von Humbolt, written several years after leaving the presidency, Jefferson elaborated on this theme and anticipated the Monroe Doctrine's principle of the non-interference of European powers in the hemispheric affairs of America: "The European nations constitute a separate division of the globe; their localities make them part of a distinct system; they have a set of interests of their own in which it is our business never to engage ourselves. America has a hemisphere to itself."[3]

These sentiments were formalized in President James Monroe's 1823 message to Congress. Monroe repeated the admonitions of his predecessors against American involvement in the quarrels of the Old World, but he framed American isolationism in the distinctive context of America's special interest in and responsibility for the hemisphere of the New World. Two decades later President James Polk restated the Monroe Doctrine in his 1845 annual message to Congress. Polk is remembered as the president of "Manifest Destiny" under whose watch the territory of the United States was greatly enlarged through the annexation of Texas and expansion west to the Pacific coast. Whereas the Monroe Doctrine enlarged the circle of American vital interests to include other independent countries in the Western hemisphere, Polk and the concept of Manifest Destiny involved a somewhat narrower conception of American interests, linking them to a sort of providential mission to expand American territory across the continent. Both the Monroe Doctrine and Manifest Destiny need to be viewed in the shadow of the European powers' presence and ambitions in the hemisphere of the Americas. Both were expressions of an American isolationism that was based on a fundamental rejection of Old World influence and an affirmation of what was seen by Americans as their unique role in world history.

The Monroe Doctrine

... The citizens of the United States cherish sentiments the most friendly in favor of the liberty and happiness of their fellow-men on [the other] side of the Atlantic. In the wars of the European powers in matters relating to themselves we have never taken any part, nor does it comport with our policy so to do. It is only when our rights are invaded or seriously menaced that we resent injuries or make preparation for our defense. With the movements in this hemisphere we are of necessity more immediately connected, and by causes which must be obvious to all enlightened and impartial observers. The political system of the allied powers is essentially different in this respect from that of America. This difference proceeds from that which exists in their respective Governments; and to the defense of our own, which has been achieved by the loss of so much blood and treasure, and matured by the wisdom of their most enlightened citizens, and under which we have enjoyed unexampled felicity, this whole nation is devoted. We owe it, therefore, to candor and to the amicable relations existing between the United States and those powers to declare that we should consider any attempt on their part to extend their system to any portion of this hemisphere as dangerous to our peace and safety. With the existing colonies or dependencies of any European power we have not interfered and shall not interfere. But with the Governments who have declared their independence and maintained it, and whose independence we have, on great consideration and on just principles, acknowledged, we could not view any interposition for the purpose of oppressing them, or controlling in any other manner their destiny, by any European power in any other light than as the manifestation of an unfriendly disposition toward the United States.

Excerpts from President James Monroe's Annual Message to Congress, December 2, 1823.

This role—really a sense of providential mission—seldom has been expressed as clearly as in President McKinley's 1898 speech after the Spanish-American War, explaining why the United States should retain the Philippines. "We will not renounce," he declared, "our part in the mission of our race, trustee, under God, of the civilization of the world. And we will move forward to our work, not howling out regrets like slaves whipped to their burdens, but with gratitude for a task worthy of our strength, and thanksgiving to Almighty God that he has marked us as his chosen people, henceforth to lead in the regeneration of the world." This sounds, of course, very much like Rudyard Kipling's famous poem on "The White Man's Burden" (1899) to bring civilization and progress to "backward" societies. And it appears to mark quite a departure from the isolationism of Washington, Jefferson, Monroe, and Polk.

In fact, however, the willingness, even eagerness, of the United States to intervene in Pacific affairs under McKinley and Theodore Roosevelt—the Great White Fleet of American warships was launched under Theodore Roosevelt, himself a hero of the Spanish-American War and perhaps the first imperialist to occupy the White House—did not signify the end of isolationism in American politics. As Henry Steele Commager observes, "it has long been one of the paradoxes of American policy and public opinion, that American isolationism has been directed to Europe alone, and that the most ardent isolationists have customarily been those most eager to intervene in Far Eastern affairs."[4] This was written half a century ago, but until the debacle of Vietnam it remained true that the struggle between isolationist and internationalist ideas in American foreign policy was focused chiefly on America's relationship to Europe.

Throughout the twentieth century isolationism and internationalism waged war in American public opinion. The inability of President Wilson to persuade Congress to ratify American participation in the League of Nations signaled a clear defeat for the president's idealistic internationalism. Before the Japanese attack on Pearl Harbor, American public opinion was strongly opposed to the United States becoming involved in World War II. One month before the attack, only one-fifth of Americans agreed that the United States should take steps, at the risk of war, to prevent Japan from becoming too powerful militarily.[5] Pearl Harbor and American involvement in World War II represented a watershed. In the wake of the Allied victory, a majority of Americans supported their country's entry into the United Nations. American participation in the North Atlantic Treaty Organization (NATO) and its assumption of the role of leader of the Free World during the Cold War indicated that the pendulum of public opinion had swung toward internationalism.

There were limits, however, to Americans' support for their country's new leadership role in what immediately became a Cold War struggle between the West, led by the United States, and the communist world under Soviet leadership. The Korean War, fought at the cost of roughly 54,000 American lives and resulting in a sort of stalemate with a Korea divided between the communist North and the pro-American South, contributed to a dramatic decline in President Truman's popular support. During the presidency of Dwight Eisenhower, the limits of Americans' support for internationalism were not tested by major military engagements and loss of American lives abroad. There was, however, a steady build-up of American forces in Western Europe under the aegis of the NATO alliance. The widespread belief among Americans that Soviet-led communism ran directly counter to American values and the American way of life and that this menace would spread throughout Europe unless dissuaded by American troops and missiles ensured popular support for America's role as the leading defender of capitalist democracy. The Soviet Union's launch of the Sputnik satellite in

1957 and its early lead in what was known as the "space race" reinforced the American public's perception that Soviet communism posed a real threat to American interests in the world. When John F. Kennedy became president in 1961, his inaugural address focused mainly on America's role in the world and expressed an idealistic internationalism that suited the generally optimistic spirit of the times.

Internationalism remained ascendant until the mid- to late-1960s, when mounting American casualties abroad and domestic unrest during the protracted Vietnam campaign produced a popular backlash against the United States playing a role that a generation of Americans had come to accept as normal. Public support for American military involvement fell dramatically during the second half of the 1960s across virtually all major segments of the population but particularly among the most highly educated.

For almost three decades after the 1973 American withdrawal from Vietnam, the competing pulls of isolationism and engagement favored a much more wary and limited role for America in the world than that which the country had assumed after World War II. *Disengagement* is the term often used to characterize this sentiment. This sense that the United States should avoid falling into circumstances that might lead to another Vietnam was only slightly related to the older isolationist sentiments that had prevailed during the country's first century and again between World Wars I and II. Retreat from the world was no longer a serious option. However, no president articulated a robustly internationalist vision for American foreign policy and America's role in the world similar in ambition to those expressed by Woodrow Wilson, Franklin D. Roosevelt, and John F. Kennedy until George W. Bush articulated such a vision after the attacks of 9/11.

It is, in the end, simplistic and misleading to use the labels isolationist and internationalist in characterizing American sentiment when it comes to foreign policy. The messy reality of public opinion is that Americans support more or less engagement, in some parts of the world, in particular circumstances. "The American people are not isolationist," argues Brett Schaefer, "rather they are largely indifferent to foreign policy issues."[6]

Indifference rather than isolation: this may appear to be a distinction without a difference. But in fact there is a real difference between the general indifference that tends to characterize American public opinion when it comes to world affairs and the active hostility toward the world outside their borders—in particular toward Europe—that characterized the old isolationism of the nineteenth century and the interwar years. American public opinion is far more nuanced, containing both internationalist and isolationist impulses.

President Kennedy's Commitment to Internationalism

Let every nation know, whether it wishes us well or ill, that we shall pay any price, bear any burden, meet any hardship, support any friend, oppose any foe to assure the survival and the success of liberty.

This much we pledge—and more.

To those old allies whose cultural and spiritual origins we share, we pledge the loyalty of faithful friends. United, there is little we cannot do in a host of cooperative ventures. Divided, there is little we can do—for we dare not meet a powerful challenge at odds and split asunder.

To those new states whom we welcome to the ranks of the free, we pledge our word that one form of colonial control shall not have passed away merely to be replaced by a far more iron tyranny. We shall not always expect to find them supporting our view. But we shall always expect to find them strongly supporting their own freedom—and to remember that, in the past, those who foolishly sought power by riding the back of the tiger ended up inside.

To those peoples in the huts and villages of half the globe struggling to break the bonds of mass misery, we pledge our best efforts to help them help them-selves, for whatever period is required—not because the communists may be doing it, not because we seek their votes, but because it is right. If a free society cannot help the many who are poor, it cannot save the few who are rich.

To our sister republics south of our border, we offer a special pledge—to convert our good words into good deeds—in a new alliance for progress—to assist free men and free governments in casting off the chains of poverty. But this peaceful revolution of hope cannot become the prey of hostile powers. Let all our neighbors know that we shall join with them to oppose aggression or subversion anywhere in the Americas. And let every other power know that this Hemisphere intends to remain the master of its own house.

To that world assembly of sovereign states, the United Nations, our last best hope in an age where the instruments of war have far outpaced the instruments of peace, we renew our pledge of support—to prevent it from becoming merely a forum for invective—to strengthen its shield of the new and the weak—and to enlarge the area in which its writ may run.

Excerpts from President Kennedy's inaugural address, January 20, 1961.

Those who argue that American public opinion is isolationist usually base their argument on one or a combination of several alleged characteristics of the public mood. These include the following:

- the United States should not bear responsibility for world leadership;
- the United States should withdraw from or limit its partici-pation in the UN and other multilateral organizations;
- the United States should not send troops or use military force abroad except when its vital interests are directly affected;

- American foreign aid should be cut back;
- the United States should spend more on defense of its own territory, not defending the rest of the world.

According to Steven Kull and I.M. Destler in *Misreading the Public*,[7] each of these claims about American public opinion is false or at least misleadingly simplistic. Based on a survey of about 1,200 Americans carried out in 1996 and several other polls, they concluded that Americans were, in actual fact, more internationalist than isolationist. Here is a summary of their findings:

- About three-quarters of Americans said that the United States should do its fair share in multilateral efforts, compared to only 12% who said that it should withdraw from the world, and 13% who said that it should assume the role of the pre-eminent world leader. Two-thirds of respondents said that they would vote for a congressional candidate who also believed that the appropriate American role in the world is to do its fair share in international efforts.

- Eighty per cent of respondents agreed that "Because the world is so interconnected today, the United States should participate in UN efforts to maintain peace, protect human rights, and promote economic development. Such efforts serve American interests." Seven out of ten disagreed that "[UN] efforts only make a minimal difference with little benefit to the United States. Therefore it is not in the American interest to participate in them." Only 9% of respondents to a 1997 CNN/USA Today poll agreed that the United States should give up its membership in the UN and those who favored America paying its UN dues in full outnumbered those opposed to this by a ratio of between two and three to one, according to various polls taken between 1996 and 1998.

- The vast majority of Americans—89% of respondents— agreed that "When there is a problem in the world that requires the use of military force, it is generally best for the United States to address the problem together with other nations working through the UN, rather than going it alone." When the question was rephrased to read, "It is better for the United States to act on its own rather than working through the UN, because the United States can move more quickly and probably more successfully," those disagreeing outnumbered those agreeing by more than two to one (66% versus 29%).

- While 86% of Americans surveyed in 1996 agreed that "Taking care of problems at home is more important than giving aid to foreign countries," only 8% said that the United States should eliminate foreign aid entirely, and the vast majority expressed support for various forms of foreign aid (86% for food and medical aid; 76% for economic assistance).

- About one-quarter of Americans agreed that their country should spend enough on defense to defend either the United States only or the United States and other countries on its own, compared to 71% who agreed that the United States should spend enough to protect itself *and* join in multilateral efforts to protect others.

This hardly seems the picture of an isolationist people. In order to counter the predictable and reasonable charge that people often lie to pollsters, giving them answers that they think are more socially or politically respectable than what they truly believe, Kull and Destler carried out focus groups in Boise, Idaho. Boise was chosen because of the widespread belief that isolationist opinion is probably as great or greater in the region of the Rocky Mountain states than anywhere else in the United States; moreover, the congressperson representing Boise was known to be an outspoken critic of the UN. The results of these focus groups simply corroborated the findings of the surveys. Support for American engagement in the world and through multilateral organizations was found to be high.

The picture that Kull and Destler paint is of a pro-engagement public waiting to be mobilized by politicians capable of packaging American involvement abroad and participating in multilateral organizations and operations in ways that tap into a strong but latent idealism and sense of international morality. At the same time, however, they acknowledge a vital truth: "[I]international issues tend not to be prominent in congressional elections ... [T]he electoral market does not reward members who correctly read and respond to general public attitudes on international issues. Nor does it punish members who do not."[8] Or, as former House Speaker Tip O'Neil once famously said, "All politics are local."

The widespread support for American engagement in the world that Kull and Destler found is corroborated in the Report of the Chicago Council/ German Marshall Fund *Worldviews 2002* study.[9] It found that although Americans have rarely cited an international issue as the biggest problem facing the country (see Figure 11.1), a majority have supported an active role for the United States in world affairs since World War II, even during the post-Vietnam years (see Figure 11.2). The study also found strong public support for multilateral approaches to international crises, respondents overwhelmingly agreeing that the United States "*should not* take action alone if it does not have the support of its allies" (72% "should not" versus 21% "should" in 1998; and 61% "should not" versus 31% "should" in 2002, only one year after 9/11). Americans appear to believe that their country has vital interests in much of the world, as may be seen in Figure 11.3.

This disposition in favor of internationalism needs to be viewed through the lens of some equally relevant facts when it comes to Americans' perceptions of the world and their country's role in it. These involve widespread ignorance and indifference. Consider the following findings:

- Americans aged 18–34 came in second last, just ahead of Mexicans, in a nine-country test of world geographic knowledge. Swedes, Germans, and Italians were several times more likely than Americans to have achieved high scores on this test.[10]

- On this same international test, Americans came in last in their ability to identify correctly countries on a world map, averaging 7.3 correct answers out of 16, compared to 12.7 for Swedes, 12.3 for Germans, 12 for Italians, and 11.3 for French respondents.[11]

- Fewer Americans than any of the other national populations could name Afghanistan, from a list of countries, as the home of the Taliban and the base for al Qaeda—and this was within one year of the 9/11 attacks and the invasion of Afghanistan![12]

- Fewer than half of Americans could identify the European Union from a list of five as the organization endorsing the euro for its members, compared to virtually all of the Europeans surveyed and large majorities among the Japanese, Canadians, and even Mexicans.[13]

FIGURE 11.1: FOREIGN PROBLEMS AND THE PUBLIC CONSCIOUSNESS
(problems related to foreign policy as a percentage of the total
mentions of problems facing the country)

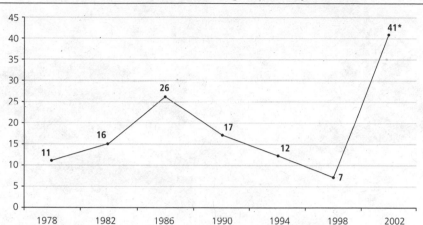

* This spike in the importance attached by the public to foreign policy problems was
prompted by the 9/11 attacks. More respondents cited terrorism as a problem.

Source: Adapted from Chicago Council/German Marshall Fund, Worldviews 2002, http://www.worldviews.org.

FIGURE 11.2: SUPPORT FOR ACTIVE AMERICAN PARTICIPATION IN WORLD
AFFAIRS (percentage who say the United States should take an
"active part" in world affairs rather than stay out, and the gap
in percentage points)

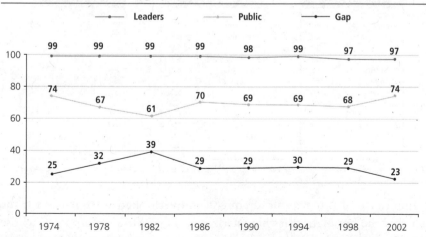

Note: Percentages for the public and leaders calculated with "don't know" excluded.

Source: Adapted from Chicago Council/German Marshall Fund, Worldviews 2002, http://www.worldviews.org.

FIGURE 11.3: AMERICAN VITAL INTERESTS

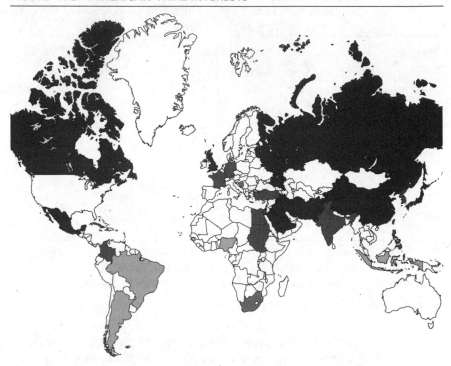

Percentage of Americans Agreeing that the US has Vital Interests in a Country

Over 70%		51% to 70%		41% to 50%	
Japan	83	South Korea	69	South Africa	49
Saudi Arabia	83	Germany	68	Bosnia	43
China	83	Taiwan	65		
Russia	81	India	65		
Israel	79	North Korea	62		
Great Britain	78	Columbia	62		
Canada	76	Philippines	62	**Under 40%**	
Pakistan	76	Cuba	60		
Iraq	76	Egypt	53	Argentina	39
Iran	75	France	53	Brazil	36
Afghanistan	73	Turkey	52	Indonesia	33
Mexico	72	Sudan	52	Nigeria	31

Source: Chicago Council/German Marshall Fund, Worldviews 2002, http://www.worldviews.org; used with permission.

Ignorance of this magnitude might be overlooked were it not for the fact that the population it characterizes is the world's superpower, whose international reach far surpasses that of any other country. However, the National Geographic cross-national survey that reported these dismal findings only looked at younger adults, ages 18 to 34. Just as those toward the older end of this age cohort had marginally better knowledge of world geography and current affairs than the younger ones, middle-aged and

older Americans are even more knowledgeable. The "60 Minutes" generation (the average viewer of this long-running CBS news and current affairs
program is in his or her late fifties or early sixties) is pretty well-informed
about these matters. Moreover, formal education makes a difference in the
United States as it does elsewhere. The National Geographic survey found
that those Americans with at least some college education knew much more
than those with only high school graduation or less, but still less than the
average Swedish, German, Italian, French, or Japanese young adult with less
education. Distressingly, National Geographic's 2006 Survey of Geographic
Literacy among Americans found that the massive media coverage of the
war in Iraq and the rise of China was not accompanied by any improvement
in young Americans' knowledge of the world.[14]

Given Americans' comparatively poor knowledge of the world outside
their borders, it comes as no surprise that they are also largely indifferent to
what happens there as well. As a general rule, information that is not chiefly
about America does not sell and is largely ignored by the news industries
that the vast majority of Americans turn to for what is happening beyond
their local community. Most American politicians avoid international issues
most of the time, knowing that the public is generally indifferent to such
matters except when they are packaged in ways that tie them very clearly
to local and domestic concerns. Likewise, television news producers and
newspaper editors know that international stories seldom present the best
choice when the goal is to maximize audience size and sell advertising time
or space.

Surveys show that television is the medium Americans rely upon most
heavily for their information about national and international current affairs.
Therefore, when discussing the general indifference of most Americans to the
world outside their borders, it makes sense to focus on television and how
it covers the international scene. This has changed dramatically over the last
generation and most sharply since the early 1990s. These changes may be
broken down as follows:

- Less time is devoted to international news stories than in the
  past, excluding those periods when coverage spikes because
  of some crisis abroad (for example, the 1990 Gulf War, the
  2001 invasion of Afghanistan, and the 2003 invasion of Iraq
  and the subsequent occupation of that country).

- The resources devoted to international reporting have
  declined dramatically.

- If the Middle East and regions of the world associated with violent hostility toward the United States are excluded from the picture, the rest of the world is, most of the time, virtually invisible when it comes to most American television news coverage. In other words, the world outside the United States is portrayed, when it is portrayed at all, as a dangerous place where nasty things happen. (In some ways, of course, this is not especially different from local television news in a city like Detroit or Houston, where the world within a ten-mile radius of most viewers' homes is commonly portrayed as a nasty place where bad things happen.)

The general indifference of Americans to the world beyond their doorstep masks the fact that, when it comes to interest in and awareness of the international scene, there are really two Americas. There is the America for whom international news is a tough sell, perhaps 80% to 90% of the population, but there is also an America that follows international news avidly. The Pew Research Center's survey of news consumption refers to this second group as the "core international news audience" and placed its size in 2002 at about 16% of the public, up from about 10% in their 2000 survey.[15] The members of this group are disproportionately white, male, highly educated, and affluent. Conservative Republicans are as likely as liberal Democrats to say that they follow international affairs "very closely."

FIGURE 11.4: ACTIVE PART IN WORLD AFFAIRS (percentage who think it is best for the future of our country if we take an active part in world affairs rather than stay out)

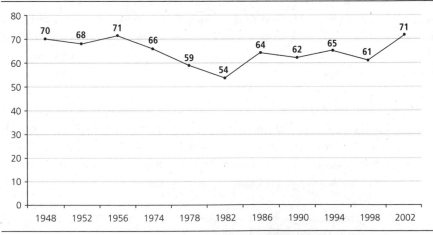

Source: Adapted from Chicago Council/German Marshall Fund, Worldviews 2002: 13, http://www.worldviews.org.

FIGURE 11.5: IMPORTANCE PLACED ON PROTECTING AMERICAN JOBS, 1970–2004 (percentage who say protecting the jobs of American works should be a "very important" goal of American foreign policy and the gap in percentage points)

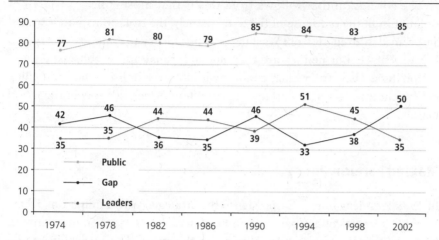

Note: Percentages for the public and leaders calculated with "don't know" excluded.
Gap equals percentage point difference between public and leader percentages.

Source: Adapted from Chicago Council/German Marshall Fund, Worldviews 2002, http://www.worldviews.org.

The attentive public that follows international affairs more closely and is more knowledgeable about the rest of the world than is the general public also tends to be considerably more internationalist. This is reflected in the significant and persistent gap that exists between the foreign policy attitudes of the American public and policy elites (the latter consisted of 397 opinion leaders, a group that included members of Congress, the administration, business leaders, and key figures from the media and some other elites). Figure 11.4 shows that while a clear majority of Americans have supported the general principle of American engagement in the world since the American withdrawal from Vietnam, support for this principle has been virtually unanimous among members of the policy elite. On the more specific issue of whether protecting American workers' jobs should be an important goal of foreign policy, the gap between leaders and the public is even greater (see Figure 11.5). At the same time, however, the 2002 *Worldviews Survey* found that the difference between the attitudes of leaders and the public on very specific foreign policy questions—such as American participation in the Kyoto Agreement on climate change or the International Criminal Court, whether the United States should take Israel's side in a Middle East conflict, and whether the country should be willing to use nuclear weapons even if it has not experienced a nuclear attack—was seldom greater than 10 percentage points.[16] The gap between the general public and policy elites on how active America should be in world affairs is much narrower when this engagement is posed in terms of specific policies and actions.

The conclusion that follows from this is that most Americans are not isolationist in the old sense of the term, namely, the isolationism that waxed and waned in strength from Washington's presidency to America's entry into World War II. But neither are they unconditional and enthusiastic internationalists. They are, rather, conditional internationalists who are mainly indifferent toward foreign affairs but for whom America's role in the world matters.

Making Foreign Policy

In 1979 President Jimmy Carter signed the Strategic Arms Limitations Treaty II with his Soviet counterpart Leonid Brezhnev. However, when he got home, he found that the Senate refused to ratify the treaty. The Soviets were perplexed. How could the President of the United States give his word and then be unable to get Congress to go along? This would not have happened in Moscow!

A couple of decades later, the Serbian government of Slobodan Milosevic was engaged in the massacre of thousands of ethnic Albanians in the Kosovo region of Serbia. The UN and European Union both proved incapable of confronting the Serbian government, and pressure mounted for American intervention to stop what was viewed as the latest round of "ethnic cleansing" in the Balkans. But in the United States neither Congress nor the American people had the stomach to tolerate the loss of American lives for a cause far from home in circumstances that were little understood. The televised spectacle of dead American troops being pulled through the streets of Mogadishu in Somalia—popularized several years later in the film "Blackhawk Down"—had turned American public opinion sharply against risky interventions abroad. In the end the Clinton administration and its NATO allies carried out an aerial bombardment of the Serbian forces, but the president made clear that no American ground troops would be committed to the enterprise. American public opinion and a Congress very sensitive to the sentiments of the electorate tied Clinton's hands, limiting the military options at his disposal.

Several years later Dubai Ports International, a United Arab Emirates (UAE)-owned company that manages ports throughout the world, purchased the British-owned Peninsular and Oriental Steam Navigation Company, which managed some of America's major port facilities through which thousands of cargo containers entered America on a daily basis. The prospect of a company owned by the UAE managing these American ports generated an explosion of protest. Although the UAE was officially supportive of the Bush administration's War on Terror, the country had a history of supporting terrorism that included support for some of those responsible for the 9/11 attacks. The White House argued that the ports deal did not pose a danger to national security. Most ports and transportation authorities agreed. But the American people did not, and members of Congress from both parties lined up in opposition to the deal. In the end, Dubai Ports International announced that it would sell its recently purchased American assets.

These three cases contain important lessons about the politics of foreign policy decision-making in the United States. The linkages between, on the one hand, domestic interests, public opinion, and Congress and, on the other hand, the president and the executive branch's apparatus of foreign and defense policy are extremely complex. As a general rule the president is more dominant in the making of foreign policy than domestic policy. However, he is very far from having a free hand, and the reality of divided powers in American governance is usually very much in evidence.

This was not always so. Until the twentieth century the president's authority in the making of foreign policy generally went unchallenged, except in matters of tariffs and trade policy. These were issues that clearly and directly affected the economic prospects of the states and districts represented by members of Congress and where they were unwilling to give the president a free hand.

This changed as American involvement in the world expanded during the early twentieth century, particularly under Presidents Theodore Roosevelt and Woodrow Wilson. Both Roosevelt and Wilson were idealists when it came to America's role in the world, although Roosevelt's was of the Manifest Destiny variety with an imperialistic edge, while Wilson's rather missionary idealism was very much about spreading American democratic ideals and institutions throughout the world. By the end of Wilson's presidency it was clear that Congress was no longer willing to defer to the executive branch in great matters of war and peace. The Senate refused to ratify the Treaty of Versailles that Wilson had negotiated on behalf of the United States. America's participation in the League of Nations, of which Wilson was the architect, was likewise rejected by Congress and found only weak support among the general population.

This assertion of Congress's ability to act as a countervailing power to the president's authority in foreign affairs lasted only as long as the mood of iso-

The Foreign Policy-Making Powers of the President Compared to Those of Other Leaders

Tocqueville thought that one of the major short-comings of the democracy that he observed in the United States was the lack of centralized author-ity in matters of war and peace. The president, he observed, competed with Congress and public opinion in deciding how to act in such matters, limi-tations that did not shackle his counterparts in other countries.

Tocqueville was comparing the United States to regimes that were either non-democratic or where public opinion was kept at a safe distance from foreign policy-making, such as his native France. But how do the foreign policy powers of the president compare today to those of his counterparts in other democracies? The answer is that they tend to be weaker and much more dependent on the presi-dent's ability to mobilize legislative support and pub-lic opinion behind his policy preferences than is true of, say, the president of France or the prime minister of either Canada or the UK.

In the case of France, the president is generally the unchallenged architect of foreign policy, a role that is only partly due to the French Constitution. At least as important is the tradition of centralized power in France, which includes the expectation that the pres-ident will have the authority to make foreign policy. In the UK and Canada the prime minister is always primus inter pares ("first among others") in the gov-ernment whose members he or she has chosen and typically plays the dominant role in determining the government's domestic and foreign-policy objectives. Minority governments can limit the prime minister's ability to act in the face of significant opposition from the legislature and the public. Divisive circum-stances may also be limiting, although British Prime Minister Tony Blair weathered them in supporting the American-led invasion of Iraq in 2003 and dur-ing the turbulent occupation period that followed.

Canadian Prime Minister Paul Martin (2004–06) was probably inclined to accept the American govern-ment's offer to participate in a continental missile defense system, but he buckled to pressure within his own cabinet and from the Quebec wing of his Liberal Party caucus. Normally, however, both the British and Canadian prime ministers face few seri-ous challenges to their foreign policy dominance.

Not so in the United States. With the exception of circumstances that are widely perceived as directly threatening to Americans or their interests—Pearl Harbor and the 9/11 attacks being the foremost examples—the president often has to fight hard to get his foreign policy preferences accepted by Congress and the public. The three cases described above—President Carter's failure to secure Senate ratification of the SALT II treaty, the inability of President Clinton to deliver more than aerial bom-bardment in Kosovo, and the George W. Bush administration's inability to overcome congressional and public opposition to the takeover of several American port facilities by a Dubai-based com-pany—all illustrate the limits on presidential powers in foreign policy-making. The first Bush administra-tion's 1991 decision to go to war against Iraq after the Saddam Hussein government had invaded Kuwait was only narrowly supported in the Senate. The Bush and then Clinton administrations' sup-port of the North American Free Trade Agreement faced considerable opposition in Congress and in the country and, despite strong presidential support, could well have been defeated or passed in some diminished form. The price that a president must be willing to pay if he decides to push hard for foreign policy choices that encounter significant opposition is either possible defeat or a major loss of popular support. Presidents Truman, Lyndon Johnson, and George W. Bush all discovered this.

lationism that existed in the United States between World Wars I and II. The attack on Pearl Harbor and America's entry into World War II swung the pendulum of foreign policy power decisively in the direction of the executive branch. Even before entry into the war produced this swing, a 1936 Supreme Court decision had delivered a constitutional victory to the advocates of presidential pre-eminence in foreign policy-making. In the *United States v. Curtiss-Wright Export Corporation* the Supreme Court came down solidly on the side of strong presidential authority in matters of foreign policy and, moreover, found that the Constitution established a clear distinction between the nature of the President's authority in foreign versus domestic affairs. "It is quite apparent," declared the Court, "that if, in the maintenance of our international relations, embarrassment ... is to be avoided and success for our aims achieved, congressional legislation which is made effective through negotiation and inquiry within the international field must often accord to the President a degree of discretion and freedom from statutory restriction which would not be admissible were domestic affairs alone involved."[17]

The years after World War II saw the beginning of two decades of almost unchallenged presidential domination of foreign policy. The Cold War rivalry with the Soviet Union and the international spread of communism required that the United States play an active role in world affairs, turning its back on the isolationist sentiments that had been so strong until the bombing of Pearl Harbor. This was done through support for and involvement in the architecture of international organizations that emerged after World War II, including the UN, the International Monetary Fund, the World Bank, and the General Agreement on Tariffs and Trade. It was also done on the military front, through NATO and the stationing of American troops, planes, and missiles in Western Europe, the maintenance of military bases and a naval fleet presence throughout the world, investment in the "arms race" against the Soviet Union, diplomacy and espionage, and competition for the hearts and minds of other countries (or at least of their political and military elites, in some cases).

The fact of having a clear enemy had a couple of important effects on American foreign policy. First, it generated a bipartisan consensus, bringing together Republicans and Democrats who, on many domestic issues, were generally at odds. This consensus sometimes became frayed, as happened over the Strategic Arms Limitations Treaty signed by President Carter but opposed by most Republican senators and even some Democrats. Most of the time, however, the consensus was durable.

This contributed to a second effect, the willingness of Congress to permit the president a large margin of leeway in the making and execution of foreign policy, including the use of military force. This willingness diminished as the Vietnam War dragged on and the casualty count mounted with no victory in sight. After the withdrawal of American troops from Vietnam, Congress passed the *War Powers Resolution, 1973* (often referred to as the *War Powers Act*) which appeared to place severe restrictions on the ability of the president to commit American forces abroad "into situations where imminent involvement in hostilities is clearly indicated by the circumstances." The Resolution included language requiring that the president first consult with Congress before sending troops in harm's way and that in the absence of a formal declaration of war the president would be obliged to report to Congress within 48 hours explaining the reasons for, scope of, and expected duration of the military engagement. Moreover, it appeared to give Congress the power to require that the president end such an engagement after no more than 60 days (with the possibility of a 60-day extension) or at any time if Congress directs him to through a concurrent resolution.

President Nixon vetoed this resolution, but Congress overrode his veto. The climate of the times was clearly on the side of reining in the war-making powers of the president. But the *War Powers Resolution* is probably, most jurists agree, unconstitutional and had been largely ignored until 2007 when several members of Congress proposed that it be revised and strengthened as a way of asserting Congress's opposition to the continuing deployment of American troops in Iraq.

A more effective congressional check on the president's ability to make foreign policy involves the power of the purse. During the 1980s, a Democrat-controlled Congress placed limits on presidential spending in Latin America, measures that were intended to limit President Reagan's ability to provide financial support for groups challenging Soviet-friendly governments such as the Contras who were fighting the Sandinista regime in Nicaragua. Efforts in the administration to fund the Contras in unauthorized ways ultimately led to criminal charges being brought against Oliver North and John Poindexter.

Although it is clear that the president remains the pre-eminent actor in foreign policy-making, it is also clear that the latitude that he enjoyed from World War II until the end of the Vietnam War has been diminished. Only part of this change, however, is due to Congress's efforts to assert its constitutional powers in foreign affairs. Congress was unable to impose any sort of significant restrictions on President Bush's determination to maintain the level of American troops in Iraq between 2005–07 at a time when public support for the war was weak. However, by keeping the issue of the war and the timing and scale of troop withdrawals in the press and before the public through congressional oversight, resolutions, and steady criticism of the administration, Congress was able to ensure that the president's decision not to bend to legislative pressure would carry a cost. This cost was a loss of popular support for the president and his party that led to the Republicans' loss of control in both houses of Congress in the 2006 elections. The combination of a steady barrage of criticism from Congress and fairly widespread opposition to the war—if not to the war as such, certainly to the perception that American forces were not winning—also had the effect of influencing the presidential nomination campaigns in both parties. All of this amounts to rather blunt congressional influence on foreign policy. Nevertheless, congressional oversight and criticism at the very least require that the executive branch must explain and defend its actions.

More than ever, the president must rely on the formidable public relations resources of what Theodore Roosevelt called the "bully pulpit" in order to rally support behind his foreign policy choices. Efforts by Congress to assert its powers in the area of foreign affairs is part of the explanation for this, but the bigger picture is that foreign policy-making has become a more decentralized and competitive domain as a result of globalization, the breakdown of any very meaningful distinction between foreign and domestic policy, and the dramatic growth in the number of groups who actively work to shape the foreign policy agenda and outcomes.

Figure 11.6 depicts the rather decentralized reality of contemporary foreign policy-making. The president is still very firmly at the center of this picture, but except during moments of crisis such as the year following the 9/11 attacks, his authority and preferences rarely escape significant challenges and criticism. The media have become an important countervailing power to the president in matters of foreign policy. Their coverage of issues and of disputes between Congress and the president became more intense and negative during the late years of the Vietnam War and has remained so. Interest groups organized around issues of trade, job protection, human rights, environmental concerns, foreign aid, and other issues have proliferated, as has the number of corporations doing business abroad. Many of these groups lobby Congress and the executive branch or attempt to influence the agenda and discourse of foreign policy through public relations activities intended to influence public opinion.

Shaping the agenda and terms of the foreign policy conversation is also the goal of many think tanks and academics through books, reports, and press conferences, as well as their role as expert commentators on television, radio, websites, and in the print media. "What distinguishes American think tanks from their counterparts in other parts of the world," writes

Don Abelson, "is [their ability] to participate both directly and indirectly in policy-making and the willingness of policy-makers to turn to them for policy advice."[18]

FIGURE 11.6: A MODEL OF THE FOREIGN POLICY-MAKING COMMUNITY:
            PUBLIC OPINION AND ELECTIONS

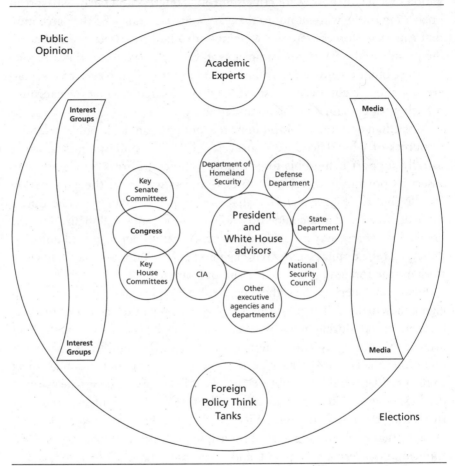

During the Reagan presidency (1981–89), it was widely believed that much of the administration's playbook for foreign policy came from expert advice provided by the conservative American Heritage Foundation. Conservative think tanks such as the Heritage Foundation, the American Enterprise Institute, and the Project for the New American Century were attributed a similarly influential role by some commentators during the presidency of George W. Bush. It is, however, extremely difficult and probably even impossible to say with any certainty how influential any particular think tank has been; however, the ideological pluralism that characterizes the think tank community guarantees that no single perspective has the airwaves and the ears of policy-makers to itself. A 2006 survey by Fairness & Accuracy in Reporting (FAIR) found that six of the ten think tanks that were most often cited in the media were ones it characterized as ideologically centrist, center-left, or progressive. Overall, centrist think tanks accounted for 45% of all media citations, right-leaning ones 40%, and 16% for left-leaning or progressive think tanks (see Table 11.1).

TABLE 11.1:   MEDIA CITATIONS OF THINK TANKS, 2006

Think Tank	Political Orientation	Number of Citations
1. Brookings Institution	Centrist	3,896
2. Council on Foreign Relations	Centrist	2,659
3. Heritage Foundation	Conservative	2,384
4. American Enterprise Institute	Conservative	2,267
5. Center for Strategic and International Studies	Conservative	1,950
6. Kaiser Family Foundation	Centrist	1,593
7. RAND Corporation	Centrist	1,450
8. Center for American Progress	Center-Left	1,309
9. Cato Institute	Conservative-Libertarian	1,250
10. Economic Policy Institute	Progressive	949

Source: Fairness in Accuracy and Reporting, March/April 2007, http://www.fair.org.

America's Role in the World Today

A popular French paperback on the United States, entitled *Les États-Unis aujourd'hui : les maîtres du monde?*[19] (*The United States Today: Masters of the World?*), features images of American military force on eight of its first 14 pages, including the book's cover. Pictures of American soldiers, helicopters, planes, and military bases abroad are plentiful throughout the book, sending a clear message that the United States is a militaristic country whose status in the world has been won and maintained largely through force of arms. A Eurobarometer survey carried out in 2003 found that a majority of Europeans believed the United States to be a threat to world peace and that as many people identified the United States as a threat as they did Iran, North Korea, and Iraq, the three countries characterized by President Bush as members of the "axis of evil."[20] Critics at home and abroad charged that the American failure to join the International Criminal Court, to sign the Kyoto Accord on global warming or the international ban on landmines, to pay its UN dues in a timely fashion, and its alleged penchant for unilateralism all showed that America's leaders were not seriously committed to supporting the international architecture for peace-building. A sort of go-it-alone global enforcer approach seemed to be preferred, they argued, by those who controlled the levers of American foreign policy-making.

Many Americans and their political leaders see things rather differently. The isolationism that Washington and Jefferson advised two centuries ago would strike them as being entirely unrealistic today, but the idealistic language that has always been used to anchor American foreign policy to democratic principles and to an image of the United States' role in the world strikes most Americans as appropriate. Partisan conflict in foreign policy has been the rule over most of the period since the end of the Cold War, Democrats often doubting the sincerity of a Republican president's motives and explanations and Republicans likewise being skeptical of Democrats in the White House. Few question the notion that American foreign policy should be linked to democratic values, and, indeed, much of the self-criticism that Americans direct against their foreign policies is generated by what they see as the failure of their government's actions to live up to these ideals.

America remains a very idealistic country. Other democracies may be idealistic too, but what is exceptional about the idealism associated with American foreign policy is the widespread belief that the United States is the *indispensable nation* in the world. The French tend to express many of the same ideals for the proper goals of foreign policy and for their country's role in the world but without a belief that their country is uniquely equipped to bring about the achievement of these goals. Indeed, the French are among the strongest supporters of multilateralism and working through international institutions, even if their governments have not always avoided unilateral action when this was perceived to be in France's national interests. Canadians tend to think of their country's role in the world as that of a peacekeeper, a modest middle power that has the respect and admiration of other countries and whose global influence depends on these soft power resources. Scandinavians see themselves and their countries as internationalist and strong supporters of bridging the gap between the developed and developing worlds.

Americans, however, not only think of their role in the world as indispensable, their leaders regularly express this view. President Clinton used the term in his 1997 inaugural address. Madeleine Albright, Clinton's Secretary of State, repeated it in defending the administration's support for regime change in Saddam Hussein's Iraq. "I am very proud of what we are doing," she said, "We are the greatest nation in the world and what we are doing is being the *indispensable nation* [my emphasis], willing to make the

Secretary of State Colin Powell on American Ideals and the Use of Force

I think our historical position is that we are a super-power that cannot be touched in this generation by anyone in terms of military power, economic power, the strength of our political system, and our value system. What we would like to see is a greater understanding of the democratic system, the open-market economic system, the rights of men and women to achieve their destiny as God has directed them to do, if they are willing to work for it. And we really do not wish to go to war with people, but, by God, we will have the strongest military around, and that's not a bad thing to have. It encourages and champions our friends that are weak, and it chills the ambitions of the evil.

From an interview with P.J. O'Rourke, "Adult-Male Elephant Diplomacy," The Atlantic (September 2004): 42.

world safe for our children and grandchildren, and for nations who follow the rules."[21]

This view of America's role in a post-Cold War world has no shortage of critics at home and abroad. At the same time, however, it is a view that cuts across partisan and ideological divisions in America. For those who believe that American unilateralism in world affairs is often necessary and justified, and needs to be backed up by the hard power arsenal of military and economic might, the idea that the United States is the indispensable nation is an article of faith. This is also the belief of most of those who advocate multilateralism and greater reliance on the soft power tools of values and diplomacy. Multilateralism without American participation, most would agree, is usually doomed to failure.

Moreover, the view that the United States is the indispensable nation in world affairs is not new. It is very clearly expressed in President Kennedy's 1961 inaugural address and the remark of Dean Acheson, Secretary of State under President Truman, that the United States was the "locomotive at the head of mankind." The idea that the United States bears a special burden in the world—one that it alone is capable of shouldering—was expressed by Harvard human rights expert Michael Ignatieff in his 2003 defense of an invasion of Iraq.[22]

Whether the United States does actually bear a unique burden in the world—whether it is, in fact, the indispensable nation—is a matter for debate. There is little doubt, however, that most of the country's political leaders believe it to be so. And it may be, as Robert Kagan argues, that the rising tide of anti-Americanism that was already evident at the time of the war in Kosovo, when Bill Clinton was in power, but that became a tsunami during the Bush administration, is a reaction to American foreign policies that are defended in the idealistic language of this self-image.[23] "Mr. Big" is never popular, Josef Joffe observes, least of all when he reminds others that he is indeed the biggest on the block.[24]

Still the Indispensable Nation

When the Cold War ended, it was possible to imagine that the world had been utterly changed: the end of international competition, the end of geopolitics, the end of history. When in the first decade after the Cold War people began describing the new era of "globalization," the common expectation was that the phenomenon of instantaneous global communications, the free flow of goods and services, the rapid transmission of ideas and information, and the intermingling and blending of cultures would further knit together a world that had already just patched up the great ideological and geopolitical tears of the previous century. "Globalization" was to the late twentieth century what "sweet commerce" was to the late eighteenth—an anticipated balm for a war-weary world.

In the 1990s serious thinkers predicted the end of wars and military confrontations among great powers. European "postmodernism" seemed to be the future: the abandonment of power politics in favor of international institutions capable of managing the disagreements among nations. Even today, there are those who believe the world is moving along the same path as the European Union....

Perhaps it was these grand expectations of a new era for humankind that helped spur the anger and out-

rage at American policies of the past decade. It is not that those policies are in themselves so different, or in any way out of character for the United States. It is that to many people in Europe and even in the United States, they have seemed jarringly out of place in a world that was supposed to have moved on.

As we now know, however, both nationalism and ideology were already making their comeback in the 1990s. Russia had ceased to be and no longer desired to be a "quasi-member" of the West, and partly because of NATO enlargement. China was already on its present trajectory and had already determined that American hegemony was a threat to its ambitions. The forces of radical Islam had already begun their jihad, globalization had already caused a backlash around the world, and the juggernaut of democracy had already stalled and begun to tip precariously.

... Six decades ago American leaders believed that the United States had the unique ability and the unique responsibility to use its power to prevent a slide back to the circumstances that produced two world wars and innumerable national calamities. Although much has changed since then, America's responsibility has not.

Excerpt from Robert Kagan, "End of Dreams, End of History."

Notes

1 See http://millercenter.org/scripps/archive/speeches. All presidential speeches quoted in this chapter can be found at this source.

2 Tocqueville, *Democracy in America*, Book I.

3 Thomas Jefferson, quoted in Henry Steele Commager, ed., *Living Ideas in America* (New York: Harper and Brothers, 1951) 655.

4 Commager 667.

5 Robert S. Erikson and Norman R. Luttbeg, *American Public Opinion* (New York: Wiley, 1973) 50–51.

6 Brett Schaefer, http://zeus.townhall.com.heritage/issues96/chpt20.html.

7 Steven Kull and I.M. Destler, *Misreading the Public: The Myth of a New Isolationism* (Washington, DC: Brookings Institution, 1999).

8 Kull and Destler 237.

9 Chicago Council on Foreign Relations, *Worldviews 2002: Public Opinion and Foreign Policy*, http://www.worldviews.org.

10 National Geographic-Roper 2002 Global Geographic Literacy Survey, *Final Report*, 17. See http://www.nationalgeographic.com/geosurvey2002/download/RoperSurvey.pdf.

11 National Geographic-Roper, *Final Report*, 23.

12 Chicago Council on Foreign Relations, *Worldviews 2002*.

13 Chicago Council on Foreign Relations, *Worldviews 2002*.

14 Roper Public Affairs, 2006 Geographic Literacy Study, *Final Report*, May 2006, http://nationalgeographic.com/roper2006/.

15 Pew Center for the People and the Press, *Biennial News Consumption Survey*, 9 June 2002: 20–21, http://people-press.org/reports/display.php3?ReportID=156.

16 Chicago Council on Foreign Relations 67.

17 Supreme Court of the United States, *The United States v. Curtiss-Wright Export Corporation*, 1936, 299 US 304.

18 Don Abelson, "Think Tanks and US Foreign Policy: An Historical View," November 2002, http://usinfo.state.gov/journals/itps/1102/ijpe/pj73abelson.htm.

19 Jacques Portes, *Les États-Unis aujourd'hui : les maîtres du monde?* (Paris: Petite encyclopédie Larousse, 2003).

20 See http://www.ec.europa.eu/public_opinion/index_en.htm.

21 Madeleine Albright, statement made at a public forum in Columbus, Ohio, 18 February 1998, http://edition.cnn.com/WORLD/9802/18/townmeeting.folo/.

22 Michael Ignatieff, "The Burden," *New York Times Magazine* (19 January 2003).

23 Robert Kagan, "End of Dreams, Return of History," *Policy Review* (August-September 2007).

24 Josef Joffe, "Who's Afraid of Mr. Big?," *The National Interest* (Summer 2001).

Appendices

The Declaration of Independence

In Congress, July 4, 1776.

The unanimous Declaration of the thirteen united States of America,

When in the Course of human events, it becomes necessary for one people to dissolve the political bands which have connected them with another, and to assume among the powers of the earth, the separate and equal station to which the Laws of Nature and of Nature's God entitle them, a decent respect to the opinions of mankind requires that they should declare the causes which impel them to the separation.

We hold these truths to be self-evident, that all men are created equal, that they are endowed by their Creator with certain unalienable Rights, that among these are Life, Liberty and the pursuit of Happiness.—That to secure these rights, Governments are instituted among Men, deriving their just powers from the consent of the governed, —That whenever any Form of Government becomes destructive of these ends, it is the Right of the People to alter or to abolish it, and to institute new Government, laying its foundation on such principles and organizing its powers in such form, as to them shall seem most likely to effect their Safety and Happiness. Prudence, indeed, will dictate that Governments long established should not be changed for light and transient causes; and accordingly all experience hath shewn, that mankind are more disposed to suffer, while evils are sufferable, than to right themselves by abolishing the forms to which they are accustomed. But when a long train of abuses and usurpations, pursuing invariably the same Object evinces a design to reduce them under absolute Despotism, it is their right, it is their duty, to throw off such Government, and to provide new Guards for their future security.—Such has been the patient sufferance of these Colonies; and such is now the necessity which constrains them to alter their former Systems of Government. The history of the present King of Great Britain is a history of repeated injuries and usurpations, all having in direct object the establishment of an absolute Tyranny over these States. To prove this, let Facts be submitted to a candid world.

> He has refused his Assent to Laws, the most wholesome and necessary for the public good.

> He has forbidden his Governors to pass Laws of immediate and pressing importance, unless suspended in their operation till his Assent should be obtained; and when so suspended, he has utterly neglected to attend to them.

> He has refused to pass other Laws for the accommodation of large districts of people, unless those people would relinquish the right of Representation in the Legislature, a right inestimable to them and formidable to tyrants only.

> He has called together legislative bodies at places unusual, uncomfortable, and distant from the depository of their public Records, for the sole purpose of fatiguing them into compliance with his measures.

> He has dissolved Representative Houses repeatedly, for opposing with manly firmness his invasions on the rights of the people.

> He has refused for a long time, after such dissolutions, to cause others to be elected; whereby the Legislative powers, incapable of Annihilation, have returned to the People at large for their exercise; the State remaining in the mean time exposed to all the dangers of invasion from without, and convulsions within.

> He has endeavoured to prevent the population of these States; for that purpose obstructing the Laws for Naturalization of Foreigners; refusing to pass others to encourage their migrations hither, and raising the conditions of new Appropriations of Lands.

> He has obstructed the Administration of Justice, by refusing his Assent to Laws for establishing Judiciary powers. He has made

Judges dependent on his Will alone, for the tenure of their offices, and the amount and payment of their salaries.

He has erected a multitude of New Offices, and sent hither swarms of Officers to harass our people, and eat out their substance.

He has kept among us, in times of peace, Standing Armies without the Consent of our legislatures.

He has affected to render the Military independent of and superior to the Civil power.

He has combined with others to subject us to a jurisdiction foreign to our constitution, and unacknowledged by our laws; giving his Assent to their Acts of pretended Legislation:

For Quartering large bodies of armed troops among us:

For protecting them, by a mock Trial, from punishment for any Murders which they should commit on the Inhabitants of these States:

For cutting off our Trade with all parts of the world:

For imposing Taxes on us without our Consent:

For depriving us in many cases, of the benefits of Trial by Jury:

For transporting us beyond Seas to be tried for pretended offences:

For abolishing the free System of English Laws in a neighbouring Province, establishing therein an Arbitrary government, and enlarging its Boundaries so as to render it at once an example and fit instrument for introducing the same absolute rule into these Colonies:

For taking away our Charters, abolishing our most valuable Laws, and altering fundamentally the Forms of our Governments:

For suspending our own Legislatures, and declaring themselves invested with power to legislate for us in all cases whatsoever.

He has abdicated Government here, by declaring us out of his Protection and waging War against us.

He has plundered our seas, ravaged our Coasts, burnt our towns, and destroyed the lives of our people.

He is at this time transporting large Armies of foreign Mercenaries to compleat the works of death, desolation and tyranny, already begun with circumstances of Cruelty & perfidy scarcely paralleled in the most barbarous ages, and totally unworthy the Head of a civilized nation.

He has constrained our fellow Citizens taken Captive on the high Seas to bear Arms against their Country, to become the executioners of their friends and Brethren, or to fall themselves by their Hands.

He has excited domestic insurrections amongst us, and has endeavoured to bring on the inhabitants of our frontiers, the merciless Indian Savages, whose known rule of warfare, is an undistinguished destruction of all ages, sexes and conditions.

In every stage of these Oppressions We have Petitioned for Redress in the most humble terms: Our repeated Petitions have been answered only by repeated injury. A Prince whose character is thus marked by every act which may define a Tyrant, is unfit to be the ruler of a free people.

Nor have We been wanting in attentions to our British brethren. We have warned them from time to time of attempts by their legislature to extend an unwarrantable jurisdiction over us. We have reminded them of the circumstances of our emigration and settlement here. We have appealed to their native justice and magnanimity, and we have conjured them by the ties of our common kindred to disavow these usurpations, which, would inevitably interrupt our connections and correspondence. They too have been deaf to the voice of justice and of consanguinity. We must, therefore, acquiesce in the necessity, which denounces our Separation, and hold them, as we hold the rest of mankind, Enemies in War, in Peace Friends.

We, therefore, the Representatives of the united States of America, in General Congress, Assembled, appealing to the Supreme Judge of the world for the rectitude of our intentions, do, in the Name, and by Authority of the good

People of these Colonies, solemnly publish and declare, That these United Colonies are, and of Right ought to be Free and Independent States; that they are Absolved from all Allegiance to the British Crown, and that all political connection between them and the State of Great Britain, is and ought to be totally dissolved; and that as Free and Independent States, they have full Power to levy War, conclude Peace, contract Alliances, establish Commerce, and to do all other Acts and Things which Independent States may of right do. And for the support of this Declaration, with a firm reliance on the protection of divine Providence, we mutually pledge to each other our Lives, our Fortunes and our sacred Honor.

[The 56 signatures on the Declaration appear in the positions indicated.]

Column 1
Georgia:
Button Gwinnett
Lyman Hall
George Walton

Column 2
North Carolina:
William Hooper
Joseph Hewes
John Penn

South Carolina:
Edward Rutledge
Thomas Heyward, Jr.
Thomas Lynch, Jr.
Arthur Middleton

Column 3
Massachusetts:
John Hancock

Maryland:
Samuel Chase
William Paca
Thomas Stone
Charles Carroll of Carrollton

Virginia:
George Wythe
Richard Henry Lee
Thomas Jefferson
Benjamin Harrison
Thomas Nelson, Jr.
Francis Lightfoot Lee
Carter Braxton

Column 4
Pennsylvania:
Robert Morris
Benjamin Rush
Benjamin Franklin
John Morton
George Clymer
James Smith
George Taylor
James Wilson
George Ross

Delaware:
Caesar Rodney
George Read
Thomas McKean

Column 5

New York:
William Floyd
Philip Livingston
Francis Lewis
Lewis Morris

New Jersey:
Richard Stockton
John Witherspoon
Francis Hopkinson
John Hart
Abraham Clark

Column 6

New Hampshire:
Josiah Bartlett
William Whipple

Massachusetts:
Samuel Adams
John Adams
Robert Treat Paine
Elbridge Gerry

Rhode Island:
Stephen Hopkins
William Ellery

Connecticut:
Roger Sherman
Samuel Huntington
William Williams
Oliver Wolcott

New Hampshire:
Matthew Thornton

Federalist Papers Nos. 10 and 51

Federalist Paper No. 10

The Same Subject Continued: The Union as a Safeguard Against Domestic
Faction and Insurrection
From the New York Packet.
Friday, November 23, 1787.
Author: James Madison

To the People of the State of New York:

AMONG the numerous advantages promised by a well-constructed Union,
none deserves to be more accurately developed than its tendency to break
and control the violence of faction. The friend of popular governments never
finds himself so much alarmed for their character and fate, as when he con-
templates their propensity to this dangerous vice. He will not fail, therefore,
to set a due value on any plan which, without violating the principles to
which he is attached, provides a proper cure for it. The instability, injustice,
and confusion introduced into the public councils, have, in truth, been the
mortal diseases under which popular governments have everywhere per-
ished; as they continue to be the favorite and fruitful topics from which
the adversaries to liberty derive their most specious declamations. The valuable improvements made by the American constitutions on the popular
models, both ancient and modern, cannot certainly be too much admired;
but it would be an unwarrantable partiality, to contend that they have as
effectually obviated the danger on this side, as was wished and expected.
Complaints are everywhere heard from our most considerate and virtuous citizens, equally the friends of public and private faith, and of public
and personal liberty, that our governments are too unstable, that the public

good is disregarded in the conflicts of rival parties, and that measures are too often decided, not according to the rules of justice and the rights of the minor party, but by the superior force of an interested and overbearing majority. However anxiously we may wish that these complaints had no foundation, the evidence, of known facts will not permit us to deny that they are in some degree true. It will be found, indeed, on a candid review of our situation, that some of the distresses under which we labor have been erroneously charged on the operation of our governments; but it will be found, at the same time, that other causes will not alone account for many of our heaviest misfortunes; and, particularly, for that prevailing and increasing distrust of public engagements, and alarm for private rights, which are echoed from one end of the continent to the other. These must be chiefly, if not wholly, effects of the unsteadiness and injustice with which a factious spirit has tainted our public administrations.

By a faction, I understand a number of citizens, whether amounting to a majority or a minority of the whole, who are united and actuated by some common impulse of passion, or of interest, adversed to the rights of other citizens, or to the permanent and aggregate interests of the community.

There are two methods of curing the mischiefs of faction: the one, by removing its causes; the other, by controlling its effects.

There are again two methods of removing the causes of faction: the one, by destroying the liberty which is essential to its existence; the other, by giving to every citizen the same opinions, the same passions, and the same interests.

It could never be more truly said than of the first remedy, that it was worse than the disease. Liberty is to faction what air is to fire, an aliment without which it instantly expires. But it could not be less folly to abolish liberty, which is essential to political life, because it nourishes faction, than it would be to wish the annihilation of air, which is essential to animal life, because it imparts to fire its destructive agency.

The second expedient is as impracticable as the first would be unwise. As long as the reason of man continues fallible, and he is at liberty to exercise it, different opinions will be formed. As long as the connection subsists between his reason and his self-love, his opinions and his passions will have a reciprocal influence on each other; and the former will be objects to which the latter will attach themselves. The diversity in the faculties of men, from which the rights of property originate, is not less an insuperable obstacle to a uniformity of interests. The protection of these faculties is the first object of government. From the protection of different and unequal faculties of acquiring property, the possession of different degrees and kinds of property immediately results; and from the influence of these on the sentiments and views of the respective proprietors, ensues a division of the society into different interests and parties.

The latent causes of faction are thus sown in the nature of man; and we see them everywhere brought into different degrees of activity, according to the different circumstances of civil society. A zeal for different opinions concerning religion, concerning government, and many other points, as well of speculation as of practice; an attachment to different leaders ambitiously contending for pre-eminence and power; or to persons of other descriptions whose fortunes have been interesting to the human passions, have, in turn, divided mankind into parties, inflamed them with mutual animosity, and rendered them much more disposed to vex and oppress each other than to co-operate for their common good. So strong is this propensity of mankind to fall into mutual animosities, that where no substantial occasion presents itself, the most frivolous and fanciful distinctions have been sufficient to kindle their unfriendly passions and excite their most violent conflicts. But the most common and durable source of factions has been the various and unequal distribution of property. Those who hold and those who are without property have ever formed distinct interests in society. Those who are creditors, and those who are debtors, fall under a like discrimination. A landed interest, a manufacturing interest, a mercantile interest, a moneyed interest, with many lesser interests, grow up of necessity in civilized nations, and divide them into different classes, actuated by different sentiments and views. The regulation of these various and interfering interests forms the principal task of modern legislation, and involves the spirit of party and faction in the necessary and ordinary operations of the government.

No man is allowed to be a judge in his own cause, because his interest would certainly bias his judgment, and, not improbably, corrupt his integrity. With equal, nay with greater reason, a body of men are unfit to be both judges and parties at the same time; yet what are many of the most important acts of legislation, but so many judicial determinations, not indeed concerning the rights of single persons, but concerning the rights of large bodies of citizens? And what are the different classes of legislators but advocates and parties to the causes which they determine? Is a law proposed concerning private debts? It is a question to which the creditors are parties on one side and the debtors on the other. Justice ought to hold the balance between them. Yet the parties are, and must be, themselves the judges; and the most numerous party, or, in other words, the most powerful faction must be expected to prevail. Shall domestic manufactures be encouraged, and in what degree, by restrictions on foreign manufactures? are questions which would be differently decided by the landed and the manufacturing classes, and probably by neither with a sole regard to justice and the public good. The apportionment of taxes on the various descriptions of property is an act which seems to require the most exact impartiality; yet there is, perhaps, no legislative act in which greater opportunity and temptation are given to a predominant party to trample on the rules of justice. Every shilling with which they overburden the inferior number, is a shilling saved to their own pockets.

It is in vain to say that enlightened statesmen will be able to adjust these clashing interests, and render them all subservient to the public good. Enlightened statesmen will not always be at the helm. Nor, in many cases, can such an adjustment be made at all without taking into view indirect and remote considerations, which will rarely prevail over the immediate interest which one party may find in disregarding the rights of another or the good of the whole.

The inference to which we are brought is, that the CAUSES of faction cannot be removed, and that relief is only to be sought in the means of controlling its EFFECTS.

If a faction consists of less than a majority, relief is supplied by the republican principle, which enables the majority to defeat its sinister views by regular vote. It may clog the administration, it may convulse the society; but it will be unable to execute and mask its violence under the forms of the Constitution. When a majority is included in a faction, the form of popular government, on the other hand, enables it to sacrifice to its ruling passion or interest both the public good and the rights of other citizens. To secure the public good and private rights against the danger of such a faction, and at the same time to preserve the spirit and the form of popular government, is then the great object to which our inquiries are directed. Let me add that it is the great desideratum by which this form of government can be rescued from the opprobrium under which it has so long labored, and be recommended to the esteem and adoption of mankind.

By what means is this object attainable? Evidently by one of two only. Either the existence of the same passion or interest in a majority at the same time must be prevented, or the majority, having such coexistent passion or interest, must be rendered, by their number and local situation, unable to concert and carry into effect schemes of oppression. If the impulse and the opportunity be suffered to coincide, we well know that neither moral nor religious motives can be relied on as an adequate control. They are not found to be such on the injustice and violence of individuals, and lose their efficacy in proportion to the number combined together, that is, in proportion as their efficacy becomes needful.

From this view of the subject it may be concluded that a pure democracy, by which I mean a society consisting of a small number of citizens, who assemble and administer the government in person, can admit of no cure for the mischiefs of faction. A common passion or interest will, in almost every case, be felt by a majority of the whole; a communication and concert result from the form of government itself; and there is nothing to check the inducements to sacrifice the weaker party or an obnoxious individual. Hence it is that such democracies have ever been spectacles of turbulence and contention; have ever been found incompatible with personal security or the rights of property; and have in general been as short in their lives as they have been violent in their deaths. Theoretic politicians, who have patronized this species of government, have erroneously supposed that by reducing mankind to a perfect equality in their political rights, they would, at the same time, be perfectly equalized and assimilated in their possessions, their opinions, and their passions.

A republic, by which I mean a government in which the scheme of representation takes place, opens a different prospect, and promises the cure for which we are seeking. Let us examine the points in which it varies from pure democracy, and we shall comprehend both the nature of the cure and the efficacy which it must derive from the Union.

The two great points of difference between a democracy and a republic are: first, the delegation of the government, in the latter, to a small number of citizens elected by the rest; secondly, the greater number of citizens, and greater sphere of country, over which the latter may be extended.

The effect of the first difference is, on the one hand, to refine and enlarge the public views, by passing them through the medium of a chosen body of citizens, whose wisdom may best discern the true interest of their country, and whose patriotism and love of justice will be least likely to sacrifice it to temporary or partial considerations. Under such a regulation, it may well happen that the public voice, pronounced by the representatives of the people, will be more consonant to the public good than if pronounced by the people themselves, convened for the purpose. On the other hand, the effect may be inverted. Men of factious tempers, of local prejudices, or of sinister designs, may, by intrigue, by corruption, or by other means, first obtain the suffrages, and then betray the interests, of the people. The question resulting is, whether small or extensive republics are more favorable to the election of proper guardians of the public weal; and it is clearly decided in favor of the latter by two obvious considerations:

In the first place, it is to be remarked that, however small the republic may be, the representatives must be raised to a certain number, in order to guard against the cabals of a few; and that, however large it may be, they must be limited to a certain number, in order to guard against the confusion of a multitude. Hence, the number of representatives in the two cases not being in proportion to that of the two constituents, and being proportionally greater in the small republic, it follows that, if the proportion of fit characters be not less in the large than in the small republic, the former will present a greater option, and consequently a greater probability of a fit choice.

In the next place, as each representative will be chosen by a greater number of citizens in the large than in the small republic, it will be more difficult for unworthy candidates to practice with success the vicious arts by which elections are too often carried; and the suffrages of the people being more free, will be more likely to centre in men who possess the most attractive merit and the most diffusive and established characters.

It must be confessed that in this, as in most other cases, there is a mean, on both sides of which inconveniences will be found to lie. By enlarging too much the number of electors, you render the representatives too little acquainted with all their local circumstances and lesser interests; as by reducing it too much, you render him unduly attached to these, and too little fit to comprehend and pursue great and national objects. The federal Constitution forms a happy combination in this respect; the great and aggregate interests being referred to the national, the local and particular to the State legislatures.

The other point of difference is, the greater number of citizens and extent of territory which may be brought within the compass of republican than of democratic government; and it is this circumstance principally which renders factious combinations less to be dreaded in the former than in the latter. The smaller the society, the fewer probably will be the distinct parties and interests composing it; the fewer the distinct parties and interests, the more frequently will a majority be found of the same party; and the smaller the number of individuals composing a majority, and the smaller the compass within which they are placed, the more easily will they concert and execute their plans of oppression. Extend the sphere, and you take in a greater variety of parties and interests; you make it less probable that a majority of the whole will have a common motive to invade the rights of other citizens; or if such a common motive exists, it will be more difficult for all who feel it to discover their own strength, and to act in unison with each other. Besides other impediments, it may be remarked that, where there is a consciousness of unjust or dishonorable purposes, communication is always checked by distrust in proportion to the number whose concurrence is necessary.

Hence, it clearly appears, that the same advantage which a republic has over a democracy, in controlling the effects of faction, is enjoyed by a large over a small republic,—is enjoyed by the Union over the States composing it. Does the advantage consist in the substitution of representatives whose enlightened views and virtuous sentiments render them superior to local prejudices and schemes of injustice? It will not be denied that the representation of the Union will be most likely to possess these requisite endowments. Does it consist in the greater security afforded by a greater variety of parties, against the event of any one party being able to outnumber and oppress the rest? In an equal degree does the increased variety of parties comprised within the Union, increase this security. Does it, in fine, consist in the greater obstacles opposed to the concert and accomplishment of the secret wishes of an unjust and interested majority? Here, again, the extent of the Union gives it the most palpable advantage.

The influence of factious leaders may kindle a flame within their particular States, but will be unable to spread a general conflagration through the other States. A religious sect may degenerate into a political faction in a part of the Confederacy; but the variety of sects dispersed over the entire face of it must secure the national councils against any danger from that source. A rage for paper money, for an abolition of debts, for an equal division of property, or for any other improper or wicked project, will be less apt to pervade the whole body of the Union than a particular member of it; in the same proportion as such a malady is more likely to taint a particular county or district, than an entire State.

In the extent and proper structure of the Union, therefore, we behold a republican remedy for the diseases most incident to republican government. And according to the degree of pleasure and pride we feel in being republicans, ought to be our zeal in cherishing the spirit and supporting the character of Federalists.

PUBLIUS

Federalist Paper No. 51

The Structure of the Government Must Furnish the Proper Checks and Balances Between the Different Departments
From the New York Packet.
Friday, February 8, 1788.

Author: Alexander Hamilton or James Madison

To the People of the State of New York:

TO WHAT expedient, then, shall we finally resort, for maintaining in prac-tice the necessary partition of power among the several departments, as laid down in the Constitution? The only answer that can be given is, that as all these exterior provisions are found to be inadequate, the defect must be sup-plied, by so contriving the interior structure of the government as that its several constituent parts may, by their mutual relations, be the means of keeping each other in their proper places. Without presuming to undertake a full development of this important idea, I will hazard a few general obser-vations, which may perhaps place it in a clearer light, and enable us to form a more correct judgment of the principles and structure of the government planned by the convention. In order to lay a due foundation for that sepa-rate and distinct exercise of the different powers of government, which to a certain extent is admitted on all hands to be essential to the preservation of liberty, it is evident that each department should have a will of its own; and consequently should be so constituted that the members of each should have as little agency as possible in the appointment of the members of the others. Were this principle rigorously adhered to, it would require that all the appointments for the supreme executive, legislative, and judiciary magistra-cies should be drawn from the same fountain of authority, the people, through channels having no communication whatever with one another. Perhaps such a plan of constructing the several departments would be less difficult in practice than it may in contemplation appear. Some difficulties, however, and some additional expense would attend the execution of it. Some deviations, therefore, from the principle must be admitted. In the con-stitution of the judiciary department in particular, it might be inexpedient to insist rigorously on the principle: first, because peculiar qualifications being essential in the members, the primary consideration ought to be to select that mode of choice which best secures these qualifications; secondly, because the permanent tenure by which the appointments are held in that department, must soon destroy all sense of dependence on the authority conferring them. It is equally evident, that the members of each department should be as little dependent as possible on those of the others, for the emoluments annexed to their offices. Were the executive magistrate, or the judges, not independent of the legislature in this particular, their independ-ence in every other would be merely nominal. But the great security against a gradual concentration of the several powers in the same department, consists in giving to those who administer each department the necessary constitutional means and personal motives to resist encroachments of the others. The provision for defense must in this, as in all other cases, be made commensurate to the danger of attack. Ambition must be made to counteract ambition. The interest of the man must be connected with the constitutional rights of the place. It may be a reflection on human nature, that such devices should be necessary to control the abuses of government. But what is government itself, but the greatest of all reflections on human nature? If men were angels, no government would be necessary. If angels were to govern men, neither external nor internal controls on government would be necessary. In framing a government which is to be administered by men over men, the great difficulty lies in this: you must first enable the government to control the governed; and in the next place oblige it to control itself. A dependence on the people is, no doubt, the primary control on the government; but experience has taught mankind the necessity of auxiliary precautions. This policy of supplying, by opposite and rival interests, the defect of better motives, might be traced through the whole system of human affairs, private as well as public. We see it particularly displayed in all the subordinate distributions of power, where the constant aim is to divide and arrange the several offices in such a manner as that each may be a check on the other, that the private interest of every individual may be a sentinel over the public rights. These inventions of prudence cannot be less requisite in the distribution of the supreme powers of the State. But it is not possible to give to each department an equal power of self-defense. In republican government, the legislative authority necessarily predominates. The remedy for this inconveniency is to divide the legislature into different branches; and to render them, by different modes of election and different principles of action, as little connected with each other as the nature of their common functions and their common dependence on the society will admit. It may even be necessary to guard against dangerous encroachments by still further precautions. As the weight of the legislative authority requires that it should be thus divided, the weakness of the executive may require, on the other hand, that it should be fortified. An absolute negative on the legislature appears, at first view, to be the natural defense with which the executive magistrate should be armed. But perhaps it would be neither altogether safe nor alone sufficient. On ordinary occasions it might not be exerted with the requisite firmness, and on extraordinary occasions it might be perfidiously abused. May not this defect of an absolute negative be supplied by some qualified connection between this weaker department and the weaker branch of the stronger department, by which the latter may be led to support the constitutional rights of the former, without being too much detached from the rights of its own department? If the principles on which these observations are founded be just, as I persuade myself they are, and they be applied as a criterion to the several State constitutions, and to the federal Constitution it will be found that if the latter does not perfectly correspond with them, the former are infinitely less able to bear such a test. There are, moreover, two considerations particularly applicable to the federal system of America, which place that system in a very interesting point of view. First. In a single republic, all the power surrendered by the people is submitted to the administration of a single government; and the usurpations are guarded against by a division of the government into distinct and separate departments. In the compound republic of America, the power surrendered by the people is first divided between two distinct governments, and then the portion allotted to each subdivided among distinct and separate departments. Hence a double security arises to the rights of the people. The different governments will control each other, at the same time that each will be controlled by itself. Second. It is of great importance in a republic not only to guard the society against the oppression of its rulers, but to guard one part of the society against the injustice of the other part. Different interests necessarily exist in different classes of citizens. If a majority be united by a common interest, the rights of the minority will be insecure. There are but two methods of providing against this evil: the one by creating a will in the community independent of the majority that is, of the society itself; the other, by comprehending in the society so many separate descriptions of citizens as will render an unjust combination of a majority of the whole very improbable, if not impracticable. The first method prevails in all governments possessing an hereditary or self-appointed authority. This, at best, is but a precarious security; because a power independent of the society may as well espouse the unjust views of the major, as the rightful interests of the minor party, and may possibly be turned against both parties. The second method will be exemplified in the federal republic of the United States. Whilst all authority in it will be derived from and dependent on the society, the society itself will be broken into so many parts, interests, and classes of citizens, that the rights of individuals, or of the minority, will be in little danger from interested combinations of the majority. In a free government the security for civil rights must be the same as that for religious rights. It consists in the one case in the multiplicity of interests, and in the other in the multiplicity of sects. The degree of security in both cases will depend on the number of interests and sects; and this may be presumed to depend on the extent of country and number of people comprehended under the same government. This view of the subject must particularly recommend a proper federal system to all the sincere and considerate friends of republican government, since it shows that in exact proportion as the territory of the Union may be formed into more circumscribed Confederacies, or States oppressive combinations of a majority will be facilitated: the best security, under the republican forms, for the rights of every class of citizens, will be diminished: and consequently the stability and independence of some member of the government, the only other security, must be proportionately increased. Justice is the end of government. It is the end of civil society. It ever has been and ever will be pursued until it be obtained, or until liberty be lost in the pursuit. In a society under the forms of which the stronger faction can readily unite and oppress the weaker, anarchy may as truly be said to reign as in a state of nature, where the weaker individual is not secured against the violence of the stronger; and as, in the latter state, even the stronger individuals are prompted, by the uncertainty of their condition, to submit to a government which may protect the weak as well as themselves; so, in the former state, will the more powerful factions or parties be gradually induced, by a like motive, to wish for a government which will protect all parties, the weaker as well as the more powerful. It can be little doubted that if the State of Rhode Island was separated from the Confederacy and left to itself, the insecurity of rights under the popular form of government within such narrow limits would be displayed by such reiterated oppressions of factious majorities that some power altogether independent of the people would soon be called for by the voice of the very factions whose misrule had proved the necessity of it. In the extended republic of the United States, and among the great variety of interests, parties, and sects which it embraces, a coalition of a majority of the whole society could seldom take place on any other principles than those of justice and the general good; whilst there being thus less danger to a minor from the will of a major party, there must be less pretext, also, to provide for the security of the former, by introducing into the government a will not dependent on the latter, or, in other words, a will independent of the society itself. It is no less certain than it is important, notwithstanding the contrary opinions which have been entertained, that the larger the society, provided it lie within a practical sphere, the more duly capable it will be of self-government. And happily for the REPUBLICAN CAUSE, the practicable sphere may be carried to a very great extent, by a judicious modification and mixture of the FEDERAL PRINCIPLE.

PUBLIUS.

The Constitution of the United States

The Constitution of the United States

[The following text is a transcription of the Constitution in its original form. Items in italics have since been amended or superseded.]

We the People of the United States, in Order to form a more perfect Union, establish Justice, insure domestic Tranquility, provide for the common defence, promote the general Welfare, and secure the Blessings of Liberty to ourselves and our Posterity, do ordain and establish this Constitution for the United States of America.

Article I
SECTION 1
All legislative Powers herein granted shall be vested in a Congress of the United States, which shall consist of a Senate and House of Representatives.

SECTION 2
The House of Representatives shall be composed of Members chosen every second Year by the People of the several States, and the Electors in each State shall have the Qualifications requisite for Electors of the most numerous Branch of the State Legislature.

No Person shall be a Representative who shall not have attained to the Age of twenty five Years, and been seven Years a Citizen of the United States, and who shall not, when elected, be an Inhabitant of that State in which he shall be chosen.

Representatives and direct Taxes shall be apportioned among the several States which may be included within this Union, according to their respective

Numbers, which shall be determined by adding to the whole Number of free Persons, including those bound to Service for a Term of Years, and excluding Indians not taxed, three fifths of all other Persons. The actual Enumeration shall be made within three Years after the first Meeting of the Congress of the United States, and within every subsequent Term of ten Years, in such Manner as they shall by Law direct. The Number of Representatives shall not exceed one for every thirty Thousand, but each State shall have at Least one Representative; and until such enumeration shall be made, the State of New Hampshire shall be entitled to chuse three, Massachusetts eight, Rhode-Island and Providence Plantations one, Connecticut five, New-York six, New Jersey four, Pennsylvania eight, Delaware one, Maryland six, Virginia ten, North Carolina five, South Carolina five, and Georgia three.

When vacancies happen in the Representation from any State, the Executive Authority thereof shall issue Writs of Election to fill such Vacancies.

The House of Representatives shall chuse their Speaker and other Officers; and shall have the sole Power of Impeachment.

SECTION 3

The Senate of the United States shall be composed of two Senators from each State, *chosen by the Legislature* thereof for six Years; and each Senator shall have one Vote.

Immediately after they shall be assembled in Consequence of the first Election, they shall be divided as equally as may be into three Classes. The Seats of the Senators of the first Class shall be vacated at the Expiration of the second Year, of the second Class at the Expiration of the fourth Year, and of the third Class at the Expiration of the sixth Year, so that one third may be chosen every second Year; *and if Vacancies happen by Resignation, or otherwise, during the Recess of the Legislature of any State, the Executive thereof may make temporary Appointments until the next Meeting of the Legislature, which shall then fill such Vacancies.*

No Person shall be a Senator who shall not have attained to the Age of thirty Years, and been nine Years a Citizen of the United States, and who shall not, when elected, be an Inhabitant of that State for which he shall be chosen.

The Vice President of the United States shall be President of the Senate, but shall have no Vote, unless they be equally divided.

The Senate shall chuse their other Officers, and also a President pro tempore, in the Absence of the Vice President, or when he shall exercise the Office of President of the United States.

The Senate shall have the sole Power to try all Impeachments. When sitting for that Purpose, they shall be on Oath or Affirmation. When the President of the United States is tried, the Chief Justice shall preside: And no Person shall be convicted without the Concurrence of two thirds of the Members present.

Judgment in Cases of Impeachment shall not extend further than to removal from Office, and disqualification to hold and enjoy any Office of honor, Trust or Profit under the United States: but the Party convicted shall nevertheless be liable and subject to Indictment, Trial, Judgment and Punishment, according to Law.

SECTION 4

The Times, Places and Manner of holding Elections for Senators and Representatives, shall be prescribed in each State by the Legislature thereof; but the Congress may at any time by Law make or alter such Regulations, except as to the Places of chusing Senators.

The Congress shall assemble at least once in every Year, and such Meeting shall be *on the first Monday in December*, unless they shall by Law appoint a different Day.

SECTION 5

Each House shall be the Judge of the Elections, Returns and Qualifications of its own Members, and a Majority of each shall constitute a Quorum to do Business; but a smaller Number may adjourn from day to day, and may be authorized to compel the Attendance of absent Members, in such Manner, and under such Penalties as each House may provide.

Each House may determine the Rules of its Proceedings, punish its Members for disorderly Behaviour, and, with the Concurrence of two thirds, expel a Member.

Each House shall keep a Journal of its Proceedings, and from time to time publish the same, excepting such Parts as may in their Judgment require Secrecy; and the Yeas and Nays of the

Members of either House on any question shall, at the Desire of one fifth of those Present, be entered on the Journal.

Neither House, during the Session of Congress, shall, without the Consent of the other, adjourn for more than three days, nor to any other Place than that in which the two Houses shall be sitting.

SECTION 6

The Senators and Representatives shall receive a Compensation for their Services, to be ascertained by Law, and paid out of the Treasury of the United States. They shall in all Cases, except Treason, Felony and Breach of the Peace, be privileged from Arrest during their Attendance at the Session of their respective Houses, and in going to and returning from the same; and for any Speech or Debate in either House, they shall not be questioned in any other Place.

No Senator or Representative shall, during the Time for which he was elected, be appointed to any civil Office under the Authority of the United States, which shall have been created, or the Emoluments whereof shall have been encreased during such time; and no Person holding any Office under the United States, shall be a Member of either House during his Continuance in Office.

SECTION 7

All Bills for raising Revenue shall originate in the House of Representatives; but the Senate may propose or concur with Amendments as on other Bills.

Every Bill which shall have passed the House of Representatives and the Senate, shall, before it become a Law, be presented to the President of the United States: If he approve he shall sign it, but if not he shall return it, with his Objections to that House in which it shall have originated, who shall enter the Objections at large on their Journal, and proceed to reconsider it. If after such Reconsideration two thirds of that House shall agree to pass the Bill, it shall be sent, together with the Objections, to the other House, by which it shall likewise be reconsidered, and if approved by two thirds of that House, it shall become a Law. But in all such Cases the Votes of both Houses shall be determined by yeas and Nays, and the Names of the Persons voting for and against the Bill shall be entered on the Journal of each House respectively. If any Bill shall not be returned by the President within ten Days (Sundays excepted) after it shall have been presented to him, the Same shall be a Law, in like Manner as if he had signed it, unless the Congress by their Adjournment prevent its Return, in which Case it shall not be a Law.

Every Order, Resolution, or Vote to which the Concurrence of the Senate and House of Representatives may be necessary (except on a question of Adjournment) shall be presented to the President of the United States; and before the Same shall take Effect, shall be approved by him, or being disapproved by him, shall be repassed by two thirds of the Senate and House of Representatives, according to the Rules and Limitations prescribed in the Case of a Bill.

SECTION 8

The Congress shall have Power To lay and collect Taxes, Duties, Imposts and Excises, to pay the Debts and provide for the common Defence and general Welfare of the United States; but all Duties, Imposts and Excises shall be uniform throughout the United States;

To borrow Money on the credit of the United States;

To regulate Commerce with foreign Nations, and among the several States, and with the Indian Tribes;

To establish an uniform Rule of Naturalization, and uniform Laws on the subject of Bankruptcies throughout the United States;

To coin Money, regulate the Value thereof, and of foreign Coin, and fix the Standard of Weights and Measures;

To provide for the Punishment of counterfeiting the Securities and current Coin of the United States;

To establish Post Offices and post Roads;

To promote the Progress of Science and useful Arts, by securing for limited Times to Authors and Inventors the exclusive Right to their respective Writings and Discoveries;

To constitute Tribunals inferior to the supreme Court;

To define and punish Piracies and Felonies committed on the high Seas, and Offences against the Law of Nations;

To declare War, grant Letters of Marque and Reprisal, and make Rules concerning Captures on Land and Water;

To raise and support Armies, but no Appropriation of Money to that Use shall be for a longer Term than two Years;

To provide and maintain a Navy;

To make Rules for the Government and Regulation of the land and naval Forces;

To provide for calling forth the Militia to execute the Laws of the Union, suppress Insurrections and repel Invasions;

To provide for organizing, arming, and disciplining, the Militia, and for governing such Part of them as may be employed in the Service of the United States, reserving to the States respectively, the Appointment of the Officers, and the Authority of training the Militia according to the discipline prescribed by Congress;

To exercise exclusive Legislation in all Cases whatsoever, over such District (not exceeding ten Miles square) as may, by Cession of particular States, and the Acceptance of Congress, become the Seat of the Government of the United States, and to exercise like Authority over all Places purchased by the Consent of the Legislature of the State in which the Same shall be, for the Erection of Forts, Magazines, Arsenals, dock-Yards, and other needful Buildings;—And

To make all Laws which shall be necessary and proper for carrying into Execution the foregoing Powers, and all other Powers vested by this Constitution in the Government of the United States, or in any Department or Officer thereof.

SECTION 9

The Migration or Importation of such Persons as any of the States now existing shall think proper to admit, shall not be prohibited by the Congress prior to the Year one thousand eight hundred and eight, but a Tax or duty may be imposed on such Importation, not exceeding ten dollars for each Person.

The Privilege of the Writ of Habeas Corpus shall not be suspended, unless when in Cases of Rebellion or Invasion the public Safety may require it.

No Bill of Attainder or ex post facto Law shall be passed.

No Capitation, or other direct, Tax shall be laid, *unless in Proportion to the Census or enumeration herein before directed to be taken.*

No Tax or Duty shall be laid on Articles exported from any State.

No Preference shall be given by any Regulation of Commerce or Revenue to the Ports of one State over those of another; nor shall Vessels bound to, or from, one State, be obliged to enter, clear, or pay Duties in another.

No Money shall be drawn from the Treasury, but in Consequence of Appropriations made by Law; and a regular Statement and Account of the Receipts and Expenditures of all public Money shall be published from time to time.

No Title of Nobility shall be granted by the United States: And no Person holding any Office of Profit or Trust under them, shall, without the Consent of the Congress, accept of any present, Emolument, Office, or Title, of any kind whatever, from any King, Prince, or foreign State.

SECTION 10

No State shall enter into any Treaty, Alliance, or Confederation; grant Letters of Marque and Reprisal; coin Money; emit Bills of Credit; make any Thing but gold and silver Coin a Tender in Payment of Debts; pass any Bill of Attainder, ex post facto Law, or Law impairing the Obligation of Contracts, or grant any Title of Nobility.

No State shall, without the Consent of the Congress, lay any Imposts or Duties on Imports or Exports, except what may be absolutely necessary for executing its inspection Laws: and the net Produce of all Duties and Imposts, laid by any State on Imports or Exports, shall be for the Use of the Treasury of the United States; and all such Laws shall be subject to the Revision and Controul of the Congress.

No State shall, without the Consent of Congress, lay any Duty of Tonnage, keep Troops, or Ships of War in time of Peace, enter into any Agreement or Compact with another State, or with a foreign Power, or engage in War, unless actually invaded, or in such imminent Danger as will not admit of delay.

Article II
SECTION I

The executive Power shall be vested in a President of the United States of America. He shall hold his Office during the Term of four Years, and, together with the Vice President, chosen for the same Term, be elected, as follows:

Each State shall appoint, in such Manner as the Legislature thereof may direct, a Number of Electors, equal to the whole Number of Senators and Representatives to which the State may be entitled in the Congress: but no Senator or Representative, or Person holding an Office of Trust or Profit under the United States, shall be appointed an Elector.

The Electors shall meet in their respective States, and vote by Ballot for two Persons, of whom one at least shall not be an Inhabitant of the same State with themselves. And they shall make a List of all the Persons voted for, and of the Number of Votes for each; which List they shall sign and certify, and transmit sealed to the Seat of the Government of the United States, directed to the President of the Senate. The President of the Senate shall, in the Presence of the Senate and House of Representatives, open all the Certificates, and the Votes shall then be counted. The Person having the greatest Number of Votes shall be the President, if such Number be a Majority of the whole Number of Electors appointed; and if there be more than one who have such Majority, and have an equal Number of Votes, then the House of Representatives shall immediately chuse by Ballot one of them for President; and if no Person have a Majority, then from the five highest on the List the said House shall in like Manner chuse the President. But in chusing the President, the Votes shall be taken by States, the Representation from each State having one Vote; A quorum for this purpose shall consist of a Member or Members from two thirds of the States, and a Majority of all the States shall be necessary to a Choice. In every Case, after the Choice of the President, the Person having the greatest Number of Votes of the

Electors shall be the Vice President. But if there should remain two or more who have equal Votes, the Senate shall chuse from them by Ballot the Vice President.

The Congress may determine the Time of chusing the Electors, and the Day on which they shall give their Votes; which Day shall be the same throughout the United States.

No Person except a natural born Citizen, or a Citizen of the United States, at the time of the Adoption of this Constitution, shall be eligible to the Office of President; neither shall any Person be eligible to that Office who shall not have attained to the Age of thirty five Years, and been fourteen Years a Resident within the United States.

In Case of the Removal of the President from Office, or of his Death, Resignation, or Inability to discharge the Powers and Duties of the said Office, the Same shall devolve on the Vice President, and the Congress may by Law provide for the Case of Removal, Death, Resignation or Inability, both of the President and Vice President, declaring what Officer shall then act as President, and such Officer shall act accordingly, until the Disability be removed, or a President shall be elected.

The President shall, at stated Times, receive for his Services, a Compensation, which shall neither be increased nor diminished during the Period for which he shall have been elected, and he shall not receive within that Period any other Emolument from the United States, or any of them.

Before he enter on the Execution of his Office, he shall take the following Oath or Affirmation:—"I do solemnly swear (or affirm) that I will faithfully execute the Office of President of the United States, and will to the best of my Ability, preserve, protect and defend the Constitution of the United States."

SECTION 2

The President shall be Commander in Chief of the Army and Navy of the United States, and of the Militia of the several States, when called into the actual Service of the United States; he may require the Opinion, in writing, of the principal Officer in each of the executive Departments, upon any Subject relating to the Duties of their respective Offices, and he shall have Power to grant Reprieves and Pardons for Offences against the United States, except in Cases of Impeachment.

He shall have Power, by and with the Advice and Consent of the Senate, to make Treaties, provided two thirds of the Senators present concur; and he shall nominate, and by and with the Advice and Consent of the Senate, shall appoint Ambassadors, other public Ministers and Consuls, Judges of the supreme Court, and all other Officers of the United States, whose Appointments are not herein otherwise provided for, and which shall be established by Law: but the Congress may by Law vest the Appointment of such inferior Officers, as they think proper, in the President alone, in the Courts of Law, or in the Heads of Departments.

The President shall have Power to fill up all Vacancies that may happen during the Recess of the Senate, by granting Commissions which shall expire at the End of their next Session.

SECTION 3

He shall from time to time give to the Congress Information of the State of the Union, and recommend to their Consideration such Measures as he shall judge necessary and expedient; he may, on extraordinary Occasions, convene both Houses, or either of them, and in Case of Disagreement between them, with Respect to the Time of Adjournment, he may adjourn them to such Time as he shall think proper; he shall receive Ambassadors and other public Ministers; he shall take Care that the Laws be faithfully executed, and shall Commission all the Officers of the United States.

SECTION 4

The President, Vice President and all civil Officers of the United States, shall be removed from Office on Impeachment for, and Conviction of, Treason, Bribery, or other high Crimes and Misdemeanors.

Article III
SECTION 1

The judicial Power of the United States shall be vested in one supreme Court, and in such inferior Courts as the Congress may from time to time ordain and establish. The Judges, both of the supreme and inferior Courts, shall hold their Offices during good Behaviour, and shall, at stated Times, receive for their Services a Compensation, which shall not be diminished during their Continuance in Office.

SECTION 2

The judicial Power shall extend to all Cases, in Law and Equity, arising under this Constitution, the Laws of the United States, and Treaties made, or which shall be made, under their Authority;—to all Cases affecting Ambassadors, other public Ministers and Consuls;—to all Cases of admiralty and maritime Jurisdiction;—to Controversies to which the United States shall be a Party;—to Controversies between two or more States;—*between a State and Citizens of another State;*—between Citizens of different States;—between Citizens of the same State claiming Lands under Grants of different States, and between a State, or the Citizens thereof, and foreign States, Citizens or Subjects.

In all Cases affecting Ambassadors, other public Ministers and Consuls, and those in which a State shall be Party, the supreme Court shall have original Jurisdiction. In all the other Cases before mentioned, the supreme Court shall have appellate Jurisdiction, both as to Law and Fact, with such Exceptions, and under such Regulations as the Congress shall make.

The Trial of all Crimes, except in Cases of Impeachment, shall be by Jury; and such Trial shall be held in the State where the said Crimes shall have been committed; but when not committed within any State, the Trial shall be at such Place or Places as the Congress may by Law have directed.

SECTION 3
Treason against the United States, shall consist only in levying War against them, or in adhering to their Enemies, giving them Aid and Comfort. No Person shall be convicted of Treason unless on the Testimony of two Witnesses to the same overt Act, or on Confession in open Court.

The Congress shall have Power to declare the Punishment of Treason, but no Attainder of Treason shall work Corruption of Blood, or Forfeiture except during the Life of the Person attainted.

Article IV
SECTION I
Full Faith and Credit shall be given in each State to the public Acts, Records, and judicial Proceedings of every other State. And the Congress may by general Laws prescribe the Manner in which such Acts, Records and Proceedings shall be proved, and the Effect thereof.

SECTION 2
The Citizens of each State shall be entitled to all Privileges and Immunities of Citizens in the several States.

A Person charged in any State with Treason, Felony, or other Crime, who shall flee from Justice, and be found in another State, shall on Demand of the executive Authority of the State from which he fled, be delivered up, to be removed to the State having Jurisdiction of the Crime.

No Person held to Service or Labour in one State, under the Laws thereof, escaping into another, shall, in Consequence of any Law or Regulation therein, be discharged from such Service or Labour, but shall be delivered up on Claim of the Party to whom such Service or Labour may be due.

SECTION 3

New States may be admitted by the Congress into this Union; but no new State shall be formed or erected within the Jurisdiction of any other State; nor any State be formed by the Junction of two or more States, or Parts of States, without the Consent of the Legislatures of the States concerned as well as of the Congress.

The Congress shall have Power to dispose of and make all needful Rules and Regulations respecting the Territory or other Property belonging to the United States; and nothing in this Constitution shall be so construed as to Prejudice any Claims of the United States, or of any particular State.

SECTION 4

The United States shall guarantee to every State in this Union a Republican Form of Government, and shall protect each of them against Invasion; and on Application of the Legislature, or of the Executive (when the Legislature cannot be convened), against domestic Violence.

Article V

The Congress, whenever two thirds of both Houses shall deem it necessary, shall propose Amendments to this Constitution, or, on the Application of the Legislatures of two thirds of the several States, shall call a Convention for proposing Amendments, which, in either Case, shall be valid to all Intents and Purposes, as Part of this Constitution, when ratified by the Legislatures of three fourths of the several States, or by Conventions in three fourths thereof, as the one or the other Mode of Ratification may be proposed by the Congress; Provided that no Amendment which may be made prior to the Year One thousand eight hundred and eight shall in any Manner affect the first and fourth Clauses in the Ninth Section of the first Article; and that no State, without its Consent, shall be deprived of its equal Suffrage in the Senate.

Article VI

All Debts contracted and Engagements entered into, before the Adoption of this Constitution, shall be as valid against the United States under this Constitution, as under the Confederation.

This Constitution, and the Laws of the United States which shall be made in Pursuance thereof; and all Treaties made, or which shall be made, under the Authority of the United States, shall be the supreme Law of the Land; and the Judges in every State shall be bound thereby, any Thing in the Constitution or Laws of any State to the Contrary notwithstanding.

The Senators and Representatives before mentioned, and the Members of the several State Legislatures, and all executive and judicial Officers, both of the United States and of the several States, shall be bound by Oath or Affirmation, to support this Constitution; but no religious Test shall ever be required as a Qualification to any Office or public Trust under the United States.

Article VII

The Ratification of the Conventions of nine States, shall be sufficient for the Establishment of this Constitution between the States so ratifying the Same.

The Word, "the," being interlined between the seventh and eighth Lines of the first Page, the Word "Thirty" being partly written on an Erazure in the fifteenth Line of the first Page, The Words "is tried" being interlined between the thirty second and thirty third Lines of the first Page and the Word "the" being interlined between the forty third and forty fourth Lines of the second Page.

Attest William Jackson Secretary

Done in Convention by the Unanimous Consent of the States present the Seventeenth Day of September in the Year of our Lord one thousand seven hundred and Eighty seven and of the Independence of the United States of America the Twelfth In witness whereof We have hereunto subscribed our Names,

G°. Washington, *Presidt and deputy from Virginia*

Delaware: Geo Read, Gunning Bedford jun, John Dickinson, Richard Bassett, Jaco Broom
Maryland: James McHenry, Dan of St Thos. Jenifer, Danl. Carroll

Virginia: John Blair, James Madison Jr.
North Carolina: Wm. Blount, Richd. Dobbs Spaight, Hu Williamson
South Carolina: J. Rutledge, Charles Cotesworth Pinckney, Charles Pinckney, Pierce Butler
Georgia: William Few, Abr Baldwin
New Hampshire: John Langdon, Nicholas Gilman
Massachusetts: Nathaniel Gorham, Rufus King
Connecticut: Wm. Saml. Johnson, Roger Sherman
New York: Alexander Hamilton
New Jersey: Wil. Livingston, David Brearley, Wm. Paterson, Jona Dayton
Pennsylvania: B Franklin, Thomas Mifflin, Robt. Morris, Geo. Clymer, Thos. FitzSimons, Jared Ingersoll, James Wilson, Gouv Morris

The Bill of Rights

[The following text is a transcription of the first ten amendments to the Constitution in their original form. These amendments were ratified December 15, 1791, and form what is known as the "Bill of Rights."]

The Preamble to The Bill of Rights

Congress of the United States
begun and held at the City of New-York, on
Wednesday the fourth of March, one thousand seven hundred and eighty nine.

THE Conventions of a number of the States, having at the time of their adopting the Constitution, expressed a desire, in order to prevent misconstruction or abuse of its powers, that further declaratory and restrictive clauses should be added: And as extending the ground of public confidence in the Government, will best ensure the beneficent ends of its institution.

RESOLVED by the Senate and House of Representatives of the United States of America, in Congress assembled, two thirds of both Houses concurring, that the following Articles be proposed to the Legislatures of the several States, as amendments to the Constitution of the United States, all, or any of which Articles, when ratified by three fourths of the said Legislatures, to be valid to all intents and purposes, as part of the said Constitution; viz.

ARTICLES in addition to, and Amendment of the Constitution of the United States of America, proposed by Congress, and ratified by the Legislatures of the several States, pursuant to the fifth Article of the original Constitution.

Amendment I

Congress shall make no law respecting an establishment of religion, or prohibiting the free exercise thereof; or abridging the freedom of speech, or of the press; or the right of the people peaceably to assemble, and to petition the Government for a redress of grievances.

Amendment II

A well regulated Militia, being necessary to the security of a free State, the right of the people to keep and bear Arms, shall not be infringed.

Amendment III

No Soldier shall, in time of peace be quartered in any house, without the consent of the Owner, nor in time of war, but in a manner to be prescribed by law.

Amendment IV

The right of the people to be secure in their persons, houses, papers, and effects, against unreasonable searches and seizures, shall not be violated, and no Warrants shall issue, but upon probable cause, supported by Oath or affirmation, and particularly describing the place to be searched, and the persons or things to be seized.

Amendment V

No person shall be held to answer for a capital, or otherwise infamous crime, unless on a presentment or indictment of a Grand Jury, except in cases arising in the land or naval forces, or in the Militia, when in actual service in time of War or public danger; nor shall any person be subject for the same offence to be twice put in jeopardy of life or limb; nor shall be compelled in any criminal case to be a witness against himself, nor be deprived of life, liberty, or property, without due process of law; nor shall private property be taken for public use, without just compensation.

Amendment VI

In all criminal prosecutions, the accused shall enjoy the right to a speedy and public trial, by an impartial jury of the State and district wherein the crime shall have been committed, which district shall have been previously ascertained by law, and to be informed of the nature and cause of the accusation; to be confronted with the witnesses against him; to have compulsory process for obtaining witnesses in his favor, and to have the Assistance of Counsel for his defence.

Amendment VII

In Suits at common law, where the value in controversy shall exceed twenty dollars, the right of trial by jury shall be preserved, and no fact tried by a jury, shall be otherwise re-examined in any Court of the United States, than according to the rules of the common law.

Amendment VIII

Excessive bail shall not be required, nor excessive fines imposed, nor cruel and unusual punishments inflicted.

Amendment IX

The enumeration in the Constitution, of certain rights, shall not be construed to deny or disparage others retained by the people.

Amendment X

The powers not delegated to the United States by the Constitution, nor prohibited by it to the States, are reserved to the States respectively, or to the people.

Amendments to the Constitution

Amendment XI

[Article III, section 2, of the Constitution was modified by Amendment 11.] Passed by Congress March 4, 1794. Ratified February 7, 1795.

The Judicial power of the United States shall not be construed to extend to any suit in law or equity, commenced or prosecuted against one of the United States by Citizens of another State, or by Citizens or Subjects of any Foreign State.

Amendment XII

[A portion of Article II, section 1 of the Constitution was superseded by the 12th Amendment.] Passed by Congress December 9, 1803. Ratified June 15, 1804.

The Electors shall meet in their respective states and vote by ballot for President and Vice-President, one of whom, at least, shall not be an inhabitant of the same state with themselves; they shall name in their ballots the person voted for as President, and in distinct ballots the person voted for as

Vice-President, and they shall make distinct lists of all persons voted for as President, and of all persons voted for as Vice-President, and of the number of votes for each, which lists they shall sign and certify, and transmit sealed to the seat of the government of the United States, directed to the President of the Senate;—the President of the Senate shall, in the presence of the Senate and House of Representatives, open all the certificates and the votes shall then be counted;—The person having the greatest number of votes for President, shall be the President, if such number be a majority of the whole number of Electors appointed; and if no person have such majority, then from the persons having the highest numbers not exceeding three on the list of those voted for as President, the House of Representatives shall choose immediately, by ballot, the President. But in choosing the President, the votes shall be taken by states, the representation from each state having one vote; a quorum for this purpose shall consist of a member or members from two-thirds of the states, and a majority of all the states shall be necessary to a choice. [And if the House of Representatives shall not choose a President whenever the right of choice shall devolve upon them, before the fourth day of March next following, then the Vice-President shall act as President, as in case of the death or other constitutional disability of the President. —]* The person having the greatest number of votes as Vice-President, shall be the Vice-President, if such number be a majority of the whole number of Electors appointed, and if no person have a majority, then from the two highest numbers on the list, the Senate shall choose the Vice-President; a quorum for the purpose shall consist of two-thirds of the whole number of Senators, and a majority of the whole number shall be necessary to a choice. But no person constitutionally ineligible to the office of President shall be eligible to that of Vice-President of the United States.
[*Superseded by section 3 of the 20th Amendment.]

Amendment XIII
[A portion of Article IV, section 2, of the Constitution was superseded by the 13th Amendment.] Passed by Congress January 31, 1865. Ratified December 6, 1865.

SECTION I
Neither slavery nor involuntary servitude, except as a punishment for crime whereof the party shall have been duly convicted, shall exist within the United States, or any place subject to their jurisdiction.

SECTION 2

Congress shall have power to enforce this article by appropriate legislation.

Amendment XIV

[Article I, section 2, of the Constitution was modified by section 2 of the 14th Amendment.]
Passed by Congress June 13, 1866. Ratified July 9, 1868.

SECTION 1

All persons born or naturalized in the United States, and subject to the jurisdiction thereof, are citizens of the United States and of the State wherein they reside. No State shall make or enforce any law which shall abridge the privileges or immunities of citizens of the United States; nor shall any State deprive any person of life, liberty, or property, without due process of law; nor deny to any person within its jurisdiction the equal protection of the laws.

SECTION 2

Representatives shall be apportioned among the several States according to their respective numbers, counting the whole number of persons in each State, excluding Indians not taxed. But when the right to vote at any election for the choice of electors for President and Vice-President of the United States, Representatives in Congress, the Executive and Judicial officers of a State, or the members of the Legislature thereof, is denied to any of the male inhabitants of such State, being twenty-one years of age,* and citizens of the United States, or in any way abridged, except for participation in rebellion, or other crime, the basis of representation therein shall be reduced in the proportion which the number of such male citizens shall bear to the whole number of male citizens twenty-one years of age in such State. *[*Changed by section 1 of the 26th Amendment.]*

SECTION 3

No person shall be a Senator or Representative in Congress, or elector of President and Vice-President, or hold any office, civil or military, under the United States, or under any State, who, having previously taken an oath, as a member of Congress, or as an officer of the United States, or as a member of any State legislature, or as an executive or judicial officer of any State, to support the Constitution of the United States, shall have engaged in insurrection or rebellion against the same, or given aid or comfort to the enemies thereof. But Congress may by a vote of two-thirds of each House, remove such disability.

SECTION 4

The validity of the public debt of the United States, authorized by law, including debts incurred for payment of pensions and bounties for services in suppressing insurrection or rebellion, shall not be questioned. But neither the United States nor any State shall assume or pay any debt or obligation incurred in aid of insurrection or rebellion against the United States, or any claim for the loss or emancipation of any slave; but all such debts, obligations and claims shall be held illegal and void.

SECTION 5

The Congress shall have the power to enforce, by appropriate legislation, the provisions of this article.

Amendment XV

Passed by Congress February 26, 1869. Ratified February 3, 1870.

SECTION 1

The right of citizens of the United States to vote shall not be denied or abridged by the United States or by any State on account of race, color, or previous condition of servitude—

SECTION 2

The Congress shall have the power to enforce this article by appropriate legislation.

Amendment XVI

[Article I, section 9, of the Constitution was modified by Amendment 16.] Passed by Congress July 2, 1909. Ratified February 3, 1913.

The Congress shall have power to lay and collect taxes on incomes, from whatever source derived, without apportionment among the several States, and without regard to any census or enumeration.

Amendment XVII

[Article I, section 3, of the Constitution was modified by the 17th Amendment.] Passed by Congress May 13, 1912. Ratified April 8, 1913.

The Senate of the United States shall be composed of two Senators from each State, elected by the people thereof, for six years; and each Senator shall have one vote. The electors in each State shall have the qualifications requisite for electors of the most numerous branch of the State legislatures.

When vacancies happen in the representation of any State in the Senate, the executive authority of such State shall issue writs of election to fill such vacancies: *Provided*, That the legislature of any State may empower the executive thereof to make temporary appointments until the people fill the vacancies by election as the legislature may direct.

This amendment shall not be so construed as to affect the election or term of any Senator chosen before it becomes valid as part of the Constitution.

Amendment XVIII
Passed by Congress December 18, 1917. Ratified January 16, 1919. Repealed by Amendment 21.

SECTION 1
After one year from the ratification of this article the manufacture, sale, or transportation of intoxicating liquors within, the importation thereof into, or the exportation thereof from the United States and all territory subject to the jurisdiction thereof for beverage purposes is hereby prohibited.

SECTION 2
The Congress and the several States shall have concurrent power to enforce this article by appropriate legislation.

SECTION 3
This article shall be inoperative unless it shall have been ratified as an amendment to the Constitution by the legislatures of the several States, as provided in the Constitution, within seven years from the date of the submission hereof to the States by the Congress.

Amendment XIX
Passed by Congress June 4, 1919. Ratified August 18, 1920.

The right of citizens of the United States to vote shall not be denied or abridged by the United States or by any State on account of sex.

Congress shall have power to enforce this article by appropriate legislation.

Amendment XX

[Article I, section 4, of the Constitution was modified by section 2 of this amendment. In addition, a portion of the 12th Amendment was superseded by section 3.] Passed by Congress March 2, 1932. Ratified January 23, 1933.

SECTION 1

The terms of the President and the Vice President shall end at noon on the 20th day of January, and the terms of Senators and Representatives at noon on the 3d day of January, of the years in which such terms would have ended if this article had not been ratified; and the terms of their successors shall then begin.

SECTION 2

The Congress shall assemble at least once in every year, and such meeting shall begin at noon on the 3d day of January, unless they shall by law appoint a different day.

SECTION 3

If, at the time fixed for the beginning of the term of the President, the President elect shall have died, the Vice President elect shall become President. If a President shall not have been chosen before the time fixed for the beginning of his term, or if the President elect shall have failed to qualify, then the Vice President elect shall act as President until a President shall have qualified; and the Congress may by law provide for the case wherein neither a President elect nor a Vice President shall have qualified, declaring who shall then act as President, or the manner in which one who is to act shall be selected, and such person shall act accordingly until a President or Vice President shall have qualified.

SECTION 4

The Congress may by law provide for the case of the death of any of the persons from whom the House of Representatives may choose a President whenever the right of choice shall have devolved upon them, and for the case of the death of any of the persons from whom the Senate may choose a Vice President whenever the right of choice shall have devolved upon them.

SECTION 5

Sections 1 and 2 shall take effect on the 15th day of October following the ratification of this article.

SECTION 6

This article shall be inoperative unless it shall have been ratified as an amendment to the Constitution by the legislatures of three-fourths of the several States within seven years from the date of its submission.

Amendment XXI

Passed by Congress February 20, 1933. Ratified December 5, 1933.

SECTION 1

The eighteenth article of amendment to the Constitution of the United States is hereby repealed.

SECTION 2

The transportation or importation into any State, Territory, or Possession of the United States for delivery or use therein of intoxicating liquors, in violation of the laws thereof, is hereby prohibited.

SECTION 3

This article shall be inoperative unless it shall have been ratified as an amendment to the Constitution by conventions in the several States, as provided in the Constitution, within seven years from the date of the submission hereof to the States by the Congress.

Amendment XXII

Passed by Congress March 21, 1947. Ratified February 27, 1951.

SECTION 1

No person shall be elected to the office of the President more than twice, and no person who has held the office of President, or acted as President, for more than two years of a term to which some other person was elected President shall be elected to the office of President more than once. But this Article shall not apply to any person holding the office of President when this Article was proposed by Congress, and shall not prevent any person who may be holding the office of President, or acting as President, during the term within which this Article becomes operative from holding the office of President or acting as President during the remainder of such term.

SECTION 2

This article shall be inoperative unless it shall have been ratified as an amendment to the Constitution by the legislatures of three-fourths of the several States within seven years from the date of its submission to the States by the Congress.

Amendment XXIII
Passed by Congress June 16, 1960. Ratified March 29, 1961.

SECTION 1
The District constituting the seat of Government of the United States shall appoint in such manner as Congress may direct:

A number of electors of President and Vice President equal to the whole number of Senators and Representatives in Congress to which the District would be entitled if it were a State, but in no event more than the least populous State; they shall be in addition to those appointed by the States, but they shall be considered, for the purposes of the election of President and Vice President, to be electors appointed by a State; and they shall meet in the District and perform such duties as provided by the twelfth article of amendment.

SECTION 2
The Congress shall have power to enforce this article by appropriate legislation.

Amendment XXIV
Passed by Congress August 27, 1962. Ratified January 23, 1964.

SECTION 1
The right of citizens of the United States to vote in any primary or other election for President or Vice President, for electors for President or Vice President, or for Senator or Representative in Congress, shall not be denied or abridged by the United States or any State by reason of failure to pay poll tax or other tax.

SECTION 2
The Congress shall have power to enforce this article by appropriate legislation.

Amendment XXV
[Article II, section 1, of the Constitution was affected by the 25th Amendment.] Passed by Congress July 6, 1965. Ratified February 10, 1967.

SECTION 1

In case of the removal of the President from office or of his death or resignation, the Vice President shall become President.

SECTION 2

Whenever there is a vacancy in the office of the Vice President, the President shall nominate a Vice President who shall take office upon confirmation by a majority vote of both Houses of Congress.

SECTION 3

Whenever the President transmits to the President pro tempore of the Senate and the Speaker of the House of Representatives his written declaration that he is unable to discharge the powers and duties of his office, and until he transmits to them a written declaration to the contrary, such powers and duties shall be discharged by the Vice President as Acting President.

SECTION 4

Whenever the Vice President and a majority of either the principal officers of the executive departments or of such other body as Congress may by law provide, transmit to the President pro tempore of the Senate and the Speaker of the House of Representatives their written declaration that the President is unable to discharge the powers and duties of his office, the Vice President shall immediately assume the powers and duties of the office as Acting President.

Thereafter, when the President transmits to the President pro tempore of the Senate and the Speaker of the House of Representatives his written declaration that no inability exists, he shall resume the powers and duties of his office unless the Vice President and a majority of either the principal officers of the executive department or of such other body as Congress may by law provide, transmit within four days to the President pro tempore of the Senate and the Speaker of the House of Representatives their written declaration that the President is unable to discharge the powers and duties of his office. Thereupon Congress shall decide the issue, assembling within forty-eight hours for that purpose if not in session. If the Congress, within twenty-one days after receipt of the latter written declaration, or, if Congress is not in session, within twenty-one days after Congress is required to assemble, determines by two-thirds vote of both Houses that the President is unable to discharge the powers and duties of his office, the Vice President shall continue to discharge the same as Acting President; otherwise, the President shall resume the powers and duties of his office.

Amendment XXVI
[Amendment 14, section 2, of the Constitution was modified by section 1 of the 26th Amendment.] Passed by Congress March 23, 1971. Ratified July 1, 1971.

SECTION 1
The right of citizens of the United States, who are eighteen years of age or older, to vote shall not be denied or abridged by the United States or by any State on account of age.

SECTION 2
The Congress shall have power to enforce this article by appropriate legislation.

Amendment XXVII
Originally proposed September 25, 1789. Ratified May 7, 1992.

No law, varying the compensation for the services of the Senators and Representatives, shall take effect, until an election of representatives shall have intervened.

Presidents of the United States

President	Party	Term as President	Vice-President
1. George Washington (1732–1799)	None, Federalist	1789–1797	John Adams
2. John Adams (1735–1826)	Federalist	1797–1801	Thomas Jefferson
3. Thomas Jefferson (1743–1826)	Democratic-Republican	1801–1809	Aaron Burr, George Clinton
4. James Madison (1751–1836)	Democratic-Republican	1809–1817	George Clinton, Elbridge Gerry
5. James Monroe (1758–1831)	Democratic-Republican	1817–1825	Daniel Tompkins
6. John Quincy Adams (1767–1848)	Democratic-Republican	1825–1829	John Calhoun
7. Andrew Jackson (1767–1845)	Democrat	1829–1837	John Calhoun, Martin van Buren
8. Martin van Buren (1782–1862)	Democrat	1837–1841	Richard Johnson
9. William H. Harrison (1773–1841)	Whig	1841	John Tyler
10. John Tyler (1790–1862)	Whig	1841–1845	
11. James K. Polk (1795–1849)	Democrat	1845–1849	George Dallas
12. Zachary Taylor (1784–1850)	Whig	1849–1850	Millard Fillmore
13. Millard Fillmore (1800–1874)	Whig	1850–1853	
14. Franklin Pierce (1804–1869)	Democrat	1853–1857	William King

President	Party	Term as President	Vice-President
15. James Buchanan (1791–1868)	Democrat	1857–1861	John Breckinridge
16. Abraham Lincoln (1809–1865)	Republican	1861–1865	Hannibal Hamlin, Andrew Johnson
17. Andrew Johnson (1808–1875)	National Union	1865–1869	
18. Ulysses S. Grant (1822–1885)	Republican	1869–1877	Schuyler Colfax
19. Rutherford Hayes (1822–1893)	Republican	1877–1881	William Wheeler
20. James Garfield (1831–1881)	Republican	1881	Chester Arthur
21. Chester Arthur (1829–1886)	Republican	1881–1885	
22. Grover Cleveland (1837–1908)	Democrat	1885–1889	Thomas Hendriks
23. Benjamin Harrison (1833–1901)	Republican	1889–1893	Levi Morton
24. Grover Cleveland (1837–1908)	Democrat	1893–1897	Adlai Stevenson
25. William McKinley (1843–1901)	Republican	1897–1901	Garret Hobart, Theodore Roosevelt
26. Theodore Roosevelt (1858–1919)	Republican	1901–1909	Charles Fairbanks
27. William Taft (1857–1930)	Republican	1909–1913	James Sherman
28. Woodrow Wilson (1856–1924)	Democrat	1913–1921	Thomas Marshall
29. Warren Harding (1865–1923)	Republican	1921–1923	Calvin Coolidge
30. Calvin Coolidge (1872–1933)	Republican	1923–1929	Charles Dawes
31. Herbert C. Hoover (1874–1964)	Republican	1929–1933	Charles Curtis
32. Franklin Delano Roosevelt (1882–1945)	Democrat	1933–1945	John Garner, Henry Wallace, Harry S. Truman
33. Harry S. Truman (1884–1972)	Democrat	1945–1953	Alben Barkley
34. Dwight David Eisenhower (1890–1969)	Republican	1953–1961	Richard Milhous Nixon

President	Party	Term as President	Vice-President
35. John Fitzgerald Kennedy (1917–1963)	Democrat	1961–1963	Lyndon Johnson
36. Lyndon Baines Johnson (1908–1973)	Democrat	1963–1969	Hubert Humphrey
37. Richard Milhous Nixon (1913–1994)	Republican	1969–1974	Spiro Agnew, Gerald R. Ford
38. Gerald R. Ford (1913–2006)	Republican	1974–1977	Nelson Rockefeller
39. James (Jimmy) Earl Carter, Jr. (1924–)	Democrat	1977–1981	Walter Mondale
40. Ronald Wilson Reagan (1911–2004)	Republican	1981–1989	George H.W. Bush
41. George H.W. Bush (1924–)	Republican	1989–1993	James Danforth (Dan) Quayle
42. William (Bill) Jefferson Clinton (1946–)	Democrat	1993–2001	Al Gore
43. George W. Bush (1946–)	Republican	2001–2009	Richard Cheney
44. Barack H. Obama (1961–)	Democrat	2009–	Joseph Biden

Congressional Caucuses and Committees

TABLE 1: SUBCOMMITTEES OF HOUSE STANDING COMMITTEES AND INFORMAL HOUSE CAUCUSES, 96TH-110TH CONGRESSES (1979–2008)

Congress	Number of Subcommittees	Number of Caucuses
96th Congress (1979–1980)	150	33
97th Congress (1981–1982)	140	44
98th Congress (1983–1984)	139	49
99th Congress (1985–1986)	140	49
100th Congress (1987–1988)	140	56
101st Congress (1989–1990)	138	62
102nd Congress (1991–1992)	135	69
103rd Congress (1994–1994)	115	58
104th Congress (1995–1996)	84	71
105th Congress (1997–1998)	88	106
106th Congress (1999–2000)	85	106
107th Congress (2001–2002)	88	113
108th Congress (20003–2004)	89	117
109th Congress (2005–2006)	97	114
110th Congress (2007–2008)	100	96

Sources: Subcommittee data for 96th-103rd Congresses from Joint Committee on the Organization of Congress, "Background Materials: Supplemental Information Provided to Members of the Joint Committee on the Organization of Congress," 103rd Congress (S. Prt. 103–55), 474; source for subsequent House subcommittees, 104th-108th Congresses, Congressional Staff Directory. Source of Informal Caucus data, Congressional Yellow Book, Spring issue, second session (except for 108th Congress, taken from Fall 2003 issue). Note: the above subcommittee listing only applies to standing committees and does not include any subcommittees on select committees such as the Permanent Select Committee on Intelligence or the Select Committee on Homeland Security. Data reproduced by permission of Donald R. Wolfensberger, Woodrow Wilson Center, Washington, DC.

TABLE 2:   APPROXIMATE NUMBER OF INFORMAL CONGRESSIONAL GROUPS LISTED IN CONGRESSIONAL YELLOW BOOK 96TH–110TH CONGRESSES (1979–2008)

Congress (Years)	House	Senate	Bicameral	Totals
96th (1979–80)	33	11	15	59
97th (1981–82)	44	12	14	70
98th (1983–84)	49	20	23	92
99th (1985–86)	49	23	31	103
100th (1987–88)	56	22	31	109
101st (1989–90)	62	23	31	116
102nd (1991–92)	69	23	32	124
103rd (1993–94)	58	22	33	113
104th (1995–96)	71	23	33	125
105th (1997–98)	106	24	44	174
106th (1999–2000)	106	26	42	174
107th (2001–02)	113	20	43	176
108th (2003–04)	117	21	40	178
109th (2005–06)	114	18	44	176
110th (2007–08)	96	15	38	149

Sources: Congressional Yellow Book, *Spring of even numbered years, 96th-107th Congresses; Fall, 2003 for 108th Congress.*

TABLE 3:   CATEGORIES OF INFORMAL CAUCUSES, 110TH CONGRESS LISTED IN CONGRESSIONAL YELLOW BOOK

Caucus Type	House	Senate	Bicameral	Totals
Constituency	50	10	18	78
(Industry)	(15)	(4)	(7)	(26)
(Geographic)	(12)	(2)	(4)	(44)
(Demographic)	(23)	(4)	(7)	(34)
Party	6	1	3	10
Personal Interest	40	4	17	61
TOTALS	96	15	38	149

Source: Congressional Yellow Book, *Fall, 2007.*

TABLE 4: HOUSE AND BICAMERAL CONGRESSIONAL MEMBER ORGANIZATIONS BY CATEGORY, 110th CONGRESS, *NOT* INCLUDED IN THE *CONGRESSIONAL YELLOW BOOK*

Caucus Type	House	Bicameral	Totals
Constituency	82	3	85
(Industry)	(22)	(2)	(24)
(Geographic)	(25)	(1)	(26)
(Demographic)	(35)	0	(35)
Party	0	0	0
Personal Interest	99	3	102
TOTALS	181	6	188

Source: House Administration Committee, 110th Congress, Directories of Congressional Organizations, "Congressional Member Organizations, 110th Congress," <http://cha.house.gov/index.php?option=com_content&task=view&id=45&Itemid=37> on Nov. 8, 2007.

TABLE 5: INFORMAL CAUCUSES IN THE 110TH CONGRESS LISTED IN *CONGRESSIONAL YELLOW BOOK* AND ON HOUSE ADMINISTRATION COMMITTEE WEB SITE COMBINED

Caucus Type	House	Senate	Bicameral	Totals
Constituency	132	10	21	163
(Industry)	(37)	(4)	(9)	(50)
(Geographic)	(37)	(2)	(5)	(44)
(Demographic)	(58)	(4)	(7)	(69)
Party	6	1	3	10
Personal Interest	139	4	20	163
TOTALS	277	15	44	336

Source: Combines totals from Tables 2 and 3 above.

TABLE 6:   SUBCOMMITTEES OF HOUSE STANDING COMMITTEES 107TH–110TH CONGRESSES (2001–2008)

Committee	Sub-comms 107th Cong.	Sub-comms 108th Cong.	Sub-comms 109th Cong.	Sub-comms 110th Cong.
Agriculture	5	5	5	6
Appropriations	13	13	13	13
Armed Services	5	6	6	7
Budget	0	0	0	0
Education & Workforce	5	5	5	5
Energy & Commerce	5	6	6	6
Financial Services	5	5	5	5
Foreign Affairs	6	6	6	7
Government Reform	8	8	8	5
Homeland Security	-	-	5	6
House Administration	0	0	0	2
Judiciary	5	5	5	5
Resources	6	5	5	5
Rules	2	2	2	2
Science	4	4	4	5
Small Business	4	4	4	5
Transportation & Infrastructure	6	6	6	6
Veterans' Affairs	3	3	3	4
Ways & Means	6	6	6	6
TOTAL HOUSE SUBCOMMITTEES	88	89	91	100

Abramowitz, Alan, and Kyle Saunders. "Why Can't We All Just Get Along? The Reality of a Polarized America." *The Forum: A Journal of Applied Research in Contemporary Politics* 3.2 (2005).

Walter R. Allen, Edgar G. Epps, and Nasha Z. Haniff (eds.), *College in Black and White*. Albany, NY: State University of New York Press, 1991.

Almond, Gabriel, and Sidney Verba. *The Civic Culture: Political Attitudes and Democracy in Five Nations*. Thousand Oaks, CA: Sage, 1989.

Barone, Michael. *The Almanac of American Politics 2006*. Washington, DC: National Journal Group, 2006.

Baudrillard, Jean. *America*. Trans. Chris Turner. New York: Verso, 1988.

Beard, Charles. *American Government and Politics*, 8th ed. New York: Macmillan, 1939.

——. *An Economic Interpretation of the Constitution*. 1913; Edison, NJ: Transaction, 1998.

Beauvoir, Simone de. *America Day by Day*. Trans. Carol Cosman. 1948; Berkeley, CA: University of California Press, 1999.

Biskupic, Joan, and Elder Witt. *The Supreme Court at Work*. 2nd ed. Washington, DC: Congressional Quarterly Books, 1997.

Bloom, Allan. *The Closing of the American Mind*. New York: Simon and Schuster, 1987.

Brader, Ted. *Campaigning for Hearts and Minds*. Chicago, IL: University of Chicago, 2006.

Breton, Raymond, and Jeffrey Reitz. *The Illusion of Difference*. Toronto: C.D. Howe Institute, 1994.

Brody, Richard A. "Public Evaluations and Expectations." In James Sterling, ed., *Problems and Prospects for Presidential Leadership: The Decade Ahead*. Lanham, MD: University Press of America, 1982.

Arthur Brooks, *Who Really Cares? The Surprising Truth about Truly Compassionate Conservatism*. New York: Basic Books, 2006.

Brooks, Stephen. *As Others See Us: The Causes and Consequences of Foreign Perceptions of America*. Peterborough, ON: Broadview Press, 2006.

Brown, Robert E. *Charles Beard and the Constitution*. New York: Norton, 1956.

Bryce, James. *The American* Commonwealth. New York: G.P. Putnam's Sons, 1959.

Carter, Jimmy. *Our Endangered Values: America's Moral Crisis.* New York: Simon and Schuster, 2005.

Citrin, Jack, and Samantha Luks. "Revisiting Political Trust in an Angry Age." In John R. Hibbing *et al.*, eds. *What is it about Government that Americans Dislike?* Cambridge, UK: Cambridge University Press, 2001.

Commager, Henry Steele (Ed.). *Living Ideas in America.* New York: Harper and Brothers, 1951.

Corak, Miles (Ed.). *Generational Income Mobility in North America and Europe.* Cambridge, UK: Cambridge University Press, 2005.

Dalton, Russel J. "Citizenship Norms and Political Participation in America: The Good News is ... The Bad News Is Wrong." Occasional Papers Series. Center for Democracy and Society, Georgetown University, October 2006.

Dickens, Charles. *American Notes.* London: Chapman and Hall, 1842; http://www.online-literature.com/dickens/americannotes.

D'Souza, Daniel. *Illiberal Education.* New York: The Free Press, 1991.

Edwards, Chris. "Federal Aid to the States." *Policy Analysis* 593 (22 May 2007).

Ellis, Joseph. *Founding Brothers: The Revolutionary Generation.* New York: Vintage, 2002.

Elshtain, Jean Bethke. "Religions in the Public Square," Ronald Reagan Symposium 2007, Regent University; http://regents.edu/publications/cl/features/fw_07/reagan_symposium.cfm.

Erikson, Robert S., and Norman R. Luttbeg. *American Public Opinion.* New York: Wiley, 1973.

Esping-Anderson, Gosta. *Politics Against Markets.* Cambridge, MA: Princeton University Press, 1985.

Fiorina, Morris. "What Culture Wars?" *Wall Street Journal*, 14 July 2004.

Fukuyama, Francis. "The End of History?" *The National Interest* (Summer 1989).

——. "Identity Crisis: Why We Shouldn't Worry about Mexican Immigration." *Slate* (4 June 2004).

Galbraith, James. *The Myth of America's Decline.* New York: Oxford University Press, 1990.

Gervais, Pierre. *L'avènement d'une superpuissance.* Paris: Larousse 2001.

Hacker, Andrew. *Two Nations: Black and White, Separate, Hostile, Unequal.* New York: Balantine, 1992.

Hartz, Louis. *The Liberal Tradition in America.* New York: Harcourt, Brace and World, 1955.

Hoffman, Stanley. *America Goes Backward.* New York: New York Review of Books, 2004.

Hunter, James Davison. *Culture Wars: The Struggle to Define America.* New York: Basic Books, 1991.

Huntington, Samuel. "A Revised Theory of American Party Politics." *American Political Science Review* 54 (1950).

Ignatieff, Michael. "The Burden." *New York Times Magazine* (19 January 2003).

Irving, William Julius. *The Truly Disadvantaged: The Inner City, the Underclass, and Public Policy.* Chicago, IL: University of Chicago Press, 1987.

Joffe, Josef. "Who's Afraid of Mr. Big?" *The National Interest* (Summer 2001).

Johnson, Lyndon Baines. *The Vantage Point: Perspectives of the Presidency 1963–1969.* New York: Holt, Rinehart and Winston, 1971.

Jones, Charles O. *The Presidency as a Separated System*, 2nd ed. Washington, DC: Brookings Institution Press, 2005.

Kagan, Robert. "End of Dreams, Return of History." *Policy Review* (August–September 2007).

Kennedy, Paul. *The Rise and Fall of the Great Powers: Economic Change and Military Conflict from 1500 to 2000*. New York: Vintage, 1989.

Key, V.O. *The Responsible Electorate*. New York: Vintage, 1966.

Koch, Ed. "The Mandate Millstone." *Public Interest* 61 (Fall 1980).

Kohut, Andrew, and Bruce Stokes. *America against the World: How We Are Different and Why We Are Disliked*. New York: Times Books, 2006.

Kopstein, Jeffrey, and Sven Steinmo (Eds.). *Growing Apart? America and Europe in the 21st Century*. Cambridge, UK: Cambridge University Press, 2007.

Krugman, Paul. *The Great Unraveling*. New York: Norton, 2003.

Kull, Steven, and I.M. Destler. *Misreading the Public: The Myth of a New Isolationism*. Washington, DC: Brookings Institution, 1999.

Ladd, Everett Carl, and Karyn H. Bowman. *Attitudes Toward Economic Inequality*. Washington, DC: American Enterprise Institute, 1998.

Laski, Harold. *The American Democracy*. New York: Viking Press, 1948.

Lessing, Doris. "What We Think of America." *Granta* 77 (2002).

Lévy, Bernard-Henri. *American Vertigo: Traveling America in the Footsteps of Tocqueville*. New York: Random House, 2006.

Lewis-Beck, Michael, William G. Jacoby, Helmut Norpoth, and Herbert F. Weisberg (Eds.) *The American Voter Revisited*. Ann Arbor, MI: University of Michigan Press, 2009.

Lichter, S. Robert, Stanley Rothman, and Linda Richter. *The Media Elite: America's New Power Brokers*. Bethesda, MD: Adler and Adler, 1986.

Lipset, Seymour Martin. *American Exceptionalism*. New York: Norton, 1996.

——. "Equal Chances versus Equal Results." *The Annals of the American Academy* 523 (September 1992).

McDonald, Forrest. *Novus Ordo Seclorum: The Intellectual Origins of the Constitution*. Lawrence, KS: University Press of Kansas, 1985.

——. *We The People: The Economic Origins of the Constitution*. Chicago, IL: University of Chicago Press, 1958.

Moynihan, Daniel Patrick. *The Negro Family: The Case for National Action*. Washington, DC: Department of Labor, 1965.

Mueller, Carol. "The Gender Gap and Women's Political Influence." *The Annals of the American Academy of Political and Social Science* 515,1 (1991): 23–37.

Myrdal, Gunnar. *An American Dilemma: The Negro Problem and Modern Democracy*. New York: Harper and Brothers Publishers, 1944.

National Center for Education Statistics. *Comparative Indicators of Education in the United States and Other G-8 Countries: 2006*. Washington, DC: Department of Education, August 2007.

Nie, Norman H., Sidney Verba, and John R. Petrocik. *The Changing American Voter: Enlarged Edition*. Cambridge, MA: Harvard University Press, 1980.

Portes, Jacques. *Les États-Unis aujourd'hui : les maîtres du monde?* Paris: Petite encyclopédie Larousse, 2003.

Putman, Robert. *Bowling Alone: The Collapse and Revival of American Community*. New York: Simon and Schuster, 2000.

Rehnquist, William. *The Supreme Court: How It Was, How It Is*. New York: William Morrow, 1987.

Reich, Robert. *The Work of Nations*. New York: Vintage, 1991.

Rifkin, Jeremy. *The European Dream*. New York: Tarcher, 2004.

Schattschneider, E.E. *The Semi-Sovereign People*. New York: Holt, Rinehart and Winston, 1960.

Schlesinger, Arthur Jr. *The Disuniting of America*. New York: Norton, 1993.

——. (Ed.). *History of US Political Parties*, 4 vols. New York: Chelsea, 1973.

Siaroff, Alan. "Women's Representation in Legislatures." *International Political Science Review* 21 (2000).

Stanley, H.W., and R.G. Niemi. "The Demise of the New Deal Coalition: Partisanship and Group Support, 1952–1992." In H.F. Weisberg (ed.), *Democracy's Feast: Elections in America*. Chatham, NJ: Chatham House, 1995.

Steyn, Mark. *America Alone: The End of the World As We Know It*. Washington, DC: Regnery Publishing, 2006.

Tocqueville, Alexis de. *Democracy in America*, Books I and II. From the Henry Reeve Translation, revised and corrected, 1899. University of Virginia, American Studies Program http://xroads.virginia.edu/~HYPER/DETOC/colophon.html.

Todd, Emmanuel. *Après l'empire*. Paris: Gallimard, 2002.

Trudeau, Pierre Elliott. *Memoirs*. Toronto: McClelland and Stewart, 1993.

Vedrine, Hubert. *Face à l'hyper-puissance*. Paris: Editions Fayard, 2003.

Wallerstein, Immanuel. *The Decline of American Power*. New York: The New Press, 2003.

White, John Kenneth. *The Values Divide: American Politics and Culture in Transition*. New York: Chatham House Publishers/Seven Bridges Press, 2003.

Wilson, James Q. and John J. Dilulio Jr. *American Government*. 10th ed. New York: Houghton Mifflin Company, 2007.

Zinn, Howard. *A People's History of the United States*. New York: HarperCollins, 1980.